AMERICAN CINEMA/AMERICAN CULTURE

AMERICAN CINEMA/ AMERICAN CULTURE

John Belton

Rutgers University

McGraw-Hill, Inc.
New York   St. Louis   San Francisco   Auckland   Bogotá   Caracas
Lisbon   London   Madrid   Mexico City   Milan   Montreal   New Delhi
San Juan   Singapore   Sydney   Tokyo   Toronto

AMERICAN CINEMA /AMERICAN CULTURE

Major funding for the American Cinema Project has been provided by the Annenberg/CPB Project; significant funding from the National Endowment for the Humanities and the National Endowment for the Arts; and additional funding from the CPB/PBS Program Challenge Fund and the Meadows Foundation.

This book is printed on acid-free paper.

15 16 17 18 19 20   QWF/QWF   0 5 4 3 2

ISBN 0-07-004466-X

This book was set in Palatino by Better Graphics, Inc.
The editors were Alison Husting and Curt Berkowitz;
the designer was Carol A. Couch;
the production supervisor was Leroy A. Young.

Cover photo: Leo the Lion from the M-G-M Collection.
            Still used courtesy of Turner Entertainment Co.

Library of Congress Cataloging-in-Publication Data

Belton, John.
    American cinema/American culture / John Belton.
        p.   cm.
    Includes bibliographical references, filmographies, and index.
    ISBN 0-07-004466-X (alk. paper)
    1. Motion pictures—United States—History.   2. Motion picture industry—United States—History.   3. Motion pictures—Social aspects—United States.   4. United States—Popular culture—History—20th century.   I. Title.
    PN1993.5.U6B365   1994
    791.43'0973—dc20

                                                93-25846

John Belton teaches film at Rutgers University. He is the author of *Widescreen Cinema* (1992) and several other books on film. He is a member of the National Film Preservation Board, as well as Chair of the Archival Papers and Historical Committee of the Society of Motion Pictures and Television Engineers.

To Mike Moore, a teacher of teachers

CONTENTS

This book introduces the reader to basic issues related to the phenomenon of American cinema. It looks at American film history from the 1890s through the 1990s, but it does not always explore this history in a purely chronological way. In fact, it is not (strictly speaking) a history. Rather, it is a *cultural* history, which focusses more on topics and issues than on what happened when.

It begins with a profile of classical Hollywood cinema as a unique economic, industrial, aesthetic, and cultural institution. It considers the experience of moviegoing; the nature of Hollywood story-telling; and the roles played by the studio system, the star system, and film genres in the creation of a body of work that functions not only as entertainment but as a portrait of the relationship between an American national identity and an industrialized mass culture that has slowly evolved over the past century.

This book assumes that the reader has little or no formal training in film history, theory, or aesthetics. It presents fairly basic concepts in such a way as to encourage discussion, not so much of individual films, but of films in general. For this reason, the book concentrates on large groupings of films— on genres, topics, and periods of film history.

This textbook differs from the more traditional histories of the cinema for certain specific and important reasons. Over the past 20 years, the field of film study has undergone a tremendous transformation. This change has been spearheaded by the work of a new generation of scholars who challenge the traditional way in which film history has been written and taught. Introduction to Film courses that, 20 years ago, taught film as art, drew heavily upon the approaches of New Criticism. Contemporary film courses now teach film not only as art but also as film, and they attempt to situate film as an art form within a larger industrial, economic, social, and cultural context. They rely heavily on cultural studies, new historicism, psychoanalysis, and other contemporary critical disciplines.

Film history texts have changed over the years as well. In the past, histories consisted of simple, chronological accounts of who-did-what and what-happened-when, and of the stories of great men (sic) and their achievements, and of straightforward accounts of the influence of technology and economics on the course of a history that unfolds in a linear fashion up to the present. More recently, film scholars have begun to rewrite these traditional histories, creating what Thomas Elsaesser refers to as "The New Film History." At its best, this history is driven by a sophisticated, theoretically informed revisionism. It simply refuses to accept the easy answers to basic historical questions which had been offered up by past historians. "The New Film History" can best be seen in the recent work of David Bordwell, Janet Staiger, and Kristin Thompson (*Classical Hollywood Cinema: Film Style and Mode of Production to 1960*) and of Robert Allen and Douglas Gomery (*Film History: Theory and Practice*), though it can be found in a number of other scholarly efforts as well.

The methods and discoveries of "The New Film History," however, have not yet been applied to an introductory level text surveying the history of the American cinema. This book is an attempt to put the principles of "The New Film History" into action—to present and to make accessible the findings of contemporary film studies to college students taking introductory level courses in film, American Studies, or Cultural Studies. In other words, it hopes to provide an updated map of the terrain of American cinema.

Traditional histories of the cinema rely upon certain unquestioned assumptions which underlie the way they are written and read. They assume, for example, that the meaning of history is best represented through the time-worn format of the chronological narrative of events. They suggest that the fact that one event takes place after another somehow automatically "explains" that event. In this view, each event derives from a prior event; it comes from a cause-and-effect chain that runs smoothly and linearly from some origin in the past to the present.

This book understands that history does not only consist of "one damned thing after another," but of ideas, problems, and issues. For that reason, the text gives a certain priority in its organization to thematic over chronological concerns. This textbook is designed not as a blow-by-blow account of who did what and when, but as an historically informed *portrait* of American cinema, provided through a clear and concise description of its most salient features.

Nonetheless, a sense of history strongly pervades the book, guiding the structure of specific chapters and of the book as a whole and providing a survey of the American cinema's major character traits as they take shape over the decades. Seen from the perspective of a cultural phenomenon, American cinema emerges as a stylistically unified body of work (as discussed in the chapters on classical Hollywood cinema), generated within a certain mode of production (see the chapters on the Studio System and the Star System) that is uniquely dependent upon modern technologies developed for the recording of images and sounds. These general characteristics of American cinema underlie the nature of the particular products which that cinema produces—the various genres of films discussed within the text, ranging from comedies and Westerns to war films and melodramas.

Traditional film histories tend to be unsuitable for introductory film courses in that they frequently omit any discussion of aesthetics, presuming that basic matters of film form have been dealt with in a prior course. This text, however, doubles as both a cultural history and an introduction to aesthetics and film form, introducing and explaining basic vocabulary in the chapters that discuss the narrative and stylistic practices of classical Hollywood cinema. Subsequent chapters refer back to these basic ingredients of narrative and stylistic form. Here, the function of mise-en-scene (lighting, set and costume design, camera angle and movement, etc.) and editing (eye-line matching, shot/reverse-shot editing, the 180-degree rule, parallel editing, etc.) is explored in terms of their relation to the overall system of classical Hollywood style.

Traditional film histories present themselves as purely objective accounts of "what happened in the past." They disguise their own position in relation to that past. This text, however, in addition to providing factual information and surveying what contemporary scholarship has revealed to us about the subject, develops a clearly delineated thesis and encourages instructors, students, and general readers to question and test that thesis by holding it up to close scrutiny. The core of that thesis rests on an assumption that American cinema reveals, both directly and indirectly, something about American experience, identity, and culture.

In setting forth this thesis, the book acknowledges that the relationship between American film and American social and historical reality is highly mediated and extremely complex. Films, quite clearly, cannot be viewed as simple mirrors of cultural reality. As fictional works, they do, however, have a "use-value." They can be analyzed—even psychoanalyzed—to reveal something about the cultural conditions that produced them and attracted audiences to them.

Of course, their status as objective documents that reflect the currents of American popular culture remains severely limited. For example, images of women, blacks, Native Americans, Asians, and other minorities in American cinema have only an indirect relationship to the real status of these individuals within American society. Yet those images can nonetheless be read symptomatically to locate their source in the real social tensions that underlie America's democratic ideal, in a profound sexual and racial inequality. In other words, the films do reflect American reality but in a distorted and displaced way. More often than not, they reflect back only what audiences *want* to see rather than what is really there.

This book, in turn, functions as another kind of mirror—a two-sided mirror like that found in motion pictures set in asylums or police stations. This mirror is a mirror on one side, but it is a window on the other side. A see-through mirror thus enables us to watch from one side something that takes place on the other side. The strategy that lies behind the arguments in this book is the strategy of the two-way mirror. It suggests that by *looking through* the movies, we are able to see both what takes place in them and what takes place in the audiences who watch them on the other side. By looking through the movies, we can see the process by which an American identity is both formed and reflected. In other words, by looking through and at the movies in certain ways, we can see how American identity is shaped in the movies and, at the same time, how the movies are shaped by it.

This book has been written in conjunction with the television course and series *American Cinema,* produced by the New York Center for Visual History as part of the Annenberg/CPB project collection. It also corresponds with a student study guide, written by Ed Sikov, which has been carefully designed to function equally well independently of these supplementary materials.

This book could not have been written without the help of a number of other film scholars. In particular, I would like to thank William Costanzo, Thomas Cripps, Douglas Gomery, William Paul, Ed Sikov, and Elisabeth Weis of the curriculum committee for the *American Cinema* television course project for the New York Center for Visual History, who read the bulk of this book in manuscript form and provided invaluable suggestions for improving it. Special thanks go to Angela Aleiss, Elizabeth Belton, Ellen Belton, Thomas Doherty, Howard Karren, Robert Lang, Charles Maland, Dara Meyers-Kingsley, and Alan Williams who read and commented on specific chapters. I am indebted to Jane Belton, David Bordwell, Aaron Braun, Fred Camper, Linda McCarthy, Al Nigrin, Jessica Rosner, Phil Shane, and Kristin Thompson for their advice, research help, and/or assistance in providing illustrative material for the book.

Also, I would like to thank the following for their careful reviews of the manuscript: Chuck Berg, University of Kansas; Jay Coughtry, University of Nevada, Las Vegas; Leger Grindon, Middleburg College; Douglas Gomery, University of Maryland; Eugene Huddleston, Michigan State University; Annette Insdorf, Columbia University; Kathryn Lasky, University of Southern Maine; Charles Maland, University of Tennessee; Karen Mann, Western Illinois University; David Nasaw, College of State Island; Jere Real, Lynchburg College; Margaret Schrage, SUNY College at Old Westbury; Susan Scrivner, Bemidji State University; Steven Shields, University of Wisconsin, Whitewater; Kristin Thompson, University of Wisconsin, Madison; and Albert Wendland, Seton Hill College.

Molly Ornati and Lawrence Pitkethly of the New York Center for Visual History and Lin Foa of the Annenberg/CPB project proved instrumental in bringing this book about, along with my editors at McGraw-Hill, Alison Husting, Peter Labella, and Curt Berkowitz. A special thanks to Jeanine Basinger, Senior Academic Advisor for the *American Cinema* television course, who served as a catalyst for the development of this project.

John Belton

During M-G-M's heyday as a studio, the end title of every M-G-M film read "Made in Hollywood, U.S.A." Though not every American film is or was made in Hollywood, the bulk of American cinema is the product of a specific mode of production which was perfected in Hollywood and which consists of a unique combination of various ingredients.

"Hollywood" is not only a place in California where movies are made. It does not only consist of studios, labs, and other buildings; nor of producers, stars, directors, screenwriters, and the other personnel who are actually involved in the making of movies. "Hollywood" is also a consistent and coherent set of aesthetic and stylistic conventions that audiences readily understand. Beneath these conventions lies an industrial infrastructure that works to maintain and support them. This industrial base includes the studio system and the star system, as well as the movie culture that grew up around these institutions.

Movie culture ranges in its scope from the discourses (or ways of representing things) of advertising, publicity, and fan magazines to the experience of moviegoing, which changes from decade to decade. The experience of watching a one-reel short film in a nickelodeon in 1908 differs dramatically from that of watching a silent feature film in a movie palace in the 1920s. These experiences, in turn, remain worlds apart from going to drive-ins in the 1950s, small-screen multiplexes in the 1960s and 1970s, and mall cinemas in the 1980s and 1990s.

This book explores the *phenomenon* of American cinema. It investigates what it is and how it works. In order to understand what American cinema is and how it works, it is necessary to look at it as a mode of production. Hollywood has its own way of doing things. Over the years it has developed a unique system of studios, stars, distribution, exhibition, advertising, and marketing that enables it to make a profit. This mode of production not only forms the nature of Hollywood as an industry, but it also determines the kinds of films that get made, the way those films look, and the way those films tell stories.

The first section of this text (Chapters 1–5) concentrates on the notion of "Hollywood" as a unique system designed for the efficient production of a rather unusual product—motion pictures. An initial chapter on "The Emergence of the Cinema as an Institution" traces the evolution of American filmmaking from a toy, novelty item and fairground attraction to a carefully tailored mode of production which is designed to produce seamless narratives capable of entertaining a mass audience. Subsequent chapters on "Classical Hollywood Cinema" ("Narration" in Chapter 2; "Style" in Chapter 3), "The Studio System," and "The Star System" explore the nature of this institution, providing a descriptive account of the basic elements that constitute Hollywood as a distinct mode of production.

Much as Hollywood turns the craft of film production, distribution, and exhibition into an efficient system, so it also systematizes its product. It makes and markets films according to yet another system—that of genres. The second section of the text (Chapters 6–10) looks at the way movies work by exploring the relation of major film genres to the specific industrial and cultural machinery that produced them—that is, to the institution of Hollywood and to the institution of American mass culture.

The system of genres duplicates, in the area of film product, the organizational strategies that underlie the film industry's institutional base. This system establishes broad categories of film types that have proven their economic viability over the years and that, as a result, work to stabilize the production process by reducing financial risk. Audiences go to movies that resemble films which they have seen before. That is, audiences go to comedies, melodramas, war films, Westerns, and other broad categories of film types.

This section will also relate these films to the more general cultural concerns which inform them and to which they, in turn, give form. The arrangement of these chapters follows a quasi-chronological line, corresponding roughly to the decades in which the individual genres are best represented by the production output of the studios. Thus, the chapter on melodramas, though it covers the genre from 1909 (*A Corner in Wheat*) to 1982 (*E. T.: The Extra-Terrestrial*) and even makes a case for certain melodramatic aspects that structure *Home Alone* (1990), focuses primarily on the 1920s.

Though the chapter on film comedy discusses the genre from the 1910s to the 1990s, it concentrates on the comedies of Frank Capra, Howard Hawks, and other directors of the 1930s. The chapter on the war film, though it includes discussion of Vietnam War films, devotes the bulk of its attention to the 1940s. And so on and so forth with the other genres.

In other words, each genre chapter focuses on a particular decade but also traces the history of that genre beyond that particular decade. At the same time, it attempts to link shifts within that genre's evolution to changes that occur within the larger profile of American cultural history.

Not all genres are covered here. There is no chapter on the musical, the gangster film, the horror film, the science-fiction film, or other major genres. Such coverage, though it might make the book more complete, would significantly change its focus and balance. Genres are a crucial part of the phenomenon of American cinema, but they need to be seen within the larger context of the institutional structure of the industry that produces them. And, as the chapters in the last section of the text suggest, individual genre films need to be seen within their larger cultural context—that is, within the history of culture.

Finally, the book concludes with a review of the history of recent American cinema. It provides an analysis of the postwar assaults on Hollywood by the anti-Communist witch-hunts of the late-1940s and 1950s, by the advent of television, by the social and political upheavals of the 1960s, and by the rise of new generations of filmmakers in the 1970s, 1980s, and 1990s. These filmmakers (and their audiences) grew up during the Cold War, watched television as kids, and were shaped, in one way or another, by the counterculture of the 1960s, Vietnam and Watergate in the 1970s, and Reaganite America in the 1980s.

This history of Hollywood in the postwar years describes the dismantling of the old Hollywood as a unique system of production, distribution, and exhibition and the attempts to construct a new Hollywood out of whatever pieces of the old that could be salvaged and adapted to the needs of a changing marketplace. This section looks back to both the first part of the book, which describes the classical mode of production that is transformed in the postwar years, and the second part, which outlines the histories of various genres, which are themselves altered by this new mode of production. Indeed, the discussion of genres, which notes their postwar transformation, anticipates the final section. This segment of the book also traces the contemporary cinema's attempts to recover its initial integrity as a system through its interest in certain filmmaking practices, which are discussed in "The 1960s: The Counterculture Strikes Back," "The Film School Generation," and "Into the 1990s: Bringing It All Back Home." This final chapter juxtaposes mainstream Hollywood cinema of the 1980s and early 1990s with a variety of countercurrent cinemas, ranging from films made at the fringe of the mainstream by directors such as Martin Scorsese, David Lynch, and others to films produced by independent and minority filmmakers such as Spike Lee, Jim Jarmusch, Todd Haynes, and Julie Dash.

Each chapter concludes with a chronological filmography of relevant motion pictures that the reader might wish to look at in order to explore a bit further the ideas and issues dealt with in the text. Each chapter also provides a select bibliography of books and articles that can be consulted for additional information about the subject. A glossary of technical and other terms is at the end of the text to assist the reader in defining crucial nomenclature and terminology.

The movies play a crucial role in our lives. They entertain us, but they also educate us. The education which they provide lies not so much in what they show—in what stories or situations we see on the screen. Rather it consists of the attitudes that the movies take to the underlying concerns with which our culture seems continuously preoccupied. The chief concern which this book examines is that of twentieth-century America as well—the traumatic shift in identity that takes place as the country evolves from a nineteenth-century, rural, agrarian-based, social, cultural, and economic community into a modern, urban, industrialized mass society. The movies, which were born in the midst of this crisis in American identity, emerge as a crucial factor in its resolution. They serve, in part, to help us to negotiate this transition. This book looks at how they do that.

PART I

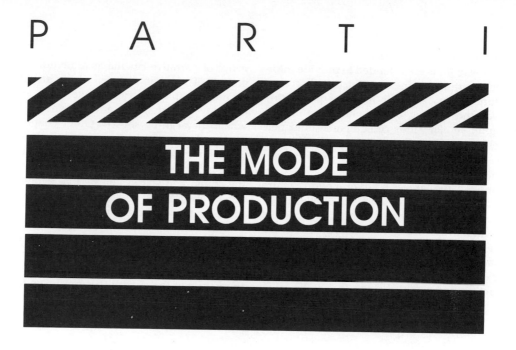

THE MODE OF PRODUCTION

Motion pictures are made in a variety of different ways. Some films, such as home movies, are inexpensively produced by individuals who own or rent amateur filmmaking equipment. They use 16mm, super 8, 8mm, or video equipment to film everyday, nonfictional occurrences, such as birthday parties, weddings, holiday celebrations, vacations, and other family-related events. They do not bother to record sound or edit (or otherwise assemble) their footage in any particular way; they show what they film as it was filmed. And they "exhibit" their films in the privacy of their own homes to audiences that consist of family members, relatives, and friends.

At the other end of the spectrum stand expensively produced, feature-length, Hollywood productions. These works boast casts of thousands, high-priced stars, lavish costumes and sets, intricate narratives, complicated special effects, dangerous stunts, meticulous sound recording, and elaborate sound design. For their successful completion they require the facilities of a major studio or an independently assembled crew of several hundred technicians and craftspersons. These films take several months to a year to produce. They require painstaking preparation in

the stage of preproduction, during which scripts are written, parts are cast, and budgets are planned. They demand the expertise of skilled professionals during the filming or production process, when the efforts of the producer, director, screenwriter, cameraperson, actors, costume and set designers, sound recordists, and scores of others are carefully coordinated to transfer the script to film. And they call upon the extensive skill and training of sound mixers, editors, and other personnel during the phase of postproduction in order to produce a high-class product that can then be sold to the general public. The distribution, advertising, marketing, and exhibition of the finished product enlist the aid of another team of experts, who design publicity campaigns and prepare marketing materials (such as posters, trailers, and television ads).

In between these two extremes are a variety of different filmmaking practices. They include avant-garde films, which are made by individuals using amateur equipment and techniques but which are designed for public exhibition. At the same time, industrial films are commercially produced using professional equipment and professionally trained staff. But, unlike experimental

1

works, these films are intended to provide information about the business products and services that fund them. Another mode of production involves the making of documentaries, which rely upon similar kinds of equipment and personnel but which are financed by public funds or grants and tend to explore topical or controversial public issues.

Although the largest body of motion picture "production" (in terms of sheer footage) undoubtedly consists of home movies, the mode of production with which the majority of Americans are most familiar is probably that of the Hollywood feature film. The chapters which follow examine the basic features of this mode of production. Individual chapters look at the emergence of narrative cinema as a medium and the growth of a movie culture, which includes the creation of an industry to make films, an audience to support them, and movie theaters in which they can be shown. Other chapters also explore the basic narrative and stylistic features of the films that dominate this industry. And still other chapters examine the industrial systems—the studio and star systems—that evolve in order to ensure that motion pictures generate a profit for those who make them.

This section of the book argues that Hollywood's mode of production plays a central role in determining the basic features of American cinema and that these features reflect, in part, the nature of the system that produced them.

CHAPTER 1

THE EMERGENCE OF THE CINEMA AS AN INSTITUTION

"THE CATHEDRAL OF THE MOTION PICTURE"

For the better part of this century, the movies have enjoyed a unique status as the premiere entertainment activity for the majority of Americans. The movies, like baseball, have become something of a national pastime. Americans not only supported their motion pictures but loved them as well. Going to the movies, though perhaps not a religious experience for most, was certainly an ecstatic experience for many. Ecstasy came not only from the movies themselves but also from the surroundings in which they were presented.

Movie palaces built in the 1910s, 1920s, and 1930s resemble gigantic cathedrals. Indeed, the 6200-seat Roxy, the world's largest theater, described itself in advertisements as "the cathedral of the motion picture." Spectacular theaters like the Roxy inspired awe, and this awe inspired, in turn, cartoons like that in the *New Yorker* in which a little girl, staring in amazement at the interior of a theater lobby, asked "Mama—does God live here?"

The cult status of movies extended to those who appeared in them. Movie fans helped to transform charismatic screen actors and actresses into movie stars, making them the objects of intense popular fascination and even idolization. Although mass-produced, movies have recovered a certain sense of "aura" or at least a unique sense of novelty and excitement for consumers of mass culture. Unlike preindustrial forms of entertainment such as the theater, the things represented (the characters, the story) were not really "there," live before the audience. Instead, they were only there indirectly; they were present in the form of images on the screen. Although they were mechanically reproduced, they nonetheless continued to create an impression of immediacy and presence. At any rate, audiences regarded them as "special." They waited for hours in lines several blocks long to see new films that had been highly publicized, critically acclaimed, or that were controversial—or which merely featured their favorite stars.

For 20 years, from the coming of sound in 1929 to the postwar period (1949), roughly 80 to 90 million Americans went to the movies *every week*. In other words, virtually every American between the ages of six and sixty went to the movies at least once a week. Although certain films, like *Gone with the Wind* (1939), drew more viewers than others, moviegoing had become a habit and increasing numbers of spectators religiously went to see whatever was

An advertisement for a new movie palace, the Paramount Theatre, describes it as "the play-ground of the millions, in a Palace worthy of a King."

playing at their neighborhood theater. Though the movies may have resembled a religious institution, they were always primarily a social institution—going to the movies became a way in which people passed their leisure time. However, in even the most common sense of the term, by the 1920s the cinema had definitely become an institution—an integral feature of the experience of being an American in the twentieth century. Going to the movies became as commonplace as going to school, to work, or to church. For earlier generations, it was as familiar an activity as watching television has become today.

DEVELOPING SYSTEMS: SOCIETY AND TECHNOLOGY

The cinema is an institution in a number of senses of the term "institution." It is an economic institution, designed to make money. In order to do this, it established itself as an industry. It is a complex organization of producers, distributors, and exhibitors whose job it is to make and market motion pictures. In order to accomplish its goals, the industry developed a basic technology that facilitates the production and exhibition of movies. It also established various "systems"—such as the star system (see Chapter 5) and the genre system—which are designed to ensure that individual films return a profit to the industry that produces, distributes, and exhibits them. Stars and genres serve as known commodities that guarantee, up front, a certain minimal amount of pleasure that can be expected by viewers. Thus, in addition to the basic technological machinery required for making and showing films, the industry developed a secondary, "mental" machinery, which makes audiences want to go to the movies.

In other words, the cinema, as an institution, developed on a variety of different levels at the same time. It functions as a social institution. That is, it is a means of providing an appropriate form of social contact for members of an emerging American populace born and bred in the world of mass culture. Indeed, it became an even more appropriate and more modern forum for leisure-time communal activity, for example, than were previous working-class, social institutions such as churches, dance halls, social clubs, and saloons, which belong, more properly, to an earlier, preindustrial culture. At the same time, the cinema evolved as a technological institution, which became dependent for its success upon products of the Industrial Revolution —cameras, celluloid, microphones, amplifiers, magnetic recording tape, film laboratories, electricity, projectors, speakers, and screens. And it serves as a psychological institution whose purpose is to encourage the moviegoing habit by providing the kind of entertainment that working-class and middle-class Americans want.

The cinematic institution has changed from period to period, responding, in part, to technological changes, to the changing demands and leisure-time activities of audiences, and to social and economic changes that take place within American culture as a whole. But these changes have taken place within a more or less fixed notion of the cinema's identity as a medium. For roughly 100 years, no matter how often the face of the cinema has changed, the underlying structure of the cinematic experience has remained more or less the same. Going to the cinema has consisted of watching life-size images projected upon a screen.

Yet even this fundamental feature of the cinema's identity was not always there. In order to understand what the cinema is and how it works, it is important to look at how it took shape. The identity of the cinema as an institution remains bound up with the sociocultural conditions within which it was conceived and developed by the growing film industry and within which it was experienced and consumed by an emerging society of habitual moviegoers.

EDISON AND THE KINETOSCOPE

Capturing Time

The origins of the cinema lie in the development of mass communication technology. The cinema serves as the culmination of an age that saw the invention of the telegraph (1837), photography (1826–1839), the typewriter (1873), the telephone (1876), the phonograph (1878), roll film (1880), the Kodak camera (1888), George Eastman's motion picture film (1889), Thomas Edison's motion picture camera (1891–1893), Marconi's wireless telegraph (1895), and the motion picture projector (1895–1896).

Edison, who had played a role in the development of the telegraph, the phonograph, and electricity, used the phonograph as a model for his "invention" of the motion picture. Actually, Edison did not so much invent as "produce" the first motion picture camera, the Kinetoscope. The actual execution of Edison's goal of creating an "instrument which [did] for the eye what the phonograph [did] for the ear" was accomplished through the effort of Edison's assistant, W. K. L. Dickson, which was itself based on earlier work by Étienne-Jules Marey.

The Kinetoscope, along with the telegraph, photography, the telephone, the phonograph, and the wireless telegraph, transformed the face of late nineteenth-century culture. Traditional notions of space and distance, which were based in part on how long it took to get from one place to another, were redefined by the virtually instantaneous transmission of information from one geographical location to another. Traditional notions of time underwent revision as still photographs captured moments of the present in ways that had eluded more "primitive" forms of representation. Photographs, unlike sketches, paintings, and sculptures, record events instantaneously before they vanish into memory. Thus the present and the past are rescued from the passage of time, lifted out of its continuous ongoing process, and frozen for all to see. Motion pictures record and reproduce the flow of time in a way that had previously been impossible, even in photography.

Photography and the motion picture introduce—and *institutionalize*—a new, modern conception of time. Time could not only be caught but also replayed. It becomes, in a sense, a commodity. In the past, time had been "spent" and then the experience of that time had disappeared. But with still photography, the phonograph, and the motion picture, time is objectified. It can be marketed, in the form of photos, records, or movies, and it can be infinitely reexperienced. In short, the new communication technologies that arose at the end of the nineteenth century helped give birth to mass culture and the era of mass consumption, in part, by transforming time into a product that can be reproduced and sold. The cinema's ability to objectify and commodify time became crucial to its success.

As a medium, the cinema realizes the goals of a twentieth-century consumer society whose desires have been shaped by the Industrial Revolution. This society is encouraged by advertising and other forms of mass persuasion to consume what machines produce for them. These mass-produced products range from material goods such as cosmetics, clothes, household furnishings, and foodstuffs, to less tangible items such as motion pictures. The cinema emerges as the perfect consumer product in that it not only gives audiences an experience to consume but it also functions as a "display window" for other mass-produced goods. As Charles Eckert argues, the movies serve as a showcase for consumer goods, including sewing machines, typewriters, telephones, automobiles, furniture, and fashions, which audiences then seek to obtain for themselves.

Peepshows versus Projectors

The cinema did not emerge as a form of mass consumption, however, until its technology evolved from its initial format of peepshow into its final form as projected images upon a screen in a darkened theater. Edison's Kinetoscope was designed for use in Kinetoscope parlors, which contained only a few individual machines and which permitted only one customer to view a short, 50-foot film at any one time. The first Kinetoscope parlors contained five machines. For the price of 25 cents (or 5 cents per machine), customers moved from machine to machine to watch five different films (or, in the case of famous prizefights, successive rounds of a single fight).

These Kinetoscope arcades were modeled on phonograph parlors which had proved successful for Edison several years earlier. In the phonograph parlors, customers listened to recordings through individual ear tubes, moving from one machine to the next to hear different recorded speeches or pieces of music. The Kinetoscope parlors functioned in a similar way. More interested in the sale of Kinetoscopes (for roughly $1000 apiece) to these parlors than in the films (which cost approximately $10 to $15 each) that would be run in them, Edison refused to develop projection technology, reasoning (quite correctly) that if he made and sold projectors, then exhibitors would purchase only one machine—a projector—from him instead of several.

Exhibitors, however, wanted to maximize *their* profits, which they could do more readily by projecting a handful of films to hundreds of customers at a time (rather than to one at a time) and by charging 25 to 50 cents admission. About a year after the opening of the first Kinetoscope parlor in 1894, show-

Edison's peepshow Kinetoscope, featuring ear tubes for sound, entertains one customer at a time.

men, such as Louis and Auguste Lumiere, Thomas Armat and Francis Jenkins, and Orville and Woodville Latham (with the assistance of Edison's former assistant, Dickson), perfected projection devices, which were used in vaudeville houses, legitimate theaters, local town halls, makeshift storefront theaters, fairgrounds, and amusement parks to show films to a mass audience.

MASS PRODUCTION, MASS CONSUMPTION

A Public Spectacle

With the advent of projection in 1895–1896, the motion pictures became the ultimate form of mass consumption. Previous audiences, of course, had viewed spectacles en masse at the theater, where vaudeville, popular dramas, musical and minstrel shows, classical plays, lectures, and slide and lantern shows had been presented to several hundred spectators at a time. But the movies differed significantly from these other forms of entertainment which depended upon either live performance or (in the case of slide and lantern shows) the active involvement of a master of ceremonies who assembled the final program.

Although exhibitors regularly accompanied movies with live acts, the substance of the movies themselves is mass-produced, prerecorded material that can easily be reproduced for audiences by theaters with little or no active participation on their part. Even though early exhibitors shaped their film programs by editing them together in whichever way they thought would be the most attractive to audiences or by accompanying them with lectures, their creative control remained limited. What audiences came to see was the technological marvel of the movies; the lifelike reproduction of the commonplace motion of trains, of waves striking the shore and of people walking in the street; and the magic made possible by trick photography and the manipulation of the camera.

With the advent of projection, the viewer's relationship with the image is no longer private, as it had been with peepshow devices such as the Kinetoscope and the Mutoscope, which was a similar machine that reproduced motion by means of successive images on individual photographic cards instead of images on strips of celluloid. It suddenly becomes public—an experience which the viewer shares with dozens, scores, and even hundreds of others. At the same time, the image which the spectator looks at expands from the minuscule peepshow dimensions of 1 or 2 inches (in height) to the life-size proportions of 6 or 9 feet. The spectator is no longer a peeping tom looking guiltily through a keyhole but a voyeur whose activity is shared (and thus semiauthorized) by a larger public.

Middle-Class Amusements

From 1896 to roughly 1905, when the nickelodeon era began, the audience which goes to the movies (in the United States, at least) is the same more or less middle-class audience that had previously gone to vaudeville shows, variety theaters, and amusement parks. Indeed, the movies become variety acts of a sort, which play alongside live acts in places which provide a broad spectrum of different kinds of popular entertainment. Although the audiences consisted of all socioeconomic classes, the cost of admission tended to exclude the lower classes as did the length of the program, which in vaudeville theaters lasted 2 hours or more. As a result, working-class laborers, who worked (ca. 1900) 60 hours a week or more and earned less than $4 a week, could only afford to attend on occasion.

The films mirror the variety contexts within which they were presented. Shown primarily in vaudeville houses until 1905, motion pictures appealed to audiences as "attractions," as a series of acts within the larger act of motion pictures, which was itself often only one of eight other "live" variety acts. The kinds of films shown were actualities (documentaries, views of famous or distant places), recorded vaudeville acts, excerpts from popular plays, phantom rides (films shot from the front of moving vehicles), and trick films, which use the techniques of slow motion, reverse motion, substitution, and multiple exposure to perform tricks or acts of "magic."

Scholars of early cinema, such as Tom Gunning, describe this cinema of attractions as essentially an "exhibitionist" cinema. As attractions, films with self-descriptive titles like *The Execution of Mary Queen of Scots* (1895) or *Electrocuting an Elephant* (1903) present or exhibit spectacles for viewers to admire. Strongmen, such as Eugene Sandow, flex their muscles for the camera and exotic dancers, such as Fatima, perform for the camera. Certain erotic films, such as *From Showgirl to Burlesque Queen* (1903), rely upon a more traditional form of exhibitionism, as women undress before and look flirtatiously at the camera.

Early, pre-1906 cinema stresses "showing" rather than "telling." The majority of films made in this period are actualities, which outnumber fiction films until roughly 1906, when the percentage of story films begins to increase dramatically and actualities become less and less popular. The shift from one kind of cinema to the other takes place rapidly. By 1908, 96 percent of all American films tell stories. The "institutionalization" of narrative as the primary category of American motion picture production marks the beginning of another stage in the development of the cinema as an institution. It is accompanied by a significant change in film exhibition.

The Nickelodeon: A Collective Experience

Starting in 1905, theaters devoted exclusively to the showing of motion picture films begin to spring up in virtually every city in the country. Referred to as "nickelodeons" because the price of admission was initially only a nickel (this figure subsequently rose to 10 cents), these small, 200-seat theaters were quickly installed in or near shopping and/or entertainment districts in former stores which were converted, often in an extremely makeshift way, to movie theaters. The low cost of admission and the abbreviated length of the program attracted a new class of patrons, whom previous (and more expensive) forms of popular entertainment had ignored—the working classes.

Previously, working-class amusements had been confined to the home, the church, the saloon, or the social club. Nickelodeons drew the poorer elements of society, including recent immigrants, out of the ethnic social life associated with their local neighborhoods into a more diversified public space, where members of different classes and religions were transformed into a community of moviegoers. At the same time, these theaters continued to attract members of the middle-class audience that had earlier seen movies in vaudeville theaters.

Although the nickelodeons were never the melting pot of American democracy that certain historians have claimed, by 1910 they did provide the 26 million Americans who attended over 10,000 nickelodeons each week a common entertainment program. For the first time, millions of Americans from different backgrounds watched the same films, and thus shared a collective experience as an invisible community. As the popularity of the nickelodeons increased and the moviegoing audience expanded, these theaters began to serve as the site for the creation of a homogeneous, middle-class American culture.

Author's collection

The exterior of a typical nickelodeon, the Cascade Theatre in New Castle, Pennsylvania (ca. 1903).

As a writer for *Harper's* magazine noted upon visiting a nickelodeon in 1913, once the various members of the ethnically, socially, and economically diverse audience had taken their seats, they became part of a single crowd, caught up in the dreamlike images on the screen. This utopian ideal of a classless (or universally middle-class) community of spectators may never have been realized, but its potential was certainly there in the form of an institution of mass production and mass exhibition that was itself national in scope.

Cleaning Up: The Benefits of Respectability

The film industry was becoming more and more stabilized. In 1908, the major film producers banded together to form the Motion Picture Patents Company (MPPC), which sought to control all aspects of motion picture production, distribution, and exhibition (see Chapter 4, "The Studio System"). Shortly after the formation of the MPPC, exhibitors and film producers sought to expand the market of habitual moviegoers to include greater and greater numbers of those who had previously attended only "high-class" amusements, such as the theater and vaudeville.

Moviegoing as a social institution: The opening night audience at the (segregated) Rex Theater on April 4, 1912. Whites sit in the orchestra while blacks are seated in the balcony.

However, in December 1908, the mayor of New York City had ordered that all nickel theaters be closed, arguing that they posed a "threat to the city's physical and moral well-being." Exhibitors and members of the MPPC responded almost immediately with a campaign to improve the content of motion pictures and the conditions of theaters. At the same time, exhibitors consciously began to court middle-class customers by becoming more "respectable." They provided half-price matinees for women and children, they upgraded the quality of the physical structure of the theaters, they eliminated lower-class elements such as ethnic films and foreign-language sing-alongs, and they raised prices.

Producers joined the program to uplift the movies by making films that appealed to a higher class of clientele. They engaged in self-censorship to control any content of motion pictures that might prove offensive to middle-class tastes. And they voluntarily submitted their films to the National Board of Censorship (an independent body of censors) for review. In an attempt to appeal to middle-class sensibilities, they drew more and more upon the classics. Prior to 1908, the source material for movies had come from newspaper headlines, vaudeville and burlesque routines, political cartoons, fairy tales, and popular songs. Between 1907 and 1911, however, Vitagraph released more than 50 films that were based upon literary, historical, or biblical sources. Filmmakers begin to adapt the works of Edgar Allan Poe, Charles Dickens, Emile Zola, Leo Tolstoy, Victor Hugo, and William Shakespeare.

SPECTACLE AND STORYTELLING: FROM PORTER TO GRIFFITH

The Camera as Recorder

The bourgeoisification of the movies involves considerably more than merely upgrading motion picture content from strongmen flexing their muscles to Shakespeare. In adapting more complex story material to the screen, film-makers are forced to upgrade their own abilities as storytellers. While early American cinema had been exhibitionist in nature, content with showing attractions, subsequent (post-1908) American cinema becomes more and more intent on the perfection of narrative skills. Mere theatrical display proves less and less capable of conveying complex character psychology or intricate narrative complications. Bourgeois, middle-class audiences who had grown up with the highly involved plots and fascinating characters of authors such as Dickens begin to demand more sophisticated film narratives than had their predecessors. Film directors like D. W. Griffith, who carefully crafted narrative personae for themselves, provide these new audiences with the kinds of narratives with which they are familiar in the theater or in literature.

Edwin S. Porter, the major filmmaker associated with early American cinema, epitomizes the presentational style of pre-Griffith cinema. Intent on a theatrical style of spectacle, Porter composes his narratives out of a succession of separate attractions. In one of his most famous films, *The Life of an American Fireman* (1903), Porter shows the fireman's dramatic rescue of a mother and her baby from the second story of a burning building. In the final version of the film, Porter presents the action of the rescue as he had originally filmed it—in two successive shots. Filmed at two separate times as two separate spectacles staged in two separate spaces, the event remained that way for the audiences who saw it in 1903.

In the first shot, audiences see the interior of a smoke-filled room; the fireman enters, rescues the woman, and returns a few moments later to rescue the infant. In the next shot, audiences see the exterior of the building; the fireman enters, rescues the woman by carrying her down a ladder, and then, informed that her child is still in the room, returns to rescue the baby. In other words, Porter shows the same action from two different perspectives successively rather than cutting back and forth from the interior to the exterior of the building to follow the unfolding of the drama as it might have been told by a storyteller more intent upon suspense and the act of narration itself. (In fact, the latter version of the film, assembled by subsequent distributors of the film, did circulate in the film library of the Museum of Modern Art for 30 or more years until the original version was discovered in the mid-1970s.)

The Camera as Narrator

Primitive cinema presents events but provides little or no "reading" of them. Events speak for themselves without the intervention of a narrator or narrating presence which attempts to read or interpret them for the audience.

Stories are told, but they are told directly; the camera does not read events but merely records them instead. The cinema of Griffith (and later) actively narrates events, shaping the audience's perception of them. This is accomplished in a variety of ways, but chief among them, for Griffith at least, is the device of parallel editing, which involves cutting back and forth from two (or more) simultaneous events taking place in separate spaces.

Gunning describes the parallel editing in Griffith's *The Drive for Life* (1909), which cuts back and forth from a man, who discovers that the woman he has jilted has sent a box of poisoned chocolates to his fiancee, to his fiancee, who is about to eat one of the pieces of candy. As the fiancee picks up a piece of chocolate and is about to eat it, Griffith cuts away, in midgesture, to her lover, speeding to her in his car to warn her of her danger. The suspense editing repeatedly interrupts her action, returning to show her being distracted by her sister, dropping the candy, or kissing it. Each time the film cuts away from her as she is about to eat the poisoned candy, the presence of Griffith as a narrator can be dramatically felt. The drama is clearly being constructed for the audience by these intrusions, as it is through similar editing patterns in *The Lonely Villa* (1909), *The Lonedale Operator* (1911), and other last-minute, race-to-the-rescue films directed by Griffith.

At the same time, Griffith uses editing to contribute to the psychological development of his characters, giving the audience a sense of what they are thinking. Thus, in *After Many Years* (1908) he cuts from a wife to the object of her thoughts—her shipwrecked husband. Other edits are used to explain the motivation or the behavior of his characters. Thus, in *Salvation Army Lass* (1908), Griffith cuts away from a burglar on his way to commit a crime to a shot of his girlfriend, still lying on the ground where he had left her after rejecting her pleas that he not go on the job. When Griffith cuts back to the burglar, who then changes his mind about going ahead with the crime, he deftly conveys to the audience the reasons for the burglar's change of heart. Similar cutaways serve to explain character behavior in Griffith's historical epic, *The Birth of a Nation* (1915).

The "Feature" Film

With the emergence of a cinema of narration, which replaced that of "monstration" or showing, classical Hollywood cinema takes one step further toward the institutionalization of the cinema as an American pastime. As narratives become more complex, the 1000-foot, one-reel (ten-to-fifteen minute) format of the motion picture, which had only recently become an industrywide standard in 1908, becomes more and more restrictive. Critics in the trade magazine *Moving Picture World* observe that "the filming of some great opera or a popular literary or dramatic or historical subject requires more than a reel" and suggest that the longer the pictures, the more exhibitors could charge audiences to see them.

Multiple-reel "feature" films from abroad, such as *Dante's Inferno* (five reels, Italy, 1911), *Queen Elizabeth* (four reels, France, 1912), *Quo Vadis* (eight reels, Italy, 1913) and *Cabiria* (ten reels, Italy, 1914) were showcased in large, first-class legitimate theaters, which charged from 25 cents to a dollar for tickets. The financial success of these multiple-reel European films prompted American producers to release longer and longer films, including Griffith's biblical spectacle, *Judith of Bethulia* (four reels, 1914), his adaptation of Poe's "The Telltale Heart" and "Annabel Lee," *The Avenging Conscience* (six reels, 1914), and his historical epic, *The Birth of a Nation* (twelve reels, 1915).

The Birth, which sustains an intricate narrative for three hours of screen time, held audiences spellbound. One of Griffith's assistants, Karl Brown, reports his reactions to seeing the fully assembled film for the first time on opening night. "What unfolded on that screen was magic itself. I knew there were cuts from this and to that, but try as I would, I could not *see* them. . . . All I knew was that between the ebb and flow of a broad canvas of a great battle, now far and now near, and the roaring of that gorgeous orchestra banging and blaring battle songs to stir the coldest blood, I was hot and cold and feeling waves of tingling electric shocks racing all over me."

The Birth ran for 44 consecutive weeks at the Liberty Theater in New York City, where reserved-seat tickets were sold at the unprecedented price of $2. Its success transformed the nature of American film production and exhibition. It marks the end of "the lowly nickelodeon storefront theater, with its tinny honky-tonk piano and its windowless, foul-air smelliness" and introduces "the grandeur of a great auditorium with a great orchestra and a great picture that ran for three hours and filled an entire evening with thrills and excitement in a setting of opulent luxury such as the great masses of working people had never dreamed possible for them."

PRESENTING . . . THE MOVIE PALACE

"Gardens of Dreams"

The advent of multiple-reel, feature-length films is accompanied by a dramatic change in motion picture presentation as the uncomfortable, small, makeshift nickelodeons give way to luxurious movie palaces and other large theaters especially built for the showing of motion pictures. Though the majority of movie theaters built in the 1910s and 1920s tend to be modest in size, seating from 500 to 800 spectators, more and more large movie palaces, seating from 1500 to over 6000 spectators, were built in urban areas. In contrast to the congestion and oppressive sense of city life experienced by urban residents outside the theater, inside the typical movie palace customers enjoy the luxury of spacious, stately surroundings and a staff of obliging theater attendants who seek to answer their every need.

Movie palaces, boasting a palatial decor that ranged from the classical to the exotic, provide "an acre of seats in a garden of dreams." Contemporary interior decorator Harold Rambusch declared, in 1929, that "in our big modern movie palaces are collected the most gorgeous rugs, furniture and fixtures that money can produce. No kings or emperors have wandered through more luxurious surroundings. In a sense, these theatres are social safety valves in that the public can partake of the same luxuries as the rich."

The interior of a typical movie palace, the Brooklyn Paramount.

The Great Showmen

The era of the movie palace begins in 1913 with the opening of the 2460-seat Regent, "the first de luxe theatre built expressly for showing movies in New York." Shortly after the Regent opened, showman S. L. Rothapfel was hired to manage it. He made it the premier motion picture theater in the world. Like the movie palaces that follow it, the Regent features an organ, an orchestra, a chorus and/or opera singers, ushers to show patrons to their seats, and a lavish, atmospheric interior adorned with gilt.

Rothapfel, or "Roxy" as he was called by his associates, was subsequently lured away from the Regent, which was located uptown at 116th Street and Seventh Avenue, to operate the 3500-seat Strand (1914), which was downtown at Broadway and 47th Street. The *New York Times* reviewed opening night, was impressed by the neo-Corinthian decor and the plush seats, and compared the experience to "going to a Presidential reception." Roxy later lent his flair for extravagant motion picture presentation to the 1900-seat Rialto, when it opened on Times Square in 1916.

By this time, the entertainment program of the movie palace has expanded to include, in addition to the theatre orchestra's overture and musical accompaniment of the silent feature, dancers, opera singers, and other performers in live skits. The film program has also evolved to consist of not only the feature film but a newsreel and a comedy short as well. In fact, the feature presentation tends to occupy only about 68 percent of the entire program.

Roxy continued to provide bigger and better shows in a series of other New York theaters. He took over the management of the 2100-seat Rivoli (built in 1917) and of the 5300-seat Capitol (built in 1919, managed by Roxy in 1920), and then of his own 6200-seat Roxy theatre (1927). By the time he built the Roxy, the art of exhibition had developed into a science. Not only are uniformed ushers and other theater personnel drilled in their duties like military cadets, but spectators become part of this streamlined system of efficiency as well. As Richard Koszarski points out, "each seat in the Roxy was wired to a central console so the house staff could immediately direct patrons to new vacancies."

In Los Angeles, impresario Sid Grauman followed Roxy's example, launching a series of movie palaces which were each more lavish than the other. While Roxy gives his audiences an entertainment program consisting of a variety of different live acts to accompany the film, Grauman provides a "Prologue," a show thematically related to the motion picture. His theater empire begins with the Million Dollar Theatre (2100 seats) in 1917, then the Egyptian (1900 seats) in 1922, the Metropolitan (3485 seats) in 1923, and the Chinese (2500 seats) in 1927. As the names "Egyptian" and "Chinese" sug-

Grauman's Chinese Theater in the late 1920s.

Author's collection

gest, a number of movie palaces of the 1920s adopt exotic architectural styles, employing Oriental, Hindu, Italian, Persian, Moorish, or Spanish decor in order to create a romantic atmosphere within which audiences could consume onscreen fantasies.

Other major cites, such as Chicago, built movie palaces of their own. Theater magnates A. J. Balaban and Sam Katz, following the major routes of urban mass-transit lines, put their theaters within reach of a growing urban middle class, building the 2400-seat Central Park Theatre in 1917; both the 4700-seat Tivoli Theatre and the 3900-seat Chicago Theatre in 1921; and the 4000-seat Uptown Theatre in the mid-1920s. In addition to the mighty Wurlitzer organ, full orchestras, and live stage shows, Balaban & Katz theaters provide patrons with "free child care, attendant smoking rooms, foyers and lobbies lined with paintings and sculpture, and organ music for those waiting in line." A staff of nurses and mother's helpers take care of the young children of patrons in the theater basement, which was equipped like a neighborhood playground with slides and sandboxes. At the same time, starting in 1921, Balaban & Katz theaters also have air conditioning, which gives them a crucial advantage over their competition throughout the summer months.

Noting the success of the Balaban & Katz theaters in Chicago, Paramount joined forces with their organization and put Sam Katz in charge of all Paramount theaters. As a result, the model for movie palaces developed by Balaban & Katz found widespread adoption within the Paramount theater circuit. It quickly spread to the circuits of other major studios as well, becoming the standard used by the film industry as a whole.

With the construction of theaters especially designed for the exhibition of motion pictures, with the shift from one-reel films to the new phenomenon of the feature-length film which presents narratives and characters as sophisticated as those found in other typically middle-class forms of representation, and with the development of a habitual, movie-going audience composed of a broad spectrum of the general public, the basic elements of the cinematic institution fell into place.

AN EVOLVING INSTITUTION

The cinema began as a technological marvel, as the latest invention from Thomas Edison, the "wizard of Menlo Park." The early cinema of the pre-nickelodeon days evolved from a primitive cinema of attractions into a modern cinema of compelling characters, engrossing stories, and hypnotic illusionism. Throughout the 1920s, the presentation of motion pictures retains its origins in the world of amusement parks, vaudeville, and burlesque. The movie palaces are themselves spectacles which frequently overwhelm the films which are shown in them. House orchestras and stage shows also foster an air of variety as does the presence of newsreels, comedy shorts, and other filmed material which round out the program. Yet the feature film holds its own among these other attractions. Its ability to give expression to its characters' emotions, to explore their psyches, to trace their pursuit of their goals—in short, to tell their stories—has evolved to a point of near perfection. The coming of sound, color, widescreen, and stereo sound will add somewhat to the feature film's expressive capabilities, but will not profoundly alter classical Hollywood cinema's ability to function as an efficient system of storytelling. Today's filmmakers draw on essentially the same set of stylistic practices and narrative techniques as those forged by Griffith and others during the period in which the fundamental elements of the feature film were established.

Other features of the cinematic institution, however, have been dismantled. The 1920s witnessed the creation of a general, moviegoing public, which habitually patronized the nation's cinemas. For over 20 years, from 1929 to 1949, an average of 83 million Americans went to the movies every week. In 1991, the average weekly attendance stands at 19 million, where it has been (with only minor variation) since 1967. The age of the nickelodeon gives way to that of the movie palace in the 1910s and 1920s. In the 1960s, the gigantic movie palaces of the past give way to the new nickelodeons of the present—to small, minimally decorated multiplexes and mall cinemas. The Roxy was torn down in 1961. Radio City Music Hall, though still standing, ceased showing motion pictures on a regular basis in 1978. The cinematic institution of Hollywood past has disappeared. It slowly transformed itself, during the 1950s, 1960s, 1970s, and 1980s, into a new institution, designed to serve the different needs of contemporary audiences and of an ever-changing, modern motion picture marketplace.

The chapters which follow are designed to provide an in-depth portrait of the cinematic institution in its heyday. They look at its stylistic foundations in classical Hollywood's stylistic and narrative practices, at its industrial roots in the studio system, and at its basic economic underpinnings in the star and genre systems. Its goal is not only to draw a map of the terrain of the institution of American cinema but to recover for today's generation of moviegoers some sense of the *experience* which previous generations had when they went out to movies.

SELECT FILMOGRAPHY

The Life of an American Fireman (1903)
After Many Years (1908)
Salvation Army Lass (1908)

The Drive for Life (1909)
The Lonely Villa (1909)
The Lonedale Operator (1911)
The Birth of a Nation (1915)

SELECT BIBLIOGRAPHY

Bordwell, David, Janet Staiger, and Kristin Thompson. *The Classical Hollywood Cinema: Film Style and Mode of Production to 1960.* New York: Columbia University Press, 1985.

Bowser, Eileen. *The Transformation of Cinema: 1907–1915.* New York: Scribner, 1990.

Brown, Karl. *Adventures with D. W. Griffith.* New York: Farrar, Straus & Giroux, 1973.

Eckert, Charles. "The Carole Lombard in Macy's Window," *Quarterly Review of Film Studies* 3, 1 (Winter 1978).

Elsaesser, Thomas, ed. *Early Cinema: Space, Frame, Narrative.* London: BFI Publishing, 1990.

Gomery, Douglas. *Movie History: A Survey.* Belmont, CA: Wadsworth, 1991.
_____. *Shared Pleasures: A History of Movie Presentation in the United States.* Madison: University of Wisconsin Press, 1992.

Gunning, Tom. "The Cinema of Attractions: Early Film, the Spectator and the Avant-Garde," and "Weaving a Narrative: Style and Economic Background in Griffith's Biograph Films," in Thomas Elsaesser, ed., *Early Cinema: Space, Frame, Narrative.* London: BFI Publishing, 1990.

Hall, Ben M. *The Best Remaining Seats: The Story of the Golden Age of the Movie Palace.* New York: Bramhall House, 1961.

Hansen, Miriam. *Babel & Babylon: Spectatorship in American Silent Film.* Cambridge: Harvard University Press, 1991.

Kern, Stephen. *The Culture of Time and Space, 1880–1918.* Cambridge: Harvard University Press, 1983.

Koszarski, Richard. *An Evening's Entertainment: The Age of the Silent Feature Picture, 1915–1928.* New York: Scribner, 1990.

May, Lary. *Screening Out the Past: The Birth of Mass Culture and the Motion Picture Industry.* Chicago: University of Chicago Press, 1980.

Mayne, Judith. "Immigrants and Spectators," *Wide Angle* 5, 2 (1982).

Musser, Charles. *The Emergence of Cinema: The American Screen to 1907.* New York: Scribner, 1990.

CHAPTER 2

CLASSICAL HOLLYWOOD CINEMA: NARRATION

A NATIONAL STYLE

"The Temper of an Age . . ."

A work of art is customarily associated with the name of the artist, and the history of an art form is traditionally written in terms of those names. Such a history assumes that individual artists either live and work in a social vacuum or so transcend the constraints of time and place that their work stands outside of social history. But if the individual artist transcends society, we should remember that society is also and above all *within* that artist and that every work bears at least two signatures—that of the artist and that of the world in which the work was created.

In the field of art history, Heinrich Wolfflin introduces the concept of "a history of art without names." Wolfflin writes that history in terms of a typology of artistic styles or "schools" rather than in terms of isolated, individual works. By subsuming the individual styles of the Great Masters within the larger styles of the school or country at that particular moment in history in which they work, he draws attention to the multifaceted nature of style, which becomes for him an "expression of the temper of an age and a nation as well as an expression of the individual temperament."

The history of the cinema that is offered to students in introductory film courses has traditionally been written as a history of names, as a history of actors, directors, producers, and writers whose works transcend the times and places within which they are produced. But in the American cinema, individual artistic styles exist within the context of a larger, "national" style. It is against the background of this general style, which has come to be known as "classical Hollywood style," that the distinct individual styles of directors such as John Ford, Alfred Hitchcock, Howard Hawks, Josef von Sternberg, Orson Welles, Martin Scorsese, and others take shape.

Every American film, from recognized masterpieces such as *Citizen Kane* (1941), which transcends stylistic convention, to run-of-the-mill program pictures such as *Andy Hardy Gets Spring Fever* (1939), which merely observes convention, draws upon the fundamental stylistic principles of classical Hollywood cinema for its means of expression and, in doing so, conveys "the temper of an age and a nation" as well as that of the artists who produce it. Yet every film also articulates this style in a different way, inflecting the larger, "national" style with the individual accent(s) of particular studios, producers, directors, writers, stars, camerapersons, and other craftspeople who make them.

A Narrative Machine

Unlike the periods of art history, such as the Gothic, Renaissance, or Baroque, in which the overall stylistic features of each period are quite apparent even to the untrained eye, classical Hollywood cinema possesses a style which is largely invisible and difficult for the average spectator to see. Its invisibility is, in large part, the product of American cinema's proficiency as a narrative machine. Like the industry-based, assembly-line process innovated by Henry Ford and his peers in the business world to make the production of auto-mobiles and other consumer goods as streamlined and as economical as possible, American movies rapidly evolved during the 1910s and 1920s into a highly efficient mode of telling stories. Every aspect of the production opera-tion gears itself up to facilitate the smoothest possible flow of the narrative process.

As a result, the narrative is delivered so effortlessly and efficiently to the audience that it appears to have no source. It comes magically off the screen as if spontaneously creating itself in the presence of the spectators in the movie theater for their immediate consumption and pleasure. But, in fact, it is created; it is made according to classical principles of clarity, simplicity, elegance, order, economy, and symmetry. Classical works thus traditionally avoid excess, subjectivity, and undue emotionalism, striving for the Greek ideal of *maden agan*, or "nothing in excess."

EQUILIBRIUM AND DISRUPTION

Narrative process follows an orderly pattern in which an initial state of affairs is introduced, after which something occurs to disturb this equilibrium. Subsequent events attempt to restore the original status quo, but this is repeatedly frustrated, and order is recovered only at the end of the film.

For instance, Alfred Hitchcock's *Rear Window* (1954) begins with a state-ment of the narrative status quo, presenting a survey of the courtyard within which the action of the film will be set. The next few minutes of the film introduce the minor characters who live in the courtyard, as well as the film's major character, the news magazine photographer L. B. Jeffries (James Stew-art), whose point of view provides us with a perspective on the action that will follow.

Once the world of the film is described, its equilibrium is suddenly dis-rupted with the introduction of a lovers' quarrel between Jeffries and his girlfriend, Lisa (Grace Kelly), and with a scream from a woman across the way, whom Jeffries subsequently suspects was murdered by her husband. The action which follows moves toward a resolution of the conflict between Jeffries and his girlfriend, toward the proof that a murder has taken place,

Courtesy of Paramount

The narrative status quo—the courtyard within which the action of *Rear Window* is set.

and toward a solution of that crime. With the completion of these actions, order is restored and the film concludes with another survey of the courtyard, revealing the new status quo.

Classical narratives routinely begin with an act which disturbs the original state of things and which is answered, by the film's end, with another act which reestablishes the initial order or balance. Thus a murder mystery, whether a private-eye film of the 1940s (*The Maltese Falcon,* 1941) or an action picture of the 1980s (*Beverly Hills Cop,* 1984), will begin with the discovery of a dead body and end with the solution of the crime.

An adventure story or quest (*Raiders of the Lost Ark,* 1981) is launched with the loss, absence, or lack of a desired object and concludes with its attainment (or at least discovery). A love story (*Pretty Woman,* 1990) starts with a chance encounter and culminates with a marriage. A monster (*Jaws,* 1975) or horror (*Halloween,* 1978; *The Silence of the Lambs,* 1991) film begins with the death of an innocent victim and ends with the actual or symbolic death of the thing, which is routinely reincarnated for the sequel(s).

In between the beginning and the end of the film's overall narrative action, a series of additional, smaller disturbances take place, followed by tentative restorations of order, with each scene or sequence recapitulating the larger process of balance, disruption, and rebalancing of the film as a whole. In this way, the narrative moves ceaselessly toward closure, completion, conclusion.

CHARACTERS AND GOALS

Problem Solving

As David Bordwell explains, classical Hollywood cinema is primarily a character-centered cinema. Its characters are more or less stable, knowable, and psychologically coherent individuals who possess clearly defined, specific goals. Although this cinema is also a plot-driven or action cinema, characters stand at the center of the action and interact with events. Filmmakers use these interactions in accordance with the classical principles of narrative economy and efficiency to further the exposition of their characters. Plot expectations are set by the specific goals which individual characters possess or by the problems they are asked to solve.

Over the course of the narrative, characters struggle to achieve their goals or solve their problems. They overcome those who stand in their way (such as the villains), triumph over adverse circumstances (such as physical disability, nature, or some other force), and/or transcend their own limitations (such as individual fears or weaknesses). The narrative ends with the character's triumph or failure, with the resolution (or conclusive nonresolution) of the problem, and with the attainment (or clear-cut nonattainment) of the goal.

In *Vertigo* (1958), former detective Scottie Ferguson (James Stewart), who suddenly discovers that he suffers from acrophobia, becomes the unwitting victim of an elaborate murder scheme which takes advantage of his fear of heights in order to commit a perfect crime. Though Scottie's larger goals in the narrative remain obscure, by the end of the film, his more immediate goals have been satisfied. He reestablishes the balance or equilibrium with which the film begins: he not only discoveres the deception and solves the mystery, but also cures his vertigo (although he loses the great love of his life in the process).

Much as classical mystery narratives, like *Vertigo*, enlist audiences in the process of problem solving, classical suspense narratives regularly take shape around the forward movement of characters' attempts to attain goals and around the backward or sideways movements of the delays they experience in trying to overcome the various obstacles that stand (or are placed) between them and their goals. For example, the action in *The Terminator* (1984) is constructed around the efforts of a cyborg (played by Arnold Schwarzenegger) who was sent back in time by a totalitarian regime in the future (ca. 2029). He has been programmed to kill a woman, Sarah Connor (Linda Hamilton), in order to prevent her from bearing a child who is destined to lead a rebellion against that dictatorship.

At the same time, Kyle Reese (Michael Biehn), a (human) rebel freedom fighter, is also sent back in time to prevent the cyborg, or Terminator, from accomplishing its task. The dramatic structure of the film consists of alternating sequences in which each of these major characters sets about attempting to solve problems and to reach their goals only to discover that their attempts have been frustrated by the counter-effort of the other. Both Reese and the Terminator pursue their goals relentlessly—to their own self-destruction. At this point, the film concludes (with Reese dead but victorious)—only to find its narrative resolution reopened seven years later in *Terminator 2: Judgment Day* (1991).

Through Time and Space

Often the goals that organize a classical Hollywood narrative are given a precise temporal dimension—a specific deadline has to be met or a certain task has to be completed by a definite time. Near the start of *Brewster's Millions* (1985), the sixth remake of a popular plot idea that first reached the screen in 1914, Brewster (Richard Pryor) is told by a somewhat sadistic philanthropist that he will be given $300 million, provided that he can spend $1 million a day for 30 days without acquiring any tangible property or assets. The remainder of the film documents his efforts to meet this deadline.

Buster Keaton also milks the inheritance idea for suspense comedy in *Seven Chances* (1925), in which his character discovers that he will inherit $7 million if he can get married by 7 P.M. on his twenty-seventh birthday, which happens to be that very day. After getting a quick brush-off from his first seven chances as possible brides, Keaton literally runs through the rest of the movie looking for someone to marry, racing against the clock to meet the 7 P.M. deadline. In *48 Hours* (1982), the deadline gimmick plays a central role in a plot in which a detective (Nick Nolte) gives a convict (Eddie Murphy) 48 hours to help him catch a couple of cop killers, promising to reward the latter with a parole if they succeed.

In a similar way, stories are routinely designed along spatial lines, with their characters moving toward precise destinations or geographical goals. Journeys and cross-country treks have served as the fundamental organizing principle for narratives since Homer's *Odyssey*. The journey provides the basic structure for a number of extremely popular motion pictures, ranging from *The Wizard of Oz* (1939), *Around the World in 80 Days* (1956), and *North by Northwest* (1959), to *2001: A Space Odyssey* (1968), *Close Encounters of the Third Kind* (1977), *Apocalypse Now* (1979), and *Thelma & Louise* (1991). Even in those instances in which the final destination is never announced, made clear, or even reached, the voyage becomes sufficient in itself to hold the narrative on course, giving it an all-important sense of forward movement.

By the ends of these journeys, the characters not only move from point A to point Z, but they realize other nonspatial goals as well, making deadlines, solving mysteries, falling in love, discovering new worlds, and coming to terms with themselves and/or their fellow travelers. The purely physical movement of the characters through space provides a sense of narrative development that is immediately coherent, no matter how obscure or incoherent the logic of the dramatic action actually is (as in *2001*). The journey film always looks forward to getting there; and, as a result, the spectator always does, even when the characters do not and even when "there" is only a hastily tacked-on title that reads "The End."

Courtesy of M-G-M

A journey structures the narrative in *2001: A Space Odyssey*.

The Audience's Journey

In the broadest possible sense then, every film is a journey which begins with the distributor's logo and the credits and ends with an end title; and every spectator is a traveler whose trip to the theater and whose short sojourn there takes him or her on a narrative journey that only ends when the lights come up. The popularity of goal-centered, deadline-driven, and journey narratives undoubtedly owes something to the ways in which these particular narrative forms rework the all-too-familiar movie-going experience in the most exciting and pleasurable ways imaginable. The invisibility of the narrative patterns of classical Hollywood cinema remain indebted, in part, to such "cloaking devices."

Going to the movies becomes "going to the movies." What we see on the screen is what we are doing at that very moment; that is, looking for goals, participating in deadlines, and undertaking journeys. The invisibility of classical Hollywood cinema is an integral product of its transparency—in both senses of the word. By concealing all signs of their artifice and constructedness, the movies encourage us to see through them, and what we see is what they are. They are us going to the movies; we identify with onscreen characters who do what we do—who look for clues and solve problems; who look forward to, yet also dread, the deadline that marks the end of the film; and who reach our destination at the same time that they reach theirs.

HIGH ARTIFICE, INVISIBLE ART

Denial and Recognition

Ironically, the invisibility of classical Hollywood cinema is the result of great artifice. Its transparency is only an illusion. Beneath the apparent artlessness of the surface lies a solid foundation of highly crafted narrative techniques that all share the same common goal and participate in the same dual mission.

They function to deliver the story as powerfully as possible without interrupting its flow with intrusive marks or signs that might betray the fact that the story is itself a product of careful construction.

Most spectators are aware, either consciously or unconsciously, that films are not real—that is, that the blood they see in the shower sequence of *Psycho* (1960) is really chocolate sauce; that the dangerous stunt sequences in the Indiana Jones films are made using doubles; that the attack on the Death Star in *Star Wars* (1977) is shot using models and miniatures at George Lucas' special-effects house, Industrial Light & Magic; and that no one really dies during the making of either of the Terminator films. At the same time, most spectators also deny—out of necessity—their awareness of this artifice, or the fiction of the reality, in order to participate in the reality of these fictions.

Moviegoing engages audiences in what is known as a "willing suspension of disbelief"; and audiences are all the more willing to do this because the pleasures provided by doing so prove to be both rewarding and significant. Although a certain amount of denial works wonders in enabling audiences to enter into the onscreen fiction, considerable pleasure also derives from the recognition of the artifice. Audiences appreciate what they refer to as "particularly good films," that is, technically well-crafted films or stories that are told in an especially exciting manner; and they distinguish these works from what they consider to be "average" films.

The pleasures of watching a Hitchcock film, for example, come as much from the audience's complicity with the storytelling interventions of the director, who repeatedly nudges his viewers to notice this or that important detail or encourages them to react in this or that specific way, as it does from their absorption into the fictional world of the narrative. Hitchcock describes his films as "slices of cake" rather than "slices of life." By this, Hitchcock means that his films are not merely transparent records of reality.

Defining drama as "life with the dull bits cut out," Hitchcock cuts those dull bits out with a razor-sharp narrative sensibility and rearranges the exciting bits that are left over into breathtaking suspense thrillers. Yet unlike other, more self-effacing directors, Hitchcock leaves his mark on the finished film, and his imprint becomes an integral element of the film's appeal, openly acknowledging its status as a concoction, that is, as a "slice of cake." As a result, Hitchcock enjoys a special relationship with his audiences, who both lose themselves in the story that he tells and simultaneously derive pleasure from a recognition of how it is being told.

Underlying Patterns

The narrative patterns of mainstream Hollywood cinema are less clearly visible than the storytelling presence that can be found in every Hitchcock film; but, even so, they function to provide audiences with pleasure. But while the structure of a Hitchcock narrative lies more or less on or near the surface of the film, the structure in the typical classical Hollywood film is buried much deeper; it shapes audiences' responses on a less visible level.

Audiences unconsciously sense the classic principles of economy, regularity, symmetry, and order which inform the most compelling narratives to emerge from this system of storytelling and derive pleasure from the order which these elements impose upon the entertainment experience. Any attempt to come to grips with the phenomenon of classical Hollywood cinema must therefore acknowledge the importance of these basic narrative patterns and examine the role they play in the overall effectiveness of classical Hollywood cinema as a system.

Average spectators are fully aware that the films they watch are constructed out of bits and pieces of celluloid that have been shot at a variety of different times and in an assortment of different settings and that have been assembled to tell a specific story in a certain way. Every time they watch a film, they are necessarily reminded of its artifice by a number of factors—not the least of which is the opening or closing credit sequence full of the names of those who worked on the film. However, spectators rarely *experience* films in this way.

ANALYZING FILM NARRATIVES: SEGMENTATION

Though 90- to 120-minute films consist, on the average, of 600 to 800 individual shots and 5 to 40 separate sequences, audiences generally experience films as continuous instead of fragmented, as seamless wholes rather than as a string of discrete episodes. As we shall see in the next chapter, this illusion of continuity is the product of a body of stylistic practices which are specifically designed to conceal the essential discontinuity of the filmmaking process. In order to understand how narratives work, film studies has developed an analytical technique designed to expose this underlying discontinuity. It breaks the film down into its basic narrative units. This process of structural analysis is known as *segmentation*, which is a term that has been used in literacy studies to describe the process of dividing works into their constituent parts in order to study them in greater detail.

Segmentation can be used in the analysis of single scenes, parts of scenes, or of entire films. Various criteria can also be used to organize the segmentation, based on their appropriateness to the narrative structures of individual films. In general, the strategy involved in the segmentation of entire films is to break the films down into their largest units, which can then be subdivided into increasingly smaller units. These larger units tend to be based on the traditional *dramatic unities* (as they are defined by Aristotle and others); that is, the unities of action, time, and/or space.

For example, Sophocles' *Oedipus the King* possesses all three unities: it consists of a single action—Oedipus' investigation into the causes of the plague which besets Thebes; it takes place more or less continuously during the course of at single day; and it plays itself out in a single setting in front of the king's palace at Thebes. Analyzed using these three traditional criteria, *Oedipus* would thus "break down" into only one segment.

Only a handful of motion pictures observe all three unities as thoroughly as does Sophocles in *Oedipus*. Hitchcock's *Rope* (1948) is one of them. *Rope* is an adaptation of a play which is set in the living room of the central characters' apartment (unity of space). It takes place in real time; that is, without any abridgement or expansion of the time of the action (unity of time). And it traces the beginning, middle, and end of a single action—a murder—which is committed, then concealed, and finally discovered (unity of action). *Rope*, like *Oedipus*, can possibly be segmented according to the arrivals and departures of various characters, but, in terms of its action, time, and space, it is not segmentable.

Other Hitchcock films, such as *Lifeboat* (1944) and *Rear Window* (1954), observe the unities of action, dealing with the survivors of a shipwreck and with a murder mystery, respectively, and of space—they are set in a lifeboat and in a Greenwich Village courtyard. But they do this without strict observance of the unity of time: *Lifeboat's* action occupies roughly a week, *Rear Window's* approximately four days.

Most films, however, violate the traditional unities. They lend themselves quite readily to segmentation, and the process of breaking them down into large units quite often reveals crucial elements of their dramatic structure. This structure, in turn, can be "read" in terms of the role it plays in shaping the film's thematic concerns. In other words, segmentation serves as a potentially productive first step in the larger process of film analysis.

A CIRCULAR PATTERN: CHAPLIN'S *THE GOLD RUSH*

Charles Chaplin's *The Gold Rush* (1925), if broken down into spatial units, proves to be a paradigm of classical narrative construction. A segmentation of the film into large units, organized around its various locations and/or settings, discloses the following seven-part, circular pattern:

    I. Prologue (journey to the Alaskan gold fields by Charlie, the lone prospector)

    II. The Cabin (Charlie and Big Jim take refuge in the outlaw Black Larsen's cabin during a snow storm; Larsen leaves to get help; Charlie and Big Jim enjoy a Thanksgiving feast of "boiled boot"; the storm subsides and they set off on their separate ways)

    III. The Dance Hall (in town, Charlie discovers Georgia and falls in love with her at first sight, though she ignores him)

    IV. The Cabin in Town (on New Year's Eve, Charlie prepares dinner for Georgia and her girlfriends, falls asleep when she stands him up, dreams that she is there, and performs "the dance of the rolls" to entertain her)

    V. The Dance Hall (Georgia apologizes to Charlie; Big Jim rediscovers Charlie and "falls in love with" [pursues] him, much as Charlie had pursued Georgia earlier)

Courtesy of United Artists

The Cabin—Charlie tries to protect himself from Big Jim, who is crazed with hunger in *The Gold Rush*.

VI. The Cabin (Charlie and Big Jim return to the cabin—this time with plenty of food—in search of Big Jim's claim; another snow storm; the storm returns Big Jim to the exact spot where he was at the start of segment II)

VII. Epilogue (Charlie and Big Jim, having struck it rich, return by boat to the States; Charlie is reunited with Georgia who mistakes him for the lone prospector whom she met in segment III)

Symmetry

Chaplin's narrative observes a strict classical symmetry. The Prologue (I), in which Charlie travels to Alaska, is answered by an Epilogue (VII), in which he returns to the States, casting the narrative in the form of a journey. An initial cabin sequence (II) introduces the characters of Big Jim and Black Larsen; Big Jim reappears in the final cabin sequence (VI). The first cabin sequence also introduces the characters' fixation upon material or physical needs (the desire for gold, then for food), which is answered in the final cabin sequence when physical survival once again becomes paramount as the cabin is blown about in a blizzard and finally settles on the edge of a cliff where it teeters precariously.

By an uncanny coincidence, the wandering cabin ends up at the exact spot where Big Jim is introduced discovering gold. Thus the pursuit of wealth, which motivates Charlie's journey to the gold fields in the Prologue and which is echoed and "doubled" in the figures of Big Jim and Black Larsen whom he meets in the cabin (II), finds resolution in segment VI in which all these elements reappear.

If the search for gold structures the overall narrative, other goals emerge to give shape to the central section of the film, which is set in the town rather than in the wilderness. These three segments introduce another set of characters and a second body of thematic concerns. This time, Charlie interacts not with men but with women (Georgia and her friends), and his chief desire is not for gold or for physical survival but for more abstract needs—he longs for Georgia's love. In this central narrative section, two public scenes in the dance hall (III, V) frame a more private sequence (IV) in the cabin which Charlie is taking care of for a friend.

The film's two fantasy or dream sequences, which provide one of the film's many parallel or paired scenes, underscore this thematic turnabout. During Thanksgiving at the wilderness cabin, Big Jim fantasizes that Charlie is a chicken, turning him into food. On New Year's Eve at the cabin in the settlement, Charlie transforms food into a phantasmical person, combining his own head with dinner rolls on the ends of forks to produce the dance of the rolls. In the former sequence, physical appetite produces the fantasy; in the latter, romantic desire feeds Charlie's imagination. The contrast between the two holidays and the two settings is further driven home by another variation on the film's central theme. In one scene, Charlie turns a boot into a meal; in the other, he turns food into feet, transcending the purely physical world of blizzards, hunger, and greed for gold with an escapist fantasy that celebrates imagination, creativity, and romance.

At the Center: Imagination

The film reveals itself to be a perfect example of the interdependency of form and function in classical Hollywood cinema. The narrative organization of *Gold Rush* is designed around the central character, Charlie, whose goals the plot explores and whose personality serves as a barometer that governs the audience's perception of and reaction to the events which take place. Charlie's desire, feelings, and imagination stand at the literal center of the film—segment IV—in which he "realizes" his romantic desires through a fantasy sequence. This central sequence looks back to the physical hardship which precedes it in the Prologue and in the wilderness cabin sequence, and it looks forward to the Epilogue, in which this fantasy is made real. Charlie, now a millionaire but dressed once again in his Tramp's outfit for news photographers, is reunited with Georgia, who, unaware of his wealth, befriends him, much as he had befriended her in his New Year's Eve dream sequence.

JOURNEY TO A NEW PLACE: *SOME LIKE IT HOT*

Flight and Pursuit

The orderly narrative patterns of classical Hollywood cinema are not always circular. The journey format often takes characters into new, unexplored terrains. That is, it takes them to a destination other than where it begins, as is the case in *Some Like It Hot* (1959). The action of the film begins in Prohibition-era Chicago and follows its central characters, a saxophone player named Joe (Tony Curtis) and a bass player named Jerry (Jack Lemmon), on their journey to Florida in flight from gangsters who want to kill them because they are the sole surviving witnesses to the St. Valentine's Day Massacre.

The narrative pattern of the film is simple, with the action falling under three basic spatial groupings which range from Chicago, to the train, and finally to Florida. The goals that drive the narrative are similarly simple, even though their comic realization seems a bit improbable. Joe and Jerry need jobs and to get out of Chicago if they are to escape "Spats" Columbo (George Raft) and his mob. Having no money, they are forced to take jobs impersonating women musicians in an all-female jazz band on its way to Miami.

On the train to Miami, they meet Sugar Kane (Marilyn Monroe), the band's lead singer, who is, like them, also in flight. However, the men she flees are not gangsters but rather saxophonists, with whom she always falls in love but who always abandon her, leaving her holding what she describes as "the fuzzy end of the lollipop."

In Florida, the characters' initial goals are modified; instead of focusing upon flight, they shift their attention to pursuit. Sugar hopes to change her luck and find a millionaire to marry. Joe, who has fallen in love with Sugar, concocts a plan that would permit him to become her millionaire. To do this, however, he is forced into yet another impersonation—he plays the role of "Shell Oil, Jr." "Shell Oil, Jr." is the sexually impotent, millionaire yachtsman who seeks Sugar's help in restoring his interest in women. Meanwhile, Jerry, masquerading as Daphne, enjoys unprecedented success as a woman. S/he is romanced by a genuine millionaire, Osgood, who showers her/him with expensive gifts and even proposes marriage.

Just as the characters are about to realize their romantic goals (even Jerry/ Daphne looks forward to marrying Osgood and then divorcing him for a nice alimony settlement), the gangsters reappear, having come to Miami from Chicago for a convention of "The Friends of Italian Opera." Pursued by "Spats" and his men, Joe and Jerry take refuge under a banquet table, where they once again witness a mob bloodbath. "Spats" is rubbed out in retribution for his murder of Toothpick Charlie and others at the St. Valentine's Day Massacre. Although "Spats" has been eliminated as a threat, Joe and Jerry suddenly find themselves pursued by a new mob for observing the murder of "Spats."

As Josephine and Daphne, they "elope" with Sugar and Osgood, fleeing to the supposed safety of the latter's yacht. For this escape, however, Joe and

Jerry remove rather than put on (their) disguises; Joe confesses to Sugar that he is not only Josephine, but "Shell Oil, Jr." as well; and Jerry informs Osgood that he cannot marry him because he is a man. The film ends with Osgood's reply: "Nobody's perfect."

Narrative Structure and Sexuality

Some Like It Hot uses the journey format to provide a background for its central characters' sexual odyssey, which takes them from a comic-book world of sexual stereotypes (Chicago), through a duplicitous, unstable world of disguise and sexual role-playing (the train, Florida), to an uncharted world where sexual differences no longer determine social structure (the boat trip in the last scene). In Osgood's world, nobody is perfect; that is, no one's sexuality is perfect and traditional notions of sexual difference no longer have any significance. As in Shakespeare's *The Tempest*, the film's characters survive a harrowing experience and enter "a brave new world," having "suffer[ed] a sea-change into something rich and strange." At any rate, they are not in Chicago anymore.

Chicago emerges as the city of gangsters. It is dominated by male violence. "Spats" and his henchmen, ironically referred to as "all Harvard men," are caricatures of masculinity. They are two-dimensional tough guys with too

Courtesy of United Artists

In *Some Like It Hot*, Joe/Josephine (Tony Curtis) and Jerry/Daphne (Jack Lemmon) flee the male world of Chicago gangsters for the female world of Sugar (Marilyn Monroe) and "Sweet Sue and Her Society Syncopaters."

many muscles and too few brains. In Chicago, Joe embodies male insensitivity, repeatedly taking advantage of women. He borrows money from the girls in the chorus without intending to pay it back and sweet-talks Nellie, an agent's receptionist, into lending him her car.

When Joe and Jerry are forced to become Josephine and Daphne, they are plunged into the all-female world of "Sweet Sue and Her Society Syncopaters," where they find themselves on the other end of male insensitivity and sexism. This world is dominated by the "masculine" presence of Sue, the leader of the band, and by the effeminate presence of Mr. Bienstalk, the band's manager. In Florida, the reversal of sexual roles continues. Gold diggers in the band, like Sugar, aggressively pursue local millionaires who, like "Shell Oil, Jr.," are inadequate as men; and millionaires, like Osgood, whose sexuality is similarly "abnormal," fall in love with men in drag, like Daphne. Joe's creation of "Shell Oil, Jr." serves as an unconscious expression of his own sense of male inadequacy and as an indirect critique of the hypermasculinity which characterizes his own earlier attitudes toward women as the womanizer, Joe.

Resolution/Irresolution

The sexual confusion of the central section of the film is resolved by the reinstitution of clear-cut sexual differences, in the form of the excessively masculine gangsters, who, unlike Osgood, see through Joe's and Jerry's masquerades. Through their threatening presence, they force the reinstitution of a simplistic sexual duality, whereby men are men and women are women.

Yet the film suggests that their stereotypical male sexuality is inadequate, much as is that of Sugar's ideal man, whom she envisions as "gentle, sweet, and helpless." Sugar's ideal proves to be pure fantasy, and she is ultimately forced to recognize and give in to her irrational desire for tenor saxophone players (Joe). On the other hand, if Daphne is Osgood's ideal, then Jerry emerges as the next best thing, as an imperfect Daphne. *Some Like It Hot* illustrates how the impossible perfection imagined in the romantic dreams and sexual fantasies of the central characters gives way to the more immediate, concrete realities of their sexual desires. In other words, all of them, even Osgood, discover that nobody is perfect.

NARRATIVE VIOLENCE: *GOODFELLAS*

The narrative structure of a number of recent Hollywood films repeatedly violates the reassuring order and economic design of classical Hollywood cinema, but they still possess patterns that lend coherence to films that increasingly test the limits of the classical paradigm. Martin Scorsese's *Goodfellas* (1990), which documents the rise and fall of an actual New York gangster named Henry Hill, reviews the major events of his life as a mafioso in an episodic series of scenes that are organized temporally. The film traces Hill's activities for over 25 years, from his first contact with the mob in 1955 until he leaves it to enter the witness protection program in the 1980s. A temporal/spatial segmentation of the film would look as follows:

I. The Prologue/credit sequence. New York, 1970 [Tommy (Joe Pesci), Jimmy (Robert De Niro), and Henry (Ray Liotta) stop their car on a highway and kill a man (Billy Batts) whom they have locked up in their trunk]

II. East New York, Brooklyn, 1955 (Henry becomes a member of Paul Cicero's mob, cuts school, sells stolen cigarettes, and wins the respect of his fellow gang members by refusing to ''rat'' on them when he is arrested)

III. Idlewild Airport, 1963 [Henry, Jimmy, and Tommy plan and carry out a robbery of Air France; Henry meets, courts, and marries Karen (Lorraine Bracco), who becomes accustomed to life as a mobster's wife]

IV. Queens, New York, June 11, 1970 (giving a context to segment I, segment IV recounts Tommy's argument with Billy Batts, who, as ''a made man'' or member of a Mafia family, enjoyed a special, ''untouchable'' status; Batts is murdered, and his body must then be buried by Henry, Jimmy, and Tommy without the knowledge of their superiors in the mob)

    a. Queens, six months later [Henry cheats on his wife with Janice; Tommy recklessly shoots Spider, a waiter at the mob's social club; Henry is sent by Pauli (Paul Sorvino) to Florida to collect on a debt]

    b. Tampa, Florida, two days later (Henry and Jimmy are arrested for threatening the debtor; Henry goes to jail and begins to deal drugs on the inside)

    c. Four years later (upon his release from jail, Henry is told by Pauli not to deal drugs, but continues to do so, using the apartment of another mistress, Sandy, as a distribution center; Henry, Jimmy, Tommy, and others engineer the famous, multi-million-dollar Lufthansa heist; Jimmy begins to kill off participants in the robbery, fearing that they might betray him; Tommy is killed in retribution for his slaying of Billy Batts)

V. Sunday, May 11, 1980 (over the course of a day, Henry runs errands in his car while being followed by a helicopter; he tries to deliver guns to Tommy; he picks up his kid brother at the hospital; he begins to cook dinner; he puts together a drug deal; he sets out to drive the courier, his babysitter, to the airport, and he is busted by the police)

VI. The Aftermath (unable to get help from Pauli and afraid that Jimmy will kill him, Henry decides to enter the witness protection program and to testify against Jimmy and Pauli, who are sent to prison; Henry ends up living more or less anonymously under a phony name in the suburbs)

Rising and Falling: A Quest for Identity

The narrative of the film follows, in fairly strict chronological order, the rise and fall of Henry Hill, who narrates most of the story from a point in the recent past (that is, from the end of segment VI); Henry's wife, Karen, narrates part of segment III. Henry's goals are clearly stated in his voice-over narration at the end of segment I: "As far back as I could remember, I always wanted to be a gangster." Segment II documents his initiation into "the life," that is, the world of power, wealth, and privilege enjoyed by members of the Mafia.

For Henry, being a gangster means, as he puts it in segment II, being "somebody in a neighborhood full of nobodies." Over the course of the film, Henry evolves from a nobody to a somebody (a kid working at the cab stand, a member of the mob, a participant in the Lufthansa heist) and finally to a nobody ("Today, everything is different. . . . I'm an average nobody. I get to live the rest of my life like a schnook.") The film's narrative structure traces out Henry's quest for identity, outlines its construction in segment II, its

Living "the life"—Henry (Ray Liotta) gets his cut of the Lufthansa heist from Jimmy (Robert De Niro) in *Goodfellas*.

confirmation in segment III, its hour-by-hour dissolution in segment V, and its disappearance in segment VI.

Henry's identity is rooted in this membership in the Mafia; the major phases of its evolution can be gauged in terms of his relation to the mob, which is, in turn, marked by his various arrests. His arrest at the close of segment II seals his membership in the mob. His arrest in the middle of the film—in segment IVb—leads to his movement away from the family as he begins to deal drugs in jail against Pauli's specific orders. His arrest at the end of segment V finalizes his break with the underworld through his deliberate violation of the code of silence which he had observed at the end of segment II. With this breach of mob ethics, Henry's original desire to be a gangster takes him full circle; in order to survive, he is forced to rat on his friends and to leave "the life."

Henry's nostalgia for "the life" dominates segments II and III, in which vast periods of time are condensed into a dreamlike flow of images evoking the "golden age" of organized crime—that is, the predrug era of the 1950s and 1960s when mobsters "were treated like movie stars with muscles" and "had it all just for the asking." By the 1970s and 1980s, however, all of that has changed. In segment V, time is no longer condensed in vibrant memory images of grandeur. Instead, the day is broken down into an episodic laundry list of unbearably tedious and mundane errands, which Henry performs almost mechanically while high on cocaine.

The turning point for Henry proves to be quite literally in the center of the film—in segment IV, where Henry, Tommy, and Jimmy violate one of the taboos of the underworld by killing a "made man" (Billy Batts) and concealing this fact from the mob. Indeed, the entire film grows out of this "original sin." The film starts with this sequence, then flashes back to Henry's youth. This violation of the otherwise strict chronology followed elsewhere underscores its centrality in the narrative. It is what prompts Henry's flashback, serving as a point of departure for the story of his fall from gangland grace that follows.

Unconventional Gangsters

Although *Goodfellas* observes the rise-and-fall narrative pattern of the traditional gangster film for much of its course, it departs from it in several key ways. Its gangster hero is neither killed (as in *The Public Enemy*, 1931; *Little Caesar*, 1930; and *Scarface*, 1932) nor catapulted to a position of leadership at the end (*The Godfather*, 1972; or *Mobsters*, 1991); he simply walks away from it all. Indeed, *Goodfellas'* conclusion violates a central precept of classical narrative—its invisibility. When Henry, while continuing his voice-over narration during the final courtroom sequence, rises from the witness stand, walks toward the camera, and directly addresses the audience, he calls attention to both the camera and to the convention of voice-over narration, exposing the essential artifice of the narrative process.

MODERNIST NARRATION: *CITIZEN KANE*

Unresolved Questions

Goodfellas employs the techniques and devices of classical Hollywood cinema, yet it also calls them into question. To the extent that it deliberately violates those techniques, it functions not as a classical but as a modernist work. Modernist texts convey the spirit of crisis which characterizes the modern (post–Industrial Revolution, twentieth-century) age. They do this, in part, by rejecting the principles of order, regularity, and invisibility which dominate representation in its classical, romantic, and realist forms. The particular form that modernism takes depends upon the particular tradition which it rebels against; within American narrative filmmaking, modernism is best exemplified by *Citizen Kane* (1941), a film that breaks the rules of classical narration in several ways.

Kane belongs to several film genres; on one level, it is a newspaper film; on another, a mystery; on yet another, it is a fictional biography (or biopic). If it is difficult to classify *Kane* in terms of its exact narrative type, it is also hard to identify its central character. Is it Charles Foster Kane, who dies in its opening minutes? Or is it Thompson, the investigative reporter who is assigned to solve the mystery of Kane's last word—"rosebud"?

What are the goals of these characters? If what both Kane and Thompson want is "rosebud," then neither succeeds in getting it. "Rosebud" remains, as far as Kane is concerned, a lost object that he both possesses and can never find; it lies concealed within the vast storehouse of Kane's possessions. For Thompson, "rosebud" remains a mystery which he never solves. In other words, the goal which structures the narrative is never reached by its central characters (though the audience does penetrate at least one layer of the mystery of "rosebud" in discovering the object to which the word refers).

Artifice Exposed

The narrative structure of *Kane* also plays havoc with the norm; it is built around a complex series of overlapping flashbacks in which five different characters present their perceptions of Kane. Though Thompson serves as the audience's guide through the maze of information presented about Kane, he never processes that information for us. In fact, he refuses, declaring that he "doesn't think any word [could] explain a man's life" and that "rosebud" is "just a piece in a jigsaw puzzle—a missing piece."

Thus, the audience is left with the difficult task of assembling these separate portraits of Kane into a coherent figure. The persistent refusal of the film to give the audience access to its central character serves as the chief mark of its modernism. "No Trespassing" signs greet us at the beginning of the film; doors are repeatedly closed in our faces; and, once we finally get to see "rosebud" at the end, it goes up in smoke just as we begin to grasp at its possible meanings.

Charles Foster Kane (Orson Welles) looks directly at the camera and strikes a pose on a streetcorner strewn with newspapers in *Citizen Kane*.

Kane stands at the very fringe of classical Hollywood cinema and draws much of its power from its violation of the codes and conventions that audiences take for granted when they go to the movies. *Kane* makes visible much of that which the machinery of Hollywood cinema seeks to keep invisible. But even this visibility, in films like *Kane* and *Goodfellas*, provides pleasure for audiences, engaging them on a heightened level of narrative awareness that plays a crucial role in their understanding of the narrative. These narratives not only echo the modern condition in their formal rebelliousness but *become about it*, representing a contemporary sense of frustration, lack of closure, and dissolution. In other words, they serve, much as does the seamless classical Hollywood cinema of the past, as an "expression of the temper of an age and a nation as well as an expression of the individual temperament" of the artists who make them.

SELECT FILMOGRAPHY

The Gold Rush (1925)
Citizen Kane (1941)
Rear Window (1954)
Vertigo (1958)

Some Like It Hot (1959)
The Terminator (1984)
Goodfellas (1990)

SELECT BIBLIOGRAPHY

Bordwell, David. "Classical Hollywood Cinema: Narration Principles and Procedures," in Philip Rosen, ed., *Narrative, Apparatus, Ideology.* New York: Columbia University Press, 1986.

Bordwell, David. *Narration in the Fiction Film.* Madison: University of Wisconsin Press, 1985.

Bordwell, David, Janet Staiger, and Kristin Thompson. *The Classical Hollywood Cinema: Film Style and Mode of Production to 1960.* New York: Columbia University Press, 1985.

Bordwell, David, and Kristin Thompson. *Film Art: An Introduction*, 4th ed. New York: McGraw-Hill, 1993.

Branigan, Edward. *Narrative Comprehension and Film.* New York: Routledge, 1992.

Gaines, Jane, ed. *Classical Hollywood Narrative: The Paradigm Wars.* Durham, NC: Duke University Press, 1992.

Wolfflin, Heinrich. *Principles of Art History.* Translated by M. D. Hottinger. New York: Dover Publications, 1932.

CLASSICAL HOLLYWOOD CINEMA: STYLE

FILM FORM AND CHARACTER DEVELOPMENT

Classical Hollywood cinema is a character-centered cinema. Not only are narratives structured around the goals of individual characters, but basic elements of film style are also put at the service of character exposition and dramatic development. Even at the level of setting, the narrative machinery seeks to maximize its use of the medium—to use it to describe character psychology, to visualize the goals and desires of characters, and to convey their development as characters through the action which follows.

Classical Economy: The Opening Sequence of *Shadow of a Doubt*

The introductory sequence of Alfred Hitchcock's *Shadow of a Doubt* (1943) provides a perfect example of classical economy and efficiency in character delineation. A series of establishing shots connected by dissolves identify the setting of the action as a lower-class neighborhood in Philadelphia. Establishing shots function to present the spatial parameters within which the subsequent action of a scene takes place. Here, long shots of the city, with derelicts, trash, and abandoned cars in the foreground, establish an aura of decadence and decay that dominate our perception of the world into which the dissolves bring us and of the character who occupies the center of that world. Dissolves, a fluid form of shot transition which involves fading out on one shot while fading in on another, gradually narrow the spectator's field of view from the entire city, to a specific block, to kids playing stickball in the street, to a rooming house on that block, and finally to a specific window in that rooming house.

The camera looks up from below at the second-story window of the rooming house. Then there is a dissolve to the second-floor interior. The camera tracks (that is, moves bodily) across a room to reveal Uncle Charlie (Joseph Cotten), lying fully dressed in a business suit on a bed in midday and smoking a cigar. On the nightstand next to him lies a wad of high-denomination currency; some of the bills have fallen to the floor; there is also a half empty whiskey glass.

The landlady enters through the door, pulls down the blinds of the window, and announces that two men have called looking for him. The lowering

Author's frame enlargement

Uncle Charlie (Joseph Cotten) lies stretched out on a bed in a rooming house in the opening sequence of *Shadow of a Doubt.*

of the blinds casts shadows on Charlie's face. Once she has left, Uncle Charlie rises, drinks the whiskey, and angrily throws the empty glass into the basin in the adjoining bathroom, smashing it. Then he walks to the window, raises the blinds, and looks out onto the street where the two men stand. In an internal monologue in which we hear his thoughts, Charlie challenges the men to prove that he has done anything wrong, declaring that they have nothing on him. Finally, Charlie leaves the room, defiantly walks by the men, and subsequently eludes them in a chase through the surrounding tenements.

The Art of Details

This introductory scene establishes Uncle Charlie as an enigmatic figure. His clothing and bearing suggest that he is clearly out of place in this lower-class setting. Yet the money, the whiskey, and his violent reaction to the news that he is being followed suggest that he belongs in a criminal milieu. The mise-en-scene (that is, the staging of the sequence) presents Charlie as a man who is at the end of his rope. His posture is that of a dead man, a fully dressed corpse stretched out on a bier in the funeral parlor. The crumpled bills on the floor convey his disregard for money. His depressed state is clearly less a result of material wants than of unstated spiritual needs.

Yet there is also something monstrous about him. Charlie rises, like Dracula from his coffin, when the room is made dark by the landlady's lowering of the blinds. His subsequent behavior expresses his potential for violence: when he gets up, one of the first things he does is to smash his glass by throwing it across the room into the bathroom sink. At the same time, his actions express tremendous hubris: his internal monologue voices defiance toward his pursuers. At the end of the scene, he goes out to confront them, behaving like a character in a Dostoevski novel who is driven by a desire for such challenges.

At the same time, the sequence epitomizes the narrative economy and efficiency of classical Hollywood cinema. Every detail in the scene serves a purpose, advances the narrative, and gets "used up" by the conclusion of the scene. The window is there for the camera to enter at the beginning of the scene, for the landlady to pull the blinds down upon, and for Charlie to raise the blinds on and look through to see the men outside. The bed is there for Charlie to lie upon and get up from; the nightstand is there to provide a surface on which the money and the whiskey can be placed. The whiskey glass is there for Charlie to drink out of and the bathroom sink is there for him to use to smash the whiskey glass. The door is there for the landlady to enter and for Charlie to use upon his exit. By the time Uncle Charlie leaves, every prop and every feature of the room has been used to advance the narrative; the room has been narratively exhausted, so to speak, and it is time to move on to the next space.

MISE-EN-SCENE

Not every Hollywood film is so meticulous in its use of decor and mise-en-scene; *Citizen Kane*, for example, overwhelms the spectator with detail, much of which never finds its way into the narrative except as "atmosphere." But films like *Shadow of a Doubt* reflect the general principles of narrative economy which informs the majority of Hollywood films and sets a standard for efficiency that a surprising number of narratives meet. Elements of film style are not merely ornamental. They are not the superficial coating of a story that could be told in a thousand different ways. Classical Hollywood style becomes *the means by which* narratives are realized; it provides the formal system that enables them to be told. Elements of style serve to shape the narrative. They function to "read" it for the audiences. They draw attention to, underline, and point out what it is that the audience needs to see or hear in order to read or understand the scene.

In presenting stories on the screen, the cinema relies upon actors and actresses to stage events, much as they are staged in the theater. The term "mise-en-scene" describes this activity. Mise-en-scene encompasses a variety of "theatrical" categories related to the staging of action. These range from purely theatrical areas of expression, such as set design, costume design, the blocking of actors, performance, and lighting to purely filmic techniques, such as camera movement, camera angle, camera distance, and composition. Strictly speaking, mise-en-scene (or "putting on the stage") includes the relation of everything within the shot to everything else within the shot—of actors to the decor; of decor and actors to the lighting; of actors, decor, and lighting to the camera position; and so forth.

In the theater, mise-en-scene serves as a "reading" of the action. Set design, costume, lighting, and the movement of actors are designed by the stage director (or producer) to present the ideas in the script to the audience in a more or less predigested way. That is, these elements of stagecraft, which are used to organize the drama, "process" the action for the audience. Mise-en-scene translates the contents of a scene into the language of the theater, producing a reading of the action that guides the audience's attention in specific ways.

THE CAMERA

In the cinema, theatrical mise-en-scene provides a primary interpretation of the drama. Costume and set design become a reflection of character, as we saw in the introduction of Uncle Charlie lying fully dressed on a bed at midday in *Shadow of a Doubt*. Lighting becomes an extension of the character's psychological make-up into the surrounding space. The shadow of the blind which falls over Charlie's face entombs him helplessly on his bed in the room and conveys the concern that creeps over him about the two men waiting outside for him in the street. The mise-en-scene's "theatrical" reading of the action is driven home, in turn, by means of a variety of uniquely cinematic techniques, such as camera position (which includes the camera's angle on and distance from the action) and camera movement (which includes pans, tracks, zooms, and combinations of all three).

Thus, the low-angle shot of Uncle Charlie from below as he looks out of the window, coupled with the high-angle shot from above of what he sees (the two men outside), communicate ideas. They function in terms of both their narrative context and their relation to one another in a system of other shots to convey a sense of conflict or opposition between his view and physical position in space and theirs. These two seemingly insignificant shots help to set up the tense confrontation which follows, when Charlie walks directly toward, then past the two men.

Meaning through Context: Camera Angle and Distance

Camera angle and distance become expressive devices as a result of their participation in systems of difference. They possess no absolute meaning, but derive their meaning through a relative process that depends upon the specific dramatic context in which they are used and upon their relation to other possible angles and distances. Thus, a low-angle shot, in which the camera looks up at the action, might acquire meaning through a process of association, becoming identified with a specific character or situation that it is repeatedly used to film.

At the same time, the particular meaning of a low-angle shot derives not only from the content of the shot but also from the relation of that particular angle to the other angles used in the film, that is, from its place in a system of differences. Thus, a particular low-angle shot differs not only from other low-angle shots (which look up at different angles), but also from eye-level and high-angle shots, in which the camera looks at the action straight on or from above, respectively.

It is often tempting to view low- or high-angle shots in somewhat literal terms as descriptive of the relative power of a character; thus, when the camera looks up at a character, it (and we) occupy an inferior position in relation to that character. As a result, our impression of that character's power or stature is thereby magnified. Similarly, high-angle shots automatically position viewers above the action, giving them a quasi-omniscient, quasi-omnipotent, god's-eye view of the action, indicating the relative weakness or inferiority of any onscreen character. However, this literal interpretation of camera angle proves to be rather limited, especially when it ignores the context in which the shot occurs.

Thus the low-angle shot of Charles Foster Kane (Orson Welles) in *Citizen Kane* (1941) as he stands in his deserted campaign headquarters and talks to his friend Jed Leland (Joseph Cotten) after his defeat in the race for state governor conveys contradictory ideas. Kane's power and mystery are suggested in the camera angle—yet in losing the election he has just proven how vulnerable he is. The extremity of the low angle actually captures his powerful powerlessness, making it appear as if the character is about to topple over.

Something similar takes place at the end of *Ace in the Hole* (1951). The film's central character, a newspaper reporter named Chuck Tatum (Kirk Douglas), turns the simple rescue of a man trapped in a cave accident into a sensational front-page story, then delays the rescue process in order to further his own career as a journalist.

Frame enlargement by Kristin Thompson

A low-angle shot of Kane (Orson Welles) and his friend Leland (Joseph Cotten) after Kane's defeat at the polls.

After the man dies, Tatum is himself fatally wounded by the man's wife. Back at his newspaper office, Tatum renounces the fame he has won through his coverage of the story. As he does so, director Billy Wilder films him in an extreme low-angle shot. The exaggeration of the angle serves to caricature his excessive abuse of the power of the press and look askance at his greed and self-interest; the shot concludes as Tatum drops dead on the floor, falling right into the camera. This particular low-angle shot can hardly be understood as a signifier of his power; rather it dramatizes the terrible consequences of too much power.

Systematic Meaning: Some Definitions

At the same time, camera angle and distance determine meaning systematically. They participate in a system of differences which varies from film to film. Thus the extreme camera angles and distances employed in a Welles film, such as *Citizen Kane,* differ significantly from the more moderate angles and distances found in a film directed by Howard Hawks, such as *Bringing Up Baby* (1938) or *His Girl Friday* (1940). In *Kane,* the extreme close-up of Welles's lips as he utters the word "rosebud" and then dies *underlines* the importance of that moment and that word in a way that would be unthinkable in a Hawks film. In other words, the Welles system depends upon exaggeration for effect, while the Hawks system employs a more subtle variation from shot to shot to drive home the meaning of its scenes.

Although camera distance is clearly a relative phenomenon, the terms used to describe it are more or less fixed. The scale upon which the terms rely is that of the human body (though the content of shots, of course, is not restricted to human or even animate forms). Thus an extreme close-up presents only a portion of the face—Kane's mouth in *Kane* or the gunfighters' eyes as they face off against one another in *Forty Guns* (1957). A close-up frames the entire head, hand, foot, or other object, such as the shot of the wad of money on the floor in *Shadow of a Doubt* or the close-up of Kane's hand as he drops the glass ball onto the floor in his death scene in *Kane.*

Medium close-ups give a chest-up view of individuals, as seen in most sequences in which two characters converse with one another, while medium shots tend to show the body from the waist up. Shots of characters which frame them from the knees up are referred to as medium long shots, while long shots range from full-figure images of characters, as well as a bit of the surrounding space immediately above and below them (such as the first image of Uncle Charlie lying on the bed), to shots in which the human figure is only a small part of the overall scene (as in the point-of-view shot in which the two men are seen waiting in the street below for Charlie). In extreme long shots, the human body is overwhelmed by the setting within which it is placed, as in countless Westerns in which distant figures are seen as specks in a larger landscape.

Camera Movement

Camera movement emerges as a powerful element of mise-en-scene which (in the majority of classical Hollywood films) serves the interests of narrative exposition. The term "camera movement" encompasses a variety of different formal devices, including one—the zoom—in which the camera makes no movement whatsoever. A zoom involves the use of a special lens that possesses a variety of different focal lengths which range from wide angle to telephoto. Manipulation of the lens produces the impression of movement toward or away from objects by shifting from wide-angle to telephoto focal lengths or vice versa. These shifts simply enlarge or decrease the apparent size of the image.

Since the camera does not literally move during a zoom shot (unless it is combined with other camera movements), its sense of movement is illusory. The famous "vertigo effect" in *Vertigo,* when the acrophobic central character, Scottie, looks down from a height, is achieved by the combined effects of zooming in and tracking out. This makes the space appear to expand and to contract at the same time. Zooms, which are frequently used to designate a character's subjective point of view or reaction to something, function as a kind of consciousness which surveys, studies, or scrutinizes the drama which unfolds before it.

Actual camera movements consist of pans, tracks, and dolly or crane shots. In a pan, the camera rotates horizontally and/or vertically on its axis. Typically, it presents a panoramic view of a space by rotating from right to left (or from left to right) a certain number of degrees to reveal what lies before the camera on either side. At the start of the cattle drive in *Red River* (1948), the camera pans 180 degrees as the owner of the herd (John Wayne) surveys his cattle and the men (including his adopted son, Montgomery Clift) who will drive them to market. The pan not only conveys the enormous size of the herd, but also sets up the conflict between Wayne and Clift which will dominate the rest of the narrative.

In tracking shots, the camera moves bodily through space in any of a variety of directions parallel to the floor. To facilitate smooth movement, the camera was either mounted on tracks fixed to the ceiling (as in the long tracking shot of the man's rendezvous with the woman from the city in the swamp in *Sunrise*, 1927) or to the floor. In the majority of instances, however, it was affixed to a moveable camera support, such as a dolly, as seen in the continuous camera movements in *Rope* (1948). If mounted on a dolly, the camera can track in a variety of different directions. It can move laterally, either to follow the movements of a character walking parallel to it or explore space in one direction or the other. It can move circularly, tracking around a central subject or observing a scene that is taking place around it from the center of a circle. The camera is also capable of moving circuitously in, out, and around the scene.

The camera, mounted on a makeshift crane (center), descends to photograph the key in Ingrid Bergman's hand in *Notorious* as director Alfred Hitchcock looks on.

Most typically, the camera tracks in or out on an axis, moving at an angle to or perpendicularly to the dramatic action. In a crane shot, the camera cannot only move forward, backward, or circuitously on the ground, as in any dolly shot, but can also rise or descend. The party sequence in *Notorious* (1946) begins with a crane shot that descends from an overhead long shot of the ballroom floor and surrounding staircase to an extreme close-up of an important key clutched in the hand of the heroine (played by Ingrid Bergman). Like other camera movements, this crane shot "reads" the action for the spectator, singling out a crucial detail that might otherwise have gone unnoticed.

LIGHTING

Though set and costume design remain the most obvious and most forceful elements of expression among all the techniques of mise-en-scene, lighting comes to play an increasingly important role in the articulation of the meaning of a particular sequence. For the most part, lighting is a fundamental requirement. A certain minimal amount of lighting is necessary in order for the camera to photograph the contents of any scene. But there is more to lighting than ensuring proper exposure. Lighting becomes a tool for "reading" the contents of a scene; and directors of photography carefully "build" their lighting setups to accomplish this goal.

Three-Point Lighting

In classical Hollywood cinema, the lighting setup begins with what is called "general" set lighting, which is designed not only to ensure proper exposure but to establish overall lighting directionality. Natural or realistic lighting always establishes (or refers to) the source of the light. In exterior, daytime sequences, light typically comes from above—from the sun. For many interior daytime or nighttime sequences, the same rule also applies because most interiors are lit from lighting fixtures located on the ceiling. In these instances, the "key" or dominant source light comes from above. In other instances, however, the major illumination for a scene comes from the front, the side, or the rear. Its source is a table or floor lamp, a fireplace, or a doorway or window through which exterior light comes. These lighting setups are realistically *motivated;* their source and direction are determined by the location or setting specified in the script.

The standard lighting setup employed in Hollywood films is called "three-point lighting." The "three points" to which the term refers are dominant sources of illumination. Most three-point lighting setups involve dozens of actual lights, not just three, but they are so arranged as to suggest three basic sources or "lights." These lights are known as the key light (or chief directional light sources), the fill light (or weaker light sources which "fill in" the shadows cast by the key light), and the back light, the minor lights that are used to light the space between the back of the set and the characters in order to separate or distinguish them from the background. In certain situations, lights are also positioned to the sides or beneath characters in order to delineate important features. At the same time, a number of back lights are deployed to create the illusion of depth by lighting various levels of the set,

Artist's sketch of the three-point lighting system.

curved surfaces of the set, or the shoulders of the characters; the latter are known as "clothes lights."

High-Key/Low-Key Lighting

Three-point lighting can be manipulated to produce a variety of different lighting effects. However, most of these effects fall under two basic stylistic categories. These are either high-key or low-key lighting. The terms "high" and "low," unlike their use in connection with camera position, have nothing to do with the position of the lights. Rather, they describe the ratio of fill light to key light. In a high-key lighting system, this ratio is high; that is, there is a high amount of fill light, which washes out shadows cast by the key light. This produces a more or less brightly lit scene in which light is evenly distributed throughout the set. This style of lighting is associated with upbeat genres, such as comedies and musicals.

In a low-key lighting system, the ratio of fill to key light is low. Shadows cast by the key light are not fully filled in, producing a shadowy effect and an uneven distribution of light. This style of lighting is used in conjunction with downbeat genres, such as mysteries, thrillers, and horror films, and with films noirs. These conventional associations of different lighting systems with different moods are occasionally violated. Billy Wilder, for example, uses low-key lighting to film a number of comedies, including *Love in the Afternoon* (1957) and *The Apartment* (1960). Yet his appropriation of the low-key style is done deliberately to match the bittersweet moods that dominate these films' narrations. In other words, the low-key style retains its "darker" associations, even in a comedy.

The key light in a Western filmed outdoors in the daylight will normally be the sun. Shadows cast by the sun on the faces of actors wearing cowboy hats are regularly "filled in" with light from reflectors or lamps positioned on or near ground level. This fill light violates the logic of nature; in daylit exteriors, light always come from above and never from below. Yet it seems perfectly natural; it has established itself as a convention, which owes its existence to the necessity that faces be as legible or readable as possible. In fact, Westerns like *Tom Horn* (1980), which do not always fill in the shadows under the brims of hats, appear unrealistic because they do not abide by this time-worn lighting convention.

Star Lighting

Readability plays a major role in the development of lighting styles and conventions, serving to justify their violation of the dictates of realism and directionality. The building of the lighting setup begins with a nonrealistic foundation—with general illumination that is merely there in order to secure proper exposure (that is, to achieve literal readability). Over this is laid directional lighting, which is realistically motivated. On top of this, in turn, is

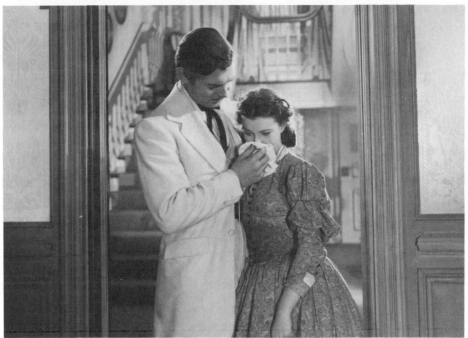

Bright, evenly lit high-key lighting in *Gone With the Wind*.

Shadowy low-key lighting in a scene from *The Grapes of Wrath*.

placed star lighting, which highlights (or conceals) certain features of the major performers and makes the expressions on their faces readable.

Star lighting singles out the chief figures in a scene by giving them their own special lighting system. Star lighting thus functions to guide the attention of the audience to the actors and actresses whose roles in the scenes are of primary importance and to relegate other figures to the literal or figurative background. At the same time, star lighting serves to heighten the charismatic presence of certain performers. Directional lighting casts shadows on the faces of the minor players, whose faces become mere surfaces which reflect light coming from elsewhere. Star lighting, on the other hand, works to transform the faces of the major performers into apparent sources of light. Since the light on their faces has no identifiable origin in the scene, it appears to come from within them—to radiate from them as if they were, indeed, astral bodies or stars. In other words, every scene in a Hollywood film combines realistic, directional, motivated lighting with unrealistic star lighting. And audiences never seem to be bothered by the apparent contradiction.

SOUND

Miking and Mixing

A blend of the realistic and the unrealistic, similar to star lighting, takes place in sound recording. Microphones are positioned to pick up sound effects and dialogue in a quasi-realistic way; the microphones duplicate, as it were, the general position of the camera, recording the sounds of what it sees. However, the intelligibility (or readability) of dialogue always takes precedence over that of other sounds in determining actual microphone positions. As a result, the overall realism and directionality of sound is combined with "star miking." Specially placed microphones ensure that the words of major performers and crucial lines of dialogue will be heard and sound-mixing practices lift them out of the general hubbub of sounds in the scene.

Sound mixing, which takes place on the set, in a recording studio, or in a sound-mixing facility, involves the combination of three different categories of film sound—dialogue, sound effects, and music. Sound mixers combine the various tracks in order to "hear" the scene for the audience. The "hearing" of a scene is the aural equivalent of the reading of the scene—that is, sound recordists and mixers provide an aural perception of the action. For example, the sound effects of the noise of an automobile engine might accompany the introduction of a scene in which two characters converse while riding in a car. But after establishing the aural atmosphere through the presence of engine noise, the sound mixer will normally lower these particular sound effects in order to make the dialogue more intelligible. The same sort of manipulation will take place with the music track during dialogue sequences.

The Musical Score

The musical score of a film, which is written by the film's composer, functions as a commentary upon the action. Music serves to direct the audience's attention to specific characters or details, to provide information about the time or place of the action, or to establish mood. Thus characters are frequently associated with or identified by specific musical motifs. In Westerns, for example, Indians will routinely be introduced with the familiar $4/4$ allegretto drumbeat that signifies "Indian territory." Melodramatic moments will be underlined with musical crescendos, and the season of the year will be cued by appropriate traditional music, such as Christmas carols, "Auld Lang Syne" (for New Year's), and so forth.

Like camera angle, distance, and movement, the musical score comments upon the action without the characters' knowledge. Much as the characters cannot (or pretend they cannot) see the camera, so they cannot hear the underscoring. However, they can obviously hear music that emanates from the space of the drama, such as that from radios, record players, and musical instruments played by characters within the fiction. The musical score provides yet another level of interpretation of the drama in addition to those already built into the mise-en-scene.

Sound and Continuity

Sound is both a feature of mise-en-scene and of editing. Sounds occurring within the shot, whether dialogue, sound effects, or music, automatically interact with one another (as do the visual elements of mise-en-scene) to provide narrative information. In other words, sound is not only a part of mise-en-scene but it also behaves and functions just as mise-en-scene does. But sound, both as a phenomenon and as an aesthetic category, cannot be as easily confined as is mise-en-scene to the borders of the frame or the limits of the shot. Off-screen sound penetrates the borders of the frame. We see characters react to unseen voices and/or noises that come from outside the frame. And sound continues over cuts. Dialogue, sound effects, and music extend from one shot to the next. Sound editing becomes an integral aspect of the film-editing process. Thus, much as film editors cut from shot to shot, they also cut from sound to sound; or they use sound to bridge those cuts and to make them less visible.

Musical scoring plays a major role in transporting spectators smoothly through highly edited sequences by giving them a melodic line that can carry them over disjunctive edits. In conversation sequences, the dialogue will provide a stream of continuous aural information that helps to bridge the cuts from one speaker to another. Sound effects are orchestrated to accomplish a similar goal. In all of these instances, the flow of the sound serves to stabilize the audience, to hold them in place across the visual discontinuities which appear on the screen.

EDITING FROM SCENE TO SCENE

Classical continuity editing serves a purpose similar to sound editing. Often referred to as "invisible editing," classical editing is designed to render more or less imperceptible the 600 to 800 separate shots that constitute the average, feature-length film. The goal of this editing strategy is to disguise the transitions from shot to shot, making the film appear to be a seamless flow of images. At the same time, invisible editing provides yet another level of interpretation of the onscreen action for audiences by singling out details or making connections from one shot to another. Thus a cut to a close-up proves to be an efficient and relatively unobtrusive way of conveying important plot- or character-related information.

Shortly after the title characters in *Strangers on a Train* (1951) accidentally meet on a train, the film cuts from a medium shot of one character, Bruno (Robert Walker), to a close-up of his lobster-patterned tie and his tie clasp. The unusual pattern of the tie and the tie clasp, which bears his name, "Bruno," communicate vital aspects of Bruno's character (his eccentricity and his narcissism), as well as his name to the audience. The physical juxtaposition of shots could be used to express ideas that cannot be conveyed through the more theatrical means of mise-en-scene. At the beginning of *Modern Times* (1936), for example, Chaplin cuts from urban workers entering the subway to a herd of sheep. This simple shot transition establishes the film's dominant metaphor—that modern workers in industrialized society are like sheep.

Transitions

Editing serves as a primary means of organizing the film. On the most basic level of organization, shots are assembled to create a scene. A shot is an unbroken strip of film made by an uninterrupted running of the camera. A scene is the film's smallest dramatic unit; it consists of one or more shots, which present an action that is spatially and temporally continuous; that is, which takes place in a single space at a single time. Certain scenes consist of two or more actions set in two or more spaces and times which are intercut to form a single, complex scene. At a larger level of organization, scenes or groups of scenes are assembled to create a sequence of scenes, a large segment, or an entire film. Thus the term "editing" encompasses two different forms of organization—editing within a scene and editing from scene to scene.

Editing from scene to scene provides the fundamental structure for the film as a whole. It employs five basic transitional devices—the cut, the fade, the dissolve, the iris, and/or the wipe. The cut is a simple break where two shots are joined together. The fade involves the gradual darkening of the image until it becomes black (the fade-out) or the gradual brightening of a darkened image until it becomes visible and achieves its proper brightness (the fade-in). The dissolve is achieved by simultaneously fading out on one shot while fading in on the next so that the first shot gradually disappears as the second gradually becomes visible; during the middle of the dissolve, the two shots will briefly be superimposed.

Though rare in contemporary cinema, the iris-in or iris-out serves as a major transition in the silent cinema; an adjustable diaphragm or iris in the camera or a moveable mask placed over the camera lens will gradually open, in an iris-in, to reveal more and more image within an expanding, geometrically shaped frame, or it will gradually close down, in an iris-out, to narrow the field of view, which is surrounded by more and more blackness. The wipe, which has also become something of a dated device, is a transition in which the second shot appears to wipe the first shot off the screen.

Cuts figure significantly in both editing from scene to scene and editing within scenes. The other transitions, however, are generally used to signify shifts from scene to scene. The fade, like the lowering or raising of the lights between scenes or acts in the theater, marks a change in time and/or place. The iris functions like the opening and/or closing of a theater curtain to designate major transitions. However, the dissolve and the wipe, which communicate similar information, provide a more fluid, less discrete marking of temporal and/or spatial change.

Editing and Narrative Structure

Editing from scene to scene provides structure for the narrative in a variety of ways. Scenes can be organized in a purely linear fashion, as seen in the journey structure of *Some Like It Hot* (1959) analyzed in the previous chapter. Or they can be narratively linear and structurally circular or symmetrical, as seen in the seven-part, A-B-C-D-C-B-A pattern found in *The Gold Rush* (1925). Or they can be organized into a flashback structure, as in *Citizen Kane* (1941), which commences with Kane's death at his mansion, Xanadu; reviews his life through five flashback interviews with his friends, associates, former wife, and butler; and concludes, roughly a week after the film began, with a return to Xanadu where the mystery of "rosebud" is solved. Yet again, films can be organized around an alternating pattern, which interweaves two or more story lines, as in D. W. Griffith's *Intolerance* (1916), which cuts back and forth from stories of social intolerance set in four different periods of history, or around the dovetailed pattern of successive stories, such as Jim Jarmusch's *Mystery Train* (1989), in which three separate plots unfold over the course of a single evening in a Memphis hotel.

Crosscutting or parallel editing provide the structural backbone of countless Hollywood narratives from the silent cinema of Griffith to the sound films of Hitchcock and George Lucas. Crosscutting or parallel action involve shifting back and forth between two or more characters and/or stories, which are occurring in two or more separate spaces more or less simultaneously. (*Intolerance* is an exception to this rule in that its events, although thematically parallel, take place in different centuries.) Hitchcock's *Strangers on a Train* alternates between the exploits of a tennis star and a psychopathic killer, while his *Family Plot* (1976) juxtaposes the actions of two couples, a phony medium and her boyfriend and a pair of kidnappers/jewel thieves, whose paths repeatedly intersect.

In *American Graffiti* (1973), Lucas' narrative shifts from character to character on a summer night in 1962. In the *Star Wars* films, Lucas cuts from the efforts of Luke Skywalker, Han Solo, Princess Leia, and their compatriots to defeat the Empire and the counterefforts of the Emperor, Darth Vader, and his underlings to suppress their rebellion. From Griffith to the present, crosscutting builds toward a climax where the various narrative strands cross and where the dramatic tensions and conflicts which they represent are finally resolved.

EDITING WITHIN SCENES

The transitions employed in editing from scene to scene are marked as such; that is, they are necessarily visible, functioning to convey dramatically significant shifts in time and/or place. Editing within scenes, on the other hand, pursues a strategy of self-effacement which disguises its operations and makes the scene appear to be more or less seamless. This is accomplished through a variety of "matching" techniques that make transitions from shot to shot smoother. These techniques involve the careful observance of narrative logic in the analytical dissection of dramatic action and the strict adherence to certain rules of thumb that ensure that the space within which the action takes place will be perceived by audiences as coherent and unified. Editing serves the narrative logic; it "reads" the drama in a purely logical and descriptive way. Thus a conversation sequence will cut back and forth from the person speaking to the reactions of those listening and then to the next speaker; the discovery of a safe that has just been robbed might be followed by a shot of the open window through which the burglar has escaped.

Scene dissection tends to follow an orderly pattern. It begins with an establishing or master shot, which is followed by a series of shots (scene dissection) that analyze the dramatic contents of the space presented within the establishing shot, and it closes with a return to either the master shot or to some other shot marking the ending of the scene. The establishing or master shot, which is frequently a long shot, establishes the space within which the subsequent action will take place. It will occasionally also indicate the time of day or year.

In *Shadow of a Doubt*, the shots of kids playing ball in the street and the crane shot up to Charlie's window serve as establishing shots, informing the viewer where and when the action was taking place. Charlie's conversation with his landlady and his subsequent behavior alone in his room constitute the body of the scene, which concludes with a medium long shot of his open door just after he has left his room to confront the men waiting outside. The interior shot of the door echoes the exterior establishing shot of the window and conveys to audiences that the scene is over.

In more recent years, a number of filmmakers have dispensed with traditional establishing shots, opting to begin scenes more abruptly in the middle of an action or with a close-up of a significant detail. In these instances, the space within which the action will occur is indicated in subsequent shots that are not reserved exclusively for establishing the location but which are part of the scene dissection.

Matches

Scene dissection relies upon a system of "matches" to provide continuity for the action. This system involves the matching of shots in such a way that potential discontinuities are cosmetically concealed. Matches include graphic matches, matches on action, and eye-line matches. In a graphic match, major features of the composition in one shot will be duplicated in the next shot, providing a graphic continuity that serves to bridge the edit. The editing of most conversation sequences employs rough graphic matches in that characters retain their approximate positions in the frame from shot to shot. The introduction of Xanadu during the opening sequence of *Citizen Kane* involves an extremely subtle series of exact graphic matches. Successive shots of the mansion from different perspectives (with different objects in the foreground) are linked together by dissolves. They are all united by a common feature—a single window with a light in it—which occupies the same place in each frame of each shot as the editing gradually brings the viewer closer and closer to the window.

Matches on action use the carryover of physical movement from one shot to the next to conceal cuts. Thus, as a character begins to sit down in medium long shot, an editor often cuts in to a closer shot as the action continues. Or as a character opens a door and begins to walk through it, there is often a cut to a different camera position on the other side of the door as the same character walks through the open door and closes it. Yet the cut and the change in camera position are more or less imperceptible, disguised by the continuity of the character's movement.

Eye-line matches and point-of-view editing play crucial roles in the continuity system, serving the interest of character exposition and character psychology. Eye-line matching involves two shots in which a character in the first shot looks offscreen at another character or object. The next shot shows what that character sees from a position which reflected, in its angle, the character's position and the direction in which he or she had looked, but which remains more or less objective in nature. That is, it does not duplicate that character's actual perspective. In effect, the second shot obliquely answers the first, presenting the space to which the character's eye line refers or looks from the neutral position of the camera.

Point-of-View Editing

Point-of-view editing is a subset of the eye-line match which involves a series of three separate shots—a shot of a character looking offscreen, a point-of-view shot of what the character sees, and a reaction shot of the character as he or she reacts to the thing that was seen. Thus in *Rear Window* (1954), Hitchcock cuts from a shot of his hero (James Stewart) looking out his window at

Author's frame enlargements

Point-of-view editing in *Rear Window:* Jeff (James Stewart) looks, an insert shot of what he sees (Miss Torso), and a shot of Jeff's reaction.

Miss Torso, one of his neighbors, to a point-of-view shot from his perspective of her dancing in a halter and shorts, and back to a reaction shot of Stewart as he smiles somewhat lecherously. Unlike the second shot in the standard eye-line match, the point-of-view shot duplicates what the character sees, representing his or her actual perspective. In other words, in point-of-view editing the second shot is subjective rather than objective. Thus while the eye-line match describes the character's interactions with others from the outside, point-of-view editing involves the audience in the mental processes of the character and gives them privileged access to character psychology.

The 180-Degree Rule

At the center of the continuity system stands its fundamental principle—the illusion of spatial reality. This illusion is created and maintained in the cinema through the observance of one simple law, which is known as the 180-degree rule. In order to guarantee matches in screen position and movement and to construct a realistic playing space for the characters, filmmakers film the action from one side of an imaginary line (the axis of action) that runs through the center of the scene's major action. By remaining on one side of this line, the camera ensures that screen direction remains constant. That is, if one character stands on the right of the frame and another on the left, those characters would retain their relative screen positions from one shot to the next (unless, of course, they moved).

If, however, the camera crosses the axis of the action after one shot and films the next shot from the other side of the 180-degree line, the original screen position of the characters would be reversed in this second shot, making them appear to switch positions as the film cuts from one shot to the next. If there is any onscreen movement from right to left (or vice versa) and the axis of action is crossed, that movement would appear to change direction from shot to shot. Certain directors, such as John Ford, repeatedly violate the 180-degree rule; others, such as Howard Hawks, scrupulously obey it. Hawks's respect for and Ford's lack of respect for the rule reflect their different attitudes toward the representation of space, which Hawks conceives of quite physically and Ford quite abstractly.

In observing the 180-degree rule, filmmakers rely extensively on shot/reverse-shot editing. This editing pattern employs paired shots to cover conversations or other actions. The shots alternate back and forth between an angled shot from one end of the 180-degree line and another from the other end. The second shot views the action from the same angle as the first, though that angle is now "reversed," that is, the shot is taken from the opposite direction.

Classical Hollywood style achieves semitransparency by putting itself at the service of film narrative. Elements of mise-en-scene and editing function to advance the narrative and/or to further character exposition. As a result, the narrative's "visibility" relegates technique to the status of a facilitating tool. Stylistic invisibility becomes a goal of the system, which its technicians and craftspersons seek to achieve on both a conscious and an unconscious level. Cinematographers, editors, and directors in Hollywood declare that if audiences notice their technique, it is no good and they immediately set to work to hide it. Ironically, their art consists of its own self-effacement. Yet that art remains visible no matter what they do to hide it. It can be seen in its invisibility, for it is a style and system of conventions that *work* to convince audiences that no work is taking place. And that *work* could never quite disappear. For in making the film legible for audiences, classical Hollywood cinema leaves the marks of this legibility on the film itself. But these marks remain hard to see because classical Hollywood style is not superficially superimposed upon the narrative. It cannot be seen as something that is separate from the narrative because it is the means by which that narrative is realized. In other words, it is invisible because it *is* the narrative.

Artist's sketch illustrating the 180-degree rule.

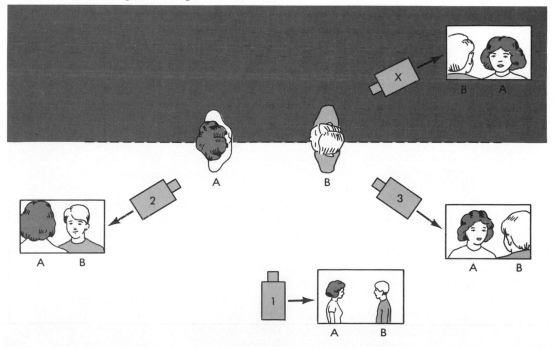

SELECT FILMOGRAPHY

Intolerance (1916)
Bringing Up Baby (1938)
His Girl Friday (1940)
Citizen Kane (1941)
Shadow of a Doubt (1943)

Notorious (1946)
Red River (1948)
Strangers on a Train (1951)
Rear Window (1954)
American Graffiti (1973)

SELECT BIBLIOGRAPHY

Alton, John. *Painting with Light.* New York: Macmillan, 1949.

Bordwell, David, and Kristin Thompson. *Film Art: An Introduction,* 4th ed. New York: McGraw-Hill, 1993.

Gorbman, Claudia. *Unheard Melodies: Narrative Film Music.* Bloomington: Indiana University Press, 1987.

Reisz, Karel, and Gavin Millar. *The Technique of Film Editing.* New York: Hastings House, 1973.

THE STUDIO SYSTEM

MANUFACTURING DREAMS

Movies and Mass Production

When Hortense Powdermaker, in her 1950 anthropological study of the movie colony describes Hollywood as "a dream factory," she puts into words the essential contradiction that lies at the heart of the American cinema: It is both an art and an industry. It manufactures images, sounds, characters, situations, and stories. Film is a product of the so-called second Industrial Revolution, the late nineteenth-century upheaval that took place in the scientific technologies of electricity, steel, chemistry, and communications. The cinema arose as a result of the scientific research and technological development of American industry—from Thomas Edison's machine shops that produced the motion picture camera; George Eastman's photographic works that innovated motion picture film; and the research labs of Bell Telephone, Western Electric, American Telephone & Telegraph, General Electric, and Westinghouse that pioneered the basic sound recording and transmission technologies, ranging from the telephone and telegraph to the phonograph and radio, which provided the foundation for the silent motion picture's subsequent transition to sound.

At the same time, the motion picture industry is genuinely an industry in that it draws upon the techniques of modern mass production—upon the centralization of production, the division of labor, the increasing specialization and professionalization of the work force, and the assembly line. Even before the studio era, film companies such as Edison and American Mutoscope relied upon cheap, sweatshop labor (consisting mostly of women) to operate film-drying drums, retouch negatives, handpaint (or tint and tone) sequences from films, and assemble prints for distribution.

The development of the studio system in the 1910s and the 1920s is based upon industrial models developed by Henry Ford and others designed to streamline the production process. Although the motion picture does not pass from hand to hand on a continuously moving conveyor belt (like the machine parts in the comic assembly line sequence of Charlie Chaplin's *Modern Times*, 1936), it nonetheless depends upon the coordinated efforts of each member of the production team, including not only highly paid producers, directors, and stars but other workers from the middle and lower end of the salary scale, such as screenwriters, art directors, costume designers, camerapeople, carpenters, electricians, and others.

Like other machine-based industries, the motion picture industry relies upon an elaborate, heavily capitalized system of production, employing precision, state-of-the-art machinery and hundreds, if not thousands, of skilled

The studio as a factory: An overview of the Warner Bros.' lot.

workers whose efforts are carefully coordinated by a centralized management. Its efficiency hinges upon the ownership or control of raw materials (including not only mechanical equipment but also, in the unique case of motion pictures, talented artists), the standardization of the production operation, and the implementation of modern mass distribution and marketing strategies that maximize the accessibility of the product for the consumer and minimize competition from others. It is no accident that the motion picture business is referred to as an "industry" and that motion picture studios are called, by Powdermaker and others, "factories."

Intangible Goods

As Powdermaker's phrase "dream factory" suggests, the products of this system of mass production are unlike the typical products of American industry; it does not make cars, household appliances, toothpaste, or laundry detergent; it manufactures dreams. The consumers of motion pictures do not purchase a "durable" good, that is, a commodity designed to last for three or more years. Nor do they purchase a "nondurable" good, an item which is intended to be used up more quickly. Instead, they purchase an "intangible" good, an entertainment experience that lasts for a few brief hours and then vanishes into memory.

Other machine-based industries produce standardized merchandise. Each bar of Ivory soap, each box of Wheaties cereal, each 1957 Cadillac Eldorado is more or less identical to each other bar, box, or car bearing the same name. It can be distributed and sold as a product to a public which knows, more or less, what it is getting. Once manufacturers have established the brand name of their wares, through advertising or other means, they can predict, with reasonable certainty, how the product will fare in the marketplace. In this way, they are able to avoid excessive underproduction or overproduction and thus stabilize their operations.

Motion pictures, however, are one-of-a-kind items. They are unique products, never before seen by an audience. Though films, in general, enjoy a relatively stable following (from the 1920s through the 1940s at least), each individual film is an unproven commodity for which there is no built-in, guaranteed audience. As a result, producers take a gamble each time they make a film. The fact that a previous film has done well at the box office in no way ensures the success of the next film. The studio system evolves to reduce the risks inherent in the production of intangible goods such as motion pictures. Its business practices develop in the way that they do in order to stabilize an unstable business.

Hollywood generates its own form of brand names—the star system, the identifiable personalities of well-known producers, directors, and screenwriters whose names attract audiences, and the familiar visual iconography and story patterns of film genres. In this way the studios attempt to provide audiences with a variety of fundamental known quantities that can serve as a basis for selling a larger, essentially unknown quantity. At the same time, producers engage in an assortment of monopolistic business practices, such as blind bidding, block booking, and runs, zones, and clearances, to ensure that whatever films they do make will provide them with a secure return on their investment.

THE MAJORS AND THE MINORS

The studio system is dominated by five major and three minor studios, most of whom continue to play a significant role in Hollywood long after the demise of the studio system. In fact, many of them continue to dominate the film industry today. The majors include Paramount, Loew's/Metro-Goldwyn-Mayer (M-G-M), Fox/20th Century-Fox, Warner Bros., and Radio-Keith-Orpheum (RKO); the minors consist of Universal, Columbia, and United Artists. These studios came into being over a relatively short, sixteen-year period, stretching from 1912 (Universal) to 1928 (RKO). (Though 20th Century-Fox was not created until 1935, the Fox Film Corporation, on which it is based, was founded in 1915.) Paramount was founded in 1914, Columbia Pictures in 1922, Warner's in 1923 (though it came into existence as a distributor in 1917), and M-G-M (formerly Metro, 1919) in 1924.

Origins

The studio system takes the place of an earlier organization, Thomas Edison's Motion Picture Patents Company (MPPC), a trust which, through its control of basic motion picture patents, governed production, distribution, and exhibition. The structure of this trust was oligopolistic; that is, it was controlled by a handful of companies, including Edison, Vitagraph, Pathé, Biograph, and others. The origins of the studio system can be traced to the attempts by independent exhibitors and distributors, such as William Fox and Carl Laemmle, to break up this trust. They finally succeeded in doing this in 1915, when U.S. courts declared the MPPC to be in violation of the Sherman Antitrust Act.

The trust had served to stabilize the industry during the nickelodeon era. Its overthrow led to the establishment of another stabilizing system, designed to suit the needs of an expanding film industry. The trust oversaw an industry in which short, one-reel films were sold, like sausages, by the foot. The dramatic content of the films played little or no part in their marketing strategy. Though the actors in trust pictures were occasionally identified in the trade press as early as 1909, the trust resisted the publicization of its stars in the popular press in a deliberate attempt to prevent the creation of a costly star system, similar to that which had developed in the legitimate theater.

Independents like Fox and Laemmle fought the trust both in the courts and in the theaters, where they gave the public what it seemed to want—feature-length films with sensational dramatic content and stars. In particular, the formation by Adolph Zukor in 1912 of the Famous Players Company, which boasted motion pictures with "famous players from famous plays," capitalized upon these two selling points to differentiate its product from the trust's more anonymous and less distinguished fare. The studio system arose to maximize the exploitation of feature-length films and the star system, dramatic innovations in the nature of the war-time and postwar film industry which the trust had ignored. But the studio system's greatest strength, as an institution, lay in its development of a vertically integrated marketplace, which virtually ensured its economic future.

Vertical Integration

The term "vertical integration" refers to the structure of a marketplace which is integrated (rather than segregated) at a variety of crucial levels; in the case of the motion picture industry, the studio system established a market in which the studios own production facilities, distribution outlets, and theaters. In other words, the studios control every level of the marketplace from the top down, from production to exhibition.

Vertical integration began in the 1910s, when the trust denied motion pictures to independent exhibitors like Fox, who refused to pay arbitrary weekly license fees to the trust to operate his theaters, and to independent distributors like Laemmle, who resented the trust's stranglehold on the supply of product, which his exchanges purchased and then rented to exhibitors.

Their search for product to distribute and to exhibit led them into production themselves. Vertical integration inspired the postwar consolidation of the studio system as national distribution companies, such as Paramount, merged with production companies, such as Famous Players and Lasky, and subsequently began to purchase theater chains; and as exhibitors such as First National added distribution and production to their overall operations.

The creation of M-G-M in the mid-1920s is exemplary of the vertical integration that was taking place during this period. In 1920, Marcus Loew, who owned an extensive chain of theaters, entered production and distribution by purchasing a small company called Metro Pictures. Early in 1924, Loew obtained another independent production company, Goldwyn Pictures, and, later that year, purchased the Louis B. Mayer Picture Corp. whose chief assets consisted of Mayer and his star producer, Irving Thalberg. The result of Loew's expansion was Metro-Goldwyn-Mayer, a fully integrated corporation that extended its control of motion picture product through the production, distribution, and exhibition stages.

All of the major studios owned theater chains; the minors, Universal, Columbia, and United Artists, did not. The minors distributed their pictures, by special arrangement, to theaters owned by the majors; and the majors regularly booked one another's films in their theaters. Vertical integration results in a fairly efficient economic system. The major studios produced from

The formation of M-G-M via a merger of Metro Pictures, Goldwyn Pictures, and Louis B. Mayer Pictures in 1924.

Author's collection

40 to 60 pictures a year—enough films to supply their own and even other studio's theaters. The majors owned only a fraction of the nation's theaters—in 1945, for example, they owned 3000 of the 18,000 theaters around the country. The remainder were owned and operated by theater chains or independents. But the theaters owned by the majors tended to be large, first-run houses, situated in the biggest cities. As a result, these theaters generated over 70 percent of all box-office receipts.

Block Booking, Blind Bidding, and Runs, Zones, and Clearances

The majors ensured the profitability of their own theaters and controlled the independents by instituting a series of special distribution practices, known as block booking, blind bidding, and runs, zones, and clearances. Block booking refers to the rental of films in large quantity. If exhibitors want to rent films, they have to rent the studio's entire yearly output. And since they contracted with distributors for films before the films had actually been made, they were forced to bid for them without seeing them—a procedure called blind bidding.

These practices evolved out of the power of the star system. In the teens, Paramount insisted that theaters who wanted to book a popular Mary Pickford or Douglas Fairbanks picture take other pictures as well, including cheaply made films which featured no stars. In this way, Paramount could sell the bad with the good, ensuring that even its worst films would find a market. The studios protected their own first-run theaters from the competition of independents and attempted to get the most rental income from first-run independent theaters by implementing a system of runs, zones, and clearances.

As a result of this system, a film that opens in the first-run movie palaces in early September will not get to play in the cheaper, neighborhood theaters until late October or early November. New films will initially be rented only to first-run theaters—to large houses which generate the lion's share of box-office receipts. The majority of these tend to be owned by the studios. At the same time, distribution is guided by a system of zones; only one theater in any particular area is permitted to exhibit a new picture. This practice also tends to favor studio-owned theaters.

Finally, smaller, second-run and sub-run theaters are forced to wait until a picture has completed its run in the larger houses before they can obtain it. As a film moves through successive runs, clearances of between 7 and 30 days are observed, during which time the film is unavailable. This practice reinforces the hierarchical structure of exhibition and protects each tier of theaters from competition with theaters farther down the scale that charge audiences less for tickets. Delays between runs are designed to renew demand for the picture.

These practices, which were subsequently outlawed by the courts, effectively prevented independent producers from entering the marketplace and competing with the eight major studios by arming the latter with contractual advantages that enabled them to control first-run exhibition. Without access to first-run exhibition, independent producers could not make a profit on their films. These procedures also served to squeeze the maximum rental income out of the marketplace. Independent producers of first-run films did exist in Hollywood. David O. Selznick, Walt Disney, Samuel Goldwyn, Walter Wanger, Howard Hughes, Alexander Korda, and others worked effectively within the studio system, largely by distributing (and occasionally financing) their films through existing studios such as United Artists, which had been established in 1919 for just such a purpose.

STUDIO PRODUCTION: FROM STORY IDEA TO AD CAMPAIGN

Under Contract

The efficient organization of distribution and exhibition operations is matched by that of actual film production. The oligopolistic control by a small cartel of major studios extends to production personnel, who are contracted to various studios or producers and who exist as a pool of resources upon which studios can draw at any time. Actors and actresses function as commodities, much as baseball players and the members of other professional athletic teams do. Unlike the stars of the silent era who secured short-term contracts for two or three pictures, studio stars worked under restrictive, long-term, seven-year contracts, which forbade them from engaging in nonapproved acting activities (such as the legitimate theater, radio, and television) and regulated their personal behavior; it demanded that they adhere to a "morals" clause and it even governed other features of their offscreen appearance, including their hair style, choice of clothing, and weight.

Studio contracts required them to act in whatever films the studios cast them (or undergo suspension without pay, which time was added to the seven years of their contract), attend studio publicity functions, publicize their own films, promote product tie-ins, and, occasionally, be loaned out to other studios to fulfill the same obligations there for one or two pictures. During the early 1930s, in particular, the actor's life was no picnic. They worked six days a week—often for fourteen hours a day. During his first year at M-G-M (1931), Clark Gable appeared in fourteen pictures; during her first year at Warner's (1932), Bette Davis made eight films. It was tough on directors as well. In the early 1930s, Michael Curtiz (who made *Casablanca* in 1942) directed, on the average, five films a year for Warner Bros.

A Self-Contained World

The studio kept everyone under contract, including producers, directors, screenwriters, cinematographers, art directors, costume designers, sound recordists, and other technical staff. With such a sizeable pool of talent held in constant readiness for each new project, it is relatively easy to cast a picture and get it into production. The physical layout of the studio is similarly designed to facilitate production. In fact, the studio functions as a self-sufficient world unto itself—with its own police force, fire, sanitation, water, and electrical departments, and with its own commissary or restaurant, gymnasium, and infirmary.

A story department houses readers whose job it is to pore through recent books, magazines, and newspapers in search of story ideas. Nearby stand the offices of studio screenwriters, who prepare story synopses or treatments, write dialogue, and generate shooting scripts for stars under contract. These scripts are then analyzed by unit managers or production assistants and broken down scene by scene by assistant directors, who estimate overall budget and shooting time and who organize a shooting schedule. This schedule will be planned in such a way as to economize on costs.

Scenes from films are rarely shot in the order in which they appear in the screenplay (in continuity), but rather they are shot out of order. Thus all the scenes staged in one setting or location will be shot back to back; scenes containing the same groups of actors or actors who are only available for a short time period will be shot together; shots requiring the rental of expensive equipment not owned by the studio, such as special camera cranes, or the use of studio equipment in high demand by other studio production units will be shot on a single day; and so forth. Shooting scripts are sent to the casting department, which suggests actors for those roles not already cast by the producer or director.

The scripts are also sent to the art department, which designs the sets and perhaps draws up a storyboard, or a sketch of what scenes will look like, for the use of the art director, costume designer, and cinematographer. Carpenters in the studio workshop build sets according to the instructions of the art director; scenic artists paint them; staff set decorators "dress" the set with tables, chairs, and other furnishings provided by the prop department, which stores a supply of such items in the prop room. A wardrobe department is staffed with seamstresses to make alterations in existing costumes, which are stored on the lot (or rented from Western Costume), and to execute designs for new costumes.

The studio's camera and sound departments provide the necessary equipment for filming scenes and recording dialogue and sound effects (and repair this equipment when necessary). Additional equipment for the filming of stunts or sequences involving special effects, such as explosions, bullet holes, or fires, are made in the studio's special-effects department. Electricians wire the set for both on-camera props, such as table lamps, and off-camera equipment, such as incandescent or arc lamps, cameras, sound-recording equipment, and other machinery to produce special effects such as wind, rain, snow, or fog.

The Chain of Command

The coordination of all of these individual efforts is the responsibility of the producer and/or director and their assistants, who rely upon the screenplay to serve as a blueprint for production. During shooting, the division of labor is coordinated according to various areas of specialization. The director's crew, consisting of assistant directors, script girls, dialogue coaches, and second-unit directors, assist the director. Actors are attended to by make-up artists, hairdressers, lighting doubles, and stand-ins. The photography unit, consisting of camera operators, grips, and gaffers, assist the cinematographer; and the sound unit, including boom operators and technicians who lay cables and place microphones, facilitate the job of the sound recordist.

After filming, editors prepare a rough cut of the film that is synched up with dialogue and sound effects. To this is added a musical score written by a studio composer and recorded by the studio orchestra. The montage department assembles montage sequences, which condense the passage of time or space (as seen in montages of newspaper headlines which summarize the course of events over time or in travel montages which convey the characters' European vacation through stock shots of the House of Parliament in London, the Eiffel Tower in Paris, and the Coliseum in Rome); the studio's own laboratory adds optical effects, such as fades, dissolves, or wipes; and the titling department prepares the credit sequence and any intertitles to be inserted in the film.

At the top of the production process stands the studio's chief executive or head of production—Jack Warner at Warner Bros., Darryl Zanuck at 20th Century-Fox, Louis B. Mayer at M-G-M, or Harry Cohn at Columbia. Actual production is supervised by a team of unit producers, like Irving Thalberg, Harry Rapf, Eddie Mannix, Hunt Stromberg, and others at M-G-M during the early 1930s. These producers select story properties and plan a program of films to be put into production for the year; the unit producer is responsible for selecting a director, helps in the casting of the film, and supervises the preproduction, production, and postproduction phases, including the final editing of the film.

Next in command is the director. Certain major directors work with the producer and screenwriter in preproduction, consulting on the preparation of

Harry Cohn (left), head of production at Columbia, and Frank Capra share an Academy Award for Best Picture for *You Can't Take It With You* (1938).

Author's collection

the script and the casting of actors. Other directors might be assigned to the picture only a few days before actual shooting is to begin. In the former case, the director consults with the art director and costume designer in working out the overall design of the film. In either instance, the director is responsible for rehearsing and directing the actors, staging the action, and giving instructions to the cinematographer on how each shot should look in terms of lighting, camera angle and distance, and camera movement. After shooting is completed, the director supervises postproduction, working with the editor, sound mixer, and composer on a version of the film that might be screened for audiences at a sneak preview. In general, the unit producer has final say on changes made to the film between the preview and its release to theaters.

During production and just prior to the film's release, the publicity department orchestrates promotion for the film in the media, designing posters and ad campaigns as well as supervising the production of publicity photographs and pressbooks to be sent to newspapers, magazines, and exhibitors, and of trailers to be run in theaters.

STUDIO STYLE

The structure of the studio results not only in the streamlining of the production process but in the creation of a studio style or look. The seven-year contract keeps actors, producers, directors, art directors, cinematographers, and composers at individual studios for decades. Gable remained under contract at M-G-M from 1931 to 1954. Producers Henry Blanke and Bryan Foy worked for Warners from 1928 through the mid-1950s. Cecil B. De Mille directed films for Paramount for over 40 years from 1914 (*The Squaw Man*) to 1956 (*The Ten Commandments*)—except for one brief six-year stretch (1925–1931) when he worked first as an independent producer and then at M-G-M, where he made his first sound films. Michael Curtiz and Roy Del Ruth directed films for Warner's from 1926 to 1953–1954.

Cedric Gibbons supervised art direction at M-G-M for over 30 years from 1924 to 1957; Anton Grot served as a production designer for Warner Bros. from 1929 to 1950; and Hans Drier worked more or less exclusively for Paramount from 1924 to 1951. Arthur Miller was a director of photography at Fox from 1932 through 1950; William Daniels, Greta Garbo's cinematographer of choice, was under contract to M-G-M from 1923 to 1946; and Charles B. Lang shot films at Paramount from 1926 to 1952. Alfred Newman scored films for 20th Century and 20th Century-Fox from 1934 to 1962; Max Steiner did the same for both Warner Bros. and RKO from 1929 to 1956.

The presence of these and other contract personnel contributes to the unique stylistic and thematic personality which each studio constructs for itself during different periods of the studio era. As a result, the studio system permits each studio, by focusing upon certain kinds of genre story types and establishing an individual style, to differentiate its product from that of the other studios. A comparable system of product differentiation exists today on television. Thus the Fox network pitches its programming to a hip, teen market. Cable channels provide viewers with markedly different programming; there are, for example, shopping, weather, news, sports, children's, classic movie, and new movie channels. The studios functioned in a somewhat similar way. Along with their movement toward the standardization of production, which was built into the structure of the studio system, there was a complementary drive for product differentiation.

M-G-M and Paramount

The most visible form of product differentiation is the star. M-G-M, which boasted "more stars than there are in heaven," developed a roster of glamorous actresses who dominated the screen from the late 1920s to the 1940s.

M-G-M's stable of stars in 1948–1949.

1st row (left to right for all rows): Lionel Barrymore, June Allyson, Leon Ames, Fred Astaire, Edward Arnold, Mary Astor, Ethel Barrymore, Spring Byington, James Craig, Arlene Dahl, Lassie

2nd row: Gloria De Haven, Tom Drake, Jimmy Durante, Vera-Ellen, Errol Flynn, Clark Gable, Ava Gardner, Judy Garland, Betty Garrett, Edmund Gwynn, Kathryn Grayson, Van Heflin

3rd row: Katharine Hepburn, John Hodiak, Claude Jarmon, Jr., Van Johnson, Jennifer Jones, Louis Jourdan, Howard Keel, Gene Kelly, Alf Kjellin, Angela Lansbury, Mario Lanza, Janet Leigh

4th row: Peter Lawford, Ann Miller, Ricardo Montalban, Jules Munchen, George Murphy, Reginald Owen, Walter Pidgeon, Jane Powell, Ginger Rogers, Frank Sinatra, Red Skelton

5th row: Alexis Smith, Ann Sothern, J. Carroll Naish, Dean Stockwell, Lewis Stone, Clinton Sundberg, Robert Taylor, Audrey Totter, Spencer Tracy, Esther Williams, Keenan Wynn

Author's collection

Garbo, Joan Crawford, Norma Shearer, Louise Rainer, Myrna Loy, and Greer Garson brought sincerity, refinement, and sophistication to their screen roles. (There were, of course, exceptions to M-G-M's image of polish and gloss, for the studio was also home to the more earthy Marie Dressler and to Lassie; it was also the producer of Tod Browning's *Freaks*, 1932, which functioned as a kind of *Grand Hotel* for freakish circus attractions.) By contrast, Paramount's leading ladies, such as Clara Bow, Marlene Dietrich, Mae West, Claudette Colbert, and Carole Lombard, combined sexual savoir-faire with tongue-in-cheek wit.

The differences between the two studios can best be illustrated by contrasting the anarchic, pretension-deflating comedies made by the Marx Brothers for Paramount (such as *Animal Crackers*, 1930; *Monkey Business*, 1931; *Horse Feathers*, 1932; and *Duck Soup*, 1933) with the more sober, restrained, calculated comedies they made a few years later for M-G-M (*A Night at the Opera*, 1935; *A Day at the Races*, 1937; and *Room Service*, 1938). Even Paramount's Jeannette MacDonald, who costarred with Maurice Chevalier in a series of Ruritanian musical romances, shed her self-irony and penchant for sexual innuendo when she moved to the more restrained operettas at M-G-M, where she teamed up with the decidedly less continental Nelson Eddy.

Paramount's deft European stylishness, epitomized in the subtle ironies of Ernst Lubitsch's comedies (such as *The Love Parade*, 1929; *Monte Carlo*, 1930; *Trouble in Paradise*, 1932; and *Design for Living*, 1933) and in the exotic erotic

The famous Bronson Gate, as seen in Paramount's *Sunset Boulevard* (1950).

Courtesy of Paramount

fantasies concocted by Josef von Sternberg for Marlene Dietrich (such as *Morocco*, 1930; *Shanghai Express*, 1932; and *The Scarlet Empress*, 1934) find their counterpart in the earnest celebration of American middle-class family values in M-G-M's series of Andy Hardy comedies and teen musicals, starring either Mickey Rooney or Judy Garland or both (*Babes in Arms*, 1939, and *Strike Up the Band*, 1940) or in the solid seriousness of prestige melodramas such as *The Good Earth*, 1937; *Boys Town*, 1938; *Mrs. Miniver* and *Random Harvest*, 1942; *Madame Curie*, 1943.

Warner Bros.

In contrast to the middlebrow style and content of M-G-M, Warner Bros. earned its reputation as the working man's studio. Photographic style at M-G-M is carefully polished; that at Warner's looks hasty and rough and conveys a gritty realism that suited the studio's narrative interests. Warner's specializes in gangster films, such as *Little Caesar* (1930), *The Public Enemy* (1931), *The Petrified Forest* (1936), and *The Roaring Twenties* (1939), starring tough-guy performers like James Cagney, Edward G. Robinson, and Humphrey Bogart whose proletarian acting style matches the looks and sounds of the ethnic characters they were asked to play.

Even the swashbuckling action heroes played by Errol Flynn in Warner's costume dramas champion the downtrodden lower echelons of society as the unjustly imprisoned doctor-turned-pirate in *Captain Blood* (1935) and as the title character in *The Adventures of Robin Hood* (1938). Exposés such as *I Was a Fugitive from the Chain Gang* (1932), *Wild Boys of the Road* (1933), and *Confessions of a Nazi Spy* (1939) are ripped from the headlines of the tabloids and pitched, like these newspapers, at a lower- and lower-middle-class audience. Warner's actresses, like Ruby Keeler, Joan Blondell, Bette Davis, Olivia de Havilland,

Errol Flynn in Warner Bros.' *The Adventures of Robin Hood* (1938).

Courtesy of Warner Bros.

Ida Lupino, Ann Sheridan, and Lauren Bacall, play girls-next-door, gold diggers, molls, and/or down-to-earth dames who can trade wisecracks with the guys without losing their femininity.

20th Century-Fox

Warner's pitched its product to an urban audience, tailoring its crime films, mysteries, films noirs, musicals, and even costume pictures to blue-collar workers and shop girls who appreciated hard-hitting films with a social conscience. 20th Century-Fox, jokingly referred to by rival studios as "16th Century-Fox" because of all the period and costume pictures it produced, targeted a rural rather than an urban audience. Major Fox stars of the 1930s, such as Will Rogers, Stepin Fetchit, Shirley Temple, and (in the late-1930s) Henry Fonda, speak to an agrarian, preindustrial, populist concern for homespun, grass-roots values. Even Fox stars of the 1940s, such as Tyrone Power, Betty Grable, and Don Ameche, are all-American types who bear no traces of the urban ethnicity found in Warner's stars, such as Robinson, Cagney, and even Paul Muni.

Fox, which was run by an Irish Catholic ex-cop named Winfield Sheehan and then by a Methodist from Nebraska named Darryl Zanuck, was also known as "the goy studio" because, after the ouster of its founder William Fox in 1930, it was the only studio that was neither owned nor operated by

Olivia de Havilland and Leo Genn in 20th Century-Fox's *The Snake Pit* (1948).

Courtesy of 20th Century-Fox

Jews (though the Jewish Joe Schenck did serve as chairman of the board and executive producer during Zanuck's reign). This image only served to reinforce the studio's appeal to nonurban audiences in the Midwest and the South. Ironically, while Jewish executives at Paramount, M-G-M, Warner's, Columbia, Universal, and elsewhere rarely dealt with subject matter that might be considered Jewish or that openly condemned anti-Semitism at home or abroad, Zanuck, perhaps because of Fox's reputation as a Christian studio, was one of the first studio heads to sponsor an exposé of anti-Semitism in his production of *Gentleman's Agreement* (1947), starring Gregory Peck. Zanuck discovered that there was a market for films with a certain social consciousness and prided himself on his productions of John Steinbeck's *The Grapes of Wrath* (1940), which dealt with exploited migrant farm workers; Erskine Caldwell's *Tobacco Road* (1941), a drama about the plight of sharecroppers; *The Ox-Bow Incident* (1943), a Western in which vigilantes lynch the wrong man; *Boomerang* (1947), an exposé of legal corruption; *The Snake Pit* (1948), a story about mental illness that looks at the brutal conditions in American mental asylums; and *Pinky* (1949), a film that deals with racial prejudice.

RKO

RKO, famous for an unlikely combination of films which range from *King Kong* (1933) to Fred Astaire and Ginger Rogers musicals and *Citizen Kane* (1941), was governed by a succession of different heads of production during the 1930s and 1940s, including David Selznick (*What Price Hollywood?* and *Bill of Divorcement,* 1932); Merian C. Cooper (*The Lost Patrol,* 1934); George Schafer (*Abe Lincoln in Illinois,* 1940; *Citizen Kane,* 1941; Charles Koerner (Val

Fred Astaire and Ginger Rogers in RKO's *Shall We Dance?* (1937).

Courtesy of RKO

Lewton's films such as *The Cat People*, 1942, and *I Walked with a Zombie*, 1943; *The Spiral Staircase*, 1946); Dore Schary, who supervised a number of films noirs (*Crossfire, Out of the Past*, 1947; *They Live by Night*, 1948); and, finally, Howard Hughes (*I Married a Communist*, 1950; *Vendetta*, 1946–1950; *Jet Pilot*, 1950–1957), whose mismanagement of the studio led to its sale and dismantlement in 1955. Though certain directors (John Ford, George Stevens, Robert Siodmak, Jacques Tourneur) and stars (Katharine Hepburn, Cary Grant, Robert Mitchum) worked for the studio at various times during this period, RKO lacks the thematic and stylistic consistency enjoyed by the other majors. United Artists, which merely distributed the work of independent producers such as Samuel Goldwyn, David Selznick, and Walter Wanger, shares a similar fate.

Columbia Pictures

Columbia earned a reputation for witty and urbane screenwriting and served as the home base for much of the screwball comedy talent in Hollywood. It is also the studio where Frank Capra directed populist melodramas (*American Madness*, 1932; *The Bitter Tea of General Yen* and *Lady for a Day*, 1933; *Lost Horizon*, 1937; *Mr. Smith Goes to Washington*, 1939) and comedies (*It Happened One Night*, 1934; *Mr. Deeds Goes to Town*, 1936; *You Can't Take it With You*, 1938)

Gary Cooper in Columbia's *Mr. Deeds Goes to Town* (1936).

Courtesy of Columbia Pictures

for over ten years (1928–1939). Capra's own *It Happened One Night* is generally acknowledged as the "first" screwball comedy, but Howard Hawks's contribution to Columbia comedies, *Twentieth Century* (1934), written by Ben Hecht and Charles MacArthur, runs a close second.

Columbia scenarists such as Robert Riskin, Sidney Buchman, Jo Swerling, Vina Delmar, Donald Ogden Stewart, Hecht, and MacArthur lend their big city cynicism to a string of screwball comedies at Columbia in the 1930s, including John Ford's *The Whole Town's Talking* and Gregory La Cava's *She Married Her Boss*, 1935; Richard Boleslawski's *Theodora Goes Wild*, 1936; Leo McCarey's *The Awful Truth*, 1937; George Cukor's *Holiday*, 1938; Hawks's *His Girl Friday*, 1940; Alexander Hall's *Here Comes Mr. Jordan*, 1941; and George Stevens's *The Talk of the Town*, 1942.

Forced to borrow stars, such as Clark Gable, Gary Cooper, James Stewart, Cary Grant, and others, from other studios for Columbia pictures in the 1930s, studio chief Harry Cohn decided to build his own stable of stars in the 1940s, including William Holden (*Golden Boy*, 1939; *Picnic*, 1955); Rita Hayworth (*Cover Girl*, 1944; *Gilda*, 1946; *The Lady from Shanghai*, 1948; *Salome* and *Miss Sadie Thompson*, 1953; *Fire Down Below*, 1957); Kim Novak (*Picnic*, 1955; *Bell, Book and Candle*, 1958); Judy Holliday (*Born Yesterday*, 1950; *The Marrying Kind*, 1952; *The Solid Gold Cadillac*, 1956); and Glenn Ford (*Gilda*, 1946; *Loves of Carmen*, 1948; *The Big Heat*, 1953; *Jubal*, 1956; *3:10 to Yuma*, 1957).

Universal Pictures

The golden age of Universal Pictures takes place in the first half of the 1930s when the studio was under the guidance of Carl Laemmle, Jr., who supervised the production of two innovative sound films in 1930, the Academy Award winning *All Quiet on the Western Front* and a Technicolor musical, *The King of Jazz*. He also launched a series of classic horror films, stretching from Bela Lugosi's *Dracula* (1931) and Boris Karloff's *Frankenstein* (1931) to *The Mummy* (1932), *The Invisible Man* (1933), *The Black Cat* (1934), and *The Bride of Frankenstein* (1935). At the same time, John Stahl directed a series of emotionally restrained melodramas, *Back Street* (1932), *Imitation of Life* (1934), and *Magnificent Obsession* (1935), which bring a sophistication and elegance to the studio that gives way, in the 1940s and early 1950s to crude program pictures for Abbott and Costello, Ma and Pa Kettle, and Francis, the Talking Mule. Douglas Sirk remade a number of Stahl's melodramas in the mid-1950s, including *Magnificent Obsession* (1954) and *Imitation of Life* (1959), and brought both prestige and profits back to the studio.

Sirk helped to build Universal's latest leading man, Rock Hudson, into a star in *Has Anybody Seen My Gal?*, 1952; *Magnificent Obsession* and *Taza, Son of Cochise*, 1954; *Captain Lightfoot* and *All That Heaven Allows*, 1955; *Written on the Wind*, 1956; *Battle Hymn*, 1957; and *Tarnished Angels*, 1958. The studio subsequently took over where Sirk left off, pairing Hudson and Doris Day together in a series of financially successful sex comedies such as *Pillow Talk* (1959) and *Lover Come Back* (1961).

Zazu Pitts and Lew Ayres in Universal's *All Quiet on the Western Front* (1930).

Poverty Row

These eight studios dominated a system that included a number of smaller studios, such as Republic and Monogram, which sprouted up in the early 1930s to make "B" pictures to accompany the major studios' more expensively produced "A" picture on the bottom half of a double bill. The demand for cheaply made "B" films gave rise to other poverty row studios, such as Grand National, Producers Releasing Corporation (PRC), Eagle-Lion, Allied Artists, and others. The advent of broadcast television in the postwar era eliminated the demand for "B" pictures, although certain producers of teen-exploitation films, such as American International Pictures, survived into the 1970s.

COLLAPSE: THE END OF THE STUDIO ERA

Divestment, Independent Production, and a Changing Marketplace

The dismantling of the studio system began just before World War II when the U.S. Department of Justice's Antitrust Division filed suit against the eight majors, accusing them of monopolistic practices in their use of block booking, blind bidding, and runs, zones, and clearances. Hollywood avoided prosecution by agreeing to refrain from some of these practices, but in 1944 the government, after hearing complaints from independent exhibitors that the studios had persisted in antitrust activity, reopened the suit. The Paramount Case, as the suit was now called, was finally settled in May 1948 when the U.S. Supreme Court ruled against the studios. The majors were forced to divorce their operations from one another, separating production and distribution from exhibition. They were also forced to divest themselves of their theater chains, which were to be sold off or operated by a separate group of owners who had no involvement in production and distribution. United Artists, Columbia, and Universal, though named in the suit as coconspirators for collaborating with the Big Five studios in these practices, owned no theaters and thus were not subject to this ruling. The major studios delayed the process of divorcement and divestiture as long as possible, maintaining a certain degree of control over their theaters until the mid- to late 1950s. As a result, the initial mechanism or structure that gave rise to the studio system remained more or less in place until roughly 1960.

Other factors contributed to the demise of the studio system, including lengthy postwar strikes against the studios by labor unions, changing patterns in leisure-time entertainment that resulted in a sharp drop in attendance (see Chapter 12, "Hollywood in the Age of Television"), competition with television, and the rise of independent production. After the war, actors and directors went into business for themselves, forming their own production companies. Instead of weekly salaries, they negotiated for lump-sum payments made to their privately owned corporations. Instead of being taxed as income, these payments were taxed at a much lower rate as corporate capital gains.

During the war, actor James Cagney had formed an independent production company with his brother William, financing and distributing films through United Artists. In 1946, directors Frank Capra, William Wyler, George Stevens, and producer Sam Briskin formed Liberty Films, which folded after the release of its one production, *It's a Wonderful Life* (1946). Alfred Hitchcock and British theater owner Sidney Bernstein set up Transatlantic Pictures in 1948, releasing *Rope* (1948) and *Under Capricorn* (1949) under that logo. Humphrey Bogart's Santana Productions, named after his yacht, produced *Knock on Any Door* (1949), *In a Lonely Place* (1950), and several other pictures which were released through Columbia. In 1951, John Wayne set up Batjac, which produced *Blood Alley* (1955), *The Alamo* (1960), *The Green Berets* (1968), and many other pictures starring Wayne. In 1956, producer Harold Hecht, screenwriter-director James Hill, and actor Burt Lancaster created their own company, which produced *Sweet Smell of Success* (1957), *Run Silent, Run Deep* (1958), and three other films.

At the same time, fewer, more expensive films were being made to satisfy a changing market of fewer, more demanding spectators. The era of the blockbuster had begun, and the studio system was not equipped to service that mode of production with any efficiency. As the studios lost their grip on major talent and as fewer and fewer films were put into production, they deliberately let other contract personnel go, closed down their newsreel and animation departments, rented out empty studio space to producers of television shows, and entered television production themselves.

Near the end of the 1960s, a number of studios, including Fox and M-G-M, began to sell off their back lots, which now had more value as real estate than as production space. M-G-M even auctioned off its collection of props and costumes, including Dorothy's ruby red slippers from *The Wizard of Oz* (1939). Symbolically, the studio era was over.

Starting from Scratch: The New "Studios"

Today, many of the studios of the old studio era exist but do so primarily as the distributors of films produced by a growing number of independents. Ironically, each time a new film is made today, a "studio" must be assembled from scratch to produce it. Screenwriters must be found to produce treatments and shooting scripts; producers, directors, stars, cinematographers, art directors, costume designers, and others must be assembled before production can go ahead; and, most crucially, financing must be secured from banks or other investors. Picture making today takes more time than it ever did; the six-week shooting schedules of the 1930s and 1940s have given way to three- to four-month shooting schedules. Pictures formerly made in two or three months now take a year or more to finish. As Billy Wilder once said, "in the old days we used to spend our time making pictures; these days we spend it making deals."

And since time is money, the cost of making motion pictures has skyrocketed as well; the average negative cost (the cost required to produce a finished negative excluding print costs and advertising and distribution expenses) has grown from $200,000 to $400,000 in the 1930s and $1 to $3 million in the 1950s to $27 to $30 million in the early 1990s. With the collapse of the studio system, another system has taken its place. Since the courts have outlawed the practices which formerly reduced the financial risks of film production, producers today face greater and greater uncertainty when they make a film. Since the system which guaranteed a profit has disappeared, these guarantees must be built into the films themselves in the form of bankable stars, sequelization, and presales to cable television.

With the demise of the studios, the production of motion pictures has left the factory and returned to a kind of preindustrial workshop in which the final product is custom-made to express the unique interests of the transitory assortment of artists who come together for this particular project, then move on to new ventures. Though we still refer to the motion pictures as an industry, the traditional industrial model, based on principles of mass production, no longer applies. Indeed, with the loss of a mass audience, mass production suddenly became inappropriate. Now Hollywood tailor-makes films for a diminishing film-going elite. The term "studio," which once served as a euphemism for "factory," has finally become a studio in fact as well as in name. It has become an interrelated group of artisans whose unique talents contribute to the handcrafting of individual motion pictures.

SELECT STUDIO PRODUCTIONS
(From Four Sample Studios)

COLUMBIA

It Happened One Night (1934)
Twentieth Century (1934)
Mr. Deeds Goes to Town (1936)
Lost Horizon (1937)
The Awful Truth (1937)
Holiday (1938)
Golden Boy (1939)
Mr. Smith Goes to Washington (1939)
His Girl Friday (1940)
Here Comes Mr. Jordan (1941)
Cover Girl (1944)
Gilda (1946)
The Jolson Story (1946)
The Lady from Shanghai (1948)
All the King's Men (1949)
Born Yesterday (1950)
The Big Heat (1953)
From Here to Eternity (1953)
On the Waterfront (1954)
Picnic (1955)
The Solid Gold Cadillac (1956)
Pal Joey (1957)

M-G-M

Greed (1924)
The Merry Widow (1925)
The Big Parade (1925)
Ben-Hur (1926)
Flesh and the Devil (1927)
Anna Christie (1930)
Grand Hotel (1932)
A Night at the Opera (1935)
Camille (1936)
The Good Earth (1937)
The Wizard of Oz (1939)
Goodbye Mr. Chips (1939)
Mrs. Miniver (1942)

Meet Me in St. Louis (1944)
The Pirate (1948)
Singin' in the Rain (1952)
The Band Wagon (1953)
Ben-Hur (1959)
Home from the Hill (1960)

PARAMOUNT

Manslaughter (1922)
Manhandled (1924)
It (1927)
Wings (1927)
Morocco (1930)
Trouble in Paradise (1932)
Shanghai Express (1932)
Duck Soup (1933)
She Done Him Wrong (1933)
I'm No Angel (1933)
The Scarlet Empress (1934)
Cleopatra (1934)
Desire (1936)
Swing High, Swing Low (1937)
Midnight (1939)
The Lady Eve (1941)
Going My Way (1944)
The Lost Weekend (1945)
Sunset Boulevard (1950)
A Place in the Sun (1951)
Roman Holiday (1953)
The Ten Commandments (1956)
Vertigo (1958)

UNIVERSAL

Blind Husbands (1919)
Foolish Wives (1922)
Phantom of the Opera (1925)
The Cat and the Canary (1927)
Lonesome (1928)

All Quiet on the Western Front (1930)
Dracula (1931)
Frankenstein (1931)
Back Street (1932)
The Mummy (1932)
The Invisible Man (1933)
Imitation of Life (1934)
Magnificent Obsession (1935)
Destry Rides Again (1939)
Cobra Woman (1944)
Phantom Lady (1944)
Scarlet Street (1945)

The Killers (1946)
Letter from an Unknown Woman (1948)
Winchester '73 (1950)
All I Desire (1953)
The Glenn Miller Story (1954)
The Far Country (1955)
All That Heaven Allows (1955)
Written on the Wind (1956)
The Incredible Shrinking Man (1957)
Touch of Evil (1958)
Imitation of Life (1959)
Pillow Talk (1959)

SELECT BIBLIOGRAPHY

Bordwell, David, Janet Staiger, and Kristin Thompson. *The Classical Hollywood Cinema: Film Style and Mode of Production to 1960.* New York: Columbia University Press, 1985.

French, Philip. *The Movie Moguls: An Informal History of the Hollywood Tycoons.* London: Weidenfeld and Nicolson, 1969.

Gomery, Douglas. *The Hollywood Studio System.* New York: St. Martin's, 1986.

Gussow, Mel. *Don't Say Yes Until I Finish Talking: A Biography of Darryl F. Zanuck.* New York: Doubleday, 1971.

Pirie, David, ed. *Anatomy of the Movies.* New York: Macmillan, 1981.

Schatz, Thomas. *The Genius of the System: Hollywood Filmmaking in the Studio Era.* New York: Pantheon, 1988.

THE STAR SYSTEM

THE MECHANICS OF STARDOM

Making Stars

Exposed Artifice: *Singin' in the Rain*

In the late 1920s, it was estimated that over 32,250,000 fan letters were received each year by movie stars in Hollywood. From the mid-1930s through the early 1950s over 500 journalists and newspaper correspondents gave Hollywood as their dateline, generating over 100,000 words per day about the film industry and making Hollywood the third largest source of "news" information in the country, lagging behind only New York and Washington. Most of that news concerned the public and private activities of movie stars.

Though motion pictures may have been an industry, the general public has always tended to see Hollywood less as a factory town than as a place where royalty resides. Indeed, few eyebrows were raised when screen stars such as Pola Negri, Gloria Swanson, or Grace Kelly married European counts, princes, and even kings. Stars inhabit a different world from the rest of us and live by different rules. To paraphrase Lina Lamont (Jean Hagen) in *Singin' in the Rain* (1952), stars are not "people." They are celestial bodies.

Convinced by the media of her own stardom, Lina (quoting a newspaper puff piece) explains that she is a "shimmering, glowing star in the cinema firmament." But Lina, alas, is not a "real" star; she does not radiate her own light but merely reflects that cast upon her by others. Her image as a star has been carefully fabricated. It is partly the product of studio press releases, which are reprinted verbatim by the media and consumed without question, not only by the public but by Lina herself. And it is partly the product of film technology that functions to conceal her flaws. Though Lina may look like a star, she doesn't sound like a star—her shrill, lower-class voice lacks refinement and fails to match the glamour and sophistication of her visual appearance.

This imperfection, which the silent cinema easily ignored, threatens to betray her when she is forced to speak in the talkies. Her image, however, is preserved when another actress, Kathy Seldon (played by Debbie Reynolds), "dubs" her, substituting her own voice for Lina's in all of Lina's dialogue and song sequences. Lina's phoniness is ultimately unmasked, however, when the curtains are drawn back to disclose to the public part of the previously invisible "machinery" that had made Lina a star; we see Reynolds—now revealed as the "real" star—singing the film's title song in the background as Lina pathetically lip syncs the lyrics in the foreground.

In the opening sequence of *Singin' in the Rain*, a radio columnist (Dora) interviews stars attending the preview of a new Lockwood and Lamont picture. Dora's presence indicates, in part, the role that the media play in Hollywood's construction of stardom. She becomes the willing vehicle for the transmission of Don Lockwood's (Gene Kelly) exaggerated reconstruction of his past to the listening public. Yet again, the film exposes the artifice involved in the construction of stardom through a mismatch of voice and image.

Lockwood's duplicity differs from that of Lina's in one crucial way, however. Here, we *see* the "truth"—Lockwood's less than glamorous personal history—while we *hear* the "official," sanitized studio biography, which paints a far more elegant self-portrait. With Lina, the audience has been tricked into forming a certain set of expectations (into assuming her perfection as a star)—an expectation which is then revealed to have been incorrect. With Lockwood, there is no deception because his verbal construction of his image is simultaneously undercut by what we see on the screen. Our knowledge of the "truth" turns us into his allies and makes us complicit in his playful manipulation of the press. At the same time, the images reveal Don to be hardworking, forthright, and unpretentious—unlike Lina, who emerges as a self-centered prima donna.

Lockwood has concocted a charming tale, carefully tailored to project a "dignified" image that matches the elegance of his onscreen roles. The story he tells is designed for the consumption of not only the radio gossip columnist but also the public, whose fascination with stars drives the economy of two interrelated industries: it draws cash customers to the box office; and it supports the fan magazines (which can be seen in the hands of members of the crowd waiting for the arrival of stars outside the preview of the new Lockwood and Lamont film) and other popular publications that seek to satisfy the public's almost insatiable appetite for news about stars.

Stars, Fans, and Profits

Indeed, it was a film studio that gave birth to the first fan magazine. In 1911, Vitagraph's head of production, J. Stuart Blackton, launched *The Motion Picture Story Magazine*, the first film magazine designed for a general readership, which publicized Vitagraph's players and recent releases. Carl Laemmle at Universal followed suit in 1913 with *Moving Picture Stories.* The independently produced *Photoplay*, which was published once a month from 1911 to 1980 and which enjoyed a circulation of more than 2 million in the 1920s, took up where the studios left off, providing photo-illustrations of the stories of films and feature articles on film stars. Major fan magazines of the sound era, such as *Modern Screen, Photoplay, Silver Screen*, and *Movie Stars*, enjoyed wide circulation (in 1950, *Photoplay* had 1.2 million readers) and furnished, through their probes into the offscreen lives of movie stars and their rehashes of studio press releases, free publicity for the studios, which, in turn, indirectly supported a number of these publications by advertising heavily in them.

Producer Samuel Goldwyn would have us believe that, "God makes the stars. It's up to the producers to find them." God, however, has little to do with it. The industry that makes motion pictures also manufactures, with the aid of the press and other media, movie stars, who have played and continue to play a crucial economic role in the history of that industry. In a business in which each new picture is an unproven commodity, the presence of an established star guarantees a certain return on the high-venture capital invested in a film. Since a star's name on the marquee drew audiences, it was to the advantage of the studios to perpetuate the star system.

The star provides the studio with a tangible attraction, with an image that could be advertised and marketed, offsetting the less tangible qualities of the story, direction, acting, art direction, costume design, and overall studio style. Though these latter elements could be marketed as well, they rarely achieved the identifiability of the star and could not, in themselves, guarantee that a film would make a profit.

Mary Pickford's popularity in the late 1910s (she was receiving 18,000 fan letters per month in 1919) not only ensured the profitability of her pictures but enabled her studio, Paramount, to sell its other, non-Pickford films as well, instituting a system of block booking and blind bidding that was forced upon exhibitors who wanted to rent Pickford's films (see Chapter 4, "The Studio System"). Years later, Mae West, the buxom burlesque and vaudeville performer who gave new meaning to the art of sexual innuendo through her double entendres and her tongue-in-cheek delivery, was credited with saving Paramount when it went into receivership and was taken over by its creditors in 1933. M-G-M owes its survival during the Depression to its stable of stars, which included Greta Garbo, Joan Crawford, Clark Gable, Marie Dressler, Norma Shearer, Mickey Rooney, Judy Garland, and Spencer Tracy; while the youthful singing star Deanna Durbin is said to have rescued Universal in the recession of 1938.

Authenticity: Actors and Their Talent

The Real and the Phony
Although the ultimate "reality" of a star is his or her economic clout at the box office, the currency with which stars purchase their popularity with the public derives from another kind of "reality" which is less economic than artistic; it stems from their *authenticity* as stars. This notion of the "reality" of the star can be seen in *Singin' in the Rain* which distinguishes between real and phony stars. Lina, the phony star, is described as a triple threat—she can't sing, dance, or act. Her lack of talent casts her into the purgatory of would-be stars.

Kathy and Don inhabit the paradise of real stars, not only because they possess talent but also because they are essentially honest with themselves about the nature of their talent. When Lockwood creates an exaggerated impression of his sophistication in his "dignity—always dignity" speech to the radio columnist, he simultaneously shares his somewhat "vulgar," actual

A "real" star, Gene Kelly (seen here with dancer Cyd Charisse), proves he can sing and dance, as well as act, in *Singin' in the Rain* (1952).

past with us through the images that accompany and undermine his narration. By tacitly acknowledging that which is false in his star image, he wins our trust. Normally, the juxtaposition of real and false images would tend to tear down the latter, yet Lockwood's collusion with the film's audience in the subversion of his own screen image effectively reassembles that image on a more ironic plane. Unlike Lina, he knows how to distinguish the real from the phony, and this is what guarantees the authenticity of his stardom.

The film legitimates itself in much the same way that Lockwood does. It takes us behind the scenes of moviemaking in Hollywood during the late 1920s and shows us how a fantasy world of swashbuckling heroes and idealized heroines was created. But, though it exposes the illusionism that underlies the making of the 1920s film-within-a-film, Monumental Pictures' *The Dancing Cavalier*, and thus convinces us that it is being honest with us, it refuses to examine itself. In other words, it doesn't show us the making of the 1950s M-G-M film called *Singin' in the Rain*, which remains the "real" world from which the "fake" world of 1920s studio filmmaking is perceived.

Gene Kelly: A Case Study

By the same token, the film analyzes the creation of the star image of the character Don Lockwood, but takes the actor Gene Kelly for granted. However, the greater "realism" (than Lina's) of Lockwood/Kelly's stardom is ironically rooted in the greater artifice of the former. Lockwood (and Kelly) simply have greater talent. In this way, "real" stardom depends upon a certain kind of phoniness or artfulness. Real stars are not born—they are made. And M-G-M star Gene Kelly is as much a fabrication as is Monumental Pictures' Don Lockwood.

Kelly, of course, does bear some resemblance to the "real" (as opposed to "phony") Lockwood: both are fun-loving song and dance men; both possess a boyish charm and a winning smile; and both are ordinary, unassuming, essentially nice guys who are genuinely surprised and embarrassed at their unexpected success. In other words, Kelly is what critics call an exceptionally "good fit" for the character he portrays. But Kelly, the star, remains distinct from Kelly, the man. Though easygoing on the screen, Kelly was an exacting perfectionist in real life, reportedly pushing himself and others to exceptional lengths in the rehearsal of dance sequences.

M-G-M presented Kelly as "Joe Average" with "a wife, a kid, a car and house"; but Kelly was not just like millions of other guys; he was a college graduate (Penn State) who briefly attended law school, a successful choreographer, and an acclaimed dancer on the stage (in the Theater Guild's production of William Saroyan's Pulitzer Prize winning play, *The Time of Your Life*). Kelly was not the happy-go-lucky Irishman with an inane, Pepsodent smile that M-G-M sold to the public; he was both serious and hardworking. In a number of respects, the actor Gene Kelly does not merely "play himself" on the screen but creates a different personality for himself to play—that of the star, Gene Kelly.

Persona

A Variety of Masks

Every star houses several different personalities, though they all tend to coexist graciously with one another rather than battle for control. At the base of the human pyramid known as the star lies an actual person, whose physical attributes and, in some instances, psychological make-up provide the foundation for the construction of the personality of the actor, or actress, who appears on screen.

The phenomenon of the star "Cary Grant" thus begins with the biological birth of Archibald Leach who would subsequently change his name to Cary Grant; that of "Judy Garland" can be traced back to Frances Gumm, the name with which she was born. Archie Leach and Frances Gumm, however, remain inaccessible to us for the most part, as do the "real" Harrison Ford, Michael Douglas, Glenn Close, and Meryl Streep. Even if we met them in the flesh, so to speak, our firsthand knowledge of them would be limited to the public persona, or "game face" which they put on for personal appearances. Our knowledge of movie stars is necessarily secondhand; we can only experience screen personalities *as personalities*. We have contact with them only through the roles they play and come to know them as personae rather than as persons.

Literally, the term "persona" refers to the mask worn by a character on the ancient Greek stage. Actors develop a persona or portrait of themselves out of the personalities of the various characters they have played over the course of their careers and out of elements of their personal lives that have become public knowledge. Actors either use these traits in their performances, or audiences impose them upon the actors, reinvesting their performances with added significance, as was the case with James Dean, whose accidental death in a highway accident became part of his star legend.

John Wayne's persona, for example, includes the inflexible, sometimes violent determination of the Western (*The Searchers*, 1956) and war (*Sands of Iwo Jima*, 1949) heroes he played as well as his public political stance as an anti-Communist (*Big Jim McLain*, 1952), a conservative Republican (*The Alamo*, 1960), and a supporter of the war in Vietnam (*The Green Berets*, 1968). Even his highly publicized personal bout with cancer, which prompted him to proclaim after one of his lungs was removed that "I licked the big C," provides crucial material for his last film, *The Shootist* (1976), in which he plays an aging gunfighter dying of cancer. Wayne himself died of cancer three years after the film was made.

Stars essentially consist of three personalities—the star, the actor, and the "actual" person. Each of these personalities consumes the entity which lies immediately beneath it. With actors, the real person disappears in the creation of a fictional character. Indeed, some actors so transform their physical features, including their voice and bodily appearance that they give the illusion not only of becoming the characters they play but of becoming different characters from film to film. They efface themselves not only as persons but also *as actors*, as in the case of chameleonlike performers such as Jeremy Irons who convincingly portrays twin gynecologists in *Dead Ringers* (1988) only to reincarnate himself, virtually unrecognizably, a few years later as Claus von Bulow in *Reversal of Fortune* (1990).

Types and Typecasting

More commonly, actors become "typed," playing similar kinds of characters from film to film. Over the course of several films, these actors develop a distinct persona, or public image. In certain instances, an actor will become associated with a specific character, whose attributes become fused with his or her own. Thus Charles Chaplin becomes identified with the Tramp, Sean Connery and Roger Moore with James Bond, William Shatner with Capt. James Kirk, and Sylvester Stallone with Rocky Balboa and John Rambo.

More frequently, an actor will consistently play a certain character type from film to film. Thus Humphrey Bogart tends to play hard-boiled, anti-authoritarian, romantically vulnerable tough guys (*The Maltese Falcon*, 1941, *Casablanca*, 1942); Marilyn Monroe is regularly cast as a gold digger or dumb blonde (*Gentlemen Prefer Blondes* and *How to Marry a Millionaire*, 1953); Woody Allen plays neurotic, New York Jewish intellectuals who quote Kierkegaard, hate Los Angeles, and fantasize about love and death (*Annie Hall*, 1977; *Manhattan*, 1979); and Julia Roberts (her recent role as Tinker Bell notwithstanding) plays street-smart, lower-class working girls who "sell" themselves

Courtesy of Universal

Sean Connery, in a departure from his role as James Bond, plays opposite Tippi Hedren in Alfred Hitchcock's "sex mystery," *Marnie* (1964).

to the highest bidder only to discover that this is the man of their dreams (*Pretty Woman*, 1990; *Dying Young*, 1991).

Many actors resist typecasting and try to alter the kinds of characters they play on the screen from film to film. Dustin Hoffman, for example, goes from a female impersonator–soap opera queen in *Tootsie* (1982) to Tom Cruise's autistic older brother in *Rain Man* (1988). Even those actors closely identified with specific roles will cast themselves against type in an attempt to broaden their range and thus rewrite their screen persona. Sean Connery resisted his James Bond image from the very start, taking parts as a Philadelphia publisher sexually intrigued by a neurotic kleptomaniac in Alfred Hitchcock's *Marnie* (1964) and a rebellious prisoner of war in Sidney Lumet's *The Hill* (1965). Later, Connery even took off his toupee to play older parts such as the seasoned soldier of fortune in John Huston's *The Man Who Would Be King* (1975) and the aging, incorruptible Irish cop in Brian DePalma's *The Untouchables* (1987).

Stardom and Mass Culture: From Persona to Star

The Role of the Media

Every actor and actress constructs a persona over the course of his or her career, but few become stars. A star is an actor whose persona transcends the sum total of his or her performances. The star's image may be rooted in specific roles, but it extends beyond them, establishing itself in subsidiary forms, in secondary representations of the actor's persona such as those found in fan magazines or supermarket tabloids. The star's persona recirculates in these other media, where it acquires new meanings more or less on its own, beyond the control of the individual actor or actress.

A star's persona thus differs from that of an actor. For an actor, the persona provides a primary mask, which disguises the real person underneath. For a star, the persona includes the actor's persona as well as the star's persona. This secondary mask of stardom covers over the earlier one, reproducing and reshaping the original persona and often transforming it in the process.

In other words, stardom is constructed not solely within films themselves but within the larger terrain of mass culture as well. As an image reflected back upon the performer from the mirror of popular culture, stardom colors over the actor's persona on which it is based, rewriting that personality in certain identifiable ways. Thus Elizabeth Taylor's stardom includes not only her films but her representation in the media, which has tended to portray her as a troubled figure—as a former alcoholic, plagued by recurrent weight problems and a succession of tragic or unhappy marriages. Taylor's current status as a star consists chiefly of her "performances" in the tabloids rather than her screen appearances; indeed, she has not acted in anything other than TV movies and perfume commercials since 1980.

The same might be said of Elvis Presley, whose stardom continues to thrive in the tabloids, even though he died in 1977. Repeated "sightings" of Elvis in midwestern malls and shopping centers testify to the supernatural existence which certain stars enjoy when they transcend the media (records, films) in which they originally excelled and achieve a different order of celebrity, becoming (even after their own death) stars in another medium. In other words, stars become stars when they lose control of their images, which then take on a life of their own.

By the same token, Jeremy Irons and Anthony Hopkins, in spite of their Oscars for *Reversal of Fortune* (1990) and *Silence of the Lambs* (1991) and their obvious talents as actors, have yet to become major stars, largely because (1) the different roles which they have played do not lend themselves to the construction of a coherent screen persona, (2) their images have not found widespread circulation in the media, and (3) their personal lives have remained private rather than public. As a result, the nature of their offscreen personalities is obscure and ill-defined for the majority of filmgoers.

Mickey Mouse: A Case Study

The transcendent nature of stardom is perhaps best illustrated not by Liz or by Elvis, whose physical realities serve as solid foundations for their appeal with the public, but by Mickey Mouse, whose star status rests upon a purely imaginary form of existence. Alfred Hitchcock, who once described actors as "cattle," declared Mickey Mouse to be the perfect actor because he didn't draw a salary, he did whatever you wanted him to do, he never asked what his motivation was for a scene, and he could be erased. Mickey was not only

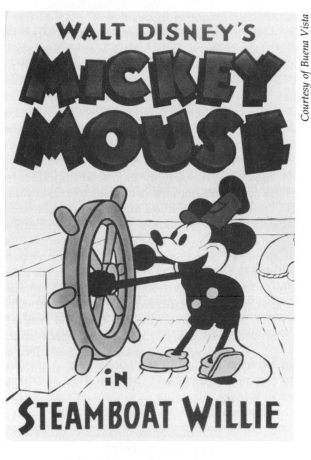

Courtesy of Buena Vista

Mickey Mouse skyrockets to stardom in *Steamboat Willie* (1928).

the perfect actor, but became a star as well, christened by no less a Hollywood luminary than Mary Pickford who once proclaimed him to be her favorite star.

Mickey's stardom was phenomenal. Mickey Mouse Clubs, introduced by theater owners in 1929 shortly after Mickey's first talkie, *Steamboat Willie*, quickly spread throughout the country and, by 1931, boasted more than a million members. Merchandising tie-ins worth tens of millions of dollars soon followed. By the mid-1930s, there were Mickey Mouse dolls, watches, stationery, ice cream cones, lunch boxes, clothing, wallpaper, toys, and games.

Though he had no private life or tabloid existence, Mickey's image was widely circulated, not only through consumer products but through the media, including newspapers, fan magazines, and comic strips, making him one of the most recognizable figures in the world. Even today, Mickey's image is better known than that of any world leader, rock star, sports figure, or any other national or international celebrity. If Mickey was the perfect actor, he was also the perfect star; he was a purely fictional construction whose image circulated independently of not only the control but also the physical existence of any real person.

Playing Themselves

It could be said of Mickey Mouse that he was a star without ever being an actor. In other words, Mickey always played himself (even when nominally playing the sorcerer's apprentice in *Fantasia*, 1940). The same thing is often said as well of star actors like John Wayne, James Stewart, and countless others. It may even account for the fact that many great stars, including Charles Chaplin, Greta Garbo, Marlene Dietrich, Cary Grant, Fred Astaire, Barbara Stanwyck, Marilyn Monroe, and Judy Garland, have never won an Academy Award for Best Actor or Actress (though Grant, Stanwyck, and Chaplin did win special, honorary, career-achievement Oscars). If stars are only playing themselves on the screen, then they are not really acting and are thus undeserving of an Oscar, or so the majority of the members of the Academy would have us believe.

Though ostensibly playing different characters, John Wayne (who finally won an Oscar in 1969 for his role as Rooster Cogburn in *True Grit*) employs the same speech and phrasing patterns, gestures, and physical movements (especially his famous walk) in roles as diverse as that of a tyrannical, empire builder in *Red River* (1948), a memory-haunted ex-prizefighter who has retired to Ireland in *The Quiet Man* (1952), and a genial naval officer serving in the Pacific on the eve of World War II in *In Harm's Way* (1965). In each instance, Wayne plays two characters—the character created in the script and John Wayne, a persona which it took the actor almost ten years (1929–1939) and scores of ''B'' Westerns and serials to create. Though Wayne's persona overlaps and creates a ''fit'' with the characters he portrays, what audiences see (and come to the movie theater to see) is not the fictional character he plays but Wayne *as* the character. In Wayne's case, the reality of the star overpowers that of the character, preventing the full realization of the character as an autonomous being.

The nature of star acting helps explain why stars have difficulty playing famous historical personages; the persona of the star refuses to ''fit'' with that of the well-known character from history. Thus, Spencer Tracy is more Spencer Tracy than Thomas Edison in *Edison, the Man* (1940), and James Stewart is more James Stewart than Glenn Miller in *The Glenn Miller Story* (1954) or Charles Lindbergh in *The Spirit of St. Louis* (1957). It's unlikely that John Wayne could have played anyone other than John Wayne, though he did take a stab at William Tecumseh Sherman in *How the West Was Won* (1962).

For this reason, Hollywood tends to cast unknowns in the parts of familiar figures; Milos Forman chose Tom Hulce, whose chief previous credit had been a supporting role in *National Lampoon's Animal House* (1978), for the role of Mozart in *Amadeus* (1984); Gary Busey plays Buddy Holly in *The Buddy Holly Story* (1978); Kurt Russell, relatively unknown at the time, stars in the TV movie *Elvis* (1979); and Ben Kingsley debuts on film as *Gandhi* (1982), winning an Oscar for his performance. *Gandhi*, however, did not turn Kingsley into a star. Nor did his Oscar translate itself into drawing power for Kingsley at the box office.

Stars, the System, and the Public

Marilyn Monroe: A Case Study

Perhaps Marilyn Monroe gave the best account of stardom when she declared that "only the public can make a star . . . it's the studios who try to make a system out of it." In other words, stars are indeed made, but it is not necessarily the studios, producers, press agents, or even the stars themselves who make them. However, once a star has been made, the studios attempt to harness the power of the star and transform it into a system.

Monroe's swipe at the studios refers, in part, to the successful efforts of her own studio, 20th Century-Fox, to build her up as a star in the early 1950s and, in part, to its less successful attempts to manufacture stars to take her place if she should ever refuse a part, fail to report to the set, chronically arrive late on the set, or temperamentally walk off the set in midproduction (which she did repeatedly in the late 1950s and early 1960s).

At first, Fox groomed the platinum-blonde starlet Sheree North to take Monroe's place, giving her the same sort of publicity buildup earlier given Monroe; but North failed to catch the attention of the public. Fox tried again in the mid-1950s, launching another shapely blonde, Jayne Mansfield, on a somewhat more successful career as a "Monroe type" in films that parody Monroe's (and Mansfield's) image as blonde bombshell like *The Girl Can't Help It* (1956) and *Will Success Spoil Rock Hunter?* (1957). Though Mansfield achieved some success, Mamie Van Doren, the next Fox entry in the field of Monroe substitutes, did not fare nearly as well, becoming a familiar fixture in teen-exploitation pictures such as *Running Wild* (1955) and *Untamed Youth* (1957), and ending her film career with *The Navy vs. The Night Monsters* (1966).

Stardom and Public Acceptance

The most famous attempts to manufacture stars are associated with the studio era (roughly from the mid-1920s through the late 1950s) when male producers reveal their obsessions with certain actresses by trying to make them stars. Thus, William Randolph Hearst established Cosmopolitan Pictures in the late 1920s to produce films for Marion Davies; Goldwyn imported Soviet actress Anna Sten in the mid-1930s, hoping to make her into another Garbo or Dietrich; Darryl Zanuck tried to turn Bella Darvi into a star in the 1950s. More recently, independent producers, agents, and publicists have tried to turn cover girls, models, or *Playboy* centerfolds into film stars and failed, as the disappointing careers of Christopher Atkins (*Blue Lagoon*, 1980), Bo Derek (*10*, 1979), Morgan Fairchild (*The Seduction*, 1982), and Pia Zadora (*Butterfly*, 1981) indicate.

If Monroe is right and it is the public that makes a star, then why does the public select certain performers for stardom and reject others? Although producers may view the public as capricious or whimsical in this regard, there is often a method to the public's madness or, to phrase this relationship more positively, a foundation for the fanaticism for certain stars.

The star answers a particular need that the public either consciously or unconsciously has at a particular time for a particular figure of identification. In other words, the star functions as a sociocultural barometer of sorts, giving expression to and providing symbolic solutions for specific fears, desires, anxieties, and/or dreams that haunt popular consciousness.

But before examining the intimate nature of the relationship between the public and its stars, it is important to recognize two significant features of this relationship. First, stars may be figures of fantasy, but their fans are not fools. Audiences are quite aware of the machinery that studios and others set in motion in their attempts to produce stars, and they knowingly participate in the manufacturing of stars. Indeed, much of their enjoyment of stars comes from this knowledge. Second, the public that makes stars can also break them, especially if the stars violate the image the public holds of them, as the much-beloved silent comedian Fatty Arbuckle did when he was accused of raping a young actress at a wild party in 1921 or as Ingrid Bergman (briefly) did when, having just starred in *Joan of Arc* (1948), she deserted her husband and daughter to live with director Roberto Rossellini, with whom she had a child out of wedlock.

Ingrid Bergman's highly publicized affair with director Roberto Rossellini clashed dramatically with her screen image as the title character in *Joan of Arc* (1948).

Courtesy of RKO

There are as many publics as there are stars. Each generation of audiences has its own stars who address its own concerns. Thus, stars of the late 1950s and early 1960s, such as Rock Hudson and Doris Day, who combine clean good looks with sexual propriety in tongue-in-cheek sex comedies such as *Pillow Talk* (1959), disappear in the late 1960s, giving way to action and adventure stars, such as Sean Connery, Clint Eastwood, Harrison Ford, Sylvester Stallone, and Arnold Schwarzenegger, in the 1970s and 1980s. And within each generation there are various segments, consisting of different age groups, races, classes, geographical regions, ethnic groups, genders, or sexual orientations that prefer one star to another.

Thus female fans will prefer Connery and Ford to Stallone and Schwarzenegger, while male fans will favor the latter over the former. A film like *The Hunt for Red October* (1990) seems designed to cross over some of these divisions by pairing a star with appeal among teen viewers, Alec Baldwin, with Sean Connery, who brings a somewhat older audience into the theater.

STARS AND CULTURE: A HISTORICAL SURVEY

The Early Years

The First Stars

The star system, of course, preexists the advent of motion pictures, thriving in the legitimate theater, vaudeville and the music hall, and the opera throughout the nineteenth century. Histories tend to cite Florence Lawrence, an actress who appeared in Biograph films in 1908–1909 and who was heavily publicized as a star by Carl Laemmle when she left Biograph in 1909 to join his IMP Company, as the first movie star. However, she was not the first star to appear on film.

In 1894, Edison's Kinetoscope Exhibition Co. signed the first movie star—the prize fighter Gentlemen Jim Corbett. His exclusive contract forbade him from appearing in anyone else's films. Edison brought before his cameras stars from a variety of fields, including wild west performers Buffalo Bill and Annie Oakley, strongman Eugene Sandow, dancers Ruth St. Denis and Annabelle, and other attractions from the New York stage and the Barnum and Bailey Circus. One of the most sensational early films, *The May Irwin–John C. Rice Kiss* (1896), was an adaptation of a scene from a Broadway stage play, *The Widow Jones,* featuring theater stars May Irwin and John Rice.

However, Lawrence, who, unlike these earlier stars, enjoyed little prior celebrity on the stage or elsewhere, was one of the first stars to have been created by the medium of film. These extracinematic stars of the cinema's first decade did not act; rather they performed feats for which they were well-known—some of which, as in the case of Sarah Bernhardt, involved the staging of famous theatrical scenes for the camera to record. For the most part, their stardom was merely recorded; it was not created on the screen, as was Lawrence's. And Lawrence's stardom derives not from studio publicity

(Biograph refused to publicize its performers) but from fans who were drawn to her without knowing her name, fascinated by her radiance, refinement, beauty, and dramatic range, which enabled her to play both comedy and tragedy. As one of a succession of Griffith heroines, including Blanche Sweet, Mary Pickford, Lillian and Dorothy Gish, and Mae Marsh, she serves as an embodiment of American energy and Victorian virtue.

Late Victorianism

The stars of the 1910s represent transitional figures for audiences whose nineteenth-century Victorianism was slowly giving way to a more modern sensibility in which many of the more restrictive aspects of Victorianism were relaxed. American Victorianism consists of somewhat more than the negative "virtues" of sexual repression and restraint. It involves a code of positive values that includes hard work and an aversion to idleness; a sense of moral orderliness and self-control, discipline, self-confidence, self-sufficiency. However, it does prize obedience and it also sets forth fairly circumscribed roles for women to play within the family and the community, relegating their activities to the private sphere of the home and barring "proper ladies" (wives, mothers, and daughters) from taking part in the more public sphere of the workplace or politics. The nineteenth-century ideal of womanhood insists, as one critic put it, upon her "piety, purity, submissiveness, and domesticity."

In *Broken Blossoms* (1919), for example, the options for Griffith's lower-class heroine, played by the delicate, Victorian ideal of femininity, Lillian Gish, consist of the virtuous drudgery of an oppressive marriage or the depraved misery of prostitution. There is no question (in Griffith's mind at least) of her getting a job, supporting herself, and living alone.

During the 1910s and 1920s, the status of women changed as the American economy shifted from a rural and agricultural to an urban and industrial base. More and more women entered the workplace, securing jobs in emerging corporations and businesses as "typewriters" (that is, office secretaries) and in the growing consumer industries such as department stores, where women found jobs as clerks and salesgirls. These economic changes produced profound social changes, resulting in—among other things—greater freedom for women. Certain stars function to bridge these transformations.

Pickford, Fairbanks, and Chaplin

Mary Pickford embodies the profound social changes taking place as she retains her screen image as "Little Mary, the girl with the long, golden curls," "America's Sweetheart," and the ideal embodiment of Victorian virtue, while a more modern, offscreen image of the actress as a working woman and as a businesswoman managing a successful career evolves alongside this earlier image. Though her screen roles, such as that in *Tess of the Storm Country* (1914) or *Rebecca of Sunnybrook Farm* (1917), continue to portray her as a doll-like child, her more modern image in the media makes her a figure of identification for an emerging class of "new women," which included independent workingwomen, suffragettes, and other nontraditional women who took their place alongside men in the post-Victorian world of modern America.

In a similar fashion, Douglas Fairbanks constructs a double image: he often plays a hard-working young businessman in an emerging corporate America; yet his occasional bouts of boredom register his frustration as an individual within a stifling atmosphere dominated by the Protestant work ethic. But rather than give in to a decadent idleness, Fairbanks energetically throws himself into the guilt-free enjoyment of pleasure and relaxation through healthy leisure-time pursuits. He engages in sports, athletic exercise, or other physical adventures.

Charles Chaplin combines, in the persona of the Tramp, the old-world, aristocratic values of Victorian society, and the new-world egalitarianism of the immigrant, whose hunger and homelessness make him the defiant opponent of all arbitrary authority—especially policemen. Thus his costume of derby, dress coat, and cane look back nostalgically to a former elegance. And his concern for proper behavior and social manners identify him with more traditional values.

The enormous popularity of Pickford, Fairbanks, and Chaplin during the 1910s testifies to their ability to address the anxieties of audiences who were themselves confronting a modern, twentieth-century world with old-fashioned, nineteenth-century values and ideas. One measure of their popularity can be seen in the dramatic escalation of their salaries: in 1909, Pickford earned $10 a day at Biograph; by 1915, she was being paid $10,000 a week by Famous Players; Chaplin's earnings grew from $150 per week (Keystone, 1913) to $10,000 a week at Mutual in 1916; Fairbanks multiplied his weekly salary from $2,000 in 1915 to $10,000 in 1916.

By the end of the decade, all three achieved per-picture salaries in excess of $150,000 as well as percentages of the box-office returns on their films, making them the most highly paid and most powerful stars in the industry. When they became so expensive that their studios, in an attempt to limit their salaries, secretly agreed not to bid against one another for their services, the stars left and formed (along with director D. W. Griffith) their own company, United Artists, which served as a distributor for their independently made films.

Exoticism, Eroticism, and Modern Morality: Stars of the 1920s

The Jazz Age

During the 1920s, more exotic and erotic stars such as Rudolph Valentino and Greta Garbo join the ranks of Pickford, Fairbanks, and Chaplin. The American nature of the latter (in spite of Pickford's Canadian and Chaplin's English origins) is expressed in both their pragmatic ingenuity and their new-world innocence. Their sexuality is that of the child or the naive adolescent rather than that of the worldly adult. The appeal of Valentino and Garbo is that of sophisticated, sexually experienced Europeans. Their popularity with American audiences reflects the new atmosphere of sexual liberation that followed the war.

The woman's suffrage movement had secured women the vote in 1920 and the women's temperance movement had played a major role in the institution of prohibition in 1919, demonstrating the power women could exert in the public sphere. But the involvement of women in political reform proves to be only the first stage of a larger social revolution in which a new generation of women begin to usurp traditionally male roles. The male double standard slowly gives way to a new permissiveness for those women who dared to enjoy it. The daughters of the women's movement discovered that it was fun to dance, drink, smoke, and "pet". And although more conservative elements of society objected, unconventional, sexually liberated young women of the roaring twenties (referred to as "flappers" and "jazz babies") defended their actions in terms of a modern morality.

The Victorian puritanism of major filmmakers of the 1910s like Griffith is replaced by a new explicitness in dealing with female desire and behavior by filmmakers such as Cecil B. De Mille. De Mille specializes in titillating topics (and film titles) such as adultery (*The Cheat*, 1915), promiscuity (*Manslaughter*, 1922), and "modern" marriages in which women and men engage equally in infidelity (*Old Wives for New*, 1918; *Don't Change Your Husband*, 1919; *Why Change Your Wife?*, 1920; *The Affairs of Anatol* and *Forbidden Fruit*, 1921). Yet, although De Mille's characters experiment with the new morality, their adventures teach them a lesson. More often than not, they return, by film's end, to the same old-fashioned values they had initially rejected, often going back to their husbands and wives with a new appreciation of the more traditional virtues of sexual fidelity, marriage, and family.

Having "It": Clara Bow and Rudolph Valentino

The extent to which the new interest in sexuality now dominates the screen can be seen in the emergence of a novel criterion for stardom—the possession of "It." Elinor Glyn, English author and Hollywood tastemaker, wrote several popular novels and more than a dozen screenplays in the 1920s about the new, sexually aggressive and sexually provocative flappers. Her 1926 novel, called *It*, was adapted for the screen and starred the quintessential Hollywood flapper—the pretty, sexy, fun-loving, impudent, worldly-wise Clara Bow. Glyn, who defines "It" as "an inner magic, an animal magnetism," declared Bow to be the "It Girl." [Glyn also acknowledged that Valentino, John Gilbert, and Rex (the horse) had "It" as well; apparently "It" was a quality that not only crosses over sexual boundaries but also those between different species.]

Although Bow's sexuality breathes rebellious life into models of female behavior in the 1920s, it remains, like that of De Mille's heroes and heroines, more or less within the moral confines of what F. Scott Fitzgerald and other spokespersons associated with the Jazz Age outline as "typical" of the wilder, more bohemian American youth of that era. Bow's characters, again like De

Courtesy of Paramount

Publicity material for Clara Bow in Elinor Glyn's *It* (1927).

Mille's, have fun and sow their wild oats but ultimately marry and settle down.

The sexuality of Valentino, Garbo, and other foreign-born screen idols of the 1920s differs in nature from the wildness of American youth epitomized by Bow. The screen behavior of the former is not part of a larger rite of passage through which they pass on their way to sexual maturity (as it is with Bow). The threat posed by Valentino, for instance, cannot be explained away as some youthful fad, though his role in *The Sheik* (1921) did produce a generation of American couples who referred to one another as "sheiks" and "shebas." As the Sheik, Valentino woos the heroine by abducting her, enslaving her, and holding her, not only against her will but under the constant threat of rape. Valentino's image as a menacing and brutal but romantic lover finds itself extended in his roles as the passionate bullfighter in *Blood and Sand* (1922) and as the vengeful woman-hater in *The Son of the Sheik* (1926); but films such as *The Four Horsemen of the Apocalypse* (1921) and *A Sainted Devil* (1924) also promote his image as a sultry Latin lover.

American men hated Valentino almost as passionately as American women loved him. Men regarded his skill as a dancer with suspicion, envied his good looks, resented his status as a great lover, considered him to be effeminate, and distrusted him as a foreigner. They preferred the more American onscreen lovemaking of male stars such as John Gilbert.

But when Valentino died suddenly in the summer of 1926, more than 100,000 fans, most of them women, mobbed the streets of New York outside the funeral home. The actress Pola Negri, with whom Valentino was reportedly having an affair, collapsed on the set of her latest film when she heard the news. When she recovered, she rushed to New York (along with a studio publicist) to be near him. And, for the past 65 years, on the anniversary of his death, a mysterious woman in black has visited his tomb and brought a bouquet of roses to place upon it.

Greta Garbo: From Divinity to Humanity

The passionate, Mediterranean sexuality introduced by Valentino ignited his female fans. The more distanced, Nordic allure of Garbo smolders on the screen, generating a more cerebral, less visceral response among her audiences. There was virtually no precedent among American actresses for Garbo's world-weary sexuality on the screen. Hollywood had created vamps before; Theda Bara enjoyed a brief career of luring men to their doom as a femme fatale in films such as *A Fool There Was* and *Carmen* (1915), *Cleopatra* (1917), and *Salome* (1918). Similar roles had subsequently been played by (and become exclusively reserved for) European actresses, such as Alla Nazimova and Negri, in the 1920s. But Garbo lacked the manipulative power that the vamp exerts over men and the destructiveness of the femme fatale. If Garbo was a femme fatale, then she was more "fatale" for herself than she was for the men who fell in love with her.

The passion of Garbo is not only romantic but religious as well. She is the Joan of Arc of screen vamps, femme fatales, and courtesans; she suffers and dies for love. Garbo's most characteristic roles are as Leo Tolstoy's Anna Karenina in *Love* (1927) and in *Anna Karenina* (1935)—as the unhappily married woman who falls desperately in love with another man and who pays for her infidelity with death. This is a part she also plays in *The Temptress* (1926), *Flesh and the Devil* (1927), *A Woman of Affairs* (1928), and a number of other films. In *Mata Hari* (1932) and *Camille* (1937), Garbo is the older, more experienced woman of the world who seduces and falls in love with younger men but dies tragically, the victim of her own self-destructive nature and past behavior.

The stars of the late silent era achieve the status of screen idols, whom fans worship from a distance. Garbo's reclusiveness, memorialized in the utterance for which she has become most famous—"I vant to be alone"—lasted even after her departure from Hollywood and her retreat to anonymity on New York City's East Side where she continued to play the moody Swede. Though Garbo's onscreen and offscreen mystery may have exceeded that of other stars, it symbolized the quasi-religious divinity that stars possessed in the eyes of the movie-going public.

But, with the down-to-earth realism associated with the coming of sound, with the social upheavals introduced by the stock market crash and the Depression, and with the redefinition of American notions of individualism brought about by the New Deal, the aloof, aristocratic nature of silent screen stars came under increasing criticism and attack. Though American audiences

Courtesy of M-G-M

Greta Garbo and John Gilbert in *Flesh and the Devil* (1927).

remain fascinated by stars, they want their stars to be more human and more accessible. The transformation of Garbo's screen persona in the 1930s provides a perfect illustration of the way in which silent stars are forced to step down off their pedestals and come alive in order to prolong their careers.

The initial stage in the dedivinization of Garbo takes place with her first sound film, *Anna Christie* (1930), which was sold to the public through an ad campaign that humanizes her by simply declaring "GARBO TALKS!" Later in the decade, when top stars such as Katharine Hepburn and Fred Astaire were denounced by exhibitors as "box-office poison" because fans supposedly found them to be too sophisticated, high-brow, and elitist, Garbo briefly reclaims her popularity by switching from tragic costume melodramas, such as *Camille* (1937), to appear in her first comedy, *Ninotchka* (1939). This film is not only done in modern dress but features Garbo as an avid consumer of contemporary female fashion (she falls in love with a hat). This time, M-G-M publicity strikes another blow in its attempt to make Garbo more accessible, proclaiming "GARBO LAUGHS!"

Depression/Repression: The 1930s

New Realities, New Images
The transition to sound ushers in a new breed of movie star made up of actors and actresses from the theater (George Arliss, Ruth Chatterton, Fredric March), vaudeville (the Marx Brothers, Mae West), the recording industry (Al

Jolson, Eddie Cantor), and radio (Bob Hope, Bing Crosby, Jack Benny). Distinct vocal styles provide the basis of stardom for many performers, ranging from the charming French and German accents of Maurice Chevalier and Marlene Dietrich, respectively; the cultivated English accents of Ronald Colman and Herbert Marshall; the urban, lower-class voices of Wallace Beery, James Cagney, Edward G. Robinson, Mae West, and Barbara Stanwyck; to the regional speech of Will Rogers and the racial dialect of Hollywood's first black star, Stepin Fetchit.

The major stars of the early 1930s (with one or two exceptions) did not belong to the sophisticated royalty of the silent era but to the working class. American audiences fall in love with burly, homely types like Wallace Beery and Marie Dressler; with hard-working shopgirls like Janet Gaynor and Joan Crawford; with proletarian tough guys like Cagney and Robinson; with homespun humorists and broad slapstick comics like Will Rogers and Joe E. Brown; and with an adorable little "orphan" whose only possessions are her dimples, her curls, and her boundless optimism for the future—Shirley Temple.

All-American Kids: Shirley Temple and Judy Garland

Between 1934 and 1938, Temple's films earned more money than those of any other star. By the mid-1930s, she was earning over $300,000 a year and received over 3500 fan letters a week. Her endorsement of products, ranging from dresses to dolls, brought in anther $300,000 a year. For Depression audiences, Temple provides sentimental solutions to national problems. In her films, Temple's character is often an orphan (*Captain January*, 1936) or motherless (*Little Miss Marker*, 1934) and comes from working-class back-grounds (*Marker, Dimples*, 1936). The perfect democrat, she befriends both servants (*Curly Top*, 1935) and blacks (*The Littlest Rebel*, 1935).

More important, she becomes the focus for a new social order. Her unqual-ified love melts the hardened hearts of both rich and poor and prompts uncharacteristic generosity among her wealthy guardians and/or benefactors, who then vow to take care of those less fortunate than themselves. Temple is America's answer to the Russian Revolution; she awakens the benign forces of paternalistic capitalism, which heal the nation's wounds and unite for-merly antagonistic factions of society. Rescued, adopted, and rewarded with untold wealth for her simple trust and love, the miraculous fortune of Tem-ple's screen characters makes her the embodiment of every spectator's de-sires.

Temple's popularity decreased as she approached puberty, but so did the dangers facing the typical American family as it weathered the economic turmoil of the 1930s. Other young stars, such as everybody's boy-next-door/ girl-next-door couple Mickey Rooney and Judy Garland, take up where Tem-ple leaves off and provide a similar optimism for audiences of the late 1930s. As Andy Hardy, Rooney applies energy and resourcefulness to the problems that beset bourgeois, middle-class America at the end of the decade. Given a meager allowance by his FDR-like father, the judge, Andy Hardy manages to

Courtesy of 20th Century-Fox

Shirley Temple dances with Bill "Bojangles" Robinson in *The Littlest Rebel* (1935).

buy a jalopy, take his girl to the drugstore for a soda, rent a tuxedo for the senior prom, and, working with the other kids in the neighborhood, assemble an amateur show or musical revue that would put Broadway to shame.

Garland, whether as Andy's sweetheart or Dorothy (of Kansas and Oz), pays similar tribute to the inventiveness and innate talent of the average American teenager. Garland infuses everything she does, from singing to coping with the trials and tribulations of adolescence, with emotion. She suggests that the happiness that lies just over the rainbow could be obtained if only you could pursue it, as Judy did, through an intense, wholehearted commitment to pure feeling.

Clark Gable: Populist Hero

The most representative star of the 1930s is not an old man (Beery, Rogers), a child (Temple), or a teen (Rooney, Garland), but rather a rugged, all-American guy. In *Broadway Melody of 1938* (1937), Garland sings to his photograph. She declares, like other female fans who worship him, that he is "Not like a real actor. . . . But like a fellow you'd meet at a party." That fellow was named Clark Gable. The foundation of Gable's screen persona was laid by Frank Capra in *It Happened One Night* (1934) in which Gable, in an Oscar-winning performance, plays a cynical, big-city newspaper reporter. His character advocates the lower-class, populist virtues of dunking donuts, eating raw carrots, hitchhiking, and giving piggyback rides just like the great Abe Lincoln used to do. Gable's regular guy educates runaway heiress Claudette

Colbert in all of the above and teaches her how to survive without money on the road in Depression America.

Whether an adventurer in *Red Dust* (1932) or *Call of the Wild* (1935), a gambler in *No Man of Her Own* (1932) or *Manhattan Melodrama* (1934), or a con man in *Hold Your Man* (1933), Gable projects a no-nonsense honesty and self-irony that make him an ideal antagonist for and complement to Scarlet O'Hara's incurably romantic and self-deluding dreamer in *Gone With the Wind* (1939).

Sex, Censorship, and Star Images

Sex continues to play a major role in the construction of stardom in the 1930s, but does so largely through its overt repression. The comparatively unbridled sexuality of stars such as Bow or Valentino in the 1920s became the object of censorship in the 1930s when the Motion Picture Producers and Distributors of America reinstituted the Production Code in 1934 in response to protests by certain civic organizations and members of the clergy.

Directed against depictions, not only of crime and violence but also of sexual themes such as adultery, scenes of passion, seduction or rape, sexual perversion, and miscegenation, the Code handcuffed the rampant sexuality of early 1930s stars such as the sexy platinum blonde Jean Harlow and the sexually suggestive Mae West. It turned the sex comedy into the screwball comedy; made stars out of presexual, child and teen performers (such as Temple, Rooney, Garland, and Deanna Durbin) and out of old men (such as Beery and Rogers). And it forced otherwise sexually healthy and attractive stars to find socially acceptable substitutes for sex, such as Joan Crawford's onscreen drive toward success in a career. In the 1920s, Rex may have had "It," but in the 1930s, Gene Autry's horse, Champion, not only didn't but couldn't.

In *It Happened One Night* (1934), which was made just after the Code was put in force, Gable finds himself in the unusual position of having to deny himself to Claudette Colbert until they can be properly married and the walls of Jericho (the makeshift curtain which Gable erects between their two, twin beds) can come tumbling down. Sexual self-censorship makes actors such as Gable even more desirable for their female fans, but it also drives sex underground where it builds up steam during the war years and finally explodes in the resexualization of Hollywood that takes place in the postwar years in film noir and in films with more sexually explicit themes and with sexier stars.

World War II and its Aftermath

A New Generation

After the Japanese attack on Pearl Harbor, a number of American actors, including Clark Gable, James Stewart, Tyrone Power, Henry Fonda, Robert Montgomery, and Mickey Rooney, enlist in the military, creating a vacuum of sorts which a new generation of male stars struggle to fill. Established male stars such as Humphrey Bogart, James Cagney, Gary Cooper, Errol Flynn,

Cary Grant, and Spencer Tracy are joined by relative newcomers such as Abbott & Costello, Don Ameche, Dana Andrews, Joseph Cotten, Bing Crosby, John Garfield, Bob Hope, Van Johnson, Ronald Reagan, John Wayne, and Orson Welles. Musical star Betty Grable becomes a favorite with the GIs in her incarnation as a pinup, whose leggy picture adorns more than 2 million posters on the walls of U.S. military barracks around the world.

At the other end of the spectrum, a desexualized Greer Garson epitomizes home-front sacrifice in/as *Mrs. Miniver* (1942). Ginger Rogers in *Tender Comrade* (1943) and Jennifer Jones in *Since You Went Away* (1944) represent the girls back home for whose safety the war is being fought, as do Judy Garland and child-star Margaret O'Brien in the period musical *Meet Me in St. Louis* (1944). Finally, Ingrid Bergman emerges as the perfect combination of romance and patriotism as a member of the Resistance in both *Casablanca* (1942) and *For Whom the Bell Tolls* (1943).

Transformations

Stardom changes during and after the war as performers begin to push the limits of classical social, sexual, and psychological behavior. Cary Grant, a handsome romantic lead in 1930s screwball comedies like *The Awful Truth* (1937), *Bringing Up Baby* and *Holiday* (1938), begins to explore the darker side of his screen persona as a suspected murderer in *Suspicion* (1941), as a small-town radical in flight from the police in *Talk of the Town* (1942), and as a disreputable cockney tramp in *None but the Lonely Heart* (1944). Musical comedy song and dance man Dick Powell and easy-going Fred MacMurray undergo a similar image overhaul for their roles as detective Philip Marlowe in *Murder, My Sweet* (1944) and as slick insurance salesman/husband killer Walter Neff in *Double Indemnity* (1944).

Bogart's transformation from 1930s gangster (*The Petrified Forest*, 1936; *The Roaring Twenties*, 1939) to 1940s romantic lead (*The Maltese Falcon*, 1941; *Casablanca*, 1942) represents the flip side of these attempts by leading men to redefine their images: instead of tarnishing his persona, he polishes it up; but in the process Bogart brings something of the gangster to his roles as a good guy. In all of these instances, an amalgam of opposing traits lead to the creation of the sort of antihero that would dominate film noir.

The postwar period also witnesses the reemergence of the femme fatale, but this time the femme fatales are home-grown, girl-next-door types rather than vamps from abroad. Stars such as Rita Hayworth (*Gilda*, 1946; *The Lady from Shanghai*, 1948), Lauren Bacall (*To Have and Have Not*, 1944; *The Big Sleep*, 1946), and Lana Turner (*The Postman Always Rings Twice*, 1946) bring an erotic sexuality to the screen that had formerly been reserved for European imports. (The exception that proves the rule is Theda Bara who, though born as Theodosia Goodman in the United States, was given an Afro-European ancestry and an exotic name by studio publicists in the 1910s.)

American female sexuality that had previously been channelled into the positive enterprises of creating a family or a career suddenly rebels, revealing its disastrous potential. And though this sexuality is ultimately contained, as in the case of Bacall, who is "tamed" by Bogart, or proves to be self-destructive, as in the case of Hayworth and Turner, whose greed, lust, and/or "improper" desire bring about their own deaths in *Shanghai* and *Postman*, that sexuality nevertheless emerges as revolutionary, empowering (albeit briefly) the women who possess it.

The Darker Side: Psychology and "the Method"

If perfection characterizes classical stardom, postwar stars expose and take advantage of their flaws—all in the interest of a greater realism. The good looks of a Tyrone Power, Errol Flynn, or Robert Taylor give way to the rough features of a Bogart or Robert Mitchum (who once described himself as looking "like a shark with a broken nose"). Actors begin to explore the psychological dimensions of their screen personae, revealing the apparent transparency of their mental make-up to be clouded with psychological complexities. Bogart starts talking to himself in *Treasure of the Sierra Madre* (1948) and develops psychotic tendencies in *In a Lonely Place* (1950). Edward G. Robinson hears voices in *Scarlet Street* (1945), and James Cagney becomes a psychopathic killer with an Oedipus complex in *White Heat* (1949).

James Stewart evolves from the naive, small-town, populist hero of Frank Capra's 1930s comedies (*Mr. Deeds Goes to Town*, 1936; *Mr. Smith Goes to Washington*, 1939) to the bitter, anxiety-ridden, vengeance-obsessed cowboy in Anthony Mann's 1950s Westerns (*Naked Spur*, 1953; *Man from Laramie*, 1955) and the disturbed voyeur and sexual fetishist in Alfred Hitchcock's 1950s suspense thrillers (*Rear Window*, 1954; *Vertigo*, 1958). Even John Wayne develops neuroses as the iron-willed, dictatorial cattleman in *Red River* (1948) and the socially estranged, broodingly violent, racist Indian fighter (who has a quasi-incestuous fixation on his brother's wife) in *The Searchers* (1956). But by the mid-1950s, Wayne, Stewart, and others are merely acting à la mode. Hollywood is now populated by a new generation of tormented, high strung young actors like Montgomery Clift, Marlon Brando, and James Dean, who embody the alienation, anguish, and sensitivity of 1950s teenagers.

Clift, Brando, and Dean, along with Barbara Bel Geddes, Ben Gazzara, Julie Harris, Paul Newman, Jack Palance, Lee Remick, Rod Steiger, Eli Wallach, Shelley Winters, and Joanne Woodward, had all studied acting in New York at the Actors Studio, where the dramatic theories of the Soviet theater director Constantin Stanislavski had been adopted and reworked by Lee Strasberg, Elia Kazan, and others. Stanislavski's techniques became the foundation for "the method," training exercises which require that actors use their own past experiences and emotional histories as a basis on which to build an inner identification with the characters they portray. The Actors Studio became so famous for its success in training actors in the 1950s that even established stars, such as Marilyn Monroe, began to take lessons there.

However, not all 1950s actors and actresses achieve stardom by means of "the method," that is, by baring their psyches and their souls to the public. Bob Hope, Bing Crosby, Gary Cooper, Gregory Peck, Doris Day, Rock Hudson, Jane Wyman, William Holden, and Randolph Scott dominate the box office during the decade. But the general, movie-going audience of the pre-

Director Elia Kazan (left) and actors Marlon Brando, Julie Harris, and James Dean on the Warner Bros.' lot during the making of *East of Eden* (1955).

war years had fragmented into a number of special-interest audiences in the 1950s, which ranged from rebellious teens (who idolized Dean, Brando, and [later] Elvis Presley); college-age men and women (who liked sexier, older stars such as Marilyn Monroe, Kim Novak, William Holden, and Gregory Peck); and housewives (who were fans of Rock Hudson, Jane Wyman, Ava Gardner, June Allyson, and Susan Hayward) to conservative, older viewers and family audiences who patronized Dean Martin and Jerry Lewis comedies and Biblical epics starring Robert Taylor or Charlton Heston.

Stars and Anti-Stars

Many of the more stable stars of the 1950s continue to be top box-office attractions in the 1960s. Dean had died in a car crash in 1955, after completing *Giant*; Clift had been seriously injured in another car accident while making *Raintree County* in 1957 and never quite recovered his earlier form; and Brando floundered in a series of oddball items, including *Mutiny on the Bounty* (1962), *The Ugly American* (1963), *Bedtime Story* (1964), and *The Countess from Hong Kong* (1967), though his performances in *The Chase* (1966) and *Reflections in a Golden Eye* (1967) proved that he had not lost his ability to rivet audiences.

Doris Day and Rock Hudson emerge as the biggest box-office attractions from 1960–1964, costarring in a number of bedroom farces including *Pillow Talk* (1959), *Lover Come Back* (1961), and *Send Me No Flowers* (1964). Cary Grant and John Wayne continue to hold sway over American screen comedies and Westerns, respectively, but are challenged by a new international star, Sean Connery, whose characterization of Ian Fleming's British secret agent, James Bond, made him one of the most popular male actors between the years 1962 (*Dr. No*) and 1972 (*Diamonds Are Forever*).

Resisting Tradition: Nicholson, Eastwood, and Their Peers

A number of contemporary stars resist the traditional star image. They play the role of the reluctant star or anti-star, refusing to give interviews to the press or do extensive publicity for their pictures. Apparent by-products of a 1960s counterculture, they not only refuse to behave like stars, they don't even look like stars (with the notable exceptions of Warren Beatty, Paul Newman, and Robert Redford). Many of them didn't even live in Hollywood (Woody Allen, Marlon Brando, Robert De Niro, Clint Eastwood, Paul Newman, Robert Redford, Bill Murray, George C. Scott, Shirley Maclaine, Meryl Streep, Sean Connery, Michael Caine, and Dustin Hoffman); some didn't even bother to pick up their Academy Awards on Oscar night (Allen, Brando, and Scott). Other anti-stars include Warren Beatty, Jack Nicholson, and Barbra Streisand.

Uncomfortable with celebrity, these anti-stars not only refuse typecasting, selecting parts that problematize their personae, but prefer to play anti-heroes rather than heroes. Eastwood, for example, alternates his role as Sergio Leone's man-with-no-name in the Italian spaghetti Westerns and the tough supercop, Dirty Harry Callahan, with a series of parts that explore the hypermasculinity of his screen image, questioning its rigidity and exposing its flaws. Thus, he plays a phony cowboy from New Jersey in *Bronco Billy* (1980) and a self-reflective cop who is sensitive to women's issues and critical of his own male chauvinism and excessive violence in *Tightrope* (1984).

Nicholson goes from antiauthoritarian rebel (*One Flew Over the Cuckoo's Nest*, 1975) to Mafia hit man (*Prizzi's Honor*, 1985), though a certain demented subversiveness has given some consistency to his image from his rebellious youth as an actor (*Easy Rider*, 1969, and *Five Easy Pieces*, 1970) to his more recent roles as the maniacal killer in *The Shining* (1980), the devil in *The Witches of Eastwick* (1987), and the Joker in *Batman* (1989). By contrast, more conventional stars, such as Schwarzenegger and Stallone, continue in stardom's classic mold, building consistent screen characters for themselves by playing a fairly narrow range of character types, such as Conan and the Terminator or Rocky and Rambo.

Television as Training Ground

Since the breakup of the studio system, contemporary stars have entered Hollywood from a variety of other media, developing a star status outside of motion pictures which they then translate into stardom in Hollywood. Television serves as the training ground for many actors, replacing the ''B'' picture and low-budget motion picture mill that has provided past performers with experience in front of a camera. Actors who move from a television series to motion picture stardom range from Steve McQueen, Burt Reynolds, James Garner, and Clint Eastwood, to John Travolta, Michael J. Fox, Sylvester Stallone, Robin Williams, and Bruce Willis. (Actresses seem to have been less successful.)

''Saturday Night Live'' gave us John Belushi, Eddie Murphy, Steve Martin, Chevy Chase, Dan Ackroyd, Bill Murray, and Gilda Radner, as well as

Michael Meyers and Dana Carvey of "Wayne's World." A handful of television gag writers and nightclub comics, such as Woody Allen and Mel Brooks, graduated to the motion pictures, where they perform their own material. Cher, Diana Ross, Kris Kristofferson, Dolly Parton, Liza Minnelli, and Barbra Streisand came to the cinema by way of the recording industry. Cover girls whose careers in modeling led them to the movies include Brooke Shields, Farrah Fawcett-Majors, Cybill Shepherd, and others.

Stars' Children: Déjà Vu

A related phenomenon is the emergence of second-generation stardom—the children of stars whose features and mannerisms recall those of their parents, giving audiences an uncanny sense of déjà vu. Thus Jane and Peter Fonda (children of Henry), Liza Minnelli (daughter of Judy Garland), Michael Douglas (son of Kirk), Jeff and Beau Bridges (sons of Lloyd), Emilio Estevez and Charles Sheen (sons of Martin Sheen), Keith, David, and Robert Carradine (sons of John), Isabelle Rossellini (daughter of Ingrid Bergman), Melanie Griffith (daughter of Tippi Hedren), Laura Dern (daughter of Dianne Ladd and Bruce Dern), Carrie Fisher (daughter of Debbie Reynolds), Jamie Lee Curtis (daughter of Janet Leigh and Tony Curtis), Kiefer Sutherland (son of Donald), and Timothy Hutton (son of Jim) bring to the screen a kind of self-reflexivity that is quite consistent with contemporary Hollywood's obsession with its glorious past (see Chapter 14, "The Film School Generation"). In effect, contemporary stars enable us to see the ghost of Hollywood past in the faces of Hollywood present.

Different Faces: The Rise of Black Stars

From Sidney Poitier to "Blaxploitation"

In the late 1960s, as the political and cultural climate polarized, a growing segment of the movie-going public, comprised largely of younger spectators under the age of 30, moved to the left, embracing certain aspects of the women's, youth, and civil rights movements. In the right place at the right time, Sidney Poitier enjoyed unprecedented success at the box office in this period, emerging as the first black star who could draw a significant number of white spectators. His *A Patch of Blue* landed among the top ten money-makers of 1965, earning $6.3 million; *To Sir with Love* did the same in 1967, making more than $7.2 million. Then, in 1967, *Guess Who's Coming to Dinner* placed second only to *The Graduate* in profits, returning an incredible $25.1 million to its distributor Columbia, while in 1968 another Poitier picture, *For the Love of Ivy*, pulled in $5 million.

The blaxploitation movement of the early 1970s sought to build upon Poitier's pioneering efforts in creating a crossover audience of whites who went to black films and to address the interests of an increasing number of black spectators, who, industry analysts estimated, made up from 25 to 30 percent of the total movie-going audience. The phenomenal success of *Shaft* and *Sweet Sweetback's Badasssss Song* (1971), which grossed $7 and $11 million,

Courtesy of Columbia

Sidney Poitier and Katharine Houghton in *Guess Who's Coming to Dinner?* (1967).

respectively, proved that black was beautiful at the box office. But unlike the Poitier vehicles, which catered to a middle-class and lower-upper-class audience, this cycle of black films addressed lower-middle-class and lower-class concerns, dramatizing crime in the streets and creating a black urban landscape peopled by private eyes, drug dealers, numbers runners, petty criminals, pimps, and prostitutes.

Fame in Other Fields

The course of stardom for young black actors and actresses in this period follows a somewhat different line of development from that taken by white performers, though black stars also come from other media. For the most part, blacks have to come from noncinematic backgrounds because Hollywood has never invested in the development of more than a handful of black stars. In the postwar era, only Poitier had evolved into a leading man, achieving celebrity in *The Defiant Ones* (1958), *Lilies of the Field* (1963), *In the Heat of the Night* and *Guess Who's Coming to Dinner* (1967). One or two other black actors such as Brock Peters (*To Kill a Mockingbird,* 1962) and James Edwards (*The Manchurian Candidate,* 1962) put together careers as talented supporting performers, but were unable to find vehicles that would secure for them the singular kind of success enjoyed by Poitier.

If television proves to be the station along the way to stardom for white actors in the 1960s and 1970s, this is not the case for black actors, who find it difficult to secure work on TV (though Bill Cosby achieves some recognition in the "I Spy" series in the late 1960s). It is not until the late 1970s that television provides roles for black actors in any significant numbers. As a result, the studios turn to black stars from other media. Hollywood had done this in the past with black performers whom it had recruited from the world of music and dance, such as Cab Calloway, Paul Robeson, Bill "Bojangles" Robinson, Pearl Bailey, Lena Horne, Harry Belafonte, and Sammy Davis, Jr.

During the 1960s and 1970s, Hollywood capitalizes upon the celebrity of blacks, but it finds them not so much in the traditional media of theater and television as in other fields in which "nonacting" skills are perfected. Black actors come from the world of fashion; white executives cast former models such as Richard Roundtree (*Shaft*, 1971) and Tamara Dobson (*Cleopatra Jones*, 1973) in films. New stars also come from the world of athletics; Hollywood turns to track and football stars such as Woody Strode (*Sergeant Rutledge*, 1960), Rafer Johnson (*Soul Soldier*, 1972), Jim Brown (*Slaughter* and *Black Gunn*, 1972), Fred Williamson (*Black Caesar*, 1973), O. J. Simpson (*The Towering Inferno*, 1974), Jim Kelly (*Enter the Dragon*, 1973), and "Rosey" Grier (*The Thing with Two Heads*, 1972).

The Eddie Murphy Generation

Unfortunately, Hollywood's interest in producing black films and developing black talent declined as the box-office revenues from blaxploitation films fell off during the mid-1970s—a turn symbolized by the failure of *The Wiz* (1978), which starred Diana Ross and Michael Jackson. Though mainstream black actors such as Poitier, Belafonte, Cosby, and Richard Pryor continue to attract large crossover audiences in films like *Uptown Saturday Night* (1974), black actor-athletes failed to establish themselves as stars. Muscle and good looks only carry black stars so far; it was raunchy nightclub comedy, however, that led the way for the next wave of black stars. The polite restraint of Cosby plays quite well on the living room TV (which proved to be the best setting for Cosby, who never enjoyed the same success in movies that he did on television). But the less conventional, "raw" humor of Pryor, who stars in a number of "concert" films as well as in the box-office smashes *Silver Streak* (1976) and *Stir Crazy* (1980), and of Eddie Murphy, who appears in a string of commercial hits in the mid-1980s ranging from *48 Hours* (1982), *Trading Places* (1983), and *Beverly Hills Cop* (I in 1984 and II in 1987) to *Coming to America* (1988), made stars out of both Pryor and Murphy and provided a new format for the showcasing of other black performers such as Whoopi Goldberg, whose skills as a comic actress produced a popular nightclub act as well as hit films like *Ghost* (1990), and Arsenio Hall, who parlayed his costarring role in *Coming to America* into a steady berth as a late-night talk show host.

During the 1980s, an increasing number of minority actors and actresses establish careers for themselves on television and in the movies, including Emilio Estevez, Raul Julia, James Earl Jones, Rae Dawn Chong, Lou Diamond

Phillips, Oprah Winfrey, James Smits, Red Foxx, and others. At the same time, black actors such as Lou Gossett, Jr. (*An Officer and a Gentlemen*, 1982), Danny Glover (the *Lethal Weapon* films), Morgan Freeman (*Driving Miss Daisy* and *Glory*, 1989), and Denzel Washington (*Glory*, 1989; *Mississippi Masala*, 1992) find more or less regular employment in a new Hollywood which is dominated by "liberal" white executives, who grew up in the 1960s. These moguls seem to have inherited some of that decade's racial sensitivity. At the very least, they see a potential market grow out of the liberal counterculture and make films for the children of those (like themselves) who grew up in the 1960s.

Economics and Contemporary Stardom

The fact that Hollywood has opened up its "heavens" for minority stars remains a significant step forward (especially for those stars of color who have made it), but this development has more to do with simple economics than it does with notions of fair play. Stars are and have always been commodities. Today's marketplace, though culturally more diverse, is nonetheless still a marketplace, where an increasing number of star images trade places with one another on the floor of the film industry's own form of stock exchange, in which images are worth money. It is from this perspective that the essential artifice of stardom emerges most clearly. Stars are not born but made; and they are made with a purpose—to sell films. Throughout the history of the theater, the movies, and television, stars have been rated in terms of their "bankability," that is, their value at the box office. The star system took shape around the economic reality into which the unique attractiveness of each star was translated. In this way the star system played a crucial role in the perpetuation of the studio system. After the demise of the studio system in the 1950s and 1960s, the star system became, along with the "genre system" (see the introduction to Part II), the most important stabilizing feature of the motion picture industry. Though the path to stardom in the contemporary film industry has become increasing complex and the attainment of stardom increasingly haphazard, the phenomenon of stardom has remained essential to Hollywood because of its ability to lure spectators into the theater.

In the early 1980s, Robert Redford's presence in a film was considered to be worth $5 million at the box office; Clint Eastwood's was worth $4 million; and Robert De Niro's, $3 million. In 1991, *Premiere* published a list of stars whose appearance in a film "virtually guarantee[d] a foreign presale [i.e., the sale of the film to potential exhibitors overseas *prior* to its production], regardless of the script, director, or other stars brought to the package." The most bankable stars included (in order of their box-office appeal) Arnold Schwarzenegger, Mel Gibson, Tom Cruise, Sean Connery, Harrison Ford, Jack Nicholson, and Julia Roberts. Stars continue to play a stabilizing role in the contemporary film industry, providing filmmakers with built-in audiences who regularly watch films in which their favorite actors and actresses appear. However, in recent years, a number of films that feature no major stars have performed exceedingly well at the box office, suggesting that those who are willing to take risks and gamble on the public's potential interest in particular projects can quite often reap even greater rewards than those who hedge their bets by hiring proven (and pricey) stars. *Variety's* list of the top-grossing films of all time includes titles such as *E.T.: The Extra-Terrestrial,* the *Star Wars* trilogy, *Batman, Home Alone, Ghostbusters, Jaws,* and the *Indiana Jones* trilogy—films which feature no well-known stars (except for Harrison Ford, who was more or less unknown at the time of *Star Wars,* and Jack Nicholson, who plays only a supporting role in *Batman*). In other words, stars are not indispensable. Yet Hollywood, the media, and motion picture audiences seem unable to do without them for any length of time.

For nearly 100 years, Hollywood's biggest attractions have been stars and stories. Audiences come to see Gentlemen Jim Corbett, Mary Pickford, Greta Garbo, Clark Gable, John Wayne, Robert Redford, Barbra Streisand, Eddie Murphy, Arnold Schwarzenegger, and others. To some extent, the stars make the stories, driving them forward with the force of their personalities. More often than not, the stars and the stories "collaborate" with one another: the stars build their screen personalities on the backs of the characters they play and on the story patterns that writers provide for them; and the fictional characters and stories come to life through/in the bodies of individual stars. Yet the pleasure that stars provide to audiences has remained unique for it always depends upon the audience's recognition of the differences between the star and the character which he or she plays. Unlike the novel in which no such distinction exists—in which there is only character—the movies can never quite collapse a star into a mere character. Our delight in stars comes from an appreciation of them *as performers*—from the interplay between star and character. Ironically, in order to be caught up in and carried away by a star we must be fully conscious of the essential artifice which underlies stardom.

SELECT FILMOGRAPHY

Tess of the Storm Country
  (1914)
The Cheat (1915)
Broken Blossoms (1919)
The Sheik (1921)
It (1927)
Steamboat Willie (1928)
It Happened One Night (1934)
The Littlest Rebel (1935)
Camille (1937)
Gone With the Wind (1939)
Ninotchka (1939)
The Maltese Falcon (1941)
Casablanca (1942)
Red River (1948)
Singin' in the Rain (1952)
Gentlemen Prefer Blondes
  (1953)
Giant (1956)
The Searchers (1956)
Will Success Spoil Rock
  Hunter? (1957)

Guess Who's Coming to
  Dinner (1967)
In the Heat of the Night (1967)
True Grit (1969)
One Flew Over the Cuckoo's
  Nest (1975)
The Shootist (1976)
Silver Streak (1976)
Annie Hall (1977)
Bronco Billy (1980)
The Shining (1980)
Stir Crazy (1980)
48 Hours (1982)
Trading Places (1983)
Beverly Hills Cop (1984)
Tightrope (1984)
Coming to America (1988)
Ghost (1990)
Pretty Woman (1990)
Reversal of Fortune (1990)

SELECT BIBLIOGRAPHY

Gledhill, Christine, ed. *Stardom: Industry of Desire.* New York: Routledge, 1991.

Morin, Edgar. *The Stars: An Account of the Star-System in Motion Pictures.* New York: Grove, 1960.

Pirie, David, ed. *Anatomy of the Movies.* New York: Macmillan, 1981.

Thompson, David. *A Biographical Dictionary of Film.* New York: Morrow, 1976.

Walker, Alexander. *Stardom: The Hollywood Phenomenon.* New York: Stein and Day, 1970.

Weis, Elizabeth, ed. *The Movie Star Book.* New York: Penguin, 1981.

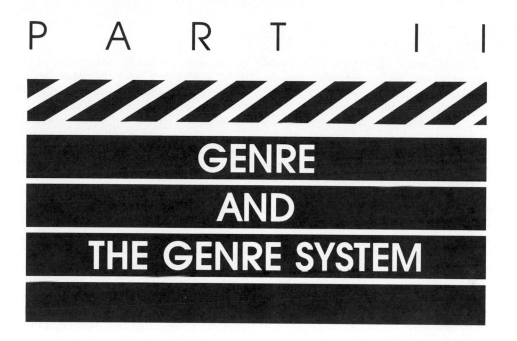

P A R T   I I

GENRE AND THE GENRE SYSTEM

"Genre" is a French word that refers to a kind, type, or category of a particular phenomenon or thing. In the cinema, genre is a term that is used to designate various categories of motion picture production. Major movie genres include such broad types of films as musicals, comedies, action and adventure films, Westerns, crime and detective films, melodramas, science-fiction and horror films, gangster films, war films, action-adventure films, suspense thrillers, epics, disaster films, and so forth.

These genres can frequently be broken down into subgenres or subdivisions of the major genre. Thus, horror films can be subdivided into specific types such as vampire, mad doctor, demon-seed/evil-child, splatter, or slasher films. Comedies can be categorized as slapstick, romantic, screwball, and so on.

Genres serve to stabilize an otherwise unstable film industry. Motion picture production is extremely expensive. In 1991, for example, the average negative cost (i.e., the amount of money it costs to produce a finished negative of the film before prints are made or costly advertising and distribution expenses are incurred) was slightly over $26 million. (By comparison, in 1950, average negative costs were approximately $1.1 mil-

lion.) Marketing, advertising, and print costs in 1991 averaged an additional $24 to $25 million. Industry analysts estimate that, for any film to break even (whether it was made in 1950 or 1991), it would have to earn roughly 2 to 2½ times its negative costs.

Given these costs, motion picture producers face tremendous risks each time they make a film. These risks are increased by the very nature of the motion picture product. Unlike other consumer products, such as cars, household appliances, and fashions, which rely upon brand name recognition for much of their market appeal, motion pictures are essentially one-of-a-kind products. Each film is necessarily different from every other film, featuring a story and a cast that is more or less unique. Each film is thus an unknown quantity; its producer has no assurance that it will make a profit at the box office because, unlike other consumer items, it has no "brand name" status in the marketplace. The star system and the genre system attempt to compensate for the dangers involved in this process. They serve to hedge producers' bets against the unknowns and variables that underlie the production of every film.

Unlike cars and other merchandise, movies

are not durable goods. They have no physical existence; they are not objects that can be bought, taken home, and used. They are, of course, consumed, but the consumer has little or nothing to show for that consumption. Audiences take home no tangible product but only the memory of an entertainment experience. The genre system, which structures the American film industry, represents an attempt by the film industry to control the entertainment marketplace in a way that is similar to the control that brand name products exert among the consumers of durable goods.

Genres result from the proven success of one-of-a-kind films in the marketplace. The box-office fortune of one particular kind of film results in the production of another film that resembles it in terms of plot and character type. The film industry assumes that the audience that came to the earlier hit will return to see a film similar in nature to it. This can be seen most clearly in the proliferation of sequels (and prequels) which accompany so many box-office hits of the 1960s, 1970s, and 1980s.

Thus the exceptional profits of the first James Bond film, *Dr. No* (1962) lead to a succession of others. This also explains the string of *Godfather, Jaws, Rocky, Star Wars, Superman, Star Trek, Indiana Jones,* and other films of the 1970s and 1980s. In terms of more traditional notions of genres (rather than the series or sequels mentioned above), the financial success of one "disaster" film, such as *Airport* (1970), leads directly to the production of others, such as *The Poseidon Adventure* (1972), *The Towering Inferno* (1974), and *Earthquake* (1974).

Films that belong to a specific genre draw from a more or less fixed body of character and story types, settings and situations, costumes and props, thematic concerns and visual iconography, and conventions that are shared by other films in that particular genre. Westerns, for example, regularly contain certain character types, such as cowboys, town marshals, Indians, dance hall girls, schoolmarms, cavalry officers, saloon keepers, Indian agents, gamblers, rustlers, and

others, who are readily identifiable in terms of the costumes they wear, the props they use, the things they do, and the situations in which they find themselves. The films will generally be set in the West and feature certain kinds of landscapes or settings, ranging from the vast stretches of the Great Plains, Rocky Mountains, and barren deserts to cattle ranches, bunkhouses, and frontier towns.

Each new film in the genre will bank on a number of familiar genre elements, motifs, and themes, but will combine them in a novel way. The audiences that go to genre films are lured to them by the promise of seeing a film that is similar in kind to films they have seen and enjoyed in the past. They are drawn to the genre much in the way they are drawn to a brand name product. But they are also enticed by the prospect of seeing a film that *differs* in a number of respects from films they have seen before. In this way, the system of genres relies on a combination of the familiar and the unknown, conventionality and novelty, similarity and difference. It will use the basic ingredients of the genre to produce certain expectations in the audience, but it will also adapt, modify, or play with those conventions in order to provide audiences with a unique entertainment experience.

Because of the economic role which genre plays in the American film industry and because the major genres not only contain a large number of films but also span several decades (or more) of film production, a study of genre and the genre system becomes crucial to any understanding of what classical Hollywood cinema is and how it works. Even more important, by looking at the large body of films within individual genres, we can see how those genres help to shape and are shaped by our understanding of American culture, character, and identity. In the following chapters, we will explore the role that a handful of American genres play in expressing "the temper of an age and a nation" and conveying the unique nature of the American experience in the twentieth century.

CHAPTER 6

SILENT FILM MELODRAMA

THE ORIGINS OF MELODRAMA

Melodrama literally means "a drama accompanied by music." The term was coined by Jean-Jacques Rousseau in 1770 to describe a dramatic monologue which he had written, entitled *Pygmalion*, which alternated speech with passages of pantomime and music. The emergence of melodrama in France in the 1770s and 1780s can be traced to the royal monopoly, which was held by officially approved, classical repertory companies, such as the Comédie Française, and which granted them the exclusive rights to stage "verbal" dramas. Secondary theater groups were restricted to nonverbal dramatic forms such as juggling or acrobatic acts, ballets, puppet shows, and pantomimes. Marcel Carne's *Children of Paradise* (France, 1945) provides a vivid portrait of this popular tradition which was built upon carnivalesque street theater and mime acts. After the French Revolution (1789), this "verbal monopoly" came to an end and all theatrical groups were able to use words. But even though melodramas could now make full use of dialogue, they never lost their ability to communicate on a nonverbal level.

Theatrical melodrama, which began without a voice, perfected the craft of visual expression, translating thought and emotion into gesture, costume, decor, and other elements of mise-en-scene. It discovered how to say all without literally saying anything. Melodrama even developed its own sign language. Adapting acting techniques from classical theater, it produced a system of gestures and hand movements, which were subsequently recorded and catalogued by a French scholar, Francois Delsarte. At the same time, melodrama manipulated traditional mise-en-scene in an attempt to wring even greater expressiveness out of it, freezing the action at particularly significant moments into a tableau. In a tableau, which frequently came at act endings, the actors assumed particularly revealing and characteristic positions and then held them for several moments in an attempt to underscore or crystallize events, feelings, or ideas for the audience.

Melodrama works on a purely emotional level, rooting its drama in a common base of feeling which crosses over all linguistic barriers. Even in contemporary film melodrama, such as the science-fiction tearjerker *E.T.: The Extra-Terrestrial* (1982), the heart of the film resides in E.T.'s large, expressive eyes and poignant facial movements rather than in anything anyone says. In another Steven Spielberg film, *Close Encounters of the Third Kind* (1977), communication between humans and aliens takes place on a purely affective level—through five musical tones. *E.T.* moves somewhat beyond that primitive stage to speech. But when words are used, as in the phrase "E.T. Phone Home!" they tend to be minimal and rudimentary—almost nonverbal. E.T.'s

Courtesy of Universal

E.T. goes home in *E.T.: The Extra-Terrestrial* (1982).

speech ignores established linguistic conventions and grammatical rules; he/it speaks directly from the heart. The expressiveness of these semiarticulate statements derive, in large part, from their childlike simplicity—from the inability of the alien to express in language the complex longings that lay behind the phrase. This is melodramatic speech.

The popularity of melodrama as a form of theater for the middle classes during the nineteenth century and its ability to convey crucial dramatic information visually made it an ideal form for the silent cinema. Virtually every silent film—including the slapstick comedies of Charles Chaplin and Buster Keaton—was, on one level or another, a melodrama. During the 1910s and 1920s, the trade press routinely described the majority of all films as melodramas. There were romantic melodramas, domestic melodramas, rural melodramas, Western melodramas, sociological melodramas, crime melodramas, society melodramas, mystery melodramas, underworld melodramas, and just plain melodramas. If the story or situation was not rooted in melodrama, then at least the acting or the mise-en-scene was. It had to be in order to communicate ideas and feelings without dialogue. Although the film melodrama successfully navigated the transition from silent to sound cinema in the late 1920s, silent melodrama, in many ways, represented the melodramatic impulse at its purest and most powerful.

TYPES OF MELODRAMA

The Melodramatic Mode

The melodrama, unlike the Western or the detective film, is a *modal* genre. But there is a genre called "the melodrama" which features conventional character types, such as heroes, heroines, and villains, as well as predictable plot elements, such as improbable reversals of fortune, accidents, and last-minute rescues. In terms of its predictable or formulaic plot patterns, a typical melodrama might begin with the disruption or disturbance of an idealized emotional paradise by some external force or act of villainy. A happy family in its home is threatened with eviction or its integrity is shattered by the abduction of one of its members; the blissful young lovers are separated or forced apart by those who would block their marriage. Subsequent action presents the struggle of the hero and/or heroine to restore this initial state of affairs by reuniting the family or removing obstacles that separate the lovers—goals which are accomplished by the end of the narrative. The plot of *Home Alone* (1990), for example, is essentially that of a melodrama: a child is accidently separated from his parents; the home is threatened by burglars; the child successfully defends the home against outside attacks; and he is finally reunited with his parents.

However, the *mode* of *Home Alone* is more comic than melodramatic. The child is fairly much in control of things and actually enjoys his experience of being home alone. That is, the *treatment* of the situation is not overtly melodramatic; the filmmakers opted for comedy instead. As a *mode*, the melodrama—or, more accurately, *the melodramatic* is less concerned with specific plot and character types than with the creation of a certain mood and of a powerful emotional response in the audience. In its status as a mode, melodrama resembles tragedy and comedy in that, though possessing a structure and identifiable motifs and character types, it crosses over from one genre to another. Thus Westerns like *Duel in the Sun* (1946), gangster films like *The Godfather* (1972), and science-fiction adventures like *E.T.* are "melodramatic." In other words, film melodrama exists primarily as an attitude or method of treatment—a melodrama is a film that features conventional character types and formulaic plot patterns which are presented in a *melodramatic* way.

A Moral Phenomenon

Like Westerns or gangster films, melodramas can also be defined in terms of their milieu. Much as Westerns are set in the West and gangster films in an urban, criminal underworld, melodramas tend to take place within the domestic space of the family or in the private, intimate space of the romantic couple. At the core of the melodrama, however, lies neither milieu nor plot but a certain mode of address to the spectator which is emotionalized by the use of melodramatic stylistic techniques. As a mode of address, the melodrama "speaks" to viewers in a way that is primarily emotional rather than logical. Indeed, one of the oppositions which characterizes traditional screen melodrama is that between emotion and reason. Characters in melodramas who are extremely articulate or presented as intellectuals are often exposed either as phonies or as emotional cripples who have lost touch with their feelings and who need to be rescued from the paralyzing forces of rationality. The "villain" in *Terms of Endearment* (1983), for example, is predictably the college professor (Jeff Daniels), who cheats on his wife (Debra Winger) with one of his female graduate students. Glib men are just not to be trusted in melodramas.

In its attempt to deal with emotional or spiritual experience, the melodrama draws upon the affective power of images and music to render the emotional dimensions of experience. That is, it attempts to depict those emotions which cannot be rendered in words. In attempting to say what cannot be said, the film melodrama traditionally relies upon stylistic excess— on an extreme camera angle, an overstated set or costume design, a delirious camera movement, or an unusual color scheme—in an attempt to make visible that which is essentially invisible. The moral forces of good and evil that lie beneath the surface of experience are pressured to the surface by melodrama's excesses and put into relief. Melodrama reveals the structure of our experience of the world as a moral and emotional phenomenon, clarifying and working out in dramatic form the emotional and moral conflicts that take place within the individual. In this respect, it is an objective rendering of subjective inner experience.

Thus in melodramas, children and animals often prove to be emotional touchstones—they are more capable of distinguishing good from bad and right from wrong than their elders. In *E.T.*, the children intuitively understand the alien from another world and prove more adept than adults when it comes to communicating with it. Family and feelings are the common denominator to which all melodramas ultimately return. Melodrama is about the loss and recovery of feelings (*Awakenings*, 1990), about the restoration of the family unit (*Home Alone*), about fathers and sons (*Kramer vs. Kramer*, 1979), about mothers and daughters (*Terms of Endearment*), about brothers (*Rain Man*, 1988), about sisters (*A League of Their Own*, 1992), and about every other possible configuration of the family from *Edward Scissorhands* (1990) and *The Prince of Tides* (1991) to *Batman Returns* (1992).

The melodrama and the melodramatic, whether in the form of a melodramatic situation, gesture, element of mise-en-scene, line of dialogue, or bar of music, have tended to be regarded by critics as second-rate forms of expression and clearly inferior to the more aristocratic forms such as tragedy and the tragic. One definition of melodrama describes it as "domestic tragedy." Tragedy was understood (by Aristotle and others) as a "serious" drama consisting of events and characters of considerable "magnitude." In other words, classical tragedy from Aeschylus to Shakespeare dealt with kings, queens, princes, and other figures of social importance whose actions determined the fate of cities, principalities, kingdoms, and nations.

The realm of melodrama, by contrast, is limited to private as opposed to public spheres. It concerns more or less ordinary characters whose actions affect the fortunes of much smaller social units; it focuses upon the fate of the couple, the family, and their immediate community. Although tragedy appealed to all classes, it emerged as the dramatic form par excellence of the nobility or social aristocracy in whose world it was situated. Melodrama, like certain forms of comedy, gives expression to the concerns of the lower ranks of society. It is the genre par excellence of (to borrow David Grimsted's term) the "historically voiceless," and its popularity in the nineteenth century accompanied the emergence of a new social order to which it appealed—that of a middle-class, mass society.

Democratic Virtue

Nineteenth-century melodrama bought with it a new vision of the universe and of the individual's place within it. Much as the French Revolution overthrew the traditional institutions of a supposedly divinely ordained, hierarchical society—the church and the monarchy—in favor of a more "democratic" social order, so the melodrama supplanted the "elitist" vision of the tragedy with a more democratic worldview. Classical tragedy, which died in the seventeenth century with Racine, could be seen as elitist largely through its concern for the fates of characters of a certain magnitude and/or social stature. But it was also aristocratic in its basic understanding of the essentially static relationship of individuals to the existing political and social order. The heroes and heroines of tragedy struggled to maintain the "natural" order of things or to repair that order when it had become "unnatural." Thus Oedipus in Sophocles' *Oedipus Rex* attempted to rid Thebes of the plague and restore it to health, much as Hamlet in Shakespeare's play concerned himself with purging the state of Denmark of something that was rotten. The heroes of tragedy sought to maintain or restore the order of the world, but that order and that world was *theirs*. For them, what was "natural" was necessarily a reflection of the value system of their particular social class. Both *Oedipus* and *Hamlet* ended with the imposition of a "new" order, but that new order was merely a more benign form of the dominant social order (i.e., monarchy) with which the drama began.

When characters in melodramas fight to maintain or repair the natural order of things, the values that inform their struggle are those of a different social class, i.e., the middle class. The stature of a character in a melodrama is a measure of his or her moral rather than social position. Virtue empowers its heroes and heroines; evil its villains. Virtue is not the exclusive property of any one class but is equally obtainable by all. The commoner has as much access to the truth as the noble. Yet it is often easier for the lower classes to discover truth, and to achieve virtue or moral wisdom because "simple people are less burdened with artificial knowledge and distinctions" than the nobility. But in tragedy, knowledge and truth tend to be the exclusive property of the aristocracy. As Grimsted argued, "the melodrama reflected and supported what is perhaps the key element in democratic psychology: the sense which individual men have of their ability to decide, and hence of their right to participate vitally in the wielding of power."

Dozens of stage melodramas (primarily those of European origin) cast the conflict between good and evil in social terms, presenting it as a class war in which the audience is encouraged to root for the underdog. Thus the villain, frequently a landlord, routinely demands the hand of his tenant's daughter when the rent is unpaid. Scores of other melodramas, especially those set in contemporary, nineteenth-century America, stage moral conflicts in terms of geography. These works explore a basic opposition between nature and culture, between the innocence of those who live in the world of nature—in small towns or on farms in the country—and the corruption and decadence of those who live in the city. For example, D. W. Griffith's *Way Down East* (1920), which is an adaptation of a popular stage melodrama, traces the journey of its innocent heroine from the small town where she lives with her mother to the big city, where she is seduced and abandoned by a member of the social aristocracy. The film concludes with her return to life in the country, where she finds a job working on a farm, and with her recovery of innocence through her contact with the purifying world of nature.

A SOCIAL VISION

Melodrama as a Tool of Reform

Melodramas may work primarily on an emotional level, but they also deal with ideas and social problems. In this way, they speak to the fundamental interests of "the people." Grimsted observes that these dramas frequently deal with social and economic issues that concern the middle and lower classes—with "the hard lot of the poor, the corrupt practices of the rich, the social threat of rapid urbanization, the evil of slavery, the injury of bad family upbringing." Novels such as Harriet Beecher Stowe's antislavery narrative *Uncle Tom's Cabin,* which was adapted for the stage shortly after its publication in 1852 and became "the greatest success in the history of the American theatre," helped to transform the theater into a popular forum for the discussion of social issues.

Melodramas also serve as tools for social reform, describing the evils of middle- and lower-class vices, such as gambling and alcohol. In one of Griffith's Biograph shorts, *A Drunkard's Reformation* (1909), the hero attends a play which dramatizes the disastrous consequences of drinking, and he vows never to touch alcohol again. Reformers praised melodramas because, as in *A Drunkard's Reformation,* they depicted the triumph of good over evil. Film in general (and film melodrama, in particular) was seen in the United States as a "grand social worker" in that it lured working-class men away from saloons and other forms of vice and promised, as Lary May points out, to teach "Anglo-Saxon ideals" to all, transforming all those who went to the movies into a "model citizenry."

Melodramas dramatized the fears of Victorian America about the toll that modernization and urbanization would take upon the institution of the family. As Griffith suggests in the modern story of his four-story epic, *Intolerance*

Parodying a typical melodramatic situation, Mack Sennett (right) ties Mabel Normand to the railroad track in *Barney Oldfield's Race for Life* (1913).

(1916), the anonymity of life in the city poses a danger to the traditional values of family and community; fatherless daughters and husbandless wives are pursued by immoral men. Greedy factory owners are shown to be anything but paternalistic; they ruthlessly exploit their workers. In other films, the clichéd image of a heroine tied to the railroad tracks gives voice to the particular concerns of a new social order—to the fears of an emerging lower- and middle-class society caught up in the onrush of fast-paced technological changes that threaten to overwhelm them. The average American was suddenly in danger of being crushed by the forces of industry, symbolized by the locomotive.

Though the melodrama was born in France, it adapted itself quite readily to the needs and demands of American audiences. Theatrical melodrama dominated the American stage in the late nineteenth century in the form of both European imports adapted for American audiences, such as Dion Boucicault's *The Poor of New York,* and domestic originals, such as *Uncle Tom's Cabin* or Augustin Daly's *Under the Gaslight.* Popular melodrama helped to shape American character, "expressing the American temperament, preaching American ideologies, embodying American aesthetic principles." Daniel Gerould sees it as having been essentially egalitarian. It was "founded on a belief in opportunity for all, and dedicated to getting ahead and making money." Unlike tragedy, melodrama is "totally devoid of fatality and inevitability. Contingency rules; things can and will be otherwise. The individual can make of himself what he will. . . . Each human being has the chance in a society unfettered by Old World hierarchies of class and profession." In this way, melodramas embody the American dream, offering success to anyone with the courage and strength to pursue it.

Politics and Melodrama

Given its associations with the French Revolution and its popular appeal in the United States, the melodrama was often identified as a tool of revolutionary change. Wylie Sypher argued that the genre conceived of things in terms of dialectical opposition—in terms of good and bad—and thus reflected the same worldview of inevitable class warfare and either/or ideology that informed Karl Marx's *Capital*. Whether melodrama was a form of revolutionary consciousness or not, it nonetheless provided a way of looking at history that proved compelling to filmmakers who occupied vastly different positions on the political spectrum.

Griffith, for example, made melodramas which, on the one hand, call for reform but which, on the other, also convey disturbing racial fears and a deep suspicion of radical change. Griffith's melodramatic polarization of society serves as a weapon against blacks in *The Birth of a Nation* (1915) and against Bolsheviks (i.e., Communists) in *Orphans of the Storm* (1922). Griffith's melodrama is essentially populist in nature. It seeks to restore an idealized, agrarian America that had been destroyed by big business, industrialization, and urbanization.

Approaching the genre in another way, the Soviet director, Sergei Eisenstein, infused his melodramas with a Marxist vision. His hero is "the masses" and his villains consist primarily of the czar and counterrevolutionary forces in films such as *Potemkin* (1925) and *October* (1928). Though both Marxists like Eisenstein and populists like Griffith use melodrama to speak out on behalf of the plain people, Marxists speak in the language of class conflict—the capitalist exploitation of the working classes. Populists speak in the language of universal, heartfelt truths which all Americans supposedly understand and respect.

The politics of America melodrama remained steadfastly populist; they were driven by a desire for reform and never embraced the revolutionary spirit of Marxism. But populism was not monolithic; it encompassed a broad spectrum of various grass-roots political positions. Rural populists, for example, consisted largely of farmers, farm workers, and residents of small towns. They tended to be Protestants whose families had lived in the United States for several generations. Urban populists were largely blue-collar laborers who worked in steel mills and factories or wage earners with jobs in department and retail stores. Many were recent immigrants, who retained strong ties to an ethnic community, and tended to be non-Protestants, such as Catholics or Jews. Both wings of the populist camp supported social reform and shared a distrust of big business, industrialization, and the growth of impersonal corporations that threatened to swallow up the individual.

TWO FILM MELODRAMATISTS: GRIFFITH AND VIDOR

An Agrarian Past

Populism is neither monolithic nor static. It changes its point of view some-what from decade to decade as the demographics of the American landscape change. It spoke, in the 1890s and 1910s, from the perspective of the agrarian majority. But in the 1920s, when the majority of Americans had moved from rural farms to live and work in the cities, populist rhetoric more and more frequently began to address the concerns of the urban working class. In particular, it attempted to deal with the problems posed to middle-class Americans by the shift which took place in American identity as it was slowly forced to confront its new foundation in urban and industrial culture. In the past, American identity had been tied to notions of individual success, which was understood to be directly related to one's character, energy, and enter-prise. In the world of the 1920s postindustrial, mass society, the ability of the individual to realize the American dream was seriously compromised by his or her powerlessness in the face of the growing industrialization and corpora-tization of modern life. This shift can best be illustrated by comparing the different visions of society and of the individual's place within it in two silent film melodramas—Griffith's *The Birth of a Nation* (1915) and King Vidor's *The Crowd* (1928).

Griffith's silent melodramas speak on behalf of nineteenth-century agrari-anism. His films look back to an earlier, more utopian, preindustrial past which was threatened by the forces of modernism. In *A Corner in Wheat* (1909), for example, the "natural" economy of the past is upset by the intervention of a greedy businessman. A farmer grows wheat out of which bread is made to feed the city's poor. But a middleman, in the form of a speculator in the grain market, interferes with this process. The speculator buys up all the wheat, then artificially drives up the price of flour in order to increase his profits, ignoring the plight of the urban poor who can no longer afford to buy a loaf of bread. Griffith's romanticized portrait of the farmer is heightened by the latter's heroic refusal to admit defeat at the hands of the stock manipulator. The film ends with the farmer's replanting of his field, but it has become clear by now that his success rests not on his own efforts but in the hands of forces beyond his control.

A Corner in Wheat deals with recent events—with the 1897–1898 attempt by a speculator to corner the wheat market on the Chicago Board of Trade (which provided, in turn, the basis for Frank Norris' novel *The Pit*, on which the Griffith film was partially based). *The Birth of a Nation* was made to celebrate the fiftieth anniversary of the end of the Civil War and was thus set in the much earlier era of the war itself (1861–1865) and Reconstruction (1865–1877). The world of the antebellum South, which provides the primary perspective from which Griffith views events, emerges as a paradise lost. In both the film and in popular mythology, the prewar agrarian South marks the final flower-ing of an old world (aristocratic) pastoral ideal before it falls victim to an unwanted industrialization that is externally imposed upon it by the North.

History as Melodrama: *The Birth of a Nation*

The Birth of a Nation begins with an idyllic portrait of the southern Cameron family, whose happiness and tranquility is disturbed by the war. Their attempts to restore this paradise lost after the war are thwarted by abolitionist politicians, northern carpetbaggers, mulattoes, and "renegade" blacks. Inspired by the traditions of his Anglo-Saxon (Scottish) heritage, Ben Cameron forms a modern-day clan—the Ku Klux Klan—in order to avenge the death of his sister and to protect southern womanhood from feared black rapists. After defeating the black militia and putting an end to black rule, the Klan restores a utopian social order. The film ends with a millennial vision in which Christ returns to Earth, puts an end to war, and presides over a "heavenly throng" who celebrate the regeneration of mankind and the return to the ultimate populist paradise—a latter-day Garden of Eden.

 The Birth of a Nation renders American history as melodrama. The Civil War takes the form of a family melodrama with the role of the villain(s) played by northern abolitionists, mulattoes, and blacks. The chief villain, however, proves to be the black race. For Griffith, the issue of slavery, introduced in the film's first shot of a slave market, leads to the outbreak of the war which then turns brother against brother. The northern Stonemans and the southern Camerons, once friends, are suddenly made unwilling enemies. The effects of

Ben Cameron (Henry Walthall, right) refuses to shake hands with the mulatto Lieutenant Governor, Silas Lynch (George Seigmann) in *The Birth of a Nation* (1915).

Author's collection

the war are presented in melodramatic terms as well. For no apparent reason, northern and southern families are forced to sacrifice their sons to the war effort—one Stoneman boy and two Camerons die in battle.

Given Griffith's racist scenario, the resolution of the conflict between North and South and the restitution of unity can only come through the reunification of the white race in the face of a common enemy—the black race. Near the conclusion of the film, the elder Camerons, their daughter, and the surviving Stoneman son take refuge from the black militia in the shack of two former Union veterans. An intertitle explains the obvious symbolism of the moment: "The former enemies of North and South are united again in common defence of their Aryan birthright."

The film's ultimate hero becomes the Ku Klux Klan, which rides to the rescue of the besieged whites. The film's ultimate solution becomes the transportation of blacks back to Africa. This action restores the purely white world which was disrupted at the beginning of the film when, as an intertitle claims, "the bringing of the African to America planted the first seed of disunion." Indeed, historians note that the film originally ended with what Griffith described as "Lincoln's solution"—the deportation of blacks to Africa. This scene was apparently later cut from the final film. Griffith's melodramatic excess led to his distortion of historical reality. His depiction of blacks and his ending of the film are pure fantasy—the product of a melodramatic imagination that had put itself at the service of a racist agenda. The phenomenal success of the film suggests that it somehow spoke to the needs of a troubled 1910s and 1920s America for a return to a simpler past and to a simplified notion of American identity based on racial purity. It also reveals the negative aspects of the populist mythology—its racism, its anti-intellectualism, its paranoia, its religious fundamentalism.

Everyman/No-Man: *The Crowd*

The Crowd deals with a more contemporary historical reality—the transformation of 1920s America into an urbanized mass society. It follows its hero, John Sims (James Murray), from his birth in small-town America in 1900 to New York City, where he moves to live and work in the 1920s. The film shows his subsequent marriage, the birth of his children, and his raising of a family, and concludes more or less in the present (1928).

In the world of *The Birth of a Nation*, it is possible for its hero not only to control events around him but even to play a role in the shaping of history. Ben Cameron's life is spared by the intervention of Abraham Lincoln, "the Great Heart," who pardons him when he is falsely charged with treason. And Cameron is, after all, the (fictionalized) founder of a powerful organization, the Ku Klux Klan. He possesses "agency," that is, he could do things that had consequence for others. The melodramatic action of *The Crowd* concerns the struggles of a character who has little or no control over his own destiny, much less that of the nation. John battles within a conformist culture to

Courtesy of M-G-M

Everyman John Sims (James Murray) enjoys a day at the beach with his wife (Eleanor Boardman) and children in *The Crowd* (1928).

establish a unique identity, which is constantly threatened by the mundane realities of day-to-day existence. He tries to assert his own unique identity amidst the drudgery of work in a large insurance office, the monotony of marriage, and the despair of failure as an employee, husband, and father.

Vidor's hero is an everyman—a man in and of the crowd. But as an everyman, he is also no-man—a nobody whose identity, goals, and desires are given to him by others rather than stemming from his own, inner needs. As a child, John is driven by his father's ambitions for him. When he and his boyhood friends tell each other what they want to be when they grow up, John proudly boasts, "My dad says I'm gonna be somebody big." Working for a large insurance company in New York, John becomes one of the crowd, behaving like everyone else. On a double date with his friend Bert and two girls, John watches Bert kiss his girl, then John kisses his date, Mary. On the subway ride home, John looks at a furniture ad which says "You furnish the girl; we'll furnish the home." He then turns to Mary, whom he had just met that night, and proposes to her.

Vidor presents John as the product of a world that lacks the romantic heroism of Ben Cameron's universe. In John's world, individual success is not tied to one's character, energy, or enterprise. Agency, the ability to shape one's own fate, is only an illusion. John is the product of the age of advertising; commercials shape John's desires and he becomes the perfect consumer in a mass society that is itself driven by the needs of a new, twentieth-century institution—mass consumption. In his spare time, John even writes copy for advertisements. Indeed, he achieves the greatest success of his life when he wins $500 for coming up with the catchy phrase: "Sleight O' Hand—The Magic Cleaner."

John's great fortune, however, is as unpredictable and uncontrollable as his misfortune, which mounts toward the end of the film. John does not distinguish himself from the crowd at work, remaining a mere clerk while his friend Bert is promoted. Later, one of his children dies in a traffic accident, he loses his job, his wife threatens to leave him, and he contemplates suicide. Through no fault of his own, John has not only failed to become "somebody big" but he has lost his identity—along with his job, his wife, and his family, who provided the only tangible signs of that identity for him. John's problems lie, in part, in his belief in the nineteenth-century notions of individualism and agency which Griffith celebrates in *Birth of a Nation* and which John's father had bequeathed to him upon his birth. Vidor's film suggests that this ideology, or system of beliefs, no longer had any connection to contemporary social and economic reality. The film's "hero" is forced to recognize his own relative powerlessness as an individual and come to terms with his new status as one of the crowd. At the very end of the film, John recovers his identity as father, husband, and workingman and rejoins the crowd from which he had earlier tried to remove himself. He discovers that a crucial aspect of his identity depends upon his identification with the crowd—that he cannot exist apart from, but must be a part of, mass society.

ESCAPE AND TRANSCENDENCE

Home as "Seventh Heaven"

In *Birth of Nation*, Griffith implicitly rejects the modern in favor of a mythic past. In *The Crowd*, Vidor demonstrates the need for the creation of a new model for understanding the relation of the individual to the world of 1920s America. In general, the film melodrama coveys either open hostility or profound ambivalence toward modern times. In films such as Frank Borzage's Academy Award winning *Seventh Heaven* (1927), it becomes something to transcend. Borzage's hero and heroine defy the original sins of contemporary mass society—despair and cynicism. They overcome the anonymity and heartlessness of the city and create a refuge or "seventh heaven" within it. ["Seventh heaven" refers to their apartment, which is on the seventh (and top) floor of an apartment house in Paris, and thus closer to the heavens than the streets below where they are first introduced.]

They are subsequently separated by the world's first truly modern war—World War I. Both remain steadfastly loyal to one another, communicating through a quasi-spiritual ceremony they perform every day at 11 A.M.. Even after the film's hero, Chico (Charles Farrell), dies in combat, the heroine,

Courtesy of 20th Century-Fox

Diane (Janet Gaynor) and Chico (Charles Farrell) find a refuge from the outside world in their "seventh heaven" in *Seventh Heaven* (1927).

Diane (Janet Gaynor) continues to be faithful to him, refusing a wealthy suitor. At the end of the film, Chico miraculously returns from the dead, and Diane, somehow sensing that he is still alive, rushes to him. The film's fairy-tale ending firmly plants it within the world of melodramatic wish fulfillment, which can overcome all the obstacles that mundane, twentieth-century life places in the paths of young lovers.

The "seventh heaven" that the lovers create for themselves serves as a secular Garden of Eden amidst the turmoil of modern times. It is an idealized space that virtually every melodrama—before and since—has sought to establish and protect from the outside world. The threats to this "domestic" space come, more often than not, from forces that are produced, in large part, by an increasingly impersonal and hostile, urban mass society. In *A Man's Castle* (1933), a small wooden shack in a New York City "Hooverville," which has been built by those made homeless by the Great Depression, serves as a "safety zone" against economic despair. In *Since You Went Away* (1944), the home is described as the "fortress of the American family" and comes to symbolize the spirit of the home-front effort in World War II.

More recently, the home functions as a space that men have also begun to defend against urban corruption, crime, and violence. In *Fatal Attraction* (1987) Glenn Close repeatedly violates the space of the family as she attempts to win Michael Douglas away from his wife and child. Douglas first tries to prevent his family from learning of his affair with Close, then struggles to defend them against her increasingly violent attacks on the home (though it is only with the aid of his wife, played by Anne Archer, that he finally succeeds in warding off his demented stalker). And in *Ghost* (1990), Patrick Swayze comes back from the dead to protect his girlfriend, played by Demi Moore, from harm. At the end of the film, he quite literally defends the space of the couple, grappling with the film's treacherous villain who has invaded their newly renovated loft. The loft remains "their" space and clearly serves as a "seventh heaven" for the 1990s.

The Lure of the City: *Sunrise*

In F. W. Murnau's *Sunrise* (1927), a rural family (husband, wife, and child) is threatened by a woman, who has journeyed from the city to the country and (apparently) seduced the husband. During a late-night rendezvous in the swamp with the man, she entices him with images of life in the city and then tries to encourage him to murder his wife, sell his farm, and come back with her to the city. This woman, a prototype for the Glenn Close character in *Fatal Attraction*, plays the role of villain, as does the city itself, which seems to be the source of her destructive power. She is also a product of the times—she is a "new woman." She has a short, mannish haircut; she smokes; she dresses like a "flapper"; she is sexually liberated; and she assumes an aggressive role in her relationships with men. The man's young wife, on the other hand, looks (although pretty) like an old-fashioned, nineteenth-century "old woman," in other words, like a European hausfrau. She wears a peasant-style dress, and her hair, unlike that of the woman from the city, is long and blonde. Crosscutting between her together with her child and the woman from the city embracing her husband emphasizes their status as moral opposites. The wife is associated with home and family; the woman from the city with the swamp and adultery.

However, the simple moral opposition between nature and culture, or the country and the city, is more complex than it initially appears. The woman from the city is associated with the country—in particular, with the swamp. The regeneration of the marriage between the husband and the wife takes place in the city, where they symbolically renew their marriage vows (at the marriage of another couple), formalize their relationship with a posed photograph, and celebrate their reunion with a peasant dance, which they perform before an audience of city dwellers.

Though Murnau's film seems to present a negative view of urbanization and industrialization, it undercuts its critique of the city with a suggestion that the experiences of its rural characters within it provide a valuable perspective on their prior relationship that ultimately restores them to one another. Yet, the final reconciliation of the couple takes place in the country, in the domestic space of their bedroom, as the woman from the city returns to the city. In this way, *Sunrise* captures the ambivalence of an America that was negotiating a dramatic change in its identity from an agrarian to an urban base. The dramatic action of the film suggests that the innately "natural"

Courtesy of 20th Century-Fox

The woman from the city (Margaret Livingston) seduces the husband (George O'Brien) in the swamp in *Sunrise* (1927).

values of the country can be renewed by contact with the city—that is, that the threats of an urbanized, industrialized America can be contained. Modernity will not destroy the values that inform American identity, but will test and prove their strength, guaranteeing the continuity of the experience of America as it evolved from an agrarian to an industrial society.

SOUND AND MELODRAMA

The coming of sound, which took place between 1926 and 1929, transformed the melodrama from *the* format or mode in which the majority of all films were made into one genre among many. Sound brought about changes in acting style, making it no longer necessary (or even desirable) to say everything with the body instead of the voice. In his first sound film, *Abraham Lincoln* (1930), Griffith attempted to stylize dialogue in order to suit it to the emotionalized atmosphere of the melodrama, much as he had earlier stylized his actors' performances. He hired the Pulitzer Prize winning poet, Stephen Vincent Benét to write the script and to turn the dialogue into poeticized speech. But Griffith's melodramatization of dialogue remains an isolated experiment in an industry that regarded sound as a crucial step forward in the medium's quest for greater and greater realism. In this context, that which was "melodramatic" was looked upon as old-fashioned or, because of its overt interest in the world of emotion, as somehow appropriate only for "women's pictures." Formerly a universal cinematic "language," melodramatic style was suddenly demoted to an inferior dialect within a new, more "realistic" system of communication and signification.

Melodramas thrived during the sound era. Several of these "women's pictures," such as *Gone With the Wind* (1939) and *Rebecca* (1940), not only appealed to a general audience but also won Academy Awards, providing added prestige for the genre. The melodrama and the melodramatic continued to satisfy basic needs within audiences for certain kinds of characters, situations, and stories. But the sound melodrama necessarily distinguished itself from the silent melodrama, which was so closely identified with the silent film itself. The tradition of the theatrical melodrama, which began in France in the 1770s, dominated the nineteenth-century American stage, and provided an expressive language for early film directors like Griffith, ended with the coming of sound. Although the theatrical melodrama died, its power to address human feelings lives on in the "melodramatic," in an emotionalized way of telling stories that continues to move audiences, as the unrivalled success of *E.T.* at the box office demonstrates.

SELECT FILMOGRAPHY

A Corner in Wheat (1909)
A Drunkard's Reformation (1909)
The Birth of a Nation (1915)
Intolerance (1916)
Broken Blossoms (1919)
True Heart Susie (1919)
Way Down East (1920)
Orphans of the Storm (1922)
The Big Parade (1925)
Seventh Heaven (1927)

Sunrise (1927)
The Crowd (1928)
A Man's Castle (1933)
Gone With the Wind (1939)
Since You Went Away (1944)
Mildred Pierce (1945)
Daisy Kenyon (1947)
E.T.: The Extra-Terrestrial (1982)
Terms of Endearment (1983)
Home Alone (1990)

SELECT BIBLIOGRAPHY

Brooks, Peter. *The Melodramatic Imagination: Balzac, Henry James, Melodrama, and the Mode of Excess.* New Haven: Yale University Press, 1976.

Gerould, Daniel C. *American Melodrama.* New York: Performing Arts Journal Publications, 1983.

Gledhill, Christine, ed. *Home Is Where the Heart Is: Studies in Melodrama and the Woman's Film.* London: BFI Publishing, 1987.

Grimsted, David. "Melodrama as Echo of the Historically Voiceless," in Tamara K. Hareven, ed., *Anonymous Explorations in Nineteenth Century Social History.* Englewood Cliffs, NJ: Prentice-Hall, 1971.

Landy, Marcia. *Imitations of Life: A Reader on Film and Television Melodrama.* Detroit: Wayne State University Press, 1991.

Lang, Robert. *American Film Melodrama: Griffith, Vidor, Minnelli.* Princeton: Princeton University Press, 1989.

May, Lary. *Screening Out the Past: The Birth of Mass Culture and the Motion Picture Industry.* Chicago: University of Chicago Press, 1983.

McKenna, George, ed. *American Populism.* New York: Putnam, 1974.

Williams, Alan. "Historical and Theoretical Issues in the Coming of Recorded Sound to the Cinema," in Rick Altman, ed., *Sound Theory/Sound Practice.* New York: Routledge, 1992.

AMERICAN COMEDY

LAUGHTER AND CULTURE

Comedy, Repression, and Cultural Dreamwork

For Sigmund Freud, jokes function, on an individual level, as a form of liberation; they provide those who laugh at them with a necessary, therapeutic release from the serious worries and cares that oppress the average human being. As a mass form, the genre of comedy works to release that which society as a whole tries to hold in check. In short, whatever a society represses frequently returns in the form of comedy to taunt it. This often occurs quite literally in the figure of the Shakespearean-like fool who tells a truth that others dare not utter. Only in a comedy does one seriously entertain the idea of throwing mama from the train or of leaving small children home alone. Yet ambivalent feelings about family clearly lie beneath the surface of the modern American psyche, waiting to find expression in the form of comedy.

To study film comedy, then, is in part to look at the dreamwork of a culture's collective unconscious, to put it "on the couch," and to make it speak of the forces that led to its production. Thus if American film comedy plays with sexual, racial, ethnic, and class differences, it is because our culture as a whole denies their existence in the supposedly egalitarian democracy of contemporary America. And, because comedy is never taken seriously, American film comedy can often deal with these issues more openly than can other, more "official" genres, such as the historical film or the Western.

Silent comedy, for example, abounds in sight gags which play on racial and ethnic differences and give expression to a profound racism that crisscrosses the social structure. In *Seven Chances* (1925), Buster Keaton desperately searches for a woman to marry (before 7 o'clock on his 27th birthday) in order to inherit $7 million. He spots several likely prospects on the street but does a double take and hurries away when one of his would-be brides turns out to be black and another Jewish.

The Marx Brothers repeatedly make fun of Italian immigrants through the character of Chico, whose heavy accent and broken English become the source for extensive wordplay with Groucho; and, in *Duck Soup* (1933), they parody black musical and singing style, turning a traditional Negro spiritual "All God's Chillun" into a prowar production number entitled "All God's Chillun Got Guns." Wearing (as the script indicates) "watermelon grins" and "swaying from side to side," they sing: "They got guns,/We got guns,/All God's chillun got guns./We gonna walk all o'er the battlefield/'Cause all God's chillun got guns." For the Marx Brothers, nothing is sacred.

Even in more recent times, ethnic comedy, which has all but disappeared from the big screen, continues to thrive on television. Archie Bunker's bigotry becomes a comic centerpiece of "All in the Family" (ca. 1971), in which the central character regularly refers to Jews as "hebes," Hispanics as "spics," blacks as "coons," and Italians as "dagoes." Archie's controversial racism gets laughs not only from those who laugh with him but also from those who laugh at him. During the mid-1970s, "Saturday Night Live" featured Czechoslovakian immigrants (Steve Martin's and Dan Ackroyd's "Two Wild and Crazy Guys") and the Japanese (John Belushi's "Samurai Warrior") as targets for running gags. "In Living Color" takes deliberate tastelessness to a new level, transforming the "unconscious" racism of the past into a "conscious" racism. Comic sketches on this show explore the nooks and crannies of political incorrectness, making fun of blacks, whites, gays, and other minorities with equal abandon. As with "All in the Family," the focus of the humor here lies on exposing whatever hidden prejudice the audience might have, recasting it in a somewhat exaggerated form, and getting viewers to laugh at it.

From Racism to Social Integration

At the same time that it exploits our ethnic and racial diversity, American comedy deals with the processes by which differences are bridged and a (more or less) unified American society is constructed. As Northrop Frye suggests, "The theme of the comic is the integration of society, which usually takes the form of incorporating a central character into it." The theme of the comic includes not only the more general themes of the creation of couples through marriage (*Coming to America*, 1988) and of communities through the absorption of individuals into larger groups (*3 Men and a Baby*, 1987), but also the more uniquely American theme of the immigrant experience, recounted in film comedies ranging from Charles Chaplin's *The Immigrant* (1917), to Robin Williams' and Paul Mazursky's *Moscow on the Hudson* (1984), and Peter Weir's *Green Card* (1990).

Immigrants: Chaplin to Depardieu

The richness of the theme of the immigrant experience emerges in Chaplin, whose "Tramp" character embodies an essential ambivalence toward society. He seeks its approval and acceptance yet repeatedly finds himself unable to conform to its demands. Thus, Chaplin comedies often play against the genre's expectations, striking a note of pathos, which qualifies the comic thrust of the films as a whole. In films such as *The Circus* (1928) and *Modern Times* (1936), the Tramp reconciles himself to his outsider status and trudges off into the sunset (or sunrise) in search of a more utopian social system. Much of Chaplin's comedy stems from the tension that exists between his conscious efforts to fit in and win the acceptance of others and his inherent resistance to authority and refusal to conform socially.

By the same token, much of the humor in *Moscow on the Hudson* and *Green Card* derives from the attempts of their immigrant heroes to adapt themselves to a seemingly alien American culture. In *Hudson*, Robin Williams' odyssey in

In Paul Mazursky's *Moscow on the Hudson* (1984), a Soviet defector played by Robin Williams interacts with his new neighbors in New York City, demonstrating his ability to adapt to American culture.

search of what it means to be an American takes him from Bloomingdale's to Harlem and then to the Lower East Side in a New York City that is peopled, for the most part, by working-class blacks and Hispanics and by recent immigrants like himself. He does not so much *enter* a community as discover that he is already a part of it.

In *Green Card*, Gerard Depardieu encounters a somewhat different American culture, which consists not of lower-class ethnic types but of middle- and upper-middle-class white-collar professionals, personified in part by the woman (Andie MacDowell) whom he marries in order to secure American citizenship. Depardieu does not quite fit into the artificial and pretentious world of New York yuppies that surrounds MacDowell and from which he attempts to "rescue" her. The couple establish a separate world for themselves—a kind of greenhouse Garden of Eden which they alone inhabit. As they manufacture a past romantic history to fool the naturalization and immigration authorities, their created fiction becomes reality; their phony marriage of convenience gives way to a relationship that gradually becomes more and more intimate and caring. The film's attack on phoniness and its celebration of authentic feeling moves it, however, toward Chaplinesque pathos rather than comic triumph: Depardieu's rediscovered integrity forces

him to abandon his initial, self-centered goal of getting citizenship by whatever means possible. Under questioning, he finally confesses to the authorities the truth about his marriage to MacDowell, a gesture that ironically seals
the internal honesty of their relationship while superficially severing it at the
same time. Though Depardieu literally loses both his green card and his girl,
he wins them both back in a figurative sense, proving his worthiness, not
only as a potential citizen, but also as an object of the heroine's romantic
desire.

Integration and the Regeneration of Society

Though only a handful of American comedies deal explicitly with the immigrant experience, that experience can be seen as displaced and reworked in
hundreds of other comedies in which an individual struggles to enter society.
Through the theme of comic integration, American screen comedies demonstrate the flexibility of our democratic social structure through its ability to
absorb new members and integrate them into a new social order, whose unity
and diversity exceeds that of the old order. The typical resolution of a film
comedy will thus involve a marriage or other ritual celebration of the formation of a new community out of the old. In this way, it suggests a regeneration
of the dying world that produced the disorder with which the comedy
typically begins.

It Happened One Night (1934), for example, begins with a "bad" marriage
between an heiress (Claudette Colbert) and a playboy-socialite. The film then
spends the next 90 minutes explaining to both the heiress and the audience
exactly why this marriage is wrong. It ends with the disruption of another
false marriage—the public ceremony in which the heiress and the socialite are
scheduled to renew their initial vows. And it then celebrates the "right"
marriage: having fled the ceremony, Colbert returns to the middle-class
newspaper reporter (Clark Gable), with whom she is really in love, and then
marries him (after a hasty annulment of the initial, "wrong" marriage). This
final marriage is "right" not only because Colbert and Gable really love one
another but also because it heals the divisions within society, establishing a
new order through the symbolic marriage of representatives of different social
classes. *Splash* (1984) provides a more recent reworking of this formula. It sets
up an interspecies love story between a man (Tom Hanks) and a mermaid
(Daryl Hannah) and follows it to its improbable conclusion. At the end,
Hanks swims off with Hannah to a new life in an underwater utopia, symbolized by the idealized city beneath the sea that appears during the end credits.

Reforming the Workplace

The theme of integration often involves the outsiders' transformation of the
very social system which they enter and regenerate from within. *9 to 5* (1980)
celebrates the efforts of three secretaries, played by Jane Fonda, Lily Tomlin,
and Dolly Parton, to reclaim their office from the male-chauvinist tyranny of
their corrupt boss (Dabney Coleman), and establish a new, more benign order
in place of the old. In *Working Girl* (1988), the traditional office hierarchy (the

status quo) is upset when a lower-class secretary, Tess (Melanie Griffith), puts together a big deal without the knowledge of her upper-middle-class boss (Sigourney Weaver). Working outside the prescribed system, Tess pools her efforts with those of an upper-middle-class male executive from another company (Harrison Ford). Together they create an ideal business team, which functions more efficiently and effectively than any pairing within the existing system. This new order, which democratically combines members of different classes, ultimately triumphs over the old, more hierarchic, stratified system. Thus, the film celebrates the comic virtues of independence, innovation, and a willingness to break the rules.

Rites of Passage: Boys to Men

The comic aspects of the integration of the individual into society find perhaps their most improbable dramatization in *Big* (1988) in which a 12-year-old boy grows "big" overnight, becoming a 30-year-old man (Tom Hanks). Hanks flees to New York in search of an antidote to his magical growth, lands a job as an executive in a toy company, and gets his own apartment and a girl (Elizabeth Perkins). As an adult, he enjoys unqualified success, emerging as the "boy wonder" of his firm and the answer to his girlfriend's dreams for a more sensitive man to love. The comedy hinges upon the efforts of Hanks (who remains a kid both in mind and spirit) to pass for and be accepted as an adult.

At the same time, it plays with his dual identity as boy and man. Though outwardly successful, Hanks discovers that he is unable (and unwilling) to give up his childhood and become an instant adult. Reversing his earlier, childish wish to become big, he learns to "grow up"—but in order to do so, he has to become a child again. At the end of the film, he gives up the pleasures and pains of being an adult. He sacrifices the rewards he has earned in the adult world—his career and his girlfriend—to come back to his own world, reverting to his original size and age and returning to his mother. Thus *Big* features a double integration, focusing primarily upon Hanks' trials and tribulations in becoming an adult but framing this within the anxieties surrounding the character's struggles with adolescence at the beginning and ending of the film.

Comic Disintegration and Disorder

Men to Boys: The Marx Brothers

Comedy remains risky business in more ways than one might imagine. On the most basic level, a film's gags and jokes might not always work, leaving the screenwriter or comedian in an embarrassing limbo. But comedy is even more dangerous when it does work. Comedy dares to disrupt the orderly processes of society by unleashing the forces of chaos and disorder. These, in turn, often get out of control. The Marx Brothers, for example, assault the very foundations of bourgeois society, mocking its repressive institutions.

Courtesy of Paramount

Groucho Marx turns the affairs of government into a song and dance act in Leo McCarey's 1933 classic *Duck Soup*.

Groucho becomes president of a college in *Horse Feathers* (1932) and levels its time-honored traditions, cutting them down to the stuff of comedy. As the president of a small European country in *Duck Soup*, Groucho literally reduces the operations of government to child's play (a game of jacks) and plunges the nation into war over an insult that never occurred. Once the genius of the Marx Brothers is uncorked, there is no putting it (or them) back into the bottle again; the brothers follow absurdist logic to its "logical" conclusion. Thus Harpo, after parodying the midnight ride of Paul Revere in *Duck Soup*, winds up in bed with his horse, while the woman he has been pursuing in earlier sequences sleeps alone on a nearby cot. The Marx Brothers' anarchic brand of humor has no limits, pushing their best films, like *Duck Soup*, to the point of nihilistic self-destruction.

The Release of the Repressed: *Bringing Up Baby*
Few comedies reach the riotous peaks hit by those of the Marx Brothers. More often than not, American comedy regulates and gives order to the forces of chaos. If the zany hero and heroine, played by Cary Grant and Katharine Hepburn, in *Bringing Up Baby* (1938) unleash a wild, man-eating leopard on the quiet Connecticut countryside, you can be sure that they will somehow get it back into its cage (or convenient jail cell) before the film is over.

Ironically, in order for comedy to achieve its goal of social cohesion, integration, and regeneration, it must first unleash the leopard. That is, comedy must acknowledge the elements of disorder or difference at work in the society it seeks to depict. Once exposed, these elements must then be either erased by dissolving them into a larger unity or subsumed within an all-encompassing system of checks and balances that neutralize them or, at the very least, hold them in place.

Bringing Up Baby, for example, is *about* attempts to control the irrational or disruptive elements of nature. Its hero, David (Grant), is a paleozoologist who is first seen assembling a dinosaur in a museum. His excessive control over "nature," seen in the form of deal animals, fossils, and bones, results in his own sexual repression. His command over nature is merely an illusion. It is produced more by nature's passivity (the dinosaur is, after, all, only the skeleton of a dead animal) than by his power. When he steps outside and encounters the living forces of nature, that is, Susan (Hepburn), Baby (a tame leopard), George (a dog), and the aforementioned wild leopard, his artificial control evaporates.

Hepburn's aggressive attempts to get Grant to notice her involve a harmonic collaboration with nature—she is assisted by Baby and George (who, following his doglike instincts, steals and buries a precious dinosaur bone). Their adventures together result in bringing Grant back to life, as it were, and reviving those elements of nature within him that have become fossilized and dead. Nature, however, can be *too* natural. Baby and George, who are tame animals, represent the "proper" mixture of elements, balancing the forces of nature with those of civilization. The wild leopard represents nature in excess—it embodies the unruly aspects of nature that must be brought under control before the natural order of things can be restored. *Baby*, unlike a Marx Brothers comedy, carefully charts a course between dangerous extremes, never quite losing control of the forces of disturbance with which it plays. The wild leopard ends up back in a cage.

Containing Chaos

Capitalism Works: *Trading Places*

As *Baby* suggests, comedy functions as a kind of cultural safety valve; it lets off steam that would otherwise build up and explode, destroying the entire system. It is comedy's job to impose order on the disorderly and to contain or harness the explosive elements that it awakens and that give it its power. Many comedies begin, for example, with a lack or deficiency that suggests the failure of society to resolve problems or differences. Poverty, for example, emerges as an implicit critique of society's ability to provide adequately for all of its citizens. Comedy liquidates that lack or solves that problem.

In *Trading Places* (1983), poverty and class differences vanish with the wave of a magic wand. In order to settle a bet about the various roles that environment and heredity play in the development of a person's character and skills, Mortimer and Randolph Duke, two wealthy commodity brokers played by

Courtesy of Paramount

In John Landis' *Trading Places* (1983), commodities broker Don Ameche becomes the target of street con man Eddie Murphy. In a classical comedy turnabout, Ameche then hires Murphy to run his company.

Don Ameche and Ralph Bellamy, take a poor, black con man named Billy Ray Valentine (Eddie Murphy) in off the street and elevate him to an executive position in their firm. At the same time, they not only fire but also throw in jail the white executive, Winthorp (Dan Ackroyd), whose position in the firm he takes.

With his reputation ruined, his bank account frozen, and his credit cards confiscated, Winthorp is forced into a life of poverty, ill-health, and crime. The Dukes' initial disruption of the original status quo, which results in a reversal of fortunes, is not, of course, designed to eliminate poverty; indeed, the terms of their wager demand not only that Murphy take Ackroyd's place but that Ackroyd also take Murphy's.

However, the Dukes' scheme does inadvertently expose the source of poverty, which is seen to stem neither from environmental nor hereditary factors but rather from the whimsical nature of capitalism. Poverty emerges as the direct result of the Dukes' selfishness and comes from their willful abuse of their economic power and class privilege. Yet this potentially radical critique of capitalism gets deflected in Murphy's and Ackroyd's rush to get even with their meddlesome tormentors. Once impoverished, but now firmly entrenched (or so it seems by their dress and manner) in the upper-class, cut-throat, capitalist world of the Dukes, Murphy and Ackroyd defeat their former bosses on their own field of battle—the commodities exchange.

Their victory over the Dukes suggests that the system works; they, along with the film's other chief "lackeys" of capitalism—including a butler (Denholm Elliot) and a hooker (Jamie Lee Curtis)—become fabulously wealthy, at the expense of the now-impoverished Dukes. Basking in the sun on the beach of a tropic island, the film's victors enjoy the spoils of capitalism. At the same time, poverty, in the form of the Dukes, is banished from the screen, along with the class conflicts and economic extremes that characterize the urban jungle in which the film is earlier set.

Reforming Prostitution: *Pretty Woman*

In a similar way, *Pretty Woman* (1990) builds its comedy on potentially explosive material which it then, in turn, defuses by means of a tried-and-true, conventional comic resolution. The dynamite lies just beneath the surface of a supposed Cinderella-like plot line. Having come to Los Angeles for a week of business meetings, a high-powered executive (Richard Gere) hires a local prostitute (Julia Roberts) to act as his female companion, paying her several thousand dollars merely to escort him to a number of business-related social functions. Gere's business arrangement with Roberts tacitly acknowledges what many feminists insist is the actual status of women in a male-dominated society. They are commodities to be bought and sold—paid prostitutes whose beauty and talent primarily function within this system to enhance the stature of the men who possess them.

When Gere actually begins to fall in love with Roberts, the commercially exploitative nature of their initial relationship gradually disappears, replaced by a more "genuine" feeling. By falling in love with her and asking her to marry him, Gere snuffs the fuse on the dynamite. He redeems their relationship from the sordid realm of crass commercialism and rewrites its scandalous origins in the more proper language of middle-class morality. The disturbing disclosure of the "real" basis of sexual relations in contemporary society becomes buried beneath the film's happy ending, which showers Roberts with good fortune and bathes the audience in good feeling. Romantic fiction replaces the "reality" of class difference and bourgeois morality. At the end of the film, Gere climbs up to Roberts' balcony and proposes to her, explaining that "after all, this is Hollywood." In other words, although comedies tend to reveal cultural contradictions more clearly than do other genres, they also take great pains to resolve them, thereby undermining their status as radical works.

Comedy, Class, and Democracy

American film comedy, like comedy in general, is the genre of the people. In Latin, it would be called *vulgus*, i.e., vulgar, signifying that it belongs to the crowd. In his book on realism and representation, *Mimesis*, Erich Auerbach distinguishes ancient tragedy, which concerns the affairs of nobles and the fate of kingdoms, from ancient comedy. Comedy is situated as often in the world of household slaves (as in the plays of Menander and Plautus) as in that of their masters, and, unlike tragedy, it tends to deal with everyday incidents in the lives of the common citizen (as in the plays of Aristophanes).

American film comedy differs from that of other national cinemas. Its vitality depends upon the egalitarian nature of American society (or at least upon the common belief that America has no class system). American comedy not only celebrates the disempowered little guy—Chaplin's Tramp or Steve Martin's *Jerk* (1979)—but it is also the genre par excellence of upward social mobility, as can be seen by the rags-to-riches plot lines of *Trading Places, Pretty Woman,* and other recent films, such as *Brewster's Millions* (1985), *Working Girl* (1988), and *King Ralph* (1991).

The Discreet Charms of the Working Class

A similar populist spirit can be found in comedies in which the wealthy aristocracy is brought low by bad times and forced to join the working class. Depression audiences love it when Claudette Colbert's heiress in *It Happened One Night* learns to live by her wits on the road. When she impersonates a lower-class plumber's daughter in order to escape detectives sent by her father, her upper-class "reserve" suddenly melts away and she actually seems to enjoy the freedom of her new role. Her transformation into a "regular" girl is now complete.

Today's audiences find it amusing to watch stock market whiz kid Dan Ackroyd temporarily lose everything in *Trading Places,* especially when he hits bottom as a drunken Santa Claus who steals food at a company Christmas party. On occasion, bluebloods even willingly go slumming to see how the other half lives. Thus Eddie Murphy's African prince in *Coming to America* learns about life in New York by taking a job as a busboy at McDonald's where he discovers the simple joys and pleasures of the working class (while living on a rather generous allowance supplied by his father).

Celebrating Change

As a genre that is rooted in the popular and the vulgar, American comedy remains profoundly social. Not only do many comedies speak for those who have been disempowered by the social order, but the underlying celebration of *change* in the majority of film comedies presents an implicit threat to the status quo. Change, of course, is a feature of all narratives. Narratives not only possess a structure which implies change—that is, they feature beginnings, middles, and ends—but they regularly begin with some literal change, with a disruption of events or with a disturbance of an equilibrium that is eventually restored.

Not only does comedy undermine the status quo, but it also endorses change as a positive feature of history, unlike tragedy, which conceives of change negatively. But ultimately what is important in comedies is not so much the positive or negative aspects of change as the way in which characters in comedies respond to change. Essentially a subversive form, comedy celebrates change. It applauds flexibility—the ability of characters to adapt themselves to changing circumstances.

A SHORT HISTORY OF AMERICAN SCREEN COMEDY

Silent Comedy

Comic narratives, however, differ both from one another and from period to period in terms of the unique form which that change takes and in terms of the ways in which the films' characters respond to that change. In the 1920s, change takes place on several levels in American screen comedies. On the most superficial level, silent comedy comes of age as a format for feature-length films. Comedies expand in length from two-reel (ca. 18–25 minutes) shorts to feature-length films, running from 45 to 85 minutes in length. The feature-length format transforms the nature of comic narratives, which become more elaborate and complex.

Slapstick

Two-reel comedies, such as those produced by Mack Sennett at Keystone, consist of a series of gags, loosely strung together, that escalate from simple comic misunderstandings to physical roughhousing, such as pratfalls or the throwing of custard pies. This action, in turn, frequently leads to an extended chase sequence, often featuring the Keystone Kops. This brand of broad physical comedy is known as "slapstick," a term that refers to the flat stick clowns use to strike one another in the more physical forms of theatrical pantomime. Slapstick, which is central to the humor of a number of comedians trained in the Sennett tradition, continues to be a staple of many silent feature-length comedies. However, the major comic stars of the 1920s, such as Charles Chaplin, Buster Keaton, and Harold Lloyd, developed the art of slapstick into a form of self-expression, tailoring their comic routines to the unique nature of their screen characters.

In *The Circus* (1928), for example, Chaplin elegantly choreographs his slapstick; in one scene, he rhythmically and repeatedly whacks his antagonist over the head with a billy club under the eyes of the policeman who pursues them both while each pretends to be a mechanical figure in an amusement park attraction. The sequence reveals a quasi-sadistic, yet charmingly child-like, aspect of the Tramp's persona; the little fellow discovers a safe way to strike back at a bully, protected from reprisals by his ingenious manipulation of the codes and conventions that govern other characters' behaviors in certain situations.

Keaton's slapstick similarly becomes an extension of his character. In *Sherlock Jr.* (1924), Keaton uses the time-worn banana peel routine, carefully placing the peel to trip up his rival; the latter refuses to be baited into the trap and it is Keaton himself who ultimately slips on the peel. Much as Chaplin's slapstick is often aimed at others, Keaton's is just as frequently directed at himself.

Lloyd also makes himself the butt of physical humor, serving as a tackling dummy for the college football team in *The Freshman* (1925); but unlike Keaton, who tends to be the unintended target of gags that inadvertently boomerang back on him, Lloyd's comedy has a somewhat masochistic edge to it, complicating the audience's identification with him with a profound uneasiness.

Charles Chaplin

Chaplin's Tramp character is rooted in nineteenth-century values. Based on the archetypal American hobo (as described by Winston Churchill), "he was not so much an outcast from society as a rebel against it. He could not settle down, either in a home or a job. He hated the routine of regular employment and loved the changes and chances of the road. Behind his wanderings was something of the old adventurous urge that sent the covered wagons lumbering across the prairie towards the sunset." His character looks back to the

Charlie gets caught up in the dehumanizing machinery of modern times in *Modern Times* (1936).

Courtesy of United Artists

defiant individualism found in Romanticism, yet retains the somewhat melodramatic, rigid moral outlook of Victorianism. The target of Chaplin's resistance is the modern world. His most memorable comic battles are with machines—whether in the form of a revolving door (*The Cure*, 1917), an escalator (*The Floorwalker*, 1916), or a folding Murphy bed (*One A.M.*, 1916).

In *Modern Times* (1936), Charlie plays a factory worker who is victimized by machines; in one scene he serves as a human guinea pig in an experiment involving a machine designed to feed workers automatically which malfunctions. In another, after working a shift tightening bolts on an automated assembly line, he goes berserk with his wrenches, twisting everything in sight (from his foreman's nose to the buttons on a woman's dress). At the end of the film, Charlie and his girlfriend leave the city, walking off together into the countryside where they hope to find a pastoral paradise.

Buster Keaton

While Chaplin rejects the modern world, Keaton embraces it. More often than not, Keaton's comic costar is a machine. In *The General* (1926), it is a locomotive; in *The Navigator* (1924) and *Steamboat Bill, Jr.* (1928), it is an ocean liner and a steamboat, respectively; in *Sherlock Jr.* (1924), it is a movie projector; and in *The Cameraman* (1928), it is a motion picture newsreel camera. Buster's relationships with machines often prove more harmonious than those with human costars, especially his love interests, whom he can never quite understand as well as he can the workings of his machines. If one of the most characteristic images of Chaplin is that of him caught up in the gears of a huge machine in *Modern Times*, then that of Keaton is of him mastering a machine—as in *Sherlock Jr.*, when he uses the convertible top of his sinking automobile to transform the car into a sailboat.

Relying upon the uniquely American virtues of common sense, ingenuity, and know-how, Buster overcomes whatever human-made or natural obstacles are placed in his path. Unlike Chaplin's homeless Tramp, who resists change and who is forever at odds with modernity, Keaton adroitly adapts himself to the ever-changing rules of the world around him, demonstrating a comic flexibility that enables him to move to the pace of modern times.

While Chaplin's unskilled, working-class character is more often unemployed than not, Keaton plays middle-class types who tend to be gainfully employed and who secure places for themselves within the power structure of contemporary society that are denied to Chaplin. In *Seven Chances*, for example, Keaton belongs to the profession par excellence of the 1920s: he is a stockbroker. Yet whether Keaton is a millionaire (*The Navigator*) or a projectionist in a movie theater (*Sherlock Jr.*), he never seems to become obsessed with his class status. Though he is internally driven to achieve goals (for example, to inherit $7 million in *Seven Chances*), he seems less interested in enjoying the rewards which reaching the goal provide than in simply reaching the goal itself (for example, in getting married by 7 P.M. on his 27th birthday).

Harold Lloyd

Harold Lloyd, like Keaton, plays middle-class (generally white-collar) workers. He is a clerk in *Girl Shy* (1924); a dry goods salesman in *Safety Last* (1923); a shoe salesman in *Feet First* (1930); and an office worker in *Hot Water* (1924) and in *Mad Wednesday* (1947). Lloyd, however, is consumed with middle-class values—with his status within the community, with impressing those around him, with "making it."

As the anxiety-ridden Harold Lamb in *The Freshman* (1925), Lloyd rivets his desires on becoming popular in college, which he attempts to do by spending his money on lavish parties and winning a position on the football team. At the "Freshman Frolic," his loosely-basted-together suit comes undone, leaving him standing in front of his classmates in his shorts. Though he doesn't quite make the football team, he mistakenly believes he has when the coach permits him to work as water boy (and tackling dummy). Exposed as the "college boob," Harold refuses to give up. When his teammates are all injured in the big game, the coach reluctantly puts him in and he miraculously scores a touchdown to win the game.

Lloyd's obsession with success finds a perfect outlet in *Safety Last* in the scaling of a skyscraper, a feat that became identified with Lloyd through his repetition of it in subsequent films. Fearful that his girl will discover that he is a failure, Harold concocts a scheme for making money by staging a publicity stunt for the department store in which he works. He arranges for his friend, a professional "human fly," to attract crowds to the store by climbing the outside of the building. When, at the last minute, his friend is unable to go ahead with the stunt, Harold takes his place. Each story of the building presents him with a different challenge; not only must he scale the building's surface, but, along the way, he is forced to struggle with pigeons, a net, a dog, a mouse, a flagpole, a clock spring, and a weather vane. When he finally reaches the top, Lloyd finds his girlfriend waiting there to reward him for his ambition and courage. The moral of this and other Lloyd stories is clear: by overcoming his own fears and physical limitations, an average guy like Lloyd can prove himself worthy of success, living out the fantasy of upward mobility that preoccupies middle-class Americans of the 1920s.

The 1920s: Three Comic Visions

Chaplin, Keaton, and Lloyd translate into comic terms the social and economic upheavals of 1920s America, in which industrialization, urbanization, and the growth of a new, white-collar middle class transform traditional social customs and behaviors. Chaplin looks back, somewhat nostalgically, to an earlier era of innocence before the idyllic world of the pastoral garden is disturbed by the machines of industry. Keaton delights in the new machine age, using its tools to redefine his relationship with the world around him, which now includes machines as well as nature. Lloyd captures the fear and uncertainty of the changes that take place in the social structure during this period through the uniquely modern metaphor of the skyscraper, which epitomizes the soaring ambitions of the 1920s as well as the economic structure that threatens (as in *The Crowd*) to make anonymous those who work within it. Through his scaling of it, Lloyd demonstrates that this new world could be mastered but only by means of a physiological and psychological ordeal which just a few were capable of withstanding. The machines of industry, which transform modern America and give birth to a new society based on mass production and mass consumption, also give birth to the movies which become the chief entertainment staple which that society consumes. But by the end of the 1920s, the machines of the motion picture industry develop a new technology—sound—which, in turn, changes the nature of screen comedy.

Early Sound Comedy

The Clowns Speak

Although Chaplin, Keaton, and Lloyd continue to make pictures in the sound era, sound permanently alters the nature of film comedy. Realizing that his comic style, which is based on silent pantomime, would not translate easily to the sound film, Chaplin persists in making silent (that is, nontalking) films until 1940. Mishandled by M-G-M during the transition to sound, Keaton's star fell quickly. Within a few years, he was playing supporting roles to Jimmy Durante; by 1934, he had returned to making shorts. Only Lloyd made a successful transition to sound, though his style of comedy remained more visual than verbal.

Sound ushers in a new generation of comedians, many of whom come from the stage. The clown tradition continues to flourish in the persons of W. C. Fields, Stan Laurel and Oliver Hardy (all of whom had appeared in silent films), Mae West, the Marx Brothers, Joe E. Brown, Bert Wheeler and Robert Woolsey, and others. These performers combine slapstick with a unique, somewhat stylized verbal delivery of comic lines, which can be heard most clearly in the exaggerated speech patterns of Fields and West. The Marx Brothers provide perhaps the broadest range of comic speech styles, including not only Groucho's fast-talking urban spiel and Chico's immigrant dialect, but also Harpo's silence. Indeed, Harpo provides a bridge of sorts between the Chaplinesque pantomime of the silent screen and the verbal slapstick perfected by Groucho's and Chico's misuse of language.

Romantic Comedies

Sound draws upon other theatrical traditions as well. Romantic comedies, in which the central dramatic action involves the comic (as opposed to melodramatic) vicissitudes of a heterosexual love affair and which had been a staple of the silent screen, enjoy a new lease on life in films that combine romance with the comedy of manners. These films tend to be set in the sophisticated world of the social aristocracy, deal with the affairs and intrigues between the ladies and gentlemen who are privileged members of this world, and make fun of the rules and conventions according to which they live their lives.

The best examples of this hybrid form are films such as *The Smiling Lieutenant* (1927), *One Hour with You* (1932), and *Trouble in Paradise* (1932), which were directed by Ernst Lubitsch and written by Samson Raphaelson. Hollywood also adapts to musical comedies, such as *Glorifying the American Girl* (1929) and *Whoopee!* (1930), which were originally produced by Florenz Ziegfeld for the Broadway stage. Both of these films provide a format for a different form of humor—personified in the singing comedian with the "banjo eyes," Eddie Cantor.

And, within a few years, Hollywood begins to extend its own comic range, featuring comic performers from radio such as Jack Benny, Bob Hope, Edgar Bergen and Charlie McCarthy, George Burns and Gracie Allen, and others. At around the same time, the career of Will Rogers, the nationally known humorist, who had already established himself in the motion pictures, in radio, and in weekly newspaper columns, reaches new heights when the actor begins to make sound comedies. Thus, Hollywood ransacks a variety of media for comic performers who bring with them the various styles and formats of different comic traditions, adding multiple and varied strains of popular comedy to the expanding field of comic styles that find a common home in 1930s American cinema.

Some of these different comic traditions had intersected in earlier screen comedies; romantic plots and subplots had provided the central dramatic situation for a number of slapstick comedians, such as Keaton and Lloyd, whose films regularly conclude with their winning the heroine's hand. In *The Gold Rush* (1925), Chaplin alternates between slapstick and romantic comedy, but keeps each sexually and geographically separate from the other: slapstick is the province of men, isolated and starving in the cabin in the wilderness. Romantic comedy is reserved for mixed company, taking place in the dance hall or in the cabin in the city. Though the three Marx Brothers steer clear of romantic entanglements, most of their comedies feature romantic subplots, which are built first around Zeppo Marx, and then around singer Allan Jones.

By and large, no matter how many comic styles an individual film incorporates, "low" slapstick routines remain carefully segregated from "high" romantic comedy. Though the hero may throw custard pies in one scene, play comedy of manners in another, and woo the heroine in a third, leading ladies tend to be relegated to the more or less passive status of romantic objects to be won or lost by the hero; they rarely indulge in physical slapstick humor, which was considered unladylike.

Screwball Comedy

But in the 1930s, all this begins to change. "High" and "low" comedy begin to be mixed together with greater and greater disregard for sexual difference. Various strains and styles of comedy find their way into a single hybrid form, which is known as the screwball comedy. The screwball comedy combines "high" comedy, such as romantic comedy and comedy of manners, with "low" slapstick comedy. It does not rely on clowns who look funny, who wear comic costumes, and who possess a recognizable comic persona. Instead, it takes romantic leading men and women, such as Irene Dunne, Katharine Hepburn, John Barrymore, and Cary Grant, who had established themselves in "serious" drama, and plunges them into the madcap world of vulgar slapstick routines.

Indeed, in *Twentieth Century* (1934), Barrymore—the "Great Profile" of the legitimate theater and the silent screen—even picks his nose, while removing putty from it. In *Bringing Up Baby,* Hepburn undergoes indignities previously reserved for the lowest of "low" comedy—she becomes the butt of anal humor. As she angrily stalks off after a minor dispute with Grant in a fancy nightclub, she unknowingly tears her evening dress, losing the rear portion of her skirt and thus exposing her backside, which Grant attempts to cover as best he can with his top hat. Though Hawks handles this sexual vulgarity with characteristic good humor as a bit of good-natured "fun," it was nonetheless a far cry for Hepburn from the propriety of *Little Women* (1933).

Under Restraints: Comedy and the Code

Not every screwball comedy indulges in such overt sexual play; indeed, most of them do not; but the majority of them tend to be covertly about sexual matters. In an essay entitled "Sex Comedy without the Sex," critic Andrew Sarris suggests that the screwball comedy is about the repression of sex, which then becomes the genre's chief subtext. Sarris argues that the genre was produced, in part, by the tightening of restrictions in the Production Code in July 1934.

Changes in the Code took place in response to a campaign by the Catholic Legion of Decency to ensure the "sanctity of the institution of marriage" by banning from the screen depictions of "adultery and illicit sex," "scenes of passion," "seduction or rape," "sex perversion," "white slavery," "miscegenation," "vulgarity," "obscenity," and other acts. This campaign was prompted, in part, by the increasing sexualization of film comedy (and other genres) that took place in the early 1930s; chief target of the censors was, of course, Mae West, as well as Hollywood's original platinum blonde, Jean Harlow. Perhaps the most audacious of the pre-Code comedies is Lubitsch's *Design for Living* (1933) in which both Gary Cooper and Fredric March live out of wedlock with Miriam Hopkins in the bohemiam world of Paris.

When the Code outlawed such sexually illicit relationships, a disconcerting tension was introduced into relationships between the sexes. Men and women still wanted one another, but their desire was denied. Perhaps the best example of what the Code did to the onscreen love life of Hollywood's heroes and heroines can be found in *It Happened One Night.* In this instance, one of the screen's sexiest male performers, Clark Gable, plays a character who seems to have internalized the Code—who censors his own sexual desires. In one particularly romantic, moonlit scene, Gable has just fixed Claudette Colbert a bed of straw on the ground and fetched carrots for her to eat. They talk and almost kiss, but Gable holds back, recalling (perhaps) that she is a married woman.

Courtesy of Columbia

In Frank Capra's Academy Award winning film, *It Happened One Night* (1934), Clark Gable restores old-fashioned morality to the screen, erecting "the walls of Jericho," which serve to keep his desire for Claudette Colbert (and hers for him) in check.

When they share a motel room for the night, it is Gable who erects a curtain (which he calls "the walls of Jericho") that separates their beds. Capra underscores the sexual significance of "the walls of Jericho" by showing them undressing on either side. The walls not only satisfy the Code, but they also come to symbolize the moral barrier to the satisfaction of their desires; Gable's refusal to "topple" them until the last scene, when the couple are (finally) legally man and wife, demonstrates his own sexual restraint and sets up a tension that can only be resolved by the consummation of their relationship, which, in accordance with the codes of comic modesty, takes place offscreen.

Since the Code forbids its onscreen representation, sexuality is driven underground. In many screwball comedies it resurfaces in the form of physical slapstick. In *Holiday* (1938), Cary Grant's handsprings and backflips become a coded expression of his sexual liberation. In *Twentieth Century* and *His Girl Friday* (1940), the heroine's kicking of the hero serves as a sign of sexual intimacy, which 1930s audiences learned to read as clearly as they had the cutaway from the lovers' kiss to the outside of the closed bedroom door, or to the crisscrossed logs burning in a fireplace, or to the familiar waterfall.

But, in screwball comedy, the cutaway which symbolizes the consummation of a romantic relationship virtually never takes place. Lovers remain in an uncomfortable limbo, which best translates itself into a kind of tension or conflict, as if the characters themselves are somehow aware that, because of the Code, any final union between them will be perpetually frustrated. In *Bringing Up Baby*, a psychiatrist explains that "the love impulse in man frequently reveals itself in terms of conflict."

Screwball Slapstick

Sexual desire in the screwball comedy follows a similarly Freudian path, revealing itself in terms not only of conflict but of combat. As Ed Sikov has observed, lovers love inflicting pain upon one another: in *The Mad Miss Manton* (1938), Barbara Stanwyck slaps Henry Fonda, who then slaps her back; Barrymore jabs Lombard with a pin to improve her stage scream in *Twentieth Century*; Fredric March expresses his love for Carole Lombard in *Nothing Sacred* (1937) by socking her in the jaw; and Cary Grant bids a fond farewell to Katharine Hepburn during the opening credits of *The Philadelphia Story* (1940) by knocking her to the ground.

Though much of the "lovemaking" tends to take place in the form of male violence directed against women, women occasionally get their licks in as well. In *Mr. and Mrs. Smith* (1941), Lombard slams the door in Robert Montgomery's face, giving him a bloody nose, and Stanwyck quite literally "strikes" up a relationship with Fonda in *The Lady Eve* (1941) by tripping him as he walks past her table. Screwball comedies give a literal twist to the tried-and-true metaphor of comic sexual relations. The "battle of the sexes" becomes an unending succession of "combat" sequences that conclude with an uneasy truce.

Unlike romantic comedies, which trace the evolution of youthful heroes and heroines into harmonic couples and which tend to conclude with their blissful union or marriage, screwball comedies, rooted as they are in conflict, do not necessarily move toward the constitution of the couple or toward some other form of consummation. More often than not, they begin with a couple which is already constituted, whose harmony is then shattered, disturbed by internal strife or conflict.

Love, War, and Unresolved Endings

Thus *Mr. and Mrs. Smith* (1941), a screwball comedy of manners, opens with the Smiths (Robert Montgomery and Carole Lombard), locked in their bedroom, where they have vowed to remain until the argument which they began three days ago is settled. Once this dispute is finally resolved, their marriage picks up where it left off, only to come unraveled again when they discover that, owing to a legal technicality, they were never really married. For the remainder of the film, the couple continue to spar, waging both physical and psychological warfare with one another until the final scene when they achieve a stalemate of sorts, locked in a wrestling hold that doubles as a tentative sexual embrace.

If one of the themes of comedy is that of integration, then the screwball comedy genuinely plays with that theme, looking at it from a variety of perspectives, including not only its inverse—disintegration—but also its variations, among which number "quasi-" or "pseudo-integration." Films do not always conclude with the comic resolution of all of the problems which beset the couple. Much as screwball narratives often begin with a couple on the verge of breaking up, so they just as frequently end with a tenuous reconciliation.

By the end of *His Girl Friday*, nothing much really changes in the Cary Grant–Rosalind Russell relationship, except that he has forced her to see the absurdity of her proposed marriage to Albany insurance salesman Ralph Bellamy. The reasons that lead Russell to divorce Grant remain. However, after spending a day together trying to outwit one another, each realizes the worthiness of the other as an opponent. Russell decides that an unconventional and unstable life with Grant is better than the deadeningly conventional, dull, and ordinary marriage that awaits her with Bellamy.

Even in films such as *Bringing Up Baby*, in which a couple is created "from scratch," as it were, their courtship is far from harmonious and their final embrace far from idyllic. As Grant confesses to Hepburn, in moments of quiet he is strangely drawn to her, but "there haven't been any quiet moments . . . and [their] relationship has been a series of misadventures from beginning to end." In the final scene, after Hepburn has toppled his brontosaurus, Grant reflexively pulls her to safety and sits together with her on the top of a huge scaffold, but their misadventures as a couple are clearly not over. Hepburn's aggressive actions have, once again, left Grant speechless. When he puts his arms around her at the end, his hug is as much an acknowledgment of surrender as it is a declaration of love.

In *Twentieth Century*, Barrymore and Lombard go through romantic cycles—they become a couple, split up, then reunite. Their relationship, which begins as a struggle for power in which Barrymore dominates her, evolves through a series of themes and variations upon power, with Lombard defiantly asserting her own independence in response to each of his similar gestures. The squabbling with which the film ends becomes a form of romantic exchange, as each tries to respond in kind to the other, proving themselves equal to one another, and, through a screwball kind of logic, proving that they are thus made for each other.

The Politics of Screwball
Andrew Bergman argues that screwball comedies bridge class differences, solving the social problems of the Depression era. Capra comedies, such as *It Happened One Night* and *You Can't Take It With You* (1938) fit this formula, as do one or two films written (*Easy Living*, 1937) and/or directed (*The Lady Eve*, 1941; *Palm Beach Story*, 1942) by Preston Sturges. But an equal number of screwball comedies, especially those directed by Howard Hawks (*Twentieth Century, Bringing Up Baby, His Girl Friday*) and Leo McCarey (*The Awful Truth*, 1937), or written by Sidney Buchman (*Theodora Goes Wild*, 1936) and Ben Hecht (*Nothing Sacred*, 1937) ignore Capra's populist rhetoric, subordinating overt political issues, such as class difference, to covert sexual issues, such as

the threats posed to the male order by the sexually aggressive female, the instability of sexual relations, or simple sexual liberation.

Nonetheless, screwball comedies give expression to the political and social concerns of the period. Bergman claims that the screwball comedy is politically conservative, if not reactionary. The anarchic comedies of the Marx Brothers assault the social order; the essential cohesiveness of the screwball comedy seeks, in Bergman's view, to patch things up. But if screwball comedy is placed in the larger context of the development of screen comedy in the years between the two world wars, then it can be seen to mark a rebellious turn in the romantic comedy in response to anarchic comedy, such as that of the Marx Brothers or Wheeler and Woolsey.

Screwball comedy, like the anarchic comedian comedies, grows out of the social and economic turmoil of the stock market crash and the Depression. Much as the Marx Brothers expose the arbitrariness of established institutions and the absurdity of traditional codes of social behavior, the screwball comedy reveals the essential artifice of the conventions which govern sexual relations, attacking the supposed stability of its chief institutions, such as marriage, and exposing the tensions that lie beneath the traditional happy endings that conclude earlier romantic comedies. It reflects the reshuffling of the delicate balance of sexual power. Women already enjoyed political enfranchisement granted them under the Nineteenth Amendment and a (limited) social equality, which found women doing traditionally "male" things such as smoking, drinking, driving cars, and so on. But during the 1930s, women began to take a more aggressive role in economic affairs, becoming the breadwinners of the Depression-era family by working as unskilled help in low-paying jobs when their fathers and husbands were laid off or by pursuing white-collar careers as "working women."

Though the screwball film does not, as Bergman insists, heal class difference, it does elevate class conflict onto a higher plane, admitting lower- and middle-class types, such as reporters and secretaries, to an upper-class milieu, such as the sophisticated world of either the madcap heiress or the heir to the family business. Within this upper stratum of society, class hostility finds full expression as basic social conflicts, often cast in the form of sexual antagonism, play themselves out in an inconclusive, Beckettesque fashion. The majority of the films tend to side with the lower- or middle-class protagonist, whose cynical critique of wealth and privilege echo the democratic and populist attitudes of both the film's makers and its targeted audience.

Yet these attitudes also find acceptance among the upper-class characters against whom they are directed, who not only seem to agree with their worst critics and launch into their own self-criticism, but also reward the messengers who bring them word of their own faults. Thus, in *It Happened One Night*, the newspaper reporter marries the poor little rich girl—with her father's blessing; and in *Easy Living, You Can't Take It With You,* and *The Lady Eve*, the socially inferior heroine proves to possess a spirit and integrity that reveals her to be superior to the upper class, which she joins through marriage to the business tycoon's son.

After the Screwball

Thesis Comedy

During the 1930s, Hollywood comedy develops a political consciousness. At one edge of the comic spectrum, Ernst Lubitsch's playful, apparently frivolous comedies of manners (*Trouble in Paradise*, 1932; *The Merry Widow*, 1934; *Angel*, 1937; *Ninotchka*, 1939; and *The Shop Around the Corner*, 1941) betray a greater and greater concern for social issues as the decade progresses and as his comic settings shift from an upper-class (*Trouble in Paradise*) to a more middle-class (*Shop Around the Corner*) milieu. Chaplin and Capra pioneer the thesis comedy—comedies with overt political messages. *Modern Times* celebrates the common workingman and denounces the advent of automation and the machine age; *The Great Dictator* (1940) satirizes fascism, in the persons of two dictators, Adenoid Hynkel (Chaplin) and Benzino Napolloni (Jack Oakie), who are undisguised caricatures of Adolph Hitler and Benito Mussolini, respectively; after the war, Chaplin continues his assault on militarism, the Cold War, and the impersonality of contemporary mass culture in *Monsieur Verdoux* (1947) and *A King in New York* (1957).

Frank Capra criticizes the New Deal, intellectual pretension, and established culture in *Mr. Deeds Goes to Town* (1936); corruption in government in *Mr. Smith Goes to Washington* (1939), and the proto-fascism of big business in *Meet John Doe* (1941). He sketches out his ideal plan for an agrarian, populist paradise, which he and novelist John Hilton called Shangri-La, in *Lost Horizon* (1937).

Chaplin's and Capra's politicization of comedy becomes, in turn, the target for another comedy by screenwriter and director, Preston Sturges. Sturges' central character in *Sullivan's Travels* (1941) is a Hollywood director who suddenly develops a social consciousness, abandons the making of escapist comedies (with names such as *Ants in Your Plants of 1941*), and sets off on a cross-country journey to research a prospective film (entitled *Oh Brother, Where Art Thou?*) about the poor, the unemployed, and the homeless. On his travels, Sullivan discovers that film comedy does have tremendous social value, providing a necessary release for audiences from intolerable misery and suffering, and he resumes his career as a director of escapist comedies.

War Comedies

Wartime comedies play a similarly crucial role in boosting morale. Abbott and Costello star in a string of fifteen comedies between 1941 and 1945, including the pre-Pearl Harbor service comedy, *Buck Privates* (1941). Bob Hope entertains the troops onscreen, in films like *Star Spangled Rhythm* (1942), and offscreen, in his USO tours. In addition to his highly popular "road" pictures with Bing Crosby and Dorothy Lamour (*Singapore*, 1940; *Zanzibar*, 1941; *Morocco*, 1942; *Utopia*, 1945), Hope cringes his way through two war-related films, *Caught in the Draft* (1941) and *They Got Me Covered* (1943).

Home-front comedies provide comic relief for the more serious waging of the war, but often do so in somewhat perverse ways, getting comic mileage out of Hope's onscreen cowardice and out of problems at home, ranging from the housing shortages in Washington, DC (*The More the Merrier*, 1943) to the hypocrisy and corruption of small-town America (*Hail the Conquering Hero*, 1944). In the latter film, duplicity not only invades the private sphere of the family (a son pretends to his mother that he is serving in the marines when he is really 4-F) and the couple (his girlfriend, though believing him to be fighting overseas, nonetheless dumps him for the mayor's son), but also the public sphere of politics (the mayor, the pawn of a political boss, endorses a self-serving civic policy of "business as usual" which undermines the town's efforts in support of the war).

As a home-front morale booster, the film is profoundly ambivalent. Although it mocks such American institutions as "momism" and the cult of the returning war hero, it reinscribes those same values. The virtues of the family and of individual heroism are reinstated through the intervention of a squad of marines, veterans of the Pacific war, who both believe in mom and are genuine war heroes. The marines make everything alright, proving that the same spirit that inspires the war effort, if brought home, can restore the traditional values of small-town America which the cynicism of the war years had permitted to deteriorate.

Sex and Neurosis: The Postwar Era

After the war, comedies continue to take on topical issues, such as the intermarriage of American GIs with Europeans (*I Was a Male War Bride*, 1949), the movement of middle-class families to the suburbs (*Mr. Blandings Builds His Dream House*, 1948), and the development of radical new technologies that can transform the processes of nature (*Monkey Business*, 1952). Although the sociohistorical situations are different, the sexual dynamics of these films look back to those of the screwball comedies, which are built upon a fundamental antagonism between the sexes. Slapstick comedy enjoys a revival in the unlikely figure of Cary Grant, who excels not only in Keaton-like physical stunts (*War Bride, Monkey Business*) but in rather sophisticated character comedy as well (as seen in *Blandings*, 1948; and *The Bachelor and the Bobby-Soxer* and *The Bishop's Wife*, both 1947).

As filmmakers begin to test the limits of the Production Code, the restrictions of the Code begin to relax somewhat. In turn, screen comedy becomes more and more overt in its treatment of sexual issues, giving rise to a new subgenre—the sex comedy. Otto Preminger openly defies the Code in *The Moon Is Blue* (1953), which assaults would-be censors not only in its open discussion of premarital sex but also in its use of previously taboo words such as "pregnant," "seduction," and "mistress," and the term "professional virgin" (a phrase coined by the film to describe the sexually teasing behavior of actress Maggie McNamara).

Courtesy of 20th Century-Fox

Marilyn Monroe emerges as the realization of Tom Ewell's sexual fantasies in Billy Wilder's wide-screen sex comedy, *The Seven Year Itch* (1955).

Preminger successfully released the film without the required Production Code seal and, when it became one of the top-grossing films of the year, the rest of Hollywood took notice and sex comedies grew racier and racier. Marilyn Monroe's screen character evolved from a sexually naive gold digger who serves as the target of dumb blonde jokes (*Gentlemen Prefer Blondes* and *How to Marry a Millionaire*, 1953), into a figure of male sexual fantasy (*The Seven Year Itch*, 1955), and finally into a more worldly, sexually aware, but somewhat embittered romantic (*Some Like It Hot*, 1959). Sex comedy reaches a new low in inspired vulgarity through the collaborative efforts of Jayne Mansfield and director Frank Tashlin. In *The Girl Can't Help It* (1956), Mansfield's sexual gyrations as she walks melt the iceman's ice, boil the milkman's milk, and shatter the eyeglasses of male onlookers. In *Will Success Spoil Rock Hunter?* (1957), her kiss pops popcorn in Tony Randall's pocket, a gag which Tashlin then follows with a seemingly unending string of phallic jokes.

Beneath the apparent complacency and conformism of 1950s America lurk the tell-tale twitches, involuntary spasms, split personalities, and deep-seated neuroses of Jerry Lewis, who gives expression to the anxieties which characterize that era of Cold War politics and sexual repression. In *Artists and Models* (1955) and *Hollywood or Bust* (1956), Lewis caricatures the typical 1950s consumer, playing the part of an avid reader of horror comic books (and subscriber to their fantasy worlds) in the former film and a star-struck movie fan in the latter. Dubbed ''le roi du crazy'' (the king of crazy) by French critics, Lewis' character consumes mass culture so passionately that it drives him insane.

Comedy and Consumerism

Sex comedies of the 1950s also become the sites for a critique of contemporary mass culture. Wilder satirizes paperback publishing in *Seven Year Itch;* Tashlin rakes the pop music industry over the coals in *Girl Can't Help It* and sends up movie stars, television, and the advertising industry in *Rock Hunter*. The latter film begins with a series of derisive television commercials, lampoons 1950s breast fetishism, laughs at rampant consumerism, derides grey-flannel dreams of success on Madison Avenue, exposes the dependence of corporate executives on alcohol and tranquilizers, mocks the faddish fascination with Freudian psychoanalysis, and holds the culture's fetishization of the bathroom up to ridicule.

A few years later, Billy Wilder's *The Apartment* (1960) takes a hard look at the relationship between sex and success in contemporary corporate America, casting the various members of the business community in the unflattering roles of pimps, prostitutes, and johns. The film's nebbishlike hero (Jack Lemmon) rises spectacularly through the bureaucratic hierarchy of a New York insurance company by letting his male superiors use his apartment for adulterous affairs with female employees. The film implicitly criticizes both the old boy network of executives who take advantage of their positions to secure special favors for themselves and the ambitious young white-collar worker who learns how to play the game of office politics and who sells out to his superiors in exchange for promotion. It thus depicts a system that is dominated by corruption from top to bottom.

But the film concludes with a repudiation by those at the bottom of those at the top as Lemmon resigns from his much-coveted, executive-level position, and an executive's much-abused mistress, elevator operator Shirley Mac-Laine, finally extricates herself from an adulterous relationship and joins Lemmon in his one-man rebellion against the system.

Alienation and Self-Reflection: The 1960s and Beyond

Black Comedy of the 1960s

The bittersweet nihilism of Wilder in sex comedies such as *Irma la Douce* (1963) and *Kiss Me, Stupid* (1964) sets the mood for much of black comedy of the 1960s. The military becomes the source of dark humor in Stanley Kubrick's apocalyptic *Dr. Strangelove* (1964), which teaches us to laugh at (if not love) the bomb, in Joseph Heller's and Mike Nichols' World War II satire *Catch-22* (1970), in Robert Altman's Korean war farce *M*A*S*H* (1970), and in George Roy Hill's adaptation of Kurt Vonnegut's *Slaughterhouse Five* (1972). These critiques of the Cold War, governmental bureaucracy, and American militarism find a receptive audience in the cynical, college-age generation that led the antiwar movement in the late 1960s.

A similar, critical sensibility informs Mike Nichols' direction of *The Graduate* (1967). This study of alienated youth suggests that no one over 30 can be trusted, that the older generation is obsessed with false, materialistic values, and that parents seek to use their children as a means of realizing their own ambitions. Comic shots, framed through fish tanks or diving masks convey both the alienation and entrapment of the younger generation within a social system that threatens to suffocate them.

At the same time, the commodification of culture that was taking place in the postwar era results in the proliferation of images of commercial products on television, in newspapers, and in magazines. In response to advertisements which encourage us to consume, pop artists, such as Andy Warhol, appropriate those images, remake them, and send them back (as well as sending them up) in a transformed state. Warhol's paintings of Brillo boxes or of Campbell's Soup cans pioneer the age of the "put-on," "send-up," and spoof, which convey the jaded skepticism of the young moviegoers who had been raised in the television era and who brought a new sophistication to their consumption of images.

Soup cans are not the only mass-produced products scrutinized by Warhol and others; the movies also provide subjects for parody. Warhol's own films, such as *Lonesome Cowboys* (1968), as well as several of those which he produced, such as *Frankenstein* and *Dracula* (both 1974), spoof traditional Hollywood genres. At around the same time, mainstream humorists, like Mel Brooks, take a critical look at familiar film genres (and at brand name directors such as Alfred Hitchcock) in a series of highly popular, if not quite Pop Art, parodies of the Western (*Blazing Saddles*, 1974), the horror film (*Young Frankenstein*, 1974), the silent film (*Silent Movie*, 1976), the science-fiction film (*Spaceballs*, 1987), and the Hitchcock thriller (*High Anxiety*, 1977).

Woody Allen and the Art of Self-Reflection

Woody Allen's uniquely self-reflexive comic style proves ideal for film parody. Allen not only makes fun of his own screen character's hang-ups, fears, anxieties, and obsessions, but he casts them in a series of familiar genre situations, ranging from the crime docudrama (*Take the Money and Run*, 1969) and science-fiction thriller (*Sleeper*, 1973) to overt parodies of literary and film classics, such as *Love and Death* (1975), which reworks Leo Tolstoy's *War and Peace*; *Play It Again, Sam* (1972), which pays tribute to *Casablanca* (1942); and *Stardust Memories* (1980), which serves as Allen's *8½* (Fellini, 1963). With *Annie Hall* (1977) and *Manhattan* (1979), Allen makes semiautobiographical melodramas that document the odyssey of a New York Jewish comedian, beset by mid-life crises and plagued with Bergmanesque self-doubt, who jokes his way through the contemporary wasteland of urban existence. The richness of experience which the Allen character seems to be seeking proves to lie in the past—in the escapist movies of the 1930s, which become the focus of *The Purple Rose of Cairo* (1985) and in the postwar "glory days" of radio, which he celebrates in *Radio Days* (1987). Yet Allen's comedy, like that of Brooks, proves too idiosyncratic and too ethnic for mass tastes.

From Animal Comedies to *Home Alone*

The kinkier comedy of the "Saturday Night Live" group (Chevy Chase, Bill Murray, John Belushi, Dan Ackroyd, Eddie Murphy, and Gilda Radner) play to a demographically broader, nonethnic audience in top-grossing films such as *Ghostbusters* (1984, 1989), *Beverly Hills Cop* (1984, 1987), *National Lampoon's Animal House* (1978), and *Coming to America* (1988). A frequent guest host on "Saturday Night Live," Steve Martin single-handedly sets out to restore the romantic comedy to preeminence in films such as *The Man With Two Brains* (1983), *All of Me* (1984), and *Roxanne* (1987), as well as the family comedy in *Parenthood* (1989) and *Father of the Bride* (1991). Chevy Chase emerges as the father-knows-best of the 1970s as Clark Griswald in a series of National Lampoon *Vacation* films (1983, 1985, 1989). Yet the major contribution of this group proves to be the creation of a new comic subgenre—what William Paul refers to as the animal comedy—which begins with *Animal House,* starring John Belushi, and which continues in raunchy, exploitational teen-sex comedies such as the *Porky's* films (1981, 1983, 1985), *Bachelor Party* (1984), *Fast Times at Ridgemont High* (1982), and *Revenge of the Nerds* (1984). What characterizes these comedies is an interest in adolescent sexuality (from masturbation to intercourse), a graphical grossness (from food fights to belching), and a comic celebration of vulgarity in general, which marks a new explicitness in screen comedy rivaling that found in recent horror films.

The unending cycle of generic development saw the animal comedy replaced in popularity in the late 1980s by more traditional family comedies, ranging from the somewhat crude *Problem Child* (1990, 1991) films, which look at the doubled-edged nature of child rearing for modern parents in the 1990s, to the more refined *3 Men and a Baby* (1987), *3 Men and a Little Lady* (1990), *Parenthood* (1989), *Look Who's Talking* (1989, 1990), and *Home Alone* (1990, 1992).

Macauley Culkin braces himself for the trials of an eight-year-old living on his own when his parents leave him *Home Alone* (1990) on their Christmas vacation to Paris.

Courtesy of 20th Century-Fox

In the latter work, ambivalent attitudes toward children are submerged beneath a slapstick plot that celebrates cartoonlike violence directed toward outsiders who threaten the sanctity of the home. In *Home Alone,* audiences delight in Macauley Culkin's independence and ingenuity as an eight-year-old who is inadvertently left behind when his parents, brothers, and sisters fly to Paris for Christmas vacation. But beneath the surface of this contemporary comedy lies a deep-seated anxiety about the nuclear family in the 1990s, addressing, in particular, the unspoken guilt felt by working parents of latchkey children. But even perhaps more disturbing than its portrait of the preoccupied parent whose self-absorption results in the neglect of a child is the film's suggestion that the child can do quite well without his family—and that the most intense relationships in his life are with outsiders.

From the childlike regression of the animal comedies of the 1970s and 1980s to the rite of passage undertaken in the "kid" comedies of the 1990s, American screen comedy continues to document the growing pains of American culture. From Chaplin, Keaton, and Lloyd, to Allen, Martin, and Murphy, comedians shape a comic vision of American life that reveals its unconscious. Freud notes that "only jokes that have a purpose run the risk of meeting with people who do not want to listen to them." Beneath its witty dialogue and behind its clever sight gags, American film comedy has a latent social agenda, addressing controversial issues in such a disarming way that they appear to lose all controversy. But it is possible to look through the laughter to catch sight of the underlying issues and social problems that give rise to comedy and see that American screen comedy is not always a laughing matter, that it contains within it serious questions that society can only address to itself in nonserious ways.

SELECT FILMOGRAPHY

The Immigrant (1917)
Safety Last (1923)
Sherlock Jr. (1924)
The Freshman (1925)
Seven Chances (1925)
The General (1926)
The Circus (1928)
Design for Living (1933)
Duck Soup (1933)
It Happened One Night (1934)
Twentieth Century (1934)
Modern Times (1936)
The Awful Truth (1937)
Bringing up Baby (1938)
The Lady Eve (1941)
Sullivan's Travels (1941)
Hail the Conquering Hero (1944)
I Was a Male War Bride (1949)
The Seven Year Itch (1955)

Will Success Spoil Rock Hunter? (1957)
Some Like It Hot (1959)
The Apartment (1960)
The Graduate (1967)
M*A*S*H (1970)
Blazing Saddles (1974)
Annie Hall (1977)
National Lampoon's Animal House (1978)
Manhattan (1979)
Fast Times at Ridgemont High (1982)
Trading Places (1983)
Moscow on the Hudson (1984)
Revenge of the Nerds (1984)
The Purple Rose of Cairo (1985)
Coming to America (1988)
Working Girl (1988)
Big (1988)
Home Alone (1990)

SELECT BIBLIOGRAPHY

Bergman, Andrew. *We're in the Money: Depression America and Its Films.* New York: New York University Press, 1971.

Cavell, Stanley. *Pursuits of Happiness: The Hollywood Comedy of Remarriage.* Cambridge, MA: Harvard University Press, 1981.

Horton, Andrew, ed. *Comedy/Cinema/Theory.* Berkeley: University of California Press, 1991.

Mast, Gerald. *The Comic Mind.* Chicago: University of Chicago Press, 1979.

Paul, William. *Ernst Lubitsch's American Comedy.* New York: Columbia University Press, 1983.

————. *Laughing/Screaming.* New York: Columbia University Press, 1994.

Sarris, Andrew. "Sex Comedy without the Sex," *American Film* (March 1978).

Sikov, Ed. *Screwball: Hollywood's Madcap Romantic Comedies.* New York: Crown, 1989.

CHAPTER 8

THE WAR FILM

A WORLD OF EXTREMES

Film producer, writer, director, and World War II veteran Samuel Fuller, appearing as himself in Jean-Luc Godard's *Pierrot le fou* (1965), declares that "film is like a battleground: love, hate, action, violence, death . . . in a word, emotion." If film is like a battleground, then the war movie is potentially the ultimate form of the cinema, creating conditions in which extreme expressions of love, hate, action, violence, and death could find representation. If the cinema is, in part, a medium well-suited for the depiction of spectacle, the war film is uniquely capable of maximizing that spectacle, marshaling thousands of troops in battle formation, blowing up bridges, battleships, ammunition dumps, airfields, towns, and cities, and laying waste to not only individual armies but entire nations as well.

Much as the musical provides cathartic release from the mundane sphere of its narrative through escapist flight into a more fantastic world of song and dance, the war film has its own "production numbers" in the form of explosive action sequences, superhuman feats of bravery, and spectacular displays of mass destruction. But while characters in musicals leap into a more perfect, utopian world of harmony, energy, intensity, and abundance, characters in war films cautiously enter a hellish no-man's-land of violence and death in which life is not ideal. Rather, life in the state of war is, as Thomas Hobbes once wrote of life in the state of nature, "nasty, brutish, and short."

The war movie plunges its characters into a world of extremes where the slightest action (or even inaction) results in death—their own or that of their comrades. One of the images that best conveys the absolutist, either/or nature of human existence in the genre is that of the GI who inadvertently steps on an enemy land mine he knows will explode if he makes a move [see *Fixed Bayonets* (1951), *The Boys in Company C* (1978)]. His life, as well as that of the man standing next to him, depends upon his self-control. He is forced to remain perfectly motionless while a comrade attempts to disarm the mine. Then he and his buddies carefully retrace their steps out of the minefield. Life (if you can call it that) is lived moment by moment. Each step becomes a nightmarish choice between life and death—a choice in which there is no real choice, only luck. Michael Cimino, the director of *The Deer Hunter* (1978), sets forth a somewhat similar image, though one which proves to be more appropriate to the Vietnam war than the traditional "us" versus "them" concept of the GI in a minefield. For Cimino, the Vietnam war is intentionally self-destructive; it is like a game of Russian roulette.

BREAKING RULES

A Suspension of Morality

The battlefield is a world in which the laws, beliefs, behavior, and morality of civilization are suspended. It is not merely permitted for one man to kill another; it is imperative for him to do so. War rewrites civil and criminal law. To charge a soldier who kills the enemy with murder is, as Captain Willard (Martin Sheen) reminds us in *Apocalypse Now* (1979), "like giving out speeding tickets at the Indy 500." There are, of course, rules of war, established by the Geneva Convention. And American soldiers in World War II films attempt, for the most part, to observe them. But, in the Vietnam war film, even those rules are honored as much in the breach as in the observance. Expediency governs morality; might makes right; the ends justify the means.

Although the difference between right and wrong is somewhat obscured and thus no longer absolute in the war film, relative moral distinctions remain. The good guys (usually us) fight fair and the bad guys (usually them) do not. Our enemies are shown not only torturing captured soldiers but also killing innocent civilians. In *The Heart of Humanity* (1918), Erich von Stroheim's Prussian officer, distracted from his attempted rape of a Red Cross nurse by the screams of an infant, picks the child up out of its cradle and tosses it out of a second-story window to its death. In *Bataan* (1943), the Japanese mutilate a Filipino soldier, fire on a Red Cross ambulance, and strafe a column of refugees, killing women and children. In *The North Star* (1943), a Nazi doctor first orders the children of a captured Ukrainian village to be fed, then forces them to give blood transfusions for German wounded; one child dies when too much blood is drained out of his body.

Even the good guys break the rules on occasion, though they are generally seen as motivated by either moral outrage, expediency, or compassion. And their violations of official codes of conduct generally take place in the Korean and Vietnam wars in which America's moral status is not as clearly delineated as it was in World War II. In *The Steel Helmet* (1951), an American sergeant deliberately shoots a North Korean prisoner of war in retaliation for his callous response to the death of a young Korean boy. In *Apocalypse Now*, Willard shoots a dying Vietnamese girl rather than let his hypocritical comrades, who originally wounded her, delay his mission by taking her to a place where she might obtain medical assistance. At the end of *Full Metal Jacket* (1987), a marine known as "Joker" complies with the pleas of a wounded female Viet Cong sniper who is writhing on the floor in pain and kills her.

Deviant Narratives: From Individual to Group Goals

As an ultimate form of the cinema, the war film is empowered to suspend even the laws of classical narrative construction. Traditional Hollywood films center on the individual, whose goals and desires drive the story line and whose psychological complexity becomes the focus of narrative exposition. In war films, the needs of the individual frequently give way to those of the group. The exceptional circumstances of the battlefield force individuals to place their own needs beneath those of the platoon, squadron, division, battalion, fleet, army, and nation.

Air Force (1943) details the transformation of assorted individual characters into a cohesive fighting unit, whose own identities are subsumed within the larger identity of "Mary Ann," the B-17 bomber on which they serve during the first few days of World War II. *Twelve O'Clock High* (1949) tells a similar story of a flight commander who transforms a ragged collection of bomber pilots, navigators, bombardiers, and gunners into a precision fighting unit of 21 B-17s, which are drilled to fly together in tight formation, drop bombs in unison on their target, and protect one another from attacking enemy fighters. The "group" becomes all-important.

Indeed, individual heroism is often represented in the war film as a form of self-indulgence and thus counterproductive to the accomplishment of the collective goals of the group. Tension between the desires of the individual and the needs of the group is regularly worked out through an educational process during which the individual (such as John Garfield's Winocki in *Air Force*) learns how crucial his cooperation is to the survival of the team. Or it is resolved through the individualistic outsider's ritualistic, sacrificial death.

In both *The War Lover* and *Hell Is for Heroes* (1962), Steve McQueen plays alienated loners whose heroic actions come in direct violation of orders. Unwilling or unable to function as a member of a combat team, his reckless-

The crew in *Air Force* (1943) functions as a multicultural group: the Pole Winocki (John Garfield, left), the WASP crew chief (Harry Carey), the Jew Weinstein (George Tobias), and the Swede Peterson (Ward Wood).

Courtesy of Warner Bros.

ness endangers his comrades. He ultimately harnesses his heroism in the form of a self-destructive energy. He then uses this energy to save his crew or to transform himself into a suicidal weapon which he then directs against the enemy. Thus, in the former film, he holds his damaged plane on course, sacrificing himself so that his crew can have time to bail out. In the latter film, he straps himself with explosives, charges an enemy pillbox, and blows himself up in an attempt to destroy it. He does all this in order to put an end to the battle that continues, however, to be waged after his death.

Even in a film like *Sergeant York* (1941), which celebrates the individual, real-life exploits of one of World War I's most famous combat heroes, Alvin York (Gary Cooper) attributes his killing of 25 German soldiers and his single-handed capture of 132 others to a desire to protect his buddies, who are pinned down by enemy machine-gun fire. The only place for individual heroism in war films is in service to the larger needs of the group.

SEXUAL COMBAT: MASCULINITY IN THE WAR FILM

Oedipal Battles

Typical Hollywood plots hinge upon love triangles, trace the vicissitudes of star-crossed lovers, and conclude with the last-minute embrace of the hero and heroine. In war films, the absence of women—and even their marginal presence—results in an entirely different set of sexual dynamics. Headstrong recruits engage in oedipal romance or warfare [or both as in *Platoon* (1986)] with their top sergeants. Oedipal rivalry becomes a means of proving their courage and manhood to these older, more experienced, father figures.

In *Sands of Iwo Jima* (1949), a sensitive young marine comes to terms with his dead father through an oedipal conflict with a tough, no-nonsense sergeant (John Wayne), who served with and idolized the boy's father. In *Apocalypse Now*, Willard's similarly oedipal relationship with Colonel Kurtz (Marlon Brando) is crystallized for us on a figurative level when he finds the letter Kurtz wrote to his son in Kurtz's dossier and reads it, implicitly identifying, as its reader, with the person to whom it is addressed. It is finalized for us quite literally when, at the end, the would-be son kills Kurtz and takes his place. Willard becomes Kurtz's emissary to the world, bringing the latter's knowledge of the horror of war back with him to explain to Kurtz's son and to all others who need to understand the essential nature of war in general and that of the Vietnam war in particular.

Conventional Homoeroticism

When women enter this predominantly male world, they are often the shared objects of desire of two or more soldiers who compete with one another for her affection. This romantic rivalry provides the chief dramatic structure for both versions of *What Price Glory?* (1926, remade in 1952), the World War I comedy in which Captain Flagg battles Sergeant Quirt over the affections of a

French innkeeper's daughter, Charmaine. The reappearance of this motif in *Hot Shots!* (1991), in which the hero (Charlie Sheen) and his nemesis both court the same girl, testifies to its status as a time-worn genre convention.

In enjoying sexual relations with the same women, the men enjoy what psychoanalysts describe as a displaced homoerotic or homosocial relationship with one another in which their rivalry becomes a form not of sexual competition but of exchange. The abduction and gang rape of a Vietnamese girl by several members of an American army patrol in *Casualties of War* (1989) provides a more brutal example of the way in which the male relationships in war films are bound up, in a rather complex way, with notions of homosexual desire. Here, as in so many other instances of gang rape, the rape victim serves as a means of sexual exchange among men—as a bond which they all share and which solidifies their ties to one another.

More recently, *A Midnight Clear* (1992), set in World War II, conceives of male camaraderie in similarly homoerotic terms. The film's buddies not only all sleep with the same young girl on their last leave together, but when one of the comrades dies, they also take off their clothes and ritualistically bathe him, conducting a sexualized communion of sorts.

Masculine/Feminine

Women pose a variety of threats to men in war films. The mere appearance of a wife on screen introduces an emotional element that is often realized in terms of the man's essential vulnerability. Thus in *Thirty Seconds Over Tokyo* (1944), the syrupy scenes between Captain Ted Lawson (Van Johnson) and his wife (Phyllis Thaxter) presage his injury and the subsequent amputation of his leg. At the beginning of *Air Force*, the farewell scene between Captain Quincannon (John Ridgely) and his wife introduces an emotional vulnerability in the hero that ultimately makes him one of the most likely candidates among the crew to die before the film reaches its conclusion. The pervasive familiarity of the convention is brought home in *Hot Shots!* when one of its scenes parodies an airman's farewell to his wife just before his comic crash. The implicit message of this motif is that relations with a woman suggest a vulnerability in the hero to that which lies outside the masculine world of war—to the feminine—that will eventually destroy him.

If every human psyche consists of masculine and feminine elements, the psyche of the male soldier must be reshaped to repress the feminine—to transform him into a ruthless, unemotional, fighting machine. In every war film, masculinity is put in crisis, as it were; the toughness of the hero becomes an issue crucial to both his survival and that of his fellow soldiers. Drill sergeants in marine boot camps repeatedly refer to young recruits as "ladies" (*Boys in Company C*, 1978; *Full Metal Jacket*, 1987; *Heartbreak Ridge*, 1986). Sergeant Zack in *Steel Helmet* draws upon a similar tactic, referring to his untested troops as "ballerinas." This explicit challenge to the manhood of the recruit is designed to force him to overcome that which is considered "weak" or "feminine" in his nature and become a hardened marine—that is, to become a "man."

Courtesy of Warner Bros.

The Drill Instructor (Lee Ermey) turns basic training into a course in masculinity in *Full Metal Jacket* (1987).

In *Full Metal Jacket,* boot camp becomes a course of instruction in masculinity, including a series of exercises in which the men are forced to train while holding onto their own genitals, as if monitoring the development of their own manhood. Director Stanley Kubrick's broadly satirical gesture in *Jacket* emerges as a purely physical rendering of a process of masculinization that takes place on a more emotional level in other war films. In *Twelve O'Clock High,* General Savage (Gregory Peck) represses all emotion in his handling of his airmen, arguing that his predecessor has made them emotionally dependent upon him by treating them as children rather than as men. When he collapses before a mission and the entire squadron successfully carries it off without him, the fliers finally prove to him that they have grown from children into men.

The archetypal Hollywood combat soldier is a caricature of masculinity; his cartoonlike toughness is epitomized in Sylvester Stallone's Rambo. This character is itself a compilation of action heroes found in comic books such as *Terry and the Pirates, G.I. Joe, G.I. Combat, Sgt. Rock, Steve Canyon,* and *The 'Nam,* as well as *Captain America, Wonder Woman,* and other comic book series which feature quasi-militaristic action figures who began their careers fighting Nazis in World War II, but have rarely, if ever, worn a uniform. Though this notion of machismo is presented as essential to the success of a soldier on the battlefield, it is often revealed as out of place in the more domestic sphere of traditional sexual relationships. In *Heartbreak Ridge,* as Tania Modleski points out, Clint Eastwood's Sergeant Tom Highway, whose wife divorced him because "marriage and the Marine Corps weren't too compatible," reads women's magazines in an attempt to regain a sensitivity which his marine training has deliberately repressed. He also seems to realize that if he is to have any kind of a "normal" relationship with women, he needs to learn to speak their language instead of his own.

Back from the Front

In the war film, the "normal" world—the world of family, wives, and children—remains an alien world, which both the soldier and the returning war veteran have difficulty reentering. Willard tells us that when he went home, he wanted to be back in Vietnam and that he hardly said a word to his wife until he said "yes" to a divorce. The difficulty of the adjustment of veterans to the peacetime world of wives and children has become a familiar motif in films that deal with returning veterans. For veterans of World War II, like those in *The Best Years of Our Lives* (1946), reintegration, though difficult, is at least possible. But for those vets returning from Vietnam, as seen in *Rolling Thunder* (1977), *Coming Home* (1978), *First Blood* (1982), *Born on the Fourth of July* (1989), homecoming is decidedly more traumatic and assimilation less successful. War's overmasculinization of the men (in this latter group of films at

Courtesy of Universal

Crippled by war, returning Vietnam veteran Ron Kovic (Tom Cruise) visits the grave of the victim of his "friendly fire" in *Born on the Fourth of July* (1989).

least) has made them unfit for the traditional social order; that is, they have become masculine in excess, uncontrollable in their potential for rage or violence.

Successful reentry into society demands that they undergo a process of demasculinization. In certain instances (*Coming Home, Fourth of July*), the returning soldier is presented as a cripple, who has been "feminized" or made passive in combat and who must come to terms with his paralysis through a psychic healing process in which his initial rage at his misfortune is channeled into socially acceptable behavior. He evolves from embittered warrior into participant in the peace movement. In other instances (*Thunder, Blood*), returning veterans refuse to accept the passive status imposed upon them and direct the violence bottled up within them toward domestic enemies, recreating battle situations at home. If the veterans resist their feminization, their excessive masculinity either destroys them or forces them to become outlaws or social outcasts, as in the case of Rambo in *First Blood*.

CROSSOVERS: WAR AND GENRE

The bizarre sexual dynamics found in the war film reflect its status as a genre that occupies the extreme edges of the familiar terrain of classical Hollywood cinema. In other words, the excesses of the war film function to define, through a process of transgression, the norms of conventional cinema. The war film, however, is not entirely the "loose cannon" of all Hollywood genres that the above description of the combat film might lead us to suspect. The all-male world of the combat film with its wall-to-wall battle and action sequences is not the sum total of the war film. It merely stands at one end of a spectrum that includes a broad variety of perspectives on war. Much as war permeates every aspect of a society engaged in it, so the war film crosses over other genres. There are war comedies such as Charlie Chaplin's *Shoulder Arms* (1918), in which Charlie mocks the authoritarian discipline of boot camp and the conditions of trench warfare at the front before capturing the Kaiser.[1]

There are even war musicals (of a sort), ranging from loosely basted together narratives dealing with the entertainment of the troops, such as *Stage Door Canteen* (1943) and *For the Boys* (1991), to love stories with wartime settings, such as *South Pacific* (1958) and *The Sound of Music* (1965).[2]

The existence of war comedies and war musicals has forced critics to reconsider any narrow definition of the war film. The genre has tended to be identified as a whole with one of its subgenres—the combat film, with a single historical period—the twentieth century, and with a handful of global

[1] See also Chaplin's *The Great Dictator* (1941), Buster Keaton's *The General* (1926), the Marx Brothers' *Duck Soup* (1933), *When Willie Comes Marching Home* (1950), *Stalag 17* (1953), *Dr. Strangelove* (1964), *M*A*S*H* (1970), *Which Way to the Front?* (1970), and *Catch-22* (1970).
[2] For additional musicals, see *Thousands Cheer* (1943), *This Is the Army* (1943), *Four Jills in a Jeep* (1944), *The Glenn Miller Story* (1954); for musical love stories, see *For Me and My Gal* (1942) and *Darling Lili* (1970), and *The Gang's All Here* (1943), *Up in Arms* (1944), and *Anchors Aweigh* (1945).

Courtesy of 20th Century-Fox

A Japanese-American coproduction, *Tora! Tora! Tora!* (1970) reconstructs the Japanese attack on Pearl Harbor.

conflicts—World War I, World War II, Korea, and Vietnam. But the war film extends beyond the precise borders of the combat film, and it looks both backward and forward in time to eras other than our own. To a certain extent, every film that depicts or refers to war as well as every film made during a war functions as a war film.

From this perspective, the musical melodrama *Meet Me in St. Louis* (1944), set in turn-of-the-century America, can even be seen as a war film, celebrating home and family—traditional values for which World War II was being fought.

More explicitly, Westerns made during the Vietnam war, such as *Ulzana's Raid* (1972), are war films, refiguring the Viet Cong as Indians. However, the war film could be more usefullly defined as a representation of war from the points of view of those whose lives it touches. At the heart of this definition lies the combat film, which focuses primarily on men in war, and in which combat sequences occupy a large percentage of the overall running time of the film itself, as is the case with films like *Bataan* (1943) and *Battleground* (1949). The war film, however, also includes films about the military in which combat occupies only a small fraction of the story line, as in *From Here to Eternity* (1953), *The Wings of Eagles* (1957), *Born on the Fourth of July* (1989), and *Dances With Wolves* (1990), as well as films set outside the narrow world of the military in which there is no combat at all and war provides a background against which certain war-related dramatic conflicts are set.

Films in which involvement in a war is debated, like *Casablanca* (1942), *To Have and Have Not* (1944), *Alice's Restaurant* (1969), or *Hair* (1979) serve as one parameter of the genre while films that celebrate the efforts of those left behind to maintain the homefront, like *Since You Went Away* (1944), *Hail the Conquering Hero* (1944), or *Swing Shift* (1984) serve as another.

War can be seen not only from the perspective of civilians and the American or allied fighting forces, but also from that of the enemy, as in *All Quiet on the Western Front* (1930) or *A Time to Love and a Time to Die* (1958). On occasion, it can even be seen from both sides of a conflict, as in the case of *Tora! Tora! Tora!* (1970), a Japanese-American coproduction that tells the story of the attack on Pearl Harbor from both the Japanese and American points of view.

THE BATTLE FOR PUBLIC OPINION: PROPAGANDA AND THE COMBAT FILM

Preaching War and Peace

The nature of its subject matter has made the war film a crucial weapon in the shaping of public opinion about individual wars and war in general. The genre has become a battleground within which different political factions have fought with one another over the hearts and minds of American moviegoers. One of the first war films, *Tearing Down the Spanish Flag* (1897), which consists of a single shot of a hand ("the hand of righteous destiny") tearing down a Spanish flag, mobilized audiences in support of the recently declared war on Spain.

Antiwar films manipulated isolationist sentiment to keep America out of World War I. Thomas Ince's *Civilization* (1914), for example, argues for the inhumanity of war through an allegorical story in which the hero, a submarine commander, refuses to fire on an ocean liner, sinks his own ship, dies, and is resurrected by Christ, who sends him forth to preach for peace on earth.

Shortly after the sinking of the *Lusitania* in May 1915, J. Stuart Blackton led the prowar, anti-German cause with *Battle Cry of Peace* (1915), in which American advocates of national disarmament and peace are revealed to be dupes of foreign spies who mastermind an invasion of New York City that leaves it in ruins. Finally, in April 1917, after the sinking of four American merchant ships by German submarines, Woodrow Wilson, recently reelected on the basis of the slogan "He Kept Us Out of War," asked Congress to declare war on Germany, prompting a stream of prowar films, terminating isolationist filmmaking activities.

Prowar feeling was so predominant that one pacifist film producer, Robert Goldstein, was sentenced to ten years in jail for making an anti-British film, *The Spirit of '76*, which was released just prior to America's entry into the war on the British side. Anti-German sentiment dominated *The Kaiser, Beast of Berlin* and *To Hell with the Kaiser* (both 1917); in the latter, the Kaiser is presented as a tool of Satan, who encourages the German emperor to sink unarmed passenger ships, engage in chemical warfare, and blow up Red Cross hospitals. Even D. W. Griffith, whose *The Birth of a Nation* (1915) and *Intolerance* (1916) depict the horrors of war and end with heavenly images of world peace, joins the prowar bandwagon (at the request of the British government), directing *Hearts of the World* (1918), a war melodrama in which the Huns play the villains.

After the war, Hollywood reverts to the pacifist neutrality to which it subscribed during peacetime. *The Big Parade* (1925), *What Price Glory?* (1926), and other films dramatize the costs of war in human life and in the spirit of those who survived.[3]

Mass Conversion: The Politics of *Sergeant York*

American sentiment regarding the war in Europe remained more or less isolationist until the bombing of Pearl Harbor on December 7, 1941. Prior to that date, members of Congress carefully scrutinized Hollywood productions, suspecting certain films such as *Confessions of a Nazi Spy* (1939), *The Great Dictator* (1941), and *The Mortal Storm* (1940) to be prowar propaganda [while apparently missing the antifascist metaphorical implications of *The Sea Hawk* (1940) in which the English defeat of the Spanish Armada in 1588 is geared to arouse sympathy for a beleaguered England]. The aviator Charles Lindbergh and other members of the America First organization campaigned to maintain American neutrality.

But as world events slowly converted America to a wartime mentality, Hollywood served as a tool of antifascist filmmakers and the Roosevelt administration for the reeducation of an isolationist and pacifist populace into reluctant warriors. The conversion that takes place in *Sergeant York* (1941) of the born-again Christian Alvin York from a conscientious objector into a patriotic soldier serves as apt metaphor for the film industry's project during the months immediately preceding American entry into the war; Americans are, like York, uncertain about war. After World War I, Americans resume their predominantly isolationist stance. Though events in Europe in the 1930s prompt certain segments of society (including the president, Franklin Delano Roosevelt) to call for American intervention, many others, like York, need to be shown their larger responsibility to the world community.

York's education takes place in two, interrelated stages. Struck by lightning while raising hell outside of the local church in the backwoods of Tennessee, he undergoes a miraculous religious conversion and discovers the truth of what his pastor told him earlier—that an individual, like a tree,

---

[3] See also *Seventh Heaven* (1927), *Four Sons* (1928), *All Quiet on the Western Front* (1930), *The Dawn Patrol* (1930), *A Farewell to Arms* (1932), *Heroes for Sale* (1933), *Pilgrimage* (1933), *The World Moves On* (1934), *No Greater Glory* (1934), *The Road to Glory* (1936), *Three Comrades* (1938), and *The Roaring Twenties* (1939).

Alvin York (Gary Cooper) is issued a gun by the Army in *Sergeant York* (1941).

cannot stand alone, that "a fellow's got to have his roots in something outside his own self." Torn between his newfound religious faith, which teaches him "thou shalt not kill" and his duty as a soldier, York reconciles his obligations to both of these demands on his loyalty through a rationalization inspired by a passage in the Bible: He will render unto Caesar (the state) that which is Caesar's and unto God that which is God's. He'll obey his duty to the state and observe, as far as possible, his religious faith.

In this way, York (and America) can uphold, without rupturing them, the basic isolationist principles that underpin his (our) identity while realizing his (our) obligations to things outside of himself (ourselves). Retaining its inherent distaste for European entanglements and war, America could, at the same time, give itself over to the larger historical (and moral) necessity of fighting fascism.

The logic that underscores the World War II war film is that of the reluctant warrior, who hates war but fights nonetheless; in this way, the American war film (unlike those produced by the British, for example) is undermined with an antiwar sentiment that justifies our apparent about-face from isolationism to interventionism. British war films, like *In Which We Serve* (1942), take popular support of the war for granted. *Of course*, the Nazis, who had declared their intention of ultimately invading England need to be both fought and destroyed.

Why We Fight: Education and the War Film

The conversion process that lies at the center of *Sergeant York* reappears in dozens of combat films in the form of an educational process. This instructive aspect of the war film aligns it with the agitational and propagandistic cinema of certain state-produced foreign films such as *Battleship Potemkin* (1925) or *Triumph of the Will* (1935), as well as with America's own series of propaganda films, *Why We Fight* (1942–1945), which were produced by Frank Capra for the Army. But the propagandistic function of the American combat film is mediated somewhat by its overt *narrativization* of the educational process. Unlike Soviet and Nazi propaganda, the Hollywood war film acknowledges its status as a didactic tool, filtering its polemical arguments through characters in the narrative rather than presenting them directly. In this way, the American war film disarms potential objections to it as blatant propaganda.

However, shortly after Pearl Harbor, Hollywood was commandeered by the government to contribute to the war effort. The recently created Office of War Information (OWI) set up shop in Los Angeles where its Bureau of Motion Pictures served as a "watchful eye" over war-related productions. Its civilian members reviewed scripts, sat in on script conferences, and made suggestions about the content of finished films. The OWI's relationship with the studios remained purely advisory, serving in a capacity similar to that of the Production Code administration of the Hays office. Both the OWI and the studios dismissed any notion that the government was involved in censoring the movies, but the industry's voluntary cooperation with the Bureau of Motion Pictures undoubtedly played a role in determining the final content of a number of films made during the war.

The war film is a school for soldiers. The common soldier, whose inherent resistance to killing and to war (as well as to military discipline) is broken down in boot camp, is trained to fight and to obey (*Sands of Iwo Jima*, 1949; *Battle Cry*, 1955; *The Boys in Company C*, 1978). Having graduated from boot camp, he continues to learn—through combat—not only how to fight but why he is fighting; contact with the enemy reveals the latter's essential villainy and teaches him just how necessary the war is (*Guadalcanal Diary*, 1943; *Gung Ho!*, 1944; *The Green Berets*, 1968).

Combat convinces Ensign Torre (Brandon de Wilde) in *In Harm's Way* (1965) that what he initially refers to as "Mr. Roosevelt's war" is not merely a politically expedient plan to advance the personal interests of the president (and the Democratic party) but a "just" war to which he finds himself committed as well. The conscientious objector in *Steel Helmet* discovers that philosophical objections to war in general have no place on the battlefield; he picks up a gun and begins to shoot at North Korean soldiers.

A similar educational process takes place for civilians and other "neutral" observers. In Alfred Hitchcock's *Lifeboat* (1944), the survivors of a torpedoed ocean liner rescue the captain of the German U-boat that attacked them. The Nazi then betrays their trust, stealing more than his fair share of food and water and piloting them into enemy territory. When the others learn of what he has done, they denounce the fascist philosophy that inspires his actions and kill him.

Naive war correspondents, like Huntley Haverstock (Joel McCrea) in *Foreign Correspondent* (1940), discover the treacherous nature of the enemy through their aggressive investigative reporting. Cynical newspaper correspondents, like Williams (Henry Hull) in *Objective Burma* (1945), accompany soldiers in the field and, through their participation in combat, come to understand the true nature of the enemy. On seeing the mutilated bodies of the men in his patrol, Williams loses his objectivity and bursts into a racist diatribe against the Japanese: "I thought I've seen or read about everything one man can do to another, from the torture chambers of the middle ages to the gang wars and lynchings of today. But this—this is different. This was done in cold blood by people who claim to be civilized. Civilized! They're degenerate, moral idiots. Stinking little savages. Wipe them out, I say. Wipe them off the face of the earth."

Perhaps the most famous conversion takes place in *The Green Berets* (1968) in which a liberal, antiwar reporter (David Janssen) joins John Wayne's Green Beret unit in Vietnam to "see for himself" what the war is like. The war correspondent's skepticism colors his coverage of the war until he witnesses Viet Cong atrocities. "This is what the war is all about," a soldier tells him. "Are you gonna stand there and referee or are you gonna help us?" In an abrupt about-face, the journalist picks up a gun and helps the American forces defend themselves against an enemy attack.

The Vietnam Reversal

The educational process that takes place in the classic war film illustrates "why we fight" and rationalizes the necessity of war. In terms of this and other issues, *The Green Berets* emerges as one of the most representative of war films. Yet it is also unique in that practically every other film about the Vietnam war reverses this traditional educational process. In Vietnam, the soldier learns to question the simplistic, Cold War rhetoric about the nature of the enemy and the justness of the American cause which have been the cornerstones of the lessons taught in high school history classes and in basic training.

The experience of Vietnam teaches that American involvement in the war makes little or no sense. Our fighting forces not only learn from past example that war in general is hell but also discover for themselves that this particular war is wrong; soldiers become pacifists or antiwar activists, as in *Getting Straight* (1970) and *Coming Home*. In *Born on the Fourth of July*, paraplegic Vietnam veteran Ron Kovic (Tom Cruise) reviews his participation in the war from the perspective of a rat-infested VA hospital in the Bronx and is radicalized, becoming a leader of the antiwar movement.

The *Boys in Company C* discover that all that matters in Vietnam is the delivery of luxury items to the general for his personal amusement and the securing of good "body counts" for the reports sent back to headquarters. War becomes a game, like the soccer match they play against the South Vietnamese at the end of the film, a game they realize they are expected to lose. Finally, army private Eriksson (Michael J. Fox) in *Casualties of War* (1989) learns about the nature of the American presence in Vietnam when he is confronted with the moral corruption of other members of his squad who have abducted, raped, and killed a Vietnamese girl; he first tries to prevent them from harming her and, having failed, eventually blows the whistle on them, a gesture which figuratively represents his rejection of American behavior in the war itself.

RACE, ETHNICITY, AND THE WAR FILM

Earlier war films celebrate American intervention overseas, using the occasion to present an idealized portrait of American democracy. American identity is at risk in World War II, and it is the particular virtues of that identity—democratic equality—that will win it. Thus the combat films celebrate group teamwork, as we have seen earlier in our examination of *Air Force* and other films. The group is shown as consisting of various ethnic and social types, imitating the melting-pot ideal of American culture. As Jeanine Basinger points out, the tough career sergeant regularly has under his command a rich kid from the suburbs, a poor kid from the inner-city ghetto, a lower-middle-class cab driver from Brooklyn, a Jew, a Hispanic, an Italian-American, a Polish-American, and a black.

By cooperating with one another, they win the war as well as demonstrate that the idea of America really works. Unfortunately, history tells us something different. For example, though blacks are occasionally depicted as serving together with whites, as in *Crash Dive*, *Sahara* (1943), and *Bataan* (1943), the Armed Forces were not integrated until 1948, when President Truman "officially" ended segregation in the military. Though blacks served valiantly in World War II, they did so, much as they had in World War I and in the Civil War (see *Glory*, 1989), in segregated units commanded by white officers.

The reality of domestic racial tension is exemplified by race riots in Detroit and other cities in 1943; by the call, within the black community, for a "Double V"—a victory over the Axis in Europe and Jim Crow at home; and by a 1942 survey reporting that 49 percent of Harlem blacks believed they would be no worse off if Japan were to win the war. Domestic racism remained in place. For example, public fear of a Mexican-American "crime wave" led to the racially motivated police harassment of Mexican-American teenagers ("zoot suiters" who wore oversize sport coats and peg-top pants) in Los Angeles in 1942–1943. Wartime racism surfaced in continuing discrimination against blacks, Mexican-Americans, and other minorities such as Native Americans.

Perhaps the most scandalous act of racism was the internment of thousands of Japanese-Americans in detention camps during the war and the confiscation of their property—a policy the Office of War Information attempted to justify in a documentary newsreel, *Japanese Relocation*, which was released at the end of 1942. It wasn't until after the war, however, that Hollywood took a more critical stance toward relocation, treating it as an embarrassing moment in American history in films such as *Go for Broke!* (1951), *Bad Day at Black Rock* (1955), *Hell to Eternity* (1960), and, more recently, *Come See The Paradise* (1990).

But all of this wartime racial tension is rewritten into onscreen racial harmony, which is a more expedient "reality." Any notion of segregation or racism within the armed forces would clearly undermine the ideal of equality for which we are supposedly fighting. Racism at home is, therefore, sup-

The demonization of the enemy: a Japanese officer (Richard Loo) looms over his American prisoners of war in this publicity material for *The Purple Heart* (1944).

pressed, or rather displaced onto a race that it is permissible to hate. This is our enemy, the Japanese, who, once the Japanese-Americans have been eliminated from view, could become visible signs of difference, of racial otherness against which animosity could be directed, as Hollywood did in *Across the Pacific* (1942), *Air Force* (1943), *Objective Burma* (1945), *The Purple Heart* (1944), and dozens of other films.

CONFLICTED: THE PSYCHIC VIOLENCE OF WAR

The Enemy Is Us

During peacetime, Hollywood was free to produce war films to express antiwar sentiment that exposes the hypocrisy, incompetence, and/or insanity of the military establishment, as in *Paths of Glory* (1957), *Anzio* (1968), *Dr. Strangelove* (1964), and *M*A*S*H* (1970); the corruption and cowardice of officers (*Attack!*, 1956; *Bitter Victory*, 1957); and the futility and senselessness of war (*Hell Is for Heroes*, 1962; *The Victors*, 1963; *Johnny Got His Gun*, 1971; *A Bridge Too Far*, 1977). With the exception of *The Green Berets*, which is the only film about the Vietnam war made during the war itself, virtually every other film about the Vietnam war takes an antiwar stance that is critical either of U.S. political policy that led to our involvement in the war or of the physical, emotional, and psychological damage incurred by servicemen in Vietnam.

Vietnam war films tend to undermine the traditional values celebrated in films about World War II and other wars by reversing or obscuring the clear-cut distinctions drawn in earlier war films between "us" and the enemy. Indeed, in many of the major films that deal with the Vietnam war, "we" become the enemy. In *Company C*, the black sergeant Tyrone Washington (Stan Shaw) attempts to shoot his own commanding officer whose ineptness has resulted in the deaths of several comrades. *Deer Hunter* reduces the war to a game of Russian roulette in which Americans are driven first by torture and then by psychic trauma to shoot themselves.

In the opening sequence of *Apocalypse Now*, Willard smashes his own image in the mirror; the central action of the film involves his mission, which has as its objective the "termination" of an American officer rather than the killing of the enemy, who, for the most part, remain unseen. The film concludes with Willard's ritualistic slaughter of Kurtz, with whom he identifies and whom he resembles in several ways.

Vietnam is seen as America at war with itself in *Platoon* (1986): the innocent Chris (Charlie Sheen, left) poses with the ruthless and violent Sergeant Barnes (Tom Berenger, center) and the more moderate and rational Sergeant Elias (Willem Dafoe).

Courtesy of Orion

Platoon dramatizes the internal division of America over the war through the ideological conflict between two platoon sergeants (Tom Berenger and Willem Dafoe). One American (Berenger) kills another (Dafoe) only to be slain, in turn, by a third (Charlie Sheen). More recently, *Fourth of July* depicts the war as a struggle in which Americans kill one another by accident, through "friendly fire."

The Aftermath

The metaphorical representation of Vietnam as a self-destructive conflict extends into postwar representations of the aftermath of the war, seen in the "betrayal" narratives of a series of films involving war veterans. Thus in *Good Guys Wear Black* (1977), an American politician who has originally conspired with the enemy to betray a crack American special forces unit proves to be responsible for their methodical assassination after the war.

The enemy in the POW/MIA rescue mission drama *Rambo: First Blood Part II* (1985) is as much the CIA, who tries to ensure that Rambo's mission fails, as the North Vietnamese, who continue to hold American prisoners of war. The difficult adjustment of Vietnam veterans to postwar America is frequently cast in terms of conflict between them and those who stayed behind. In *Rolling Thunder* (1977), a veteran looks on helplessly as his wife and child are slain by a gang of thieves, intent on finding the silver dollars given to him by local residents upon his return home. He subsequently tracks down the robbers and, with the help of another veteran, kills them in a military-style assault. Other veterans become vigilantes (*Slaughter*, 1972; *Gordon's War*, 1973; *Magnum Force*, 1973; *Taxi Driver*, 1976) or are portrayed as criminals capable of insane acts that threaten domestic stability (*Black Sunday* and *Twilight's Last Gleaming*, 1977; *Betrayed* and *Distant Thunder*, 1988).

Though the veterans of other wars are occasionally depicted as having difficulty in adjusting to civilian life, as seen in *Pride of the Marines* (1945), *The Best Years of Our Lives* and *Till the End of Time* (1946), their problems remain contained within the family or the workplace; they rarely result in acts of civil disorder or criminal violence.

The scars of the Vietnam war, however, extend much deeper into the American psyche, producing veterans whose violence reaches out from the confines of the family into the public sphere. The clear sense of victory (and of closure or completion) that characterizes World War II produces a cinema that is itself untroubled in its representation of war. The sense of defeat (and lack of closure) that characterizes the Vietnam war leads to a cinema that continually seeks explanations for the war's outcome and to a cinema that attempts to rewrite our defeat in Vietnam as a postwar victory. Thus Vietnam veterans return to Southeast Asia to rescue prisoners of war (*Uncommon Valor*, 1983; *Missing in Action*, 1984; *Rambo: First Blood Part II*, 1985). Or the larger loss of the war is restaged as a smaller, domestic battle that could be won (*Gordon's War*, 1973; *Slaughter*, 1976; *Rolling Thunder*, 1977; *Good Guys Wear Black* and *A Force of One*, 1979; *Forced Vengeance*, 1982; and *Eye of the Tiger*, 1986).

MEDIATION AND REPRESENTATION

The war film mediates our relationship to war, helping to prepare us for it, reconcile us to victory or defeat, and adjust us to its aftermath. The conventions of the war film continue to shape our understanding of real wars—to inspire us, on the one hand, to fight in them and, on the other, to protest against them. Though wars continue to be fought and won or lost on the battlefield, they also continue to be fought and won or lost through their representation on the movie or television screen. Images of war explain why we fight; they stage and restage war's battles; and they attempt to explain why we won or lost.

In other words, all contemporary wars are waged on two fronts—on the battlefield and on the screen. Hollywood's job has been to make sure not that we always win but that we are always right—that our victories are informed by an inherent pacifism and distaste for war that redeems us from the sins of our conscienceless enemies and that our single defeat (in Vietnam) is the product not of our consciencelessness but of our heightened conscienceness, which sets us against ourselves and provides the basis for the recasting of our defeat as a victory in Hollywood's various epilogues to the war. Whether we win or lose the battle, the movies are there to enable us to win the war.

SELECT FILMOGRAPHY

Hearts of the World (1918)
The Great Dictator (1941)
Sergeant York (1941)
Air Force (1943)
Bataan (1943)
Guadalcanal Diary (1943)
Since You Went Away (1944)
The Story of G.I. Joe (1945)
The Best Years of Our Lives (1946)
Sands of Iwo Jima (1949)
Fixed Bayonets (1951)
The Steel Helmet (1951)
Battle Cry (1955)

The Longest Day (1962)
The Dirty Dozen (1967)
The Green Berets (1968)
Rolling Thunder (1977)
The Boys in Company C (1978)
Coming Home (1978)
The Deer Hunter (1978)
Apocalypse Now (1979)
Rambo: First Blood Part II (1985)
Heartbreak Ridge (1986)
Platoon (1986)
Full Metal Jacket (1987)
Born on the Fourth of July (1989)
Casualties of War (1989)

SELECT BIBLIOGRAPHY

Basinger, Jeanine. *The World War II Combat Film: Anatomy of a Genre.* New York: Columbia University Press, 1986.

Dick, Bernard. *The Star-Spangled Screen: The American World War II Film.* Lexington: University Press of Kentucky, 1985.

Doherty, Thomas. *Projections of War: Hollywood and American Culture, 1941–1945.* New York: Columbia University Press, 1993.

Fussell, Paul. *Wartime: Understanding and Behavior in the Second World War.* New York: Oxford University Press, 1989.

Jeffords, Susan. "Friendly Civilians: Images of Women and the Feminization of the Audience in Vietnam Films," *Wide Angle* **7**, no. 4 (1985): 13–22.

Koppes, Clayton, and Gregory Black. *Hollywood Goes to War: How Politics, Profits, and Propaganda Shaped World War II Movies.* New York: Free Press, 1987.

Modleski, Tania. "A Father Is Being Beaten: Male Feminism and the War Film," in *Feminism without Women: Culture and Criticism in a "Postfeminist" Age.* New York: Routledge, 1991.

Shindler, Colin. *Hollywood Goes to War: Films and American Society, 1939–1952.* London: Routledge and Kegan Paul, 1979.

Suid, Lawrence. *Guts and Glory: Great American War Movies.* Reading, MA: Addison-Wesley, 1978.

FILM NOIR:
SOMEWHERE IN THE NIGHT

MADE IN THE U.S.A.

Film noir—literally "black film"—sounds like something French, but it is an American phenomenon made in Hollywood, U.S.A. Though several of the directors associated with film noir, such as Billy Wilder, Fritz Lang, Otto Preminger, and Edgar G. Ulmer, were foreign-born, the majority of those who explored the darker reaches of the noir experience were American, born and bred. They include, among others, Orson Welles, John Huston, Nicholas Ray, Samuel Fuller, Joseph H. Lewis, Anthony Mann, Raoul Walsh, Joseph Mankiewicz, Don Siegel, Phil Karlson, Tay Garnett, Frank Tuttle, Edward Dmytryk, Henry Hathaway, and Jacques Tourneur who, though born in Paris (1904), grew up in Hollywood (from 1914).

Even more important, the source material for the bulk of noir narratives comes from the underworld of American pulp fiction. For example, nearly 20 percent of the films noirs made between 1941 and 1948 are adaptations of hard-boiled novels written by American authors such as Dashiell Hammett, Raymond Chandler, James M. Cain, Horace McCoy, Cornell Woolrich, and others. An even greater percentage of films noirs are written by American screenwriters whose original scripts were heavily influenced by the hard-boiled style of these proletarian, tough-guy writers of the 1930s and 1940s. And, as we shall see, film noir deals with a uniquely American experience of wartime and postwar despair and alienation as a disoriented America readjusts to a new social and political reality.

There is a French connection, however. Film noir was discovered and "christened" in postwar France. On August 26, 1944, the Allies liberated Paris. During the Nazi occupation, which began in the summer of 1940, the Germans had banned the exhibition of American films in French theaters. Finally, in 1945, an enormous backlog of American films, which had been made during the war but had not been seen in Nazi-controlled territories, reached French screens.

French audiences were overwhelmed by a flood of American films, and critics were startled by the changes that had taken place in American film production during the war. The prewar, classical Hollywood cinema, which was dominated by the rationality, symmetry, and order of their favorite directors such as William Wyler, John Ford, and Frank Capra, had given way to a subversive strain of behavioral deviance in American films, which were now dominated by crime, corruption, cruelty, and an apparently unhealthy

Courtesy of Warner Bros.

The beginnings of noir: Joel Cairo (Peter Lorre) gets the drop on Sam Spade (Humphrey Bogart) in *The Maltese Falcon* (1941).

interest in the erotic. American film had suddenly—from the French perspective, at least—turned grimmer, bleaker, and blacker.

During a short period from mid-July to the end of August, 1946, a succession of extremely downbeat films opened in Paris. The cycle began with a Hammett detective yarn, *The Maltese Falcon* (Huston, 1941). It was followed by *Laura* (Preminger, 1944), an *amor fou* in which a police detective falls in love with a murder victim by looking at her portrait. Then there was a Raymond Chandler–Philip Marlowe mystery, *Murder, My Sweet* (Dmytryk, 1944); James Cain's study of corruption, distrust, and betrayal, *Double Indemnity* (Wilder, 1944); and the nightmarish *Woman in the Window* (Lang, 1944). Several months later, a second wave of similarly dark, American motion pictures hit the French capital, including *This Gun for Hire* (Tuttle, 1942), *The Killers* (Siodmak, 1946), *The Lady in the Lake* (Montgomery, 1946), *Gilda* (Vidor, 1946), and *The Big Sleep* (Hawks, 1946).

French critics were quick to recognize that many of these films possessed similar sylistic elements and settings, common character and narrative traits, and recurrent thematic concerns. They pointed out that these features resembled, in a number of ways, certain characteristics found in prewar, American hard-boiled fiction. In fact, the majority of these first ten films were adaptations of hard-boiled novels. Dozens of these novels had recently been translated into French and published as a group in a series edited by Marcel

Duhamel at Gallimard Press, which marketed them under the generic title of *Serie Noire* or "black series [of novels]."

The term "film noir" was coined by two French critics in an attempt to describe these movies. The adjective "noir" aptly conveys not only the films' antecedents in the *romans noirs* (black novels) of Dashiell Hammett, Raymond Chandler, James M. Cain, Horace McCoy, Cornell Woolrich, Graham Greene, and others but also the essential nature of the *experience* which audiences have in watching the films. These films unsettled audiences. Through their violation of the traditional narrative and stylistic practices of classical Hollywood cinema which orient and stabilize spectators, these films create an uncomfortable and disturbing malaise or anxiety in their viewers.

FILM NOIR: GENRE, SERIES, OR MODE?

Noir as Genre: A Set of Conventions

Though most critics and historians regard noir as a mode of film practice whose identity resides chiefly in its ability to make audiences uneasy, there is considerable disagreement over what *exactly* film noir is. A number of recent scholars treat film noir as a *genre*, discussing it in terms of its iconography (dark city streets glistening at night with fresh rain), fixed character types (proletarian, tough-guy, anti-heroes ensnared by treacherous femmes fatales), and predictable narrative patterns (murder plots and criminal investigations in which the hero's moral fallibility leads to his victimization and/or defeat at the hands of his enemies and often results in his death or in an otherwise unhappy ending).

For those who view it as a genre, film noir, like the Western, gangster film, or musical, relies upon a well-defined system of conventions and expectations. Yet these critics also acknowledge film noir's distinctive *style*—it is *dark*. Low-key lighting becomes the norm, replacing the pre-noir norm of cheerful, high-key lighting setups. But style is a feature which rarely, if ever, figures in the definition of a genre.

Noir as Series: A Certain Style

Others insist that film noir is not a genre but a *series* or "cycle," and view it as an aesthetic movement, somewhat like German Expressionism was in the 1920s. Though certain characters, narrative situations, and thematic concerns appear again and again in film noir, these elements tend to resist conventionalization and play against expectations. In addition, critics of the genre argument note that film noir lacks the "institutional" status of traditional genres. Producers, directors, and screenwriters of 1940s and 1950s films noirs, unlike those of Westerns, musicals, or gangster films, do not deliberately set out to make a film noir. There was no body of noir conventions for them to follow. Nor do audiences who see films noirs view them as they do conventional genre pictures. That is, they do not look at them in relation to a fixed system of prior expectations.

At the same time, a number of critics contend that film noir cannot be a genre because it crosses over traditional genre boundaries; there are noir westerns (*Pursued*, 1947; *Duel in the Sun*, 1946), gangster films (*White Heat*, 1949), melodramas (*Mildred Pierce* and *Leave Her to Heaven*, 1945), costume pictures (*Hangover Square*, 1945; *Reign of Terror*, 1949), sequences in musicals ("The Girl Hunt Ballet" in *The Band Wagon*, 1953), and even comedies (*Arsenic and Old Lace*, 1944; *M. Verdoux*, 1947).

Yet both the pro and con positions concerning noir's status as a genre have a certain validity. Like genre films, every film noir does rely, to some extent, upon identifiable character types and conventionalized narrative patterns. The detective hero falls into the clutches of the "spider woman," extricating himself from danger only by repressing those passions that drew him to her in the first place and by "sending her over" (i.e., giving her over to the police). Yet, it is just as clear that that which is *generic* in film noir is precisely that which is *not* "noir." There is nothing in the above outline of the typical detective story that is necessarily eery, disorienting, or anxiety-producing for the audience.

The problem of film noir's status lies in its essentially schizophrenic nature: film noir is not a genre, but every film noir is *also* a genre film. In other words, the conventions and systems of expectations that can be found in films noirs are those of the various genres to which these films belong—those of the detective film, the melodrama, or the Western. But what makes these films "noir" is the similar, transgeneric attitude they take toward their particular genre—the *twist* they give to conventional genre types, forms, and patterns. Thus, films noirs are all genre films; yet the genre to which they belong is not that of "film noir" but that of the detective film, the crime film, the Western, the melodrama, or some other genre.

Noir as Mode: An Uneasy Feeling

Another way of understanding the relationship of film noir to the question of genre is to return to the notion of noir as a specific emotional reaction produced by certain films in an audience. In this respect, film noir can be seen as a purely *affective* phenomenon; that is, it does things to people. Given this definition of noir, not every film noir needs to be "noir" from start to finish. It need only to be noir for a moment or two. It requires only a single character, situation, or scene that is noir to produce the disturbance or disorientation that is necessary to give the audience an unsettling twist or distressing jolt.

"Noir" thus emerges as an adjectival attribute or characteristic, functioning much as the terms "tragic," "comic," or "melodramatic" do in relation to the genres of tragedy, comedy, and melodrama; "noir" becomes a description of tone, attitude, or mood. In other words, noir, like the "melodramatic" which also crosses over generic boundaries, is not so much a genre as a *mode*—a particular *way in which* genre information is conveyed.

Traditional modes, however, do not have any temporal boundaries; they are just the *way* certain stories are told. Although that *way* of telling stories changes slightly from year to year, in general, it remains fairly consistent over extended lengths of time. Melodramatic historical pictures, for example, continue to be made from period to period, ranging from *The Birth of a Nation* (1915) and *Gone With the Wind* (1939) to *Empire of the Sun* (1987) and *Come See the Paradise* (1990). Melodramatic Westerns flourished back in the 1940s (*Duel in the Sun, Pursued*) as well as more recently in the 1980s (*Lonesome Dove*).

If film noir is a mode, should it not also transcend time? If so, then *Fatal Attraction* (1987) would be as much a film noir as earlier films, such as *Leave Her to Heaven* (1945) or *Angel Face* (1953) in which demonic women wreak their vengeance on men. But *Fatal Attraction* is not really noir; it is only pseudo-noir.

By the same token, contemporary remakes of postwar films noirs—*Body Heat* (a 1981 reworking of *Double Indemnity*), *Against All Odds* (a 1984 remake of *Out of the Past*), or *Farewell, My Lovely* (a 1975 remake of *Murder, My Sweet*)— are frequently mistaken as films noirs. A number of critics, especially those who view film noir as a genre, insist that these recent works *are* films noirs. However, others, especially Paul Schrader, contend that they are *not*, arguing that film noir, as a cycle, comes to an end in the late 1950s. Indeed, Schrader, whose own projects as a screenwriter (*Taxi Driver*, 1976) and director (*Cat People*, 1982) have clearly been heavily influenced by films noir, refuses to describe his own work or even noirish contemporary detective films, such as *Chinatown* (1974), as films noirs. For Schrader, film noir belongs to a specific historical era, lasting roughly from 1941 (*The Maltese Falcon*) to 1958 (*Touch of Evil*).

NOIR AESTHETICS, THEMES, AND CHARACTER TYPES

In other words, for Schrader, film noir, as a mode (rather than a genre), is an aesthetic movement. Like the more familiar, European aesthetic movements of German Expressionism or Italian Nonrealism, film noir emerges as a cycle or series of films. It consists of a finite group of motion pictures made during a specific historical period which share certain aesthetic traits and thematic concerns.

Aesthetically, noir relies heavily on shadowy, low-key lighting; deep-focus cinematography; distorting, wide-angle lenses; sequence shots; disorienting mise-en-scene; tension-inducing, oblique and vertical compositional lines; jarring juxtapositions betweens shots involving extreme changes in camera angle or screen size; claustrophobic framing; romantic, voice-over narration; and a complex narrative structure, characterized by flashbacks and/or a convoluted temporal sequencing of events.

Thematically, film noir grapples, as Robert Porfirio suggests, with existential issues such as the futility of individual action; the alienation, loneliness, and isolation of the individual within industrialized, mass society; the problematic choice between being and nothingness; the absurdity, meaninglessness, and purposelessness of life; and the arbitrariness of social justice, which results in individual despair, leading to chaos, violence, and paranoia.

Typical noir heroes do not need to be detectives, though the social alienation of figures in that profession makes them archetypal noir protagonists.
Often, they are merely antisocial loners—tramps or drifters as in *Detour* (1945)
and *The Postman Always Rings Twice* (1946). But even the gainfully employed,
like insurance salesman Walter Neff in *Double Indemnity* (1944) or cashier
Chris Cross in *Scarlet Street* (1945), can be subject to a certain deadpan,
existential angst, especially given their relatively faceless anonymity within a
larger, dehumanizing work environment.

But perhaps the most existential of all noir heroes is the amnesiac. In
Somewhere in the Night (1946), he is an ex-marine (played by John Hodiak) who
possesses only two enigmatic clues to his identity, and who is plunged into a
sinister underworld of crime as he follows these leads in an attempt to figure
out who he is. Similar mysteries centered around amnesiacs become the
central focus of Alfred Hitchcock's *Spellbound* (1945), in which Gregory Peck is
cured of his amnesia by a psychiatrist (played by Ingrid Bergman) with whom
he has fallen in love. The amnesiac reappears in Robert Florey's *The Crooked
Way* (1949), which tells the story of another shell-shocked veteran who becomes involved with racketeers as he investigates his own past. These amnesiacs epitomize the social estrangement and psychological confusion that has
settled in on the formerly healthy American psyche after the war. Audiences
establish a troubled identification with these heroes who have become cut off

Amnesiac and returning war veteran "George Taylor" (John Hodiak) searches for clues to his real
identity in *Somewhere in the Night* (1946).

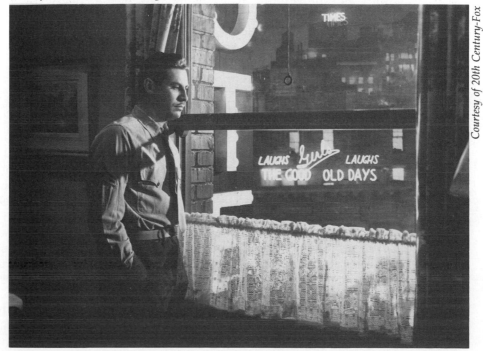

Courtesy of 20th Century-Fox

from their own pasts and whose identity crises mirror those of the nation as a whole.

As both a style and a bundle of thematic concerns, film noir initially seems to be a phenomenon that could appear at any moment in time. But, as an aesthetic movement, it is necessarily grounded in a particular historical period—that of wartime and postwar America. To what extent is it a style or (thematic) content? To what extent is it a unique feature of American film history? Clearly, noir is a combination of all of its various identities. It is part genre, part series, part mode.

Certain stylistic elements and thematic concerns associated with film noir look back to 1920s German Expressionism and 1930s French Poetic Realism. They also look forward to certain American films of the 1970s and 1980s, which appropriate noir stylistics in an attempt to capture the apocalyptic mood of an era that was disillusioned by the Watergate cover-up and psychically scarred by the Vietnam war. But they finally belong to only one period and place—to 1940s and early 1950s America.

Neither the German Expressionist *The Cabinet of Dr. Caligari* (1919) nor the French Poetic Realist *La Bête Humaine* (1938) have ever been described as films noirs. However, Hollywood's reworking of the former (*Strange Illusion*, 1945) and remake of the latter (*Human Desire*, 1954) have. Why? And why is it that Schrader and others have not accepted contemporary remakes of postwar films noirs, ranging from *Farewell, My Lovely* (1975) and *The Big Sleep* (1978) to *Body Heat* (1981) and *Against All Odds* (1984), as films noirs? The answers to these questions return us to the moment of the "discovery" of film noir in postwar France and to the notion that film noir's identity is somehow bound up with its ability to disturb audiences.

NOIR STYLISTICS: A SHIFT IN PERSPECTIVE

American Expressionism

What struck French critics about film noir was its essential *difference* from earlier American films. The narrative linearity of 1930s classical cinema had suddenly given way to narrative disjunction, fragmentation, and disorientation, as seen in the flashback-within-flashback-within-flashback structure of *The Locket* (1946). *Citizen Kane* (1941) had blazed the trail for complex narrative structure, and dozens of films noirs, even including marginal, low-budget efforts such as *Raw Deal* (1948) and *Ruthless* (1948), model themselves on Welles's masterpiece. *Kane* serves as a source for much of noir's subsequent stylistic and narrative practice, though it lacks one ingredient crucial to most definitions of noir: Its narrative is not concerned with crime nor are its characters situated in a criminal milieu.

The soft, evenly distributed, high-key lighting style of the 1930s, which functions to direct the audience's attention and to glamorize stars, has yielded virtually overnight to the harsh, low-key lighting of the 1940s, which obscures the action, deglamorizes the star, and reduces the actors to shadowy formal elements embedded within the overall design of the composition. The carefully constructed sense of space found in classical cinema, which works to maintain the spatial orientation of the spectator, disappears and is replaced by wide-angle cinematography, which, as in films like Welles's *Touch of Evil* (1958), distorts space and disorients the spectator.

Conventional eye-level camera positions give way, in films such as *Kiss Me Deadly* (Aldrich, 1955), to extreme low- and high-angle perspectives. Welles and Aldrich frequently cut from one extreme angle to another to heighten the assault upon the spectator's sense of complacency. With every violation of the norm, film noir stylistics mark an intrusive intervention between the spectator and the straightforward exposition of the story, foregrounding narrative form and thus making it visible.

From the perspective of French and presumably American audiences as well, film noir can be understood as the same old, familiar classical Hollywood cinema possessed by a new, recognizably alien spirit, which incorporates aesthetic elements and thematic concerns previously found only in "foreign" art films. Expressionistic devices, such as highly subjective, voice-over narration (*Detour*, 1945) or hallucinatory sequences (*Murder, My Sweet*, 1944), suddenly replace more conventional, less visible, narrative practices. It is all right for foreign films, like *Caligari*, to be a bit odd. American audiences expect that. But when American films begin to adopt—even for only a moment—a foreign tongue, the disquieting forces of fear and paranoia creep into what used to be, for most American audiences at least, the stabilizing and reassuring experience of going to the movies.

From Disturbing Conventions to Conventional Disturbances

If "foreign" elements had appeared in American films that had more overt artistic pretensions, they might have been understood as justified by the artistic nature of the film itself as in the case of *Citizen Kane*. But they crop up in the least likely places—in sleazy detective films, low-budget crime pictures, and run-of-the-mill melodramas. No wonder audiences become uneasy. The staple of the industry and the films most frequently identified with everyday motion picture entertainment—genre films—had developed psychotic tendencies. Something has clearly gone wrong somewhere. In other words, these films are "noir" in the context of the more conventional body of Hollywood cinema which preceded them. They were "noir" for audiences seeing them for the first time in the 1940s and 1950s. And, though they continue to appear "noir" in relation to earlier films for subsequent audiences, we tend to be less disturbed by them today than our grandparents must have been in the postwar era. Subsequent American cinema—itself influenced by film noir—has hardened us to its unsettling power.

This is clearly not the case for the *derivative* "films noirs" of the 1970s and 1980s, which look back stylistically and thematically to the *authentic* films noirs of the 1940s and 1950s. Following the publication of Schrader's "Notes on Film Noir" in 1972, screenwriters and directors deliberately set out to make films noirs, transforming the disruptive stylistic strategies and disturbing thematic obsessions of postwar film noir into a system of expectations and conventions. As they watch *The Long Goodbye* (1973) and *Chinatown* (1974), audiences recall the private-eye films of the 1940s to which these works allude. Directors in the 1970s quote film noir stylistic devices in an attempt to reconstruct the postwar period in which their films are set.

In these instances, film noir has been transformed from an aesthetic movement into a genre. Stylistic elements which, in the 1940s and 1950s, were part of a strategy to disorient spectators have been refashioned, in the 1970s, into a systematic, carefully tailored "look" designed to trigger a conventional acknowledgment on the part of viewers who identify that look with films of the late 1940s. The overall effect of these allusions to earlier films noirs upon contemporary audiences is more reassuring than unsettling. The "noir" films of the 1970s and 1980s are not noir. They are pseudo-noir.

NOIR AND THE PRODUCTION CODE

Forbidden Subjects; Twisted Treatments

The Production Code—the body of censorship regulations governing what Hollywood was permitted to show on the screen—played a crucial role in making films of the 1940s and early 1950s noir. Subsequent changes in this Code result in the production of films that are decidedly less noir. Prior to 1968, when the Production Code instituted in the 1930s, was abandoned for a version of the present film-rating system, certain subject matters were prohibited from the screen. Taboo subjects range from the depiction of nudity, homosexuality, interracial sexual activity, incest, rape, and abortion to excessive violence or brutality, profanity, the detailed depiction of criminal acts, and the use of drugs.

American films of the mid- to late 1930s rarely deal with these subjects, but film noir frequently does, often resulting in amazing displays of narrative contortion as the films allude to prohibited material without directly violating the Code. Acts of sadism and violence, such as the scalding of an individual's face with a pot of boiling hot coffee in *The Big Heat* (1953), regularly take place offscreen. Their intensity is amplified by violent or otherwise disjunctive editing or offscreen sound effects. Homosexuality figures prominently in the motivation of the plots of several original novels later made into films noirs; but on the screen this motivation is concealed, disguised, or recast in another form. It is desexualized and displaced—occasionally in ways that lay bare deep cultural fears about homosexuality with an astounding clarity. Thus the homophobia that prompts the central murder in Richard Brooks' novel, *The Brick Foxhole*, is transformed by Hollywood "self-censorship" into anti-Semitism in Edward Dmytryk's screen adaptation of the book, *Crossfire* (1947).

Courtesy of Warner Bros.

The Production Code represses the depiction of sex and drugs, complicating narrative moments such as this in *The Big Sleep* (1946) in which detective Philip Marlowe (Humphrey Bogart) investigates a crime scene.

In other instances, the presence of sexual abnormality and the use of drugs in novels are repressed altogether in their film adaptations, resulting in narrative incoherence, as in *The Big Sleep* (1946). Indeed, the centrality of drugs and sex to the Chandler novel on which the Hawks film was based forces its producers to resort to the most obscure sorts of subterfuges in an attempt to adapt the original plot to the screen. These gymnastics result in a final product that, although directed by one of the most obsessive practitioners of narrative logic—Howard Hawks—is almost incomprehensible to anyone who has not read the original Chandler novel.

The End of Censorship; the End of Noir?

The relaxation of the Production Code in the late 1950s, along with the advent of the ratings system in the late 1960s, prepares the way for a new era of explicitness in the 1970s. By that time, films deal more or less openly with adultery (*Body Heat* and *The Postman Always Rings Twice*, 1981), rape (*Straw Dogs*, 1971; *Frenzy*, 1972), incest (*Chinatown*, 1974), drugs (*The French Connection I and II*, 1971, 1975; *Farewell, My Lovely*, 1975), extreme violence (*Dirty Harry*, 1971; *Taxi Driver*, 1976), prostitution (*Hustle*, 1975; *Taxi Driver*, 1976), and, last but not least, nudity and sexual intercourse (see all of the above films and a large percentage of all 1970s films).

Michael Winner's remake of *The Big Sleep* (1978) is free to put everything back into the film that had been outlawed by censors in the 1940s, and it does so with a vengeance. But its graphicness dooms it as a film noir. No stylistic or narrational contortions are necessary to get it past the censors. Its subject matter may have been sensational (though in the context of 1970s movies it is pretty tame), but the way in which this material is presented is neither disturbed nor disturbing. It is as classically "direct" as any film from Hollywood in the 1930s. The matter-of-factness with which previously taboo material is dealt in the sexually "liberated" climate of the 1970s is what distinguishes the earlier, "authentic" films noirs of the 1940s and 1950s from the pseudo-films noirs of the 1970s and 1980s.

INNOCENCE LOST: THE LITERARY ORIGINS OF FILM NOIR

In examining film noir as an affective phenomenon—as an uncomfortable experience for spectators—we have tended so far to define it "negatively" by stating what it is not and what is not it: It is not a genre and films of the 1970s and 1980s that appropriate the style and themes of earlier films noirs are not necessarily noir. Neither genres nor pseudo-noirs are "negative" enough as phenomena; neither could generate enough negative energy to upset the traditional viewer. But it is also possible to define film noir more positively in terms of the various "negative" forces that help bring it into being. For instance, the outbreak of war in Europe, American entry into World War II, and postwar efforts to "return to normal," set the agenda for a more down-beat brand of cinema than audiences had encountered in the 1930s.

The immediate postwar era, in particular, seems to have been guided by the mistaken belief that the relatively simple world of prewar America for which returning servicemen had fought and for which they nostalgically longed could be magically re-created. The general realization that this was a delusion clearly influences both the world-weary cynicism of film noir and the sense of frustration and experience of disempowerment that stood at its center. American innocence cannot be easily recaptured.

In fact, film noir suggests that American innocence had been lost long before the war. It becomes clearer and clearer that something more than money and jobs has been lost during the Great Depression. The spirit of noir traces its origins back to certain thematic and stylistic antecedents that it shares with American popular fiction of the 1920s and 1930s.

Hard-Boiled Fiction

In both content and style, American hard-boiled novels introduce a new tradition of realism to the genre of detective fiction. This "realism" is characterized by a revolutionary shift in both the class and the technique of the detective, the milieu in which the detective works, and the language which he or she speaks. Unlike English detective fiction, which is dominated by aristocratic dabblers in detection, armchair experts in the art of deduction, or dotty old women armed with upper- or middle-class sensibilities, the novels of Hammett, Cain, McCoy, Chandler, and others feature a proletarian tough guy who lives on the fringe of the criminal world.

As Ross Macdonald, the creator of Lew Archer, explains, the protagonist of these works is "the classless, restless man [sic] of American democracy, who spoke the language of the street." As Macdonald's own language suggests, American hard-boiled detectives are, almost by definition, male. While the relative gentility of the world in which English detectives function permits female sleuths, the "mean streets" down which the hard-boiled detective walk are not safe for women.

The private eye's milieu is characterized not by garden parties, teas, masked balls, and other ceremonies of the well-to-do but by dark city streets, back alleys, grungy offices (with a pint of booze in the desk drawer), desolate hotel rooms, sleazy bars, pool halls, gambling dens, houses of prostitution, and other attractions within the neon-lit, red-light districts that dominate the wrong side of town. Hammett's Personville (pronounced "Poisonville") and Chandler's Bay City epitomize the corrupt metropolises the typical hard-boiled detective haunts. As Steven Marcus suggests, this is a Hobbesian world, in which life is nasty, brutish, and short—a world characterized by universal warfare, anarchy, and mistrust.

For the majority of these Depression-era novelists, contemporary America is an urban, industrialized landscape peopled by characters caught in the grip of passion, lust, greed, jealousy, and other naturalistic drives. The "boys in the back room," as Edmund Wilson called the "Black Mask" school of writers of pulp detective fiction, look back for inspiration neither to Wilkie Collins, the Dickensian author of *The Moonstone* and *The Woman in White*, nor to Sir Arthur Conan Doyle, but to Émile Zola and other nineteenth-century naturalists, whose matter-of-fact depiction of decadence and corruption caught their imagination.

The Detective Hero

Unlike their "European" predecessors, Edgar Allan Poe's Dupin or Conan Doyle's Sherlock Holmes, the hard-boiled detective does not rely upon the powers of deductive reasoning, acute observation, or scientific method to solve his cases but rather upon dogged perseverance, animal cunning, physical stamina, and brute force. Noir heroes, whether detectives or not, are similarly weak as intellects. In *Double Indemnity*, when insurance investigator Barton Keyes asks Walter Neff to give up his sales job to work behind a desk with him, Walter refuses. After noting that he has always considered Walter "a shade less dumb" than the other salesmen, Keyes sarcastically quips that Walter isn't really smarter than the others; he is just a bit taller.

In matching wits with Phyllis, the film's femme fatale, Walter comes in second. She successfully manipulates him into helping her do away with her husband and then, when he begins to suspect her of treachery at the end, she outmaneuvers him, countering his plot against her with a plot of her own against him. About all he can do is arrange to die last (i.e., after she has died), enjoying the fate that lies in store for most noir heroes.

Though the brawny, proletarian tough guy of American detective fiction may lack the mental powers of his brainy predecessors, he, like his successors in film noir, attempts to make up for his failings as a man of intellect with his verbal wit. Both the writer of detective fiction and the detective hero control their worlds by controlling language. They have style—verbal style. Hammett's sparse, highly verbal, prose style and straightforward syntactical style establish a no-nonsense world in which the monosyllabic directness and the dogged, one-fact/clue-after-another, linear logic of the detective hero effectively cuts through the web of lies spun by everyone he encounters, from the Fat Man and his gunsel to Joel Cairo and the femme fatale.

At the other end of the stylistic spectrum, Chandler's complex syntactical style, colorful metaphors, and descriptive excesses establish a narrative voice that values the ability to turn a phrase. The prowess of his private eye is measured by his control of language, especially witty repartee which enables him to enjoy an edge over his opponents in the verbal arena, even though they may have been able to dominate him physically. In *Farewell, My Lovely*, Marlowe even dubs one of his flat-footed, slow-witted antagonists "Hemingway." Here Chandler, through his detective hero, takes a jab at the impoverished verbal style that informs a number of Hemingway-influenced American mystery writers and confirms the privileged status, within his work at least, of verbal wit over linguistic directness.

Noir and Verbal Wit

In Chandler's reworking for the screen of Cain's *Double Indemnity*, the first encounter between Fred MacMurray's Walter Neff and Barbara Stanwyck's Phyllis Dietrichson provides the chief example of hard-boiled repartee used as a mode of playful combat. Always the glib insurance salesman trying to make a sale, Neff attempts to talk his client's wife into bed with him while she coyly counters his advances. Their conversation concludes with the following exchange:

PHYLLIS: There's a speed limit in this state, Mr. Neff. Forty-five miles per hour.

WALTER: How fast was I going, officer?

PHYLLIS: I'd say around ninety.

WALTER: Suppose you get down off your motorcycle and give me a ticket?

PHYLLIS: Suppose I let you off with a warning this time?

WALTER: Suppose it doesn't take?

PHYLLIS: Suppose I have to whack you over the knuckles?

WALTER: Suppose I bust out crying and put my head on your shoulder?

PHYLLIS: Suppose you try putting it on my husband's shoulder?

WALTER: That tears it! [*pause*] Eight-thirty tomorrow evening then?

PHYLLIS: That's what I suggested.

WALTER: Will you be here too?

PHYLLIS: I guess so. I usually am.

WALTER: Same chair, same perfume, same anklet?

PHYLLIS: I wonder if I know what you mean?

WALTER: I wonder if you wonder?

Courtesy of Paramount

Insurance salesman Walter Neff (Fred MacMurray) spars with his client's wife (Barbara Stan-wyck) in *Double Indemnity* (1944).

Double Indemnity's double entendres about "speeding" and "traffic tickets" not only introduce the couple's relationship in terms of crime and punishment, but also establish their basic sexual antagonism. This initial, seemingly harmless, sexual banter serves to structure the implicit sexual hostility that governs their relationship during the remainder of the film and prepares the groundwork for their last, nonverbal exchange when they finally stop talking and shoot one another.

WOMEN IN FILM NOIR

The origins of film noir in pulp fiction help explain its distinctive attitude toward the representation of women. The proletarian tough guy achieves his toughness by repressing all signs of weakness within him—and all weakness, for him, is associated with the feminine. At the end of *The Maltese Falcon*, Humphrey Bogart's Sam Spade deliberates between his feelings (a "feminine" virtue) for Brigid O'Shaughnessy (Mary Astor) and his loyalty to professional codes (a "male" virtue), which requires him to avenge the murder of his former partner. Spade sticks by the "male" codes of the detective and, by resisting Brigid's final appeals and turning her over to the police, rejects his "feminine" side.

Women as Social Menace

The threat that women and the feminine pose to the noir hero presents itself on two different fronts—the socioeconomic and the psychoanalytic. On the socioeconomic front, as Sylvia Harvey shows, the changing status of American women during the war and postwar period challenges male dominance. The entry of women into the workforce and their taking over of traditional male roles violate the fundamental order of sexual relations. Previously, middle-class women were confined to the home where they took care of the domestic needs of the family, while men were able to move back and forth freely between the home and the workplace. In the 1940s, women take jobs in factories, replacing men who had gone into the service (see *The Life and Times of Rosie the Riveter*, 1980). They work on assembly lines in defense plants, making tanks or airplanes (see *Swing Shift Maisie*, 1943, or *Swing Shift*, 1984).

These changes pose a threat to traditional values, which are seen as centered in the institution of the family. Film noir registers the anitfeminist backlash by providing a picture of a postwar America in which there is no family or in which the family exists chiefly as a negative phenomenon. In noir, the family is either nonexistent or negative. It is characterized either as a claustrophobic, emasculating trap (snaring the henpecked husband, Chris Cross, in *Scarlet Street*) or as a bankrupt system of perfunctory relationships, featuring murderous wives (*Double Indemnity*) and corrupt children (*Mildred Pierce*). In leaving the private sphere of home and family to enter the public sphere of work, women (like Mildred Pierce), it is assumed, have abandoned—or at least neglected—the domestic needs of their sweethearts, husbands, and/or children. Film noir dramatizes the consequences of this neglect, transforming women into willful creatures intent on destroying both their mates and the sacred institution of the family.

Classical Hollywood cinema has taken great efforts to shield the family from the world of crime. Traditional genre films routinely oppose the sacred space of the family to that of the world outside. Even gangster films seek to contrast the bonds of family with those of the gang. Crime films center dramatic conflict around the struggle of each institution with the other over the possession of the identity and/or soul of the gangster hero, a process illustrated in *Public Enemy* (1931) through the (ineffectual) efforts of Tom Powers' family to keep him from a life of crime. In film noir, the world of crime and that of the family overlap. Crime has moved from outside the family to within it, and the impetus for crime comes as often from women as from men.

Typical film noir families consist of wives who kill their husbands (*Double Indemnity*, *The Postman Always Rings Twice*), husbands who kill or try to kill their wives (*Gaslight*, *The Two Mrs. Carrolls*), children who kill or try to kill their parents or stepparents (*The Strange Love of Martha Ivers*, *Angel Face*), uncles who try to kill their nieces (*Shadow of a Doubt*), aunts who kill their nephews (*Leave Her to Heaven*), and lovers who kill one another (*Out of the Past*, *Gun Crazy*).

Women as Psychological Terror

The psychoanalytic front reflects women in film noir who present a psychic threat to the typically insecure noir hero. Laura Mulvey, following Freud, argues that the image of women on the screen functions to recall, for the male spectator, the castration anxiety he experiences on first perceiving sexual difference as a child. As an institution that supports male dominance and patriarchy, classical Hollywood cinema attempts to alleviate this anxiety through a process known as disavowal in which the female's "castrated" status is denied. This denial can be achieved either through her fetishization or through her devaluation, or both.

In fetishization, the image of the woman is *overvalued*, often through the use of lingering close-ups, glamorous costumes, or other techniques that transform her into a spectacle. In becoming pure spectacle, the lack which she signifies is thus "filled in," replaced by her objectification. Marlene Dietrich, for example, is routinely fetishized by Josef von Sternberg in films such as *The Blue Angel* and *Morocco* (1930) and *Shanghai Express* (1932), in which close-ups of her legs or her face turn her into an object of both male desire and male fantasy.

Through a process of *devaluation*, woman is seen as a guilty object—her "castration" serving as the symbol of her punishment. Thus Alfred Hitchcock, in films such as *Notorious* (1946) or *Vertigo* (1958), presents "guilty" women who are the objects of male investigations into the original source of their guilt. The heroine in the former film is a "fallen woman"—the daughter of a Nazi spy, an alcoholic, and a playmate of wealthy men; the heroine in the latter film is a paid accomplice to a murder. These women are first punished and then later, having revealed their guilty secret, rescued (or, in the case of *Vertigo*, not rescued) by the hero. A similar logic motivates the representation of women in film noir. As Mulvey explains, female sexuality is routinely devalued by the male protagonists who feel threatened by it.

Thus women in film noir tend to be characterized as femmes fatales, intent on castrating or otherwise destroying the male hero. This role is played with nightmarish fidelity by Jean Simmons in *Angel Face* (1953), Barbara Stanwyck in *Double Indemnity*, Joan Bennett in *Scarlet Street*, and by a host of other spider women.

Often, noir women are both fetishized and devalued, constructed as spectacular objects of male sexual fantasy who then turn on those whose desires initially empowered them. Thus, Stanwyck first appears in *Double Indemnity* standing at the top of the stairs, dressed only in a bath towel. Moments later, her body is fetishized through close-ups of her ankle as she descends the stairs. Yet her initial appearance as spectacle is subsequently revealed to have been staged; it is all part of her seduction and subsequent entrapment of the hero, whom she then manipulates into killing her husband.

The femme fatale in *Out of the Past* (1947) romantically materializes before the detective hero in the exotic setting of Mexico, emerging first out of the sunlight, then out of the moonlight, as he sits in a small cantina in Acapulco.

Courtesy of RKO

The iconography of film noir: In *Out of the Past* (1947), the treacherous femme fatale (played by Jane Greer, left) holds a smoking gun, while the vulnerable male hero (Robert Mitchum) smokes a cigarette.

By the end of the film, her path has been strewn with the bodies of an apparently endless succession of dead men, culminating with that of the hapless hero (Robert Mitchum) whom she shoots in the groin.

A CRITIQUE OF POPULISM

New Culture, Old Myths

The destabilization of sexual relationships found in film noir is symptomatic of a larger social disorder. Prior to World War II, American society had been held together by various myths that structured its identity as a nation. These myths rested, in large part, upon the principles of Jeffersonian democracy, which assumed a fundamental equality based upon the universal ownership of property. More specifically, Jeffersonian democracy was based upon the agrarian ideal of the yeoman farmer, whose self-sufficiency was rooted in his ability to grow enough food for himself as well as additional produce to sell to his neighbors. In other words, notions of democratic equality were founded upon the universal ownership of property. This equality-through-universal-ownership concept provided the fundamental principle for a mythology which drove nineteenth-century American expansionist ideology. The "democratic" promise of cheap or free land to those who settled the frontier thus served as the motivation for western settlement, which became, in turn, a realization of America's manifest destiny.

But the closing of the frontier, the exhaustion of free land, and the rapid industrialization of America in the latter part of the century begins a slow process of social change. The agrarian ideal gives way to an industrialized mass society. By 1920, for the first time in American history, more people live in urban than in rural areas. The "old" middle class, consisting of shopkeepers, farmers, and other property owners, gives way to a "new" middle class, dominated by hourly wage earners, who own neither land nor houses.

Though millions of laborers and white-collar workers live this new reality, they continue to subscribe to the old, preindustrial-era myths. It is only after the Depression that the power of these myths begins to waver. Film noir reflects a transitional stage in American ideology as American identity shifts from nineteenth-century, preindustrial, agrarian prototypes to twentieth-century models, which acknowledge the nation's transformation into a mass, consumer society and into an industrialized, corporate state.

Double Indemnity's Walter Neff, for example, works for a large, anonymous, consumer-based corporation—the Pacific All-Risk Insurance Co. He is a product of postwar consumer society. He lives alone in an efficiency apartment, goes bowling for fun and relaxation, has clandestine rendezvous with married women among shelves of mass-produced baby food and other mass-market products at the local supermarket, and drinks beer in his car at a drive-in restaurant. Film noir captures the emptiness of Neff's world. As a movement, it reflects the chaotic period in which old myths begin to crumble and no new myths are there to take their place—the period in which national identity is in crisis.

Capra and Film Noir

The best examples of these old myths appear in the work of Frank Capra, whose films epitomize the classicism and order of pre-noir Hollywood cinema. Capra's vision of America is set forth in a series of films made in the late 1930s, culminating in *Mr. Deeds Goes to Town* (1936) and *Mr. Smith Goes to Washington* (1939), which articulate a "populist" ideology. These films celebrate nineteenth-century agrarian values, such as hard work, frugality, honesty, good neighborliness, self-sufficiency, egalitarianism, common sense, personal authenticity (as opposed to phoniness), and moral sincerity. Through the heroic efforts of their stalwart protagonists, they attack the twentieth-century evils of industrialism, big business, special interest groups, commercialism, political machines, urban corruption, cynicism, and intellectualism—all of which threaten the populist spirit that has animated small-town America.

The threat to this idyllic world is presented most powerfully in Capra's postwar celebration of small-town American values—*It's a Wonderful Life* (1946). Here George Bailey (James Stewart), through his building and loan company, holds off the efforts of corrupt, greedy capitalists such as Mr. Potter (Lionel Barrymore) to transform the city of Bedford Falls into an ugly, modern American metropolis. George Bailey, having sacrificed his own desires and needs in the service of his family, friends, and the larger community, believes that his life has been a failure and, like the existential noir hero, is driven to contemplate suicide. But his guardian angel "rescues" him from his own self-destructive efforts and reveals to him what Bedford Falls would have been like if he had never lived.

Like the alienated hero of film noir, George wanders through Bedford Falls, which has now become "Pottersville," in search of someone who would confirm his identity and the fact of his prior existence. In a reversal of certain earlier noir films like *Somewhere in the Night* (1946), it is the town, not George, that has developed amnesia. Yet, the experience for George remains as weird and alienating as that which any of his shell-shocked predecessors had undergone. The "Pottersville" sequence reverses the populist ideal of small-town America, displaying no families, homes, or small businesses. All of these have apparently been destroyed by the forces of big business and industrialization identified with Potter, who reduces proud homeowners to tenants in slum dwellings.

For a few minutes, the corrupt nature of contemporary corporate America which this and Capra's earlier 1930s films had struggled so hard to combat and, through their heroes' ultimate triumphs, to deny, surfaces. It is a world

A depressed George Bailey (James Stewart, center) contemplates suicide in *It's a Wonderful Life* (1946).

Courtesy of RKO

in which the individual has no stake in society, and thus no power or place within a social system that is suddenly revealed to be nondemocratic (i.e., not based on an equal ownership of property). Capra, however, quickly patches up this crack in American populist ideology, relegating the "Pottersville" sequence to the status of a "bad dream" and restoring George to his family, friends, and community.

Yet, the presence of this nightmarish inversion of Capra's ideal American community in the film brilliantly illustrates film noir's subversive relationship to classical Hollywood cinema, which attempts to repress the very forces to which film noir gives voice. Film noir, as a phenomenon of the 1940s, grows out of the horrifying realization that the populist myth that had given comfort and order to American identity in the past was just that—only a myth—and that a new reality—that of Pottersville—has taken its place. It is a realization that, coupled with the trauma of war and the disillusionment of the postwar period, serves to smash the utopian fantasy world of 1930s ideology. In other words, film noir represents a remarkable epistemological shift in America's self-conceptualization. Capra's utopian, small-town America doesn't exist anymore—except in Capra pictures.

FILM NOIR: AN UNDERCURRENT WITHIN THE MAINSTREAM

Film noir, however, does not entirely dismantle American myth and American identity in the 1940s; it proves to be only one major current within (and clearly beneath) a flood of films which reaffirm traditional American values and identity. With the exception of certain downbeat items, such as *The Best Years of Our Lives* (1946) and *Duel in the Sun* (1946), the box-office champs of the postwar era tend to be films that are decidedly not noir—films like *Meet Me in St. Louis* (1944), *National Velvet* (1944), *The Bells of St. Mary's* (1945), *The Jolson Story* (1946), *Life With Father* (1947), *The Road to Rio* (1947), *Easter Parade* (1948), *Jolson Sings Again* (1949), *Samson and Delilah* (1949), *David and Bathsheba* (1951), *Show Boat* (1951), *An American in Paris* (1951), *Quo Vadis?* (1951), and *Ivanhoe* (1952).

By the late 1950s, the advent of television virtually destroyed the low-budget, B-film industry, which provided the bulk of films noirs. The mood of the country begins to reflect a newfound, postwar prosperity (indeed, economic historians begin to refer to the United States as "the affluent society"); and, at the end of the decade, the promise of John F. Kennedy's "New Frontier" turns Americans away from potentially depressing thoughts of the technological blight that had been produced by industrialization to utopian visions of a machine-age paradise, filled with labor-saving devices. The trauma of the Depression and the shell-shock of the war years, which destabilized American identity briefly in the postwar era, has supposedly been treated and cured. The films noirs that were noir "for us" no longer spoke to the needs some Americans felt for films that addressed their own existential malaise.

But the scar on the American psyche which film noir represented remains visible today for all of us to see. It is brought back to the surface of the American psyche by another war—that in Vietnam. And film noir's ability to convey a sense of paranoia and betrayal makes it the ideal form for capturing the spirit of post-Watergate America. Americans rediscover film noir in the 1970s because it provides a way of looking at experience that not only reflects that experience but also finally makes sense. Film noir of the 1940s and 1950s becomes the source material that prompts a new understanding of postwar American reality. In rediscovering it, Americans locate a more modern body of myths through which they might come to terms with contemporary American experience.

SELECT FILMOGRAPHY

Citizen Kane (1941)
The Maltese Falcon (1941)
This Gun for Hire (1942)
Double Indemnity (1944)
Murder, My Sweet (1944)
Detour (1945)
Hangover Square (1945)
Leave Her to Heaven (1945)
Mildred Pierce (1945)
My Name Is Julia Ross (1945)
Scarlet Street (1945)
The Killers (1946)
The Locket (1946)
Somewhere in the Night (1946)
The Spiral Staircase (1946)
The Strange Love of Martha Ivers (1946)

Crossfire (1947)
M. Verdoux (1947)
Out of the Past (1947)
Pursued (1947)
The Lady From Shanghai (1948)
Moonrise (1948)
The Naked City (1948)
Ruthless (1948)
Gun Crazy (1949)
Sunset Blvd. (1950)
Macao (1952)
Angel Face (1953)
The Big Heat (1953)
The Big Combo (1955)
Kiss Me Deadly (1955)
Touch of Evil (1958)

SELECT BIBLIOGRAPHY

Borde, Raymond, and Etienne Chaumeton. *Panorama du Film Noir Americain.* Paris: Editions du Minuit, 1955.

Harvey, Sylvia. "Woman's Place: The Absent Family of Film Noir," in E. Ann Kaplan, ed., *Women in Film Noir.* London: British Film Institute, 1978.

Higham, Charles, and Joel Greenberg. *Hollywood in the Forties.* New York: Barnes, 1968.

Hirsch, Foster. *The Dark Side of the Screen: Film Noir.* San Diego: Barnes, 1981.

Marcus, Steven. "Introduction" to Dashiell Hammett's *The Continental Op.* New York: Vintage, 1975.

Mulvey, Laura. "Visual Pleasure and Narrative Cinema," *Screen 16,* no. 3 (Autumn 1975).

Place, Janey. "Women in Film Noir," in E. Ann Kaplan, ed., *Women in Film Noir.* London: British Film Institute, 1978.

Porfirio, Robert G. "No Way Out: Existential Motifs in the Film Noir," *Sight and Sound 45,* no. 4 (Autumn 1976).

Schrader, Paul. "Notes on Film Noir," *Film Comment 8* (Spring 1972).

Silver, Alain, and Elizabeth Ward, eds. *Film Noir: An Encyclopedic Reference to the American Style.* Woodstock, NY: Overlook Press, 1979.

THE MAKING OF THE WEST

THE AMERICAN FILM GENRE PAR EXCELLENCE

For over 40 years, from 1926 to 1967, Hollywood produced more Westerns than it did any other kind of film. During these years, roughly one-quarter of all Hollywood films were Westerns and, though no statistics exist for the years prior to 1926, Westerns similarly dominated American silent film production. The popularity of the silent Western begins with *The Great Train Robbery* (1903), which reenacts a famous robbery by Butch Cassidy and the Wild Bunch that had occurred only a few years earlier. The genre's appeal increases with "Broncho Billy" Anderson, Thomas Ince, and D. W. Griffith Westerns. And it culminates in the box-office success of films featuring Dustin Farnum, William S. Hart, and Tom Mix. The screen personae of these Western stars captivated audiences from the mid-1910s through the late 1920s.

Though a sizeable proportion of the total number of Westerns made in Hollywood undoubtedly include many B films, the sheer quantity of Westerns produced—whether classified as A, B, or Z pictures—testifies to the overwhelming popularity of the genre. Other genres, most notably the gangster film, remain uniquely American in origin, but the Western has become the American film genre par excellence, not only in terms of the quantity and quality of films made but also in terms of its longevity as a genre.

Though almost all the great Western stars of the postwar era, such as Gary Cooper, Randolph Scott, Joel McCrea, and John Wayne, are now dead and the genre itself has been repeatedly proclaimed dead (by Pauline Kael and others), rumors of the death of the Western have, as Mark Twain might have said, been somewhat exaggerated, as recent hits such as the television miniseries *Lonesome Dove* (1989), *Dances With Wolves* (1990), *City Slickers* (1991), and *Unforgiven* (1992) suggest.

And even if the film Western were to disappear entirely, the power of the myth of the West, which gives film Westerns much of their vitality, would, in all likelihood, continue to flourish in the everyday world of modern America. We would still be listening to country and western music, performed by singers and musicians in western dress. We would still pay premium prices for "sweated" Stetsons and jeans, broken in for us by "real cowboys out West." Those of us with a bit less money would still buy new Wrangler jeans off the rack. And we would still be eating fast food at Roy's (Roy Rogers' restaurants, that is), smoking Marlboro cigarettes, and driving cars named

Thunderbird, Mustang, Colt, Bronco, Pinto, Cougar, Sundance, and Cimarron.

If nineteenth-century western myth has become so powerful in twentieth-century America, what accounts for that power? If the Western has become *the* American genre, in what way(s) is it uniquely American? How does it address American concerns, what is its relationship to American culture, and what role does it play in the construction of an American identity? How does the genre change from period to period and what accounts for the fluctuations in its popularity, which reached an all-time high in the 1950s, then suddenly dropped in the 1960s, and continued to fall in the 1970s and later? The study of the *phenomenon* of the Western which follows will attempt to answer these and other questions.

FRONTIERS: HISTORY AND CINEMA

Frederick Jackson Turner and the 1890s

The birth of the Western film is inextricably bound up with the death of the West; more specifically, with the closing of the frontier. In Chicago, at a meeting of the American Historical Association on July 12, 1893, Frederick Jackson Turner presented a paper, "The Significance of the Frontier in American History," which revolutionized traditional thinking about American history. Turner's thesis begins with a declaration that the frontier, according to the U.S. Census Report of 1890, no longer existed. He argues that the existence of the frontier had played a crucial role both in American expansion during the nineteenth century and in the shaping of American character as well.

Turner maintains that "the peculiarity of American institutions is the fact that they have been compelled to adapt themselves to the changes of an expanding people—to the changes involved in crossing a continent, in winning a wilderness, and in developing at each area of this progress out of the primitive economic and political conditions of the frontier into the complexity of city life." For Turner, the closing of the frontier marks an end not only to the first period of American history, but also to the influence of the frontier upon the development of American identity.

Turner, however, fails to reckon with the movies (and with other popular forms of entertainment within which the old West survives) that recreate the frontier and, with it, an experience (by proxy) of the frontier for subsequent generations of Americans. In other words, at around the time when the frontier begins to disappear, the Western begins to replace the West, continuing, albeit in a purely mythic way, to shape American character. Subsequent historians have called Turner's frontier thesis into question, pointing out that the development of the West (and of American identity) cannot fully be explained by looking solely at the question of the frontier.

". . . Print the Legend"

Although Turner's frontier thesis may not be entirely accurate as history, it is nonetheless compelling as myth, providing a scenario of the role the West plays in American history, which Western films and literature have told over and over again until it seems to be true. In other words, at Turner's frontier, not only does East meet West but fact also meets fiction. Indeed, fiction is ultimately what the West is about. It is a site for the telling of the *story* of American identity. As the newspaper editor explains it in *The Man Who Shot Liberty Valance* (1962), "This is the West . . . when the legend becomes fact, print the legend."

Early in May of 1893, Thomas Edison had publicly demonstrated his latest invention, the Kinetoscope, to a gathering of engineers and scientists in Brooklyn. Within a year, Edison began to record on film various attractions, including stunts from Buffalo Bill Cody's Wild West Show, featuring Cody, Annie Oakley, a group of Sioux Indians, and other performers. In addition to these early actualities of 1894, in 1898 Edison filmed two fictional scenes, *Cripple Creek Bar-room* and *Poker at Dawson City*. With these few flickering images, which lasted, in toto, less than five minutes of screen time, the film Western is born. It recreates for mass consumption one of the most dramatic periods of American development—a period which had only just come to an end and had just begun to become the stuff of legends.

The fact that the first representations of the West on motion picture film are images of a wild west show and that the first blockbuster Western, *The Great Train Robbery*, is an updated reworking of a wild west show staple—"The Attack (by outlaws or Indians) on the Deadwood Stage"—is not insignificant. Nor is it an accident that Thomas Ince's popular Bison 101 series arose, in 1911, out of a partnership between the movies and the Miller Brothers' 101 Ranch Wild West Show or that Western stars, such as Will Rogers, Tom Mix, and Tim McCoy, entered the movies from the world of rodeos and wild west shows.

Buffalo Bill's Wild West Show, which began as a Fourth of July celebration organized by Cody in North Platte, Nebraska, in 1882, celebrates a West that was rapidly disappearing or, as some historians of the West might contend, never actually existed. It involves a transformation of history into theater and of actuality into myth. By 1895, when Cody added Sitting Bull to his list of attractions, it had become clear that the strategy of the wild west show was to turn the real "old" West into a spectacle for the entertainment of the new West, the East, and Europe. The popularity of Cody's show was astounding. During the 1885–1886 season, more than 1 million people attended its performances in Madison Square Garden and over 6 million spectators saw it, over a six-month period, at the Chicago World's Fair. By 1901, Cody's show employed over 500 people and he earned over $1 million a year for his efforts.

What Cody had begun Hollywood appropriated and adapted to suit its own needs. The movies not only continue but also expand upon Cody's commercialization and commodification of the West by mass-producing the wild west show and reworking its thrills and chills into an ever-increasing

Courtesy of United Artists

Buffalo Bill (Paul Newman) serves as star and master of ceremonies of his own wild west show in *Buffalo Bill and the Indians, or Sitting Bull's History Lesson* (1976).

number of different narrative situations. Robert Altman's *Buffalo Bill and the Indians, or Sitting Bull's History Lesson* (1976), which is based on Arthur Kopit's play *Indians*, provides a satiric portrait of the essential phoniness of this tradition, debunking Cody and calling into question the way in which American history has been turned into the stuff of show business. Clint Eastwood's *Bronco Billy* (1980), on the other hand, reaffirms the values of that tradition, presenting the wild west show and the myths of the old West, which it celebrates, as a means of personal redemption in a modern-day world corrupted by selfishness and greed.

THE LITERARY WEST

Dime Novels and Pulp Magazines

The commercialization of the West does not begin with the advent of the movies or of the wild west show but dates back to the 1860s, when Erastus Beadle published the first dime novel—Ann Stephens' *Malaeska: The Indian Wife of the White Hunter* (1860). Indeed, Buffalo Bill himself owes his fame and fortune to the dime novels. An obscure cavalry scout and buffalo hunter for the Union Pacific Railroad's construction crews, Cody was "discovered" in 1869 by dime novelist Ned Buntline who retold (and greatly embellished) Cody's story in a newspaper serial entitled "Buffalo Bill, the King of the Border Men." The dime novels similarly conferred celebrity status upon Wild Bill Hickok, Calamity Jane, Billy the Kid, Jesse James, and others.

Inexpensively printed and sold at a price of from 5 to 25 cents, dime novels were mass-produced in runs of 60,000 copies and enjoyed wide circulation in the Civil War and post–Civil War era. In 1860, Beadle issued one of the most popular and profitable Western stories—Edward Ellis' *Seth Jones: Or the Captives of the Frontier*, which sold more than 600,000 copies. Between 1860 and 1865, Beadle sold more than 5 million dime novels and, over the course of the years, published more than 3100 different titles in 33 separate series.

Later, when publishers began to explore the mass distribution of popular literature through the mails, dime novels gave way to magazines, which, in 1879, Congress permitted to be sent quite cheaply through the postal service to subscribers. After that, western stories began to serve as a staple of pulp magazines, including *Argosy* (founded in 1882) and *Western Story Magazine* (founded in 1919).

From Natty Bumppo to Shane

Dime novels and pulp westerns look back, as does every story or film about the West, to the *Leatherstocking Tales*, written by James Fenimore Cooper in the 1820s. The adventures of Cooper's fictional hero, Natty Bumppo, are based, in part, on the exploits of the real-life Daniel Boone, who died in 1820, and their sagas epitomize the contradictory nature of American experience. They both live in a space that stands between two not only different but also opposed cultures and both Boone and Bumppo repeatedly move back and forth between those worlds. That space is the frontier, and it defines the nature of their characters. They not only occupy the frontier but also embody it, serving as sites where the two worlds meet.

Both Boone and Bumppo are torn between the naturalness of the wilderness and the artifice of civilization, between savagery and humanity, between the freedom of nature and the constraints of culture. Like Boone, who reportedly pulled up stakes and moved further west whenever he could see the chimney smoke of his nearest neighbor, Cooper's hero also flees before the advance of civilization. But also like Boone, Bumppo's flight into the wilderness results only in the blazing of a trail for others to follow, leading to the further encroachment of civilization upon the wilds of nature.

Cooper's frontiersman provides the archetype for the western hero that we find in dime novels and films. According to Henry Nash Smith, "of seventy-nine dime novels selected as a sample of those dealing with the West between 1860 and 1893, forty contain one or more hunters or trappers whose age, costume, weapons, and general functions entitle them to be considered lineal descendants" of Cooper's Leatherstocking. Natty Bumppo, also known as Deerslayer, and Pathfinder, literally survives in the dozen or more film adaptations of Cooper's novels.

But he also serves as a more general model for the heroes featured in scores of other films, ranging from the Boone-like backwoods hunters in *The Big Sky* (1952)[1] to the alienated anti-heroes of *Stagecoach* (1939), *Shane* (1953), and *The Searchers* (1956). This figure also provides the central focus for the James Stewart–Anthony Mann and Randolph Scott–Budd Boetticher Westerns of the 1950s; for Clint Eastwood's man-with-no-name in Sergio Leone's Italian-made, "spaghetti" Westerns; and for Eastwood (again) in his own directorial efforts in the genre, *High Plains Drifter* (1972) and *Pale Rider* (1985).

In *Shane* and *The Searchers*, for example, the hero is a social outcast who rides in from the wilderness, enters the frontier community, leads it in its struggle to "civilize" the frontier, helps defeat the hired guns or Indians who stand in the way of "progress," and then returns to the wilderness. In emerging from and retreating to the wilderness, the hero remains identified with the natural landscape and functions as a force of nature in purging that landscape of corruption.

The western hero's conflict with the Indians, however, represents a significant exception to this rule in that the Indians are not associated with corruption but rather with an "unruly" force of nature which, in the eyes of white culture, resists the "natural" development of the West into an agrarian paradise. In both instances, the hero is quite frequently identified with the violent world against which he is pitted. Thus Shane (Alan Ladd) and Ethan Edwards (John Wayne) fight the gunfighter Wilson and the Comanche warchief Scar, their alter egos; that is, men like themselves. In slaying the enemies of society, who often resemble him in appearance or character, the western hero symbolically destroys himself. Having brought peace to the community through the use of his superior strength and unique skills, this western hero is unable to enter the community because it can no longer tolerate the excessive violence with which he, like his former enemy, remains identified.

ADAPTATION: WHEN EAST MEETS WEST

Bowlers to Buckskins

The western hero is forged amidst the conflicting forces that characterize the formation of the frontier. At the frontier, nature and culture meet, an encounter which transforms both. In order to survive, the pioneer from the East must adopt the ways of the West; the colonist must put aside his or her European dress and behavior, put on buckskin and moccasins, build the log houses of the Iroquois, and learn, like the Indian, to hunt, to fish, and to read the signs of nature. Struggle for survival within the natural landscape "westernizes" the easterner. Extreme instances of this can be found in *Broken Arrow* (1950), *Run of the Arrow* (1957), *A Man Called Horse* (1970), *Little Big Man* (1970), and

---

[1] For films about hunters and backwoodsmen, see also *Across the Wide Missouri* (1951), *The Kentuckian* (1955), *How the West Was Won* (1962), and *The Way West* (1967).

Dances With Wolves (1990), in which easterners (and in one case, an English lord) abandon their own culture for that of the Indian tribes with which they live.

More typically, the easterner will adapt to the West, while retaining certain eastern traits. The eastern tenderfoot played by Robert Young in *Western Union* (1941) exchanges his city clothes for western boots, chaps, vest, and hat, a ritualistic ceremony which appears in countless Westerns and is parodied in *City Slickers* when the three heroes comically outfit themselves for the trail drive which follows. As in the latter film, this purely superficial transformation precedes Young's more thorough westernization, which takes place, under the tutelage of a western mentor (played by Randolph Scott in *Western Union* and Jack Palance in *City Slickers*), against the background of a hostile natural landscape (and, in the former film, skirmishes with renegade Indians).

Feminine Transformations

Often the process of westernization is dramatized through the transformation of eastern women into frontierswomen. As Turner points out, from the days of the Revolutionary War until the closing of the frontier, the East has never quite been able to understand the West. Easterners tend to view the frontier as a rough and uncivilized region inhabited by rude, semiliterate, semibarbaric backwoodsmen. Like many other Westerns, *Drums Along the Mohawk* (1939) plays with this prejudice. The film begins with the wedding of the hero, Gil (Henry Fonda), to Lana (Claudette Colbert), the genteel daughter of a well-to-do Albany family, who leaves behind the elegant houses and fancy gowns of the city for the wilderness of west central New York (ca. 1776).

Upon her arrival in the Mohawk Valley, the heroine becomes hysterical at the sight of Blueback (Chief John Big Tree), a friendly Indian, and is dismayed upon discovering that her new home is a crude, one-room log cabin. Her fine eastern furniture is destroyed, along with their cabin, in an Indian attack, and the couple are forced to become tenant farmers for a local widow. Gradually, the heroine's fear of the wilderness gives way to an appreciation of the self-sufficiency, courage, good neighborliness, and generosity of the frontier community, and she willingly takes her place within it.

In *The Virginian* (1929), Molly (Mary Brian), a schoolteacher from Vermont, is shocked when she discovers that the Virginian (Gary Cooper) has lynched his best friend, Steve (Richard Arlen), for cattle rustling. Vowing to return East, she declares that western justice is nothing other than cold-blooded murder. Rebuked by a homespun Wyoming frontierswoman, who explains the pragmatic necessity of the codes of the West to her, Molly learns to accept the ways of the western community, stays on as the schoolmarm, and, ultimately, marries the Virginian. The "education" of the heroine in these films provides one of the genre's most familiar dramatic patterns—a scenario that perhaps finds its fullest treatment in *High Noon* (1952) in which the hero's Quaker bride (Grace Kelly) discovers that her religious principles have little or no currency in the West, and, in the final sequence, shoots a man in the back in order to save her husband's life.

Teaching a Tenderfoot

An educational process similar to that of the eastern woman takes place in a number of Westerns in which a feminized male character, often a youth or a tenderfoot from the East, is instructed in the codes of the West by a tough representative of the masculine frontier society. One of the most familiar sequences in Westerns is the shooting lesson, in which the experienced gunfighter attempts to teach a novice how to draw his six-shooter quickly and hit a target. John Wayne frequently finds himself in this role, instructing the young Matthew Garth to outdraw his opponent by watching his eyes in *Red River* (1948); sharing his expertise about Indians with his "nephew," Martin Pauley (Jeffrey Hunter) in *The Searchers* (1956); showing the "green" lawyer from the East, Ranse Stoddard (James Stewart), how to squeeze the trigger in *The Man Who Shot Liberty Valance* (1962); and retraining knife-fighter Mississippi (James Caan) to use a sawed-off shotgun in *El Dorado* (1966). In most of these instances, the encounter between mentor and apprentice functions (as in many war films) as a stage in an elaborate rite of passage through which the younger hero is forced to repress the "feminine" elements of his character and, as a result, become a more masculine, more westernized figure.

Tom Doniphon (John Wayne) teaches tenderfoot Ranse Stoddard (James Stewart) to shoot in *The Man Who Shot Liberty Valance* (1962).

Courtesy of Paramount

Women, Civilization, and Nature

The status of women in the Western remains somewhat conventional and secondary, even when they have learned the codes of the West. More often than not, women represent the forces of civilization; they embody the values of family, community, education, domestication, and cultivation that inform the male hero's transformation of the wilderness into a garden. In short, women serve as the agents of "easternization." If a woman is "westernized" through her encounter with the landscape, then her presence also serves to "easternize" it.

In *My Darling Clementine* (1946), the Boston-bred heroine gradually enters the western community, a process which begins by her dancing with its nominal leader, Wyatt Earp, at the church dedication ceremony. Her westernization is symbolized by her subsequent abandonment of eastern for western dress (her dark, constricting, formal-looking suits give way to white blouses and flowing skirts). By the end of the film, she has become Tombstone's first schoolmarm. Following her instruction by others in the ways of the West, she begins to educate it in the ways of the East—by teaching a new generation of westerners reading, writing, and arithmetic.

Women in Westerns do not always represent eastern values. In a number of films, they symbolize the West itself and function as contested sites for the playing out of struggles between the forces of East and West or of old West and new West. *Duel in the Sun* (1946), a virtual allegorization of the dilemma that lies at the heart of the Western genre, links the identity crisis (and ultimate fate) of its central character, Pearl, to the larger identity crisis of the American nation as it settles the West. The product of an English eastern father and a western Mexican-Indian mother, the mestiza Pearl is, quite literally, the meeting place between East and West.

Forced to choose between two brothers—Jesse, who represents law, order, and the progressive domestication of the new West, and Lewt, who is tied to the lawlessness and violence of the old West—Pearl first submits herself to Jesse's civilizing, but repressive, guidance and then to Lewt's unbridled passion. Unable to repress her own sexual desires (i.e., the forces of nature) she yields to Lewt; but, aware that Lewt and what he represents must be destroyed, she kills him and is killed herself in the process. This action paves the way for the emergence of an unconflicted (that is, not internally torn between two identities as she is) new order in the West.

In a similar way, Hallie (Vera Miles) in *The Man Who Shot Liberty Valance* (1962) represents a West that gradually passes from the hands of the old West (John Wayne's Tom Doniphon) to that of the new (James Stewart's Ranse Stoddard). Stoddard "wins" Hallie, in part, by teaching her to read and write and by instilling in her his belief in law and order and his dreams of the future. Alongside the wild cactus rose, given to her by Doniphon, Stoddard plants the vision of a "real" (i.e., eastern, carefully cultivated) rose, the product of dams and irrigation projects that will transform the wilderness into a garden.

The mestiza Pearl (Jennifer Jones, left) views herself through both the racist perspective of Senator McCanles (Lionel Barrymore) and the nurturing encouragement of Mrs. McCanles (Lillian Gish) in *Duel in the Sun* (1946).

Though this transformation is necessary and inevitable, Hallie, as symbol of the West, both embraces and resists it. She marries the easterner Stoddard, but is unable to forget her feeling for the westerner Doniphon, upon whose coffin she places a wild cactus rose. Though Hallie, unlike Pearl in *Duel*, survives the implicit battle of the film's two heroes over the possession of her, something in her dies. She has lost her former energy, passion, and fiery temper. The very qualities that draw the eastern hero to her and to the West are destroyed through her easternization.

ON NATIVE GROUND: LANDSCAPE AND CONFLICT

A Struggle for National Identity

The easternization of the West is not only played out across the bodies of western heroines but across the body of the West itself—across the landscape that provides the very basis of the genre. The Western, as its name suggests, is defined, in large part, in terms of its setting. (The genre, of course, is also historically defined; the dramatic action of A Westerns is set in the time period of, roughly, 1865 to 1890; that of B Westerns, on the other hand, is frequently pushed into the twentieth century, with heroes and villains often trading horses for cars, jeeps, and airplanes and relying on telephones and shortwave radios instead of the telegraph.)

Much as the traditional space of the melodrama is the home, that of the Western is the landscape of the West. It is within this landscape that the struggle for a national identity takes place; the West is where that which is eastern, European, or Old World engages in a process of continual self-redefinition, repeatedly reborn with each further step taken toward the West.

The journey in *Stagecoach* (1939), for example, takes its passengers from the "easternized" West of Tonto, where the Ladies Law and Order League purges the town of its undesirable elements, to the wild West of Lordsburg, where gambling, prostitution, and violence such as the climactic shoot-out in the street, still prevail. From here, the tarnished hero (the outlaw Ringo, played by John Wayne) and heroine (the prostitute Dallas, played by Claire Trevor) push further "west" (actually to Mexico) toward rejuvenation in the wilderness. They are saved, as we are told by those who oversee their departure, from "the blessings of civilization."

Though Ringo and Dallas flee the advance of civilization in search of a less oppressive existence in nature, the very stagecoach that brings them to the edge of the frontier represents the forces of progress that will eventually transform the landscape. As the frontier pushes further and further to the West, forests are cleared, the range is fenced off, farms and towns are built, and stagecoach routes and railroad tracks begin to crisscross formerly uncharted territory. The stagecoach and the train come to symbolize the taming of the wilderness and the linking of the West to the East.

From Wilderness to Garden

The building of the transcontinental railroad, celebrated in *The Iron Horse* (1924), *Union Pacific* (1939), *Kansas Pacific* (1953), and other films, remains closely identified with the evolution of the West. Attacks on trains, featured in films as diverse as *The Great Train Robbery* and *Jesse James* (1939), *Duel in the Sun* (1946), and *Butch Cassidy and the Sundance Kid* (1969), are figured as defiant gestures against the inevitable progression of the West into the twentieth century. In a handful of films, such as *The Professionals* (1966) and *Once Upon a Time in the West* (1968), the railroads represent rampant eastern capitalism, which rides roughshod over all obstacles in its path.

As Leo Marx shows (in *The Machine in the Garden*), American fiction from Nathaniel Hawthorne to F. Scott Fitzgerald has concerned itself with the uniquely American experience of a pastoral ideal destroyed by the intrusion of technology. The Western's ambivalent attitude toward progress in general and toward trains in particular situates it firmly within this larger tradition and reveals deep-seated tensions that underlie the Western's account of the West's transformation from a wilderness into a garden.

At the frontier, the wilderness meets civilization and, as a consequence of this encounter, the wilderness disappears and is replaced by a frontier society that combines elements of both the wilderness and civilization. As Turner describes it, "gradually this society lost its primitive conditions, and assimilated itself to the type of the older social conditions of the East; but it bore within it enduring and distinguishing survivals of its frontier experience. Decade after decade, West after West, this rebirth of American society had gone on," transforming America from a European colony into an autonomous nation whose character is determined not by borrowing from or imitation of Old World culture but by its own unique experience of the New World.

According to Turner, successive waves of western immigration result in a series of encounters at the frontier between distinct cultures and/or societies. The various conflicts that characterize the different kinds of Westerns correspond, in large part, to the successive stages of western development from a wilderness into a garden. In each instance, the old(er) West resists the coming of the new(er) West, but the new West ultimately triumphs. All of these subgenres of the Western not only provide convincing evidence that the Western is *about* the frontier, but they also provide an attempted rationalization of history. They present the historical movement from one period to the next as inevitable and thus suggest that the product of this Darwinian process of natural selection—twentieth-century America—is itself natural and right. In this way, the Western justifies the present and reaffirms our identity as a nation, an identity that has slowly been constructed during this process.

A Clash of Cultures: Cowboys and Indians

The first major "period" of Westerns focuses primarily upon the hero's struggle for survival in a natural landscape (as in *Jeremiah Johnson*, 1972) or recounts the adventures of a Daniel Boone-like character in the wilderness (see the hunter/trapper films cited above). In these films the chief conflict lies between culture and nature. The next stage/subgenre of the Western concerns conflicts not between culture and nature but between two distinct cultures—that of whites and Native Americans. This comprises one of the largest of the Western's several subgenres, which is the cowboy/cavalry and Indian pictures. These films dominate the genre from its inception until its demise, running from *The Battle at Elderbush Gulch* (1913) to *Ulzana's Raid* (1972), *Dances With Wolves* (1990), and *Last of the Mohicans* (1992).[2]

In many of these films, Native Americans are stereotypically portrayed as violent savages. In fact, only a handful of Westerns portray Indians as fully developed, individual characters or display any sensitivity, beyond a superficial concern for accuracy in costume and artifacts, to the particulars of Indian culture. Even in the films that are most sympathetic to them, Indians are not presented as Indians, but as romantic, Rousseauesque Noble Savages living

---

[2] Other examples include *Northwest Passage* (1940), *They Died with Their Boots On* (1941), *Fort Apache* (1948), *She Wore A Yellow Ribbon* (1949), *Distant Drums* (1951), *Apache* (1954), *Drum Beat* (1954), *Hondo* (1954), *The Indian Fighter* (1955), *The Last Frontier* (1956) and *The Searchers* (1956) to *A Distant Trumpet* (1964), *Major Dundee* (1965), *Cheyenne Autumn* (1964), *The Stalking Moon* (1968), *Little Big Man* (1970). It should be noted that, although the primary conflict in these films lies between whites and Indians, villainous whites are often the source of this conflict, as in *They Died, Fort Apache, Apache, Cheyenne Autumn, Little Big Man,* and others.

in implicit defiance of a decadent European civilization. This idealized image of the Native American dominates recent revisionist Westerns, such as *A Man Called Horse* (1970), *Return of a Man Called Horse* (1976), and *Dances With Wolves* (1990). The portrayal of the Indian as nightmarish devil (as seen in the character of Scar in *The Searchers* and Silvaje in *Stalking Moon*, 1969) or as victimized saint (seen in the person of Broken Lance in *Devil's Doorway* and Cochise in *Broken Arrow*, both 1950) betrays his or her status more as a figment of the imagination of white culture than as an authentic inhabitant of the frontier.

The majority of the "Indians" who achieve recognition as heroic symbols or as figures of empowerment on the screen are played primarily by white actors as in *Apache* (1954) (Burt Lancaster), *Taza, Son of Cochise* (1954) (Rock Hudson), and *The Searchers* (1956) (Henry Brandon).[3] The Native Americans to achieve prominence as actors within the film industry are few and far between. Chief Thundercloud starred in *Ramona* (1936), enjoyed the lead in Monogram's "Trail Blazers" serials, and played character parts in Westerns for over 20 years. Chief Yowlachie, who steals scenes from Walter Brennan in Howard Hawk's *Red River* (1948), worked in movies from the mid-1920s until his death in 1960. Iron Eyes Cody began acting as a child in 1912 in Griffith's *The Massacre* and continued his career into the 1960s, playing Indians on such television series as "Gunsmoke."

Jay Silverheels won renown as Tonto in the "Lone Ranger" television series and played Geronimo in *Broken Arrow* (1950). Chief John Big Tree acted in motion pictures from 1915 to 1950 and appeared in such classic Ford Westerns as *Stagecoach* (1939), *Drums Along the Mohawk* (1939), and *She Wore a Yellow Ribbon* (1949), where he plays Pony That Walks, the "Christian" Indian who wants to spend his time smoking and getting drunk with John Wayne's Nathan Brittles. And Chief Dan George won national acclaim for his role as Old Lodge Skins in *Little Big Man* (1970).

Native Images, White Values

The majority of speaking parts in Westerns went to white actors. This phenomenon tends to confirm the suspicion that Indians in Westerns function largely as psychic projections of the fears and desires of the white frontier community and have little or no connection with the Native Americans who originally inhabited the West. Even in films supposedly sympathetic to the plight of Native Americans, such as *Dances With Wolves*, stereotypical attitudes toward Indian savagery persist. Here, "nobler," more advanced tribes—the Lakota Sioux—fight against their deadly enemy—the primitive Pawnee, who savagely murder whites and Sioux alike.

---

[3] See also *Ramona* (1936), *The Squaw Man* (1931), *The Vanishing American* (1955), and *Geronimo* (1962). This should in no way diminish the significance of Indian actors such as Chief Thundercloud (*Ramona*, 1936), Jay Silverheels (*Broken Arrow*, 1950), Chief Dan George (*Little Big Man*, 1970), and other Native Americans who starred in Hollywood Westerns.

Courtesy of Orion

In *Dances With Wolves* (1990), Lt. John Dunbar (Kevin Costner) comes to recognize the value of Kicking Bird's (Graham Greene's) Native American lifestyle.

Certain contemporary Native Americans criticize *A Man Called Horse* (1970) for its suggestions of Indian brutality in its depiction of the Ceremony of the Sun (or Sundance) initiation ritual [in which Horse (Richard Harris) is "tortured" by having wooden pins inserted under the skin of his chest and being hoisted by these pins to the rafters of a lodge house]. One could similarly fault the "positive" image of the Sioux in *Wolves* for its reliance upon a spectrum of values that depend upon "negative" images of the Pawnee. At the same time, in its treatment of conflict between whites and Native Americans, the Sioux again emerge as "more civilized" against a background of white violence and irrationality. At any rate, the depiction of the Sioux in *Wolves* merely continues the pattern of conflict between new and more civilized versus old and less civilized cultures which underlies the genre as a whole.

CYCLES: CHARACTERS AND TYPES IN THE WESTERN

Cattlemen and Prospectors

Not all "periods" of the Western are distinct from one another. The era of the cowboy and the empire-building cattleman overlaps somewhat with that of the cowboy and Indian cycle. Cattlemen in *Shane* (1953) and *Day of the Outlaw*

(1959) assert the priority of their claim (over that of homesteaders) to the open range by recounting how they had fought not only Indians but also rustlers to acquire the land and make it safe for law-abiding citizens. The saga of the cattle baron and/or epic cattle drives is dramatized in films like *Red River* (1948), which also overlaps with the cowboy and Indian cycle.[4] In this film, the heroic empire builder, Tom Dunson (John Wayne) is associated with the individualism, strength, self-reliance, and violence of the pre–Civil War, old West. Dunson must learn to submit his tyrannical will to that of the new West, represented by his adopted son, Matthew Garth (Montgomery Clift). For Garth, self-reliance has given way to communal interdependence and individual authority to democratic cooperation. Garth's success in getting the cattle to market testifies to the flexibility of the new West and to its ability to get things done.

This series of films represents a period that gives way, in turn, to another that deals with the range wars. These films pit cattlemen against rustlers (*The Virginian*, 1946; *Blood on the Moon*, 1948; and *The Missouri Breaks*, 1976), sheep-herders (*Ramrod*, 1947; *Montana*, 1950; *The Sheepman*, 1958; *Heaven With a Gun*, 1969; and *Joe Kidd*, 1972), or homesteaders (*Shane*, 1953; *The Man Who Shot Liberty Valance*, 1962; and *Silverado*, 1985).

At the same time, from the discovery of gold in California in 1848 to the 1898 and 1903 gold rushes in Alaska, a legion of prospectors and miners flood the West and populate those regions of the frontier that are unsuitable for herding cattle or growing crops. From the Black Hills (*They Died With Their Boots On*, 1941) to Colorado (*Silver River*, 1948) and Nevada (*Virginia City*, 1940), and from California (*Sutter's Gold*, 1936; *Ride the High Country*, 1962) to the Yukon (*The Far Country*, 1954), miners pursue the quest for gold and silver. They, in turn, are followed by gamblers (*My Darling Clementine*, 1946; *McCabe and Mrs. Miller*, 1971) and gold diggers of a different sort (such as Marilyn Monroe in *River of No Return*, 1954). In both *McCabe and Mrs. Miller* and *Pale Rider* (1985), mining communities provide a site for the struggle between the idiosyncratic, nineteenth-century individualism of the old West and the impersonal but efficient anonymity of the forward looking new West, which is identified with twentieth-century big business methods and corporate policies.

Marshalls and Outlaws

Hard on the heels of the cattle drive and gold rush Westerns come the "urban" horse operas in which wild and woolly cattle towns such as Abilene, Dodge City, and Wichita and "wide-open" mining towns such as Deadwood, Tombstone, and Virginia City are tamed by legendary lawmen such as Wild Bill Hickok, Wyatt Earp, and Bat Masterson. These "town-tamer" Westerns

---

[4] Other Westerns in which the cattle "industry" figures prominently are *Duel in the Sun* (1946), *The Far Country* (1954), *The Tall Men* (1955), *Cowboy* (1958), *The Big Country* (1958), *The Cowboys* (1972), and *The Culpepper Cattle Company* (1972).

like *My Darling Clementine* (1946) lead to "law-and-order" Westerns such as *Destry Rides Again* (1939) and *High Noon* (1952), in which town marshals keep the peace won by their predecessors.[5]

The final stages of the winning of the West shift the focus of law and order from the town to the wilderness, which has become the last haven for outlaws. In films like *Hang 'em High* (1967) and *True Grit* (1969), U.S. marshals track down men wanted by the territory, state, or national government and bring them to justice. Bounty hunters, often drawn from the ranks of former lawmen, scour the countryside for fugitives in *Naked Spur* (1952), *Ride Lonesome* (1959), and *The Good, the Bad, and the Ugly* (1966).[6] A similar story of flight and pursuit, told from the perspective of the outlaw, crops up in *Jesse James* (1939), *Butch Cassidy and the Sundance Kid* and *The Wild Bunch* (1969), and *The Young Guns* (1988).[7]

Out-of-Time Anti-Heroes

A handful of Westerns, made in the 1960s and early 1970s and set in the period after the closing of the frontier, look back nostalgically to the old West and feature legendary characters who have outlived the heroic gold, silver, and bronze ages of the West and who are regarded as either curiosities or unwanted embarrassments by an indifferent or openly hostile twentieth-century society. The values of the world around these old West character types have become corrupted by the forces of corporate capitalism, such as railroads, banks, mining interests, or trusts. These institutions play an increasingly significant role in the rooting out of these defiant individualists who have fallen out of step with the advancing parade of modern times.

The suicidal resistance of these western anti-heroes to the values of modernity lies at the heart of several Sam Peckinpah Westerns, including *Ride the High Country* (1962) and *The Wild Bunch* (1969), whose outlaw heroes are pursued by an ignoble assortment of bounty hunters in the employ of the railroads. This spirit also provides the dramatic core of nontraditional, "late" Westerns such as *McCabe and Mrs. Miller* (1971) in which the hero, who refuses to sell out to a mining conglomerate, is gunned down by its henchmen.

Whether lawmen, gunfighters, or outlaws, these anti-heroes live by a set of frontier codes that have become antiquated in the twentieth century. This notion of the Western hero as a dying breed is, perhaps, best exemplified in *The Shootist* (1976), in which aging gunslinger J. B. Books (John Wayne) is

---

[5] Other films in this category include *Forty Guns* (1957), *The Tin Star* (1957), *Rio Bravo* (1959), *Cat Ballou* (1965), *El Dorado* (1967), *Firecreek* (1968), *Death of a Gunfighter* (1969), *Support Your Local Sheriff!* (1969), *Rio Lobo* (1970), *Cahill—U.S. Marshal* (1973), and *Blazing Saddles* (1974).

[6] See also *The Bounty Hunter* (1954), *The Tin Star* (1957), *Comanche Station* (1960), and *For a Few Dollars More* (1965).

[7] See also *The Return of Frank James* (1940), *The Outlaw* (1943), *3 Godfathers* (1948), *The Lawless Breed* (1952), *The True Story of Jesse James* (1957), *Wild Rovers* (1971), *Bad Company* (1972), *The Great Northfield Minnesota Raid* (1972), *Pat Garrett and Billy the Kid* (1973), and *The Long Riders* (1980).

Courtesy of Dino De Laurentis

J. B. Books (John Wayne) confirms his suspicion that he has cancer when he visits Dr. Hostetler (James Stewart) in *The Shootist* (1976).

literally dying of cancer (as was Wayne himself when the film was being made). Books rides into Carson City in January 1901 on the very day on which the local newspaper headlines Queen Victoria's death. This news item not only foreshadows his own death but also symbolizes the passing of the values of the previous century, most particularly, of a certain moral integrity with which he is identified.

The townspeople of Carson City, concerned more with their own material well-being than with their loyalty to the abstract ideals of individualism and/ or community, are driven by a set of values, which might best be described as post-Victorian. Books' chief relationships are with those who seek to profit from his death by selling his horse, his life story, or clippings of his hair. Refusing to die passively in bed, Books stages a confrontation (on his birthday) with three local troublemakers who fancy themselves good with a gun. This gunfight takes on the dynamics of a last hurrah, in which the authenticity of the old (movie) West, symbolized by legendary Western film star Wayne, emerges and defeats derivative western types in the form of television Western stars, Hugh O'Brien and Richard Boone. Though he rides to the gunfight on a streetcar, Books nonetheless recaptures, through his display of traditional western courage and skill, the heroic stature of a bygone era.

CONTEMPORARY VISIONS, ENDURING MYTHS

Throughout its history, the Western has played a crucial role in dramatizing and recreating for successive generations of Americans the original experience of the frontier, which shaped (and which continues, through each new cycle of Westerns, to reshape) American character. At the same time, the Western becomes a site for the working out of problems that plague contemporary American society. In certain instances, the Western's role is fairly overt. During the Korean war, films like *Rio Grande* (1950) act out national frustration in being unable to pursue the enemy beyond the 48th parallel by sending a cavalry troop across the Mexican border to rescue children who have been abducted by Indians. During the Vietnam war, in the aftermath of the recent My Lai massacre, Westerns such as *Soldier Blue* and *Little Big Man* (both 1970) vividly portray the massacres of Indians at Sand Creek and Washita River by U.S. forces. *Ulzana's Raid* (1972) doubles as an allegory for America's misguided involvement in Southeast Asia and *Jeremiah Johnson* and *Bad Company* (both 1972) play upon antiwar sentiment.

In general, however, the Western is both a barometer of contemporary political history as well as a site for the production and perpetuation of myths that are crucial to the larger ideological demand of sustaining a nineteenth-century American identity that is repeatedly under attack in the twentieth century. The Western celebrates the values of a preindustrialized, rural, agrarian America in which an individual's contact with nature becomes a source of perpetual rejuvenation and in which the pastoral ideal of the yeoman farmer that informs Jeffersonian democracy still flourishes.

Back to the Garden

Set, for the most part, in a period prior to the closing of the frontier in 1890, the Western looks forward to the continued development of a populist paradise. Made in an increasingly industrialized and urbanized society, the Western looks backward from the vantage point of a "fallen" culture to a Garden of Eden from which it has been expelled by its own progress and development. Thus, the representation of history and progress remains profoundly ambivalent in most Westerns; the passing of the old West and its transformation into the new West necessarily involves tremendous loss. A-level Westerns set in the twentieth century tend to feature heroes who resist modernity and who struggle against its machines, whether they be trains, planes, or automobiles, or modern methods of mining, manufacture, and merchandising. (In B Westerns, however, history plays a more neutral role: contemporary technology becomes a tool that is appropriated by both good guys and bad guys; the past has little or no nostalgic value.)

Two recent Westerns, *Three Amigos!* (1986) and *City Slickers* (1991), present characters in flight from a contemporary, mechanized, depersonalized, urban America who discover an exciting world of adventure out West. The modern world (1920s Hollywood and 1990s New York, respectively) not only has turned them into alienated individuals whose contact with any larger community has been severed but also has rendered their existence artificial or in some way dishonest. The Three Amigos, for example, have lost touch with modern-day reality and believe instead in the fictions of their own Hollywood movies. The three city slickers lead lives of quiet desperation in a modern metropolis from which they periodically escape through fantasy vacations to exotic, faraway places. The West enables both groups of middle-aged men to recover a lost authenticity. Though set in a more traditionally western period, *Dances With Wolves* reveals a similar rejection of the insanity of the decadent white culture that would win the West in favor of the more natural and authentic Native American culture that was losing it.

In all three Westerns, the West functions as a paradise lost, as a world in which utopian communities reaffirm the value of the individual and provide a stable identity for that individual within it. This world no longer exists in twentieth-century mass society in which traditional notions of the individual's relationship to the community and of the individual's ability to shape or control events and/or history have been replaced by a pervasive sense of social alienation and powerlessness. Ever since the closing of the frontier and the disappearance of the old West, contemporary American audiences need the Western to provide them with a mythical, quasi-utopian past in which they are empowered as individuals and become members of a society whose values and beliefs are rooted in the stable realities of the land itself.

The desire for the mythical world of the old West also serves as the subject of another western, *Unforgiven* (1992). Unlike *City Slickers* and *Three Amigos*,

The sheriff of Big Whiskey, Little Bill Daggett (Gene Hackman), instructs outlaw Will Munny (Clint Eastwood) on the fine points of frontier law in *Unforgiven* (1992).

Courtesy of Warner Bros.

however, *Unforgiven* is not set in the present or recent past, but in the classic era of 1870 to 1890. Its hero, Will Munny (Clint Eastwood), is a former gunman and outlaw who has reformed, becoming a hog farmer and family man. During the course of the film, he slowly reverts to his former identity as a legendary killer whose avenging of unjust acts, including the disfigurement of a whore and the death of a friend (Morgan Freeman), is presented as a feat of quasi-heroic proportions, duly witnessed and recorded by a dime novelist. Although much of the film explores the nonheroic passivity of the hero and the crisis of masculine identity in the late West, it finally reaffirms the traditional myth, providing Munny with an opportunity to recover his mythical status. Once this happens, he vanishes, becoming a legendary figure of the old West. In other words, the final gunfight functions as escapist fantasy, providing the hero with a means of flight into the illusory world of Western myth.

Periods of Popularity

Americans have needed the Western more in certain periods of their history than in others. The Western flowered as a film genre in the 1950s, when over 800 were made. Its popularity gradually withered in the 1960s, when less than 200 Westerns were released, and the genre virtually disappeared in the late 1970s and 1980s. Fluctuations in its popularity reflect the genre's changing status as a means for audiences to come to terms with the modern world. It is possible to locate the origins of the Western in the disturbance of an agrarian-pastoral order introduced by the Industrial Revolution, technological innovation, urbanization, and in the transformation of small-town America into a modern, mass society. Given this origin, the proliferation of A Westerns in the years 1946–1958, a period in which explosive developments took place in the sciences, could be seen as a response to the anxiety of society as a whole over the increasingly important role that technology plays in shaping human consciousness and in increasing international instability (through the nuclear arms race and the Cold War).

Of course, the postwar concern for the bomb hardly explains prewar fascination with the Western, which led to over 1300 (mostly B) films made in the 1920s and over 1000 oaters released in each of the next two decades. In these instances, the genre's celebration of agrarianism is less clearly a response to an increasing fear of nuclear war than it is a conservative reaction to a growing dependence upon technology and to the impersonality of the consumer-oriented mass culture that accompanies the modernization of America in the 1920s and later. Thus, William S. Hart appeals, as a western hero, to the codes of a preindustrial, largely Protestant, nineteenth-century, small-town society, representing the forces of a Victorian moral order that oppose the corruption of a world which has become decadent. In *Hell's Hinges* (1916), Hart plays a good-bad man who is redeemed by the love of the virtuous sister of a minister. Wreaking an Old Testament vengeance upon those sinners who have burned down the town church, Hart corners them in the saloon and sets both it and the rest of the town of Hell's Hinges afire, purging the town of its criminal element before he and the film's heroine set off on a new life together.

Ambivalence: Land, Technology, and Utopia

Epic A Westerns of the 1920s, such as *The Covered Wagon* (1923) and *The Iron Horse* (1924), embrace the expansionist optimism and go-getter ethos of the 1920s through a celebration of the principles of Manifest Destiny. The dramatic westward expansion of the United States in the nineteenth century, which many believed was justified by God and geography, became a metaphor for the legitimation of American enterprise and the unrestrained development of the business economy in the 1920s.

Ironically, in John Ford's *Iron Horse,* an industrial techology—the first transcontinental railroad—serves as the device that links the past with the present and symbolizes the growth of America into a corporate giant. John Ford's utopian conception of the railroad persists into the 1930s, in spite of the Great Depression and the resulting cynicism it produced regarding the excesses of unregulated rugged individualism. Bankers (like the self-serving embezzler Gatewood in *Stagecoach*) take the brunt of the criticism for the nation's ills, but the railroads continue to represent the promise of a corporate capitalism that might rescue America from the contemporary cycle of hard times. Thus, by the end of Roosevelt's second term of office, *Union Pacific* (1939), which recounts the building of the first transcontinental railroad, epitomizes the (in this particular case) conservative concerns of the A Western: through heroic efforts Americans can overcome all obstacles and rebuild the greatness of the past.

B Westerns reinforce this affirmation of capitalist enterprise through an unending series of films whose plots are based upon the conflict over property; films about range wars, cattle rustling, claim jumping, or disputes over land boundaries and water rights tend to come down on the side of those whose moral (if not legal) rights to property need protection by the benevolent, intervening force of the government or its agents. Though the superficial look of the Western changes from year to year, along with its variations in plot types, its underlying principles and beliefs remain constant, planted firmly in the terrain of American populist ideology.

Westerns echo populism's dream of an agrarian utopia, populated by farmers whose stake in democratic society is assured by their ownership of land which they work themselves, which makes them economically self-sufficient, and which gives them equal footing with others in their community. The traditional enemies of these small farmers prove to be those of Depression audiences as well—bankers and big business.

Though the railroads, as the symbol of big business in the West, also became targets of populist attack, the building of the first transcontinental railroads depicted in *The Iron Horse* and *Union Pacific* function less as a symbol of big business than of a national unity achieved through the labor of the working class. *Union Pacific* even exposes the corruption of the robber barons and corporate trusts that seek to divert government funds allocated for the construction of the railroads. The "railroad" consists largely of populist individuals—an incorruptible troubleshooter (played by Joel McCrea) and a scrappy Irish postmistress (Barbara Stanwyck)—who join forces to fight off the agents of big business who try to delay construction of the railroad for their own personal profit.

But beneath this celebration of individual effort lie deep misgivings about the modern technology upon which these enterprising individuals rely. The benefits of industrial America do not always outweigh the drawbacks that accompany it. Thus, the progress achieved in another "utilities" Western, *Western Union* (1941) comes at considerable cost; telegraph lines may have been strung, but they stretch over the graves of an earlier generation of pioneering westerners (such as Randolph Scott) who give their lives for this new technology which would spawn a revolution in the fledgling communications industry.

The Western enjoys unprecedented popularity in the 1950s because it enables audiences to retreat to a world in which technology poses more promise than threat. In this respect, Westerns reflect, albeit quite indirectly, a deep-rooted uneasiness on the part of postwar America in regard to technological advancement. This uneasiness is strikingly similar to that found in 1950s science-fiction films, which dramatize the darker side of scientific development in the form of alien invasions, mutations produced by atomic explosions, and apocalyptic visions at the end of the world triggered by a rampant technology that has run amuck.

SPACE: THE FINAL FRONTIER

The popularity of the Western endures just so long as it continues to address the basic concerns of a technophobic American populace. It begins to fade just at the point that America attempts to reconcile itself with certain realities that underlie its status as a highly industrialized, mass society. In the 1890s, Turner and others noted the closing of the western frontier. In the 1960s, John F. Kennedy proclaims a "New Frontier," which, in addition to new domestic policies, including tax reform, federal aid to education, medicare, civil rights, and the Peace Corps, dramatically increases spending for the space program. Responding in part to the initiative taken by Eisenhower shortly after the Soviets launched the first satellite into space in 1958, Americans made science and mathematics a new priority in both primary and secondary educational instruction. Within a decade, there emerged a new generation of young Americans (of movie-going age) who no longer shared the deep-seated anxiety toward science and technology of their parents.

With Kennedy and Johnson, the conquest of outer space becomes a central goal around which the American pioneering spirit, engineering know-how, and technology are marshaled. With the advent of the space program, popular attitudes toward science and technology slowly begin to change. Although no one event could be said to have determined the demise of the Western, by

Courtesy of 20th Century-Fox

The Western hero resurfaces in the science-fiction film: Han Solo (Harrison Ford) functions as a futuristic cowboy in *Star Wars* (1977).

the 1970s, the West and the genre of the Western are no longer the most powerful sites for the definition of a contemporary American identity. Outer space and the "space" opera or science-fiction film has replaced the West and the horse opera in the popular imagination. No longer are Americans to be defined by the primal contact between culture and nature, but by that between culture and advanced technology.

The science-fiction films of Steven Spielberg, *Close Encounters of the Third Kind* (1977) and *E.T.: The Extra-Terrestrial* (1982), rewrite the technophobia of the 1950s as technophilia in the 1970s. Spielberg reimagines the future brought about by technological change as utopian and reconfigures technologically advanced, alien cultures (which had been regarded as threatening in the 1950s) as benign. The Western's fearful retreat to a preindustrialized past gradually gives way, in popularity, to the science-fiction film's wholehearted adoption of a technological future. Westerns, of course, continue to be made, as do technophobic science-fiction films. *Star Wars* (1977), for example, proves both technophilic, in its humanization of technology in the form of anthropomorphic robots C3PO and R2D2, and technophobic, in its adoption of the medieval codes of the Jedi knights and in its endorsement of human intuition over science (in the film's finale, Luke Skywalker [Mark Hamill] turns off his computerized gun sight and learns to "reach out with [his] feelings" in the attack on the Death Star).

Though opposed in their attitudes toward technology, the Western and the science-fiction film remain remarkably similar in their celebration of the frontier experience. Indeed, as the power of the Western faded, the science-fiction film snatched up the body of its themes, situations, icons, and motifs. *Star Wars* borrows extensively from *The Searchers*, reworking its basic plot, involving the abduction and rescue of the hero's niece/sister and reusing one of its most powerful images (the hero's discovery of a burned out ranch house containing the bodies of his dead relatives). It even includes a western saloon sequence in which first Obi-Won Kenobi (Alec Guinness) uses his light sabre to defend Luke from an alien bully and then Han Solo (Harrison Ford), dressed like a "western" hero, shoots it out with an alien bounty hunter, sent by Jabba the Hut.

But perhaps the most audacious revamping of the 1950s Western is *Outland* (1981), which restages the central dramatic action of *High Noon* (1952) on an isolated volcanic moon of Jupiter where marshal Sean Connery single-handedly defeats the representatives of a corrupt mining corporation. The familiar plots and motifs of the Western function as a way of providing audiences with access to the unfamiliar and the unknown; the otherness of outer space is likened to the wilderness of the West. We will conquer it as we have conquered alien spaces in the past. It is nothing more than a new, albeit "final" frontier.

SELECT FILMOGRAPHY

Hell's Hinges (1916)
The Iron Horse (1924)
The Virginian (1929)
Stagecoach (1939)
The Outlaw (1943)
Duel in the Sun (1946)
My Darling Clementine (1946)
Pursued (1947)
Fort Apache (1948)
Red River (1948)
She Wore a Yellow Ribbon
  (1949)
Broken Arrow (1950)
Devil's Doorway (1950)
High Noon (1952)
The Naked Spur (1952)
Shane (1953)
Apache (1954)
Johnny Guitar (1954)
The Man from Laramie (1955)

The Searchers (1956)
The Day of the Outlaw (1959)
Ride Lonesome (1959)
Rio Bravo (1959)
*The Man Who Shot Liberty
  Valance* (1962)
Ride the High Country (1962)
El Dorado (1966)
The Wild Bunch (1969)
Little Big Man (1970)
McCabe and Mrs. Miller (1971)
High Plains Drifter (1972)
Ulzana's Raid (1972)
*Buffalo Bill and the Indians,
  or Sitting Bull's History
  Lesson* (1976)
The Outlaw Josey Wales (1976)
The Shootist (1976)
Pale Rider (1985)
Dances With Wolves (1990)

SELECT BIBLIOGRAPHY

Buscombe, Ed, ed. *The BFI Companion to the Western.* London: Andre Deutsch, 1988.

Marx, Leo. *The Machine in the Garden: Technology and the Pastoral Ideal in America.* New York: Oxford University Press, 1964.

Smith, Henry Nash. *Virgin Land: The American West as Symbol and Myth.* Cambridge: Harvard University Press, 1950.

Wright, Will. *Sixguns & Society: A Structural Study of the Western.* Berkeley: University of California, 1975.

PART III

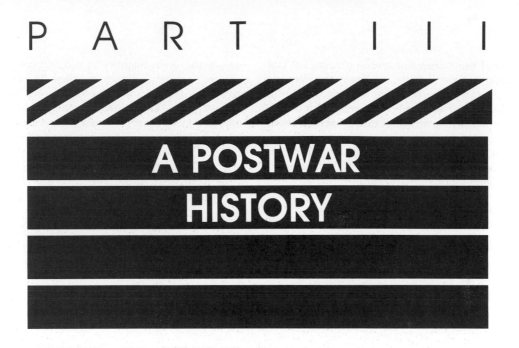

A POSTWAR
HISTORY

The institutional base for classical Hollywood cinema was established in the 1910s with the vertical integration of the film industry—that is, when studios became involved in the fields of distribution and exhibition and exhibitors entered the production and distribution arena. This industrial base remained more or less intact for almost 40 years—until 1948 when the United States Department of Justice and the Supreme Court declared the present structure of the film industry to be in violation of the Sherman Antitrust Act and ordered the studios to divest themselves of their theater holdings. Over the next decade, the studios gradually sold off their theaters. And, over the course of succeeding decades, the role of the studios gradually evolved from that of producers and distributors of motion pictures to primarily that of distributors of films that had been independently produced.

The structure of the film industry changed in response not only to court-imposed orders but also to profound changes that took place within the area of leisure-time entertainment. Postwar audiences differed dramatically from their prewar counterparts. As a result of demographic changes, which involved the shift of a significant part of the movie-going audience from the cities

to the suburbs, the traditional (habitual) movie audience gave way to a new breed of infrequent moviegoers, who could be lured out of their houses and away from their television sets only by exceptional films—by big-budget blockbusters or special-event films.

The chapters that follow chart the postwar transformation of Hollywood from its status as a semistable institution, which had been established in the first few decades of this century, to an industry that has become increasingly flexible in its structure. Indeed, during this time period, Hollywood is forced to respond to a succession of challenges that threaten its economic survival. These range from government intervention (forced divestiture in 1948, the House Un-American Activities Committee hearings in 1947 and 1953) and the competition of television in the 1950s to the advent of cable TV, the VCR, and videotape in the 1980s.

A review of these changes will show how variations within the larger cultural profile of the United States result in significant alterations in the kinds of films that are made. As the industry adapts itself to a constantly changing set of economic, social, political, and cultural demands, it gradually becomes a different kind of cinema.

Many of the features of traditional classical Hollywood cinema survive, especially the narrative patterns and stylistic forms it perfected during the heyday of the studio system. And it continues to perform a similar cultural function, representing the experience of postwar America.

But the movies no longer speak to the entire population in the way that prewar cinema did; older generations of Americans rarely go to the movies; the great majority of moviegoers grow younger and younger over the years. The largest percentage of today's audience is between 12 and 20 years of age. The following history of postwar Hollywood cinema is designed to provide an account of the forces that transformed the "old" classical Hollywood cinema into the "new" classical Hollywood cinema and to provide a portrait of the latter as an institution.

HOLLYWOOD AND THE COLD WAR

ORIGINS: COMMUNISM, HOLLYWOOD, AND THE AMERICAN WAY

Revolution and Repercussion

Unofficially, the Cold War began in 1917, when the Communist Bolsheviks came to power in Russia, after unseating the more moderate Mensheviks who ran the country after the overthrow of the Czar. The Cold War officially ended more than 70 years later, in 1991, when the Soviet Union began to unravel. America responded to the Russian Revolution with a "red scare," which was triggered in 1919 by labor unrest, strikes, and the growing unionization of the work force. Even the Boston police force formed a union and went on strike, leaving the city defenseless and forcing officials to call out the state guard. The official responsible for breaking this strike, state governor Calvin Coolidge, parlayed his antiunion stance into a probusiness platform, which later won him a nomination for Vice-President in 1920. When President Warren Harding died in 1923, Coolidge found himself President.

In 1919, anarchists, Bolsheviks, and other radical groups were suspected of sending a series of bombs through the mails to prominent political leaders and industrialists, terrorizing government officials and capitalists. In 1920, five socialists were elected to the New York State Assembly, then expelled by that body because, as socialists, they were members of "a disloyal organization composed exclusively of perpetual traitors." To many, it seemed as if the forces of revolution had spread beyond the borders of Russia and the Communist goal of worldwide revolution was threatening the United States as well. Blaming the postwar strikes by steel workers and coal miners on "the red menace," the U.S. Attorney General ordered that all Communists be rounded up and deported. Over 6000 men were arrested and over 500 were deported as undesirable aliens.

At the same time, Hollywood produced a number of anti-Communist films, including *Bolshevism on Trial* (1919), which was based on a novel by Thomas Dixon, the author of D. W. Griffith's *The Birth of a Nation* (1915). Playing upon popular fears of worldwide revolution, publicity for the film asks, "Shall [Bolshevism] travel to America, gathering in its net Western peoples and Democratic organizations?" *The Right to Happiness* (ca. 1919) seeks from its viewers the answer to a similar question: "Which would you rather have in this country—destruction under the Red flag or construction and co-operation under the American Flag?" Griffith's *Orphans of the Storm* (1922), which ostensibly dealt with the French Revolution, warns its audiences in an opening intertitle of the dangers of "Anarchy and Bolshevism,"

233

Courtesy of Paramount

"Are you now or have you ever been a Communist?" Responding to the red scare of the 1950s, Robert Walker swears to his mother (Helen Hayes) on the Bible that he is not a Communist in *My Son John* (1952).

suggesting that the film be seen as a lesson in history. "The lesson: the French Revolution RIGHTLY overthrew a BAD government. But we in America should be careful lest we with a GOOD government mistake fanatics for leaders and exchange our decent law and order for Anarchy and Bolshevism."

The red scare of the early 1920s also led to the arrest of two Italian immigrants and suspected anarchists, Nicola Sacco and Bartolomeo Vanzetti, for the murder of a payroll clerk. Their controversial trial and subsequent execution in 1927 made them internationally famous, focusing unwanted attention upon the American legal system and the country's treatment of radicals. Fear of potential "reds" spread to the motion picture industry. In 1922, the FBI opened a file on Charles Chaplin, after he had entertained a leader of the American Communist Party in his home. They continued to document his supposedly "subversive" activities and associations until 1952, when Chaplin left the United States and his reentry permit was revoked by the State Department.

The threat of worldwide revolution in the wake of the 1917 Russian Revolution began to seem a bit less likely when postwar leftist movements in Germany, Hungary, and other European countries failed to succeed in establishing Communist or socialist governments. As a result, concern about domestic radicals gradually subsided in the United States. At the same time, the prosperity of the American economy in the 1920s appeared to undermine Communist critiques of capitalism—that is, until the stock market crash in 1929.

In the Red: The Depression Era

Hollywood has never attempted to glamorize bankers, industrialists, and stock speculators. After the crash, these capitalist figures tend to be regularly identified with the fiscal mismanagement that had brought about the Great Depression, but their villainy is more often seen in terms of individual greed than of class oppression. Decades later, during the Communist witch-hunts of the late 1940s and early 1950s, right-wing novelist Ayn Rand, author of *The Fountainhead*, would read these characterizations of the business community as Communist-inspired. In her booklet *Screen Guide for Americans*, Rand warns Hollywood filmmakers "Don't Smear Industrialists," "Don't Smear the Free Enterprise System," and "Don't Smear Success." Rand also advises screenwriters, "Don't give your character—as a sign of villainy, as a damning characteristic—the desire to make money."

But the depiction of capitalists in 1930s Hollywood films, ranging from Charles Chaplin's *City Lights* (1931) to Frank Capra's *You Can't Take It With You* (1938), is inspired more by the reactionary spirit of populism, which seeks reform, than by the radical spirit of communism, which preaches revolution. In other words, the "system" works, though it often needs watching. Indeed, for every "bad" capitalist or millionaire, these movies suggest that there is a "good" capitalist, who might make things right.

However, the films that depict Communists continued to portray them negatively. In Depression-era comedies, Bolsheviks not only behave like deranged lunatics but—even worse—they have no sense of humor, style, or wit. Thus the Bolshevik in Ernst Lubitsch's *Trouble in Paradise* (1932) denounces the heroine (Kay Francis), a wealthy cosmetics manufacturer, and lectures to her that "any women who spends a fortune in times like these for a handbag—phooey, phooey, phooey!" In topical melodramas, such as *Heroes for Sale* (1933) and *Little Man, What Now* (1934), Communists are exposed as essentially selfish phonies who are unconcerned with the genuine poverty and hardship of others.

In *Heroes*, for example, the European inventor is a Bolshevik who is described by another character as "kinda cracked." He quotes Lenin, speaks of "class servitude," denounces "dirty capitalists," and refers to the workers as "sheep." But, he abruptly changes his tune when his invention turns him into a millionaire, describing the poor and the needy as "a cancer on civilization." When the hero objects, saying "I thought you hated all employers and capitalists,"the former radical replies: "I despise them, I spit on them. But I'm willing to get rich with them." The film carefully distinguishes the unemployed "heroes" referred to in its title from foreign subversives. When vigilante groups force an army of homeless and jobless men to board a train that will get rid of them by shipping them across the state line, they refer to the men as "reds." But the hero quickly corrects them, declaring "we're not reds; we're ex-servicemen!"

Although studios such as Warner Bros. openly supported much of the social reform proposed by Franklin Roosevelt's New Deal, Hollywood drew the line when it came to more radical politics. In 1934, muckraking author and millionaire-socialist Upton Sinclair campaigned for the office of governor of California, promising to "End Poverty in California." Working together with the conservative press, the studios launched a negative publicity campaign against Sinclair, describing him as a "dangerous Bolshevik beast." M-G-M produced fake newsreels, depicting hordes of tramps besieging little old ladies on their porches, and newspapers reproduced photographs of hoboes and criminals aboard trains bound for California, intent on taking advantage of Sinclair's promise. The photos were later identified as stills (featuring professional actors) from a Warner Bros. movie about homeless teenagers, *Wild Boys of the Road* (1933). Needless to say, Sinclair lost the election.

Anti-Fascists, Populists, and "Dupes"

During the Spanish Civil War, Hollywood's anti-communism was tempered somewhat by its anti-fascism. The specter of yet another Fascist dictatorship in Spain, supported by those already in place in Hitler's Germany and Mussolini's Italy, prompted many liberals to support the Communist-backed Loyalists in their fight against Generalissimo Francisco Franco's Fascists. Screenwriter Dorothy Parker and playwright Lillian Hellman organized a group of Loyalist supporters in Hollywood into the Motion Picture Artists Committee to Aid Republican Spain. Members included writers Dashiell Hammett, Dudley Nichols, and Julius and Philip Epstein; directors John Ford and Lewis Milestone; and actors Louise Rainer, Melvyn Douglas, Fredric March, Paul Muni, John Garfield, and others. Ford donated an ambulance to the American Abraham Lincoln Brigade, which fought on the side of the Loyalists.

Producer Walter Wanger, together with screenwriter John Howard Lawson, made a film about the Spanish Civil War, *Blockade* (1938), which was released by United Artists. However, pressure from the Hays Office and the Roosevelt administration, which were nervous about taking sides in the conflict, undermined the project, which had been designed as a warning about the dangers of the spread of fascism in Europe. As a result, the film becomes a simple love story about an idealistic farmer (Henry Fonda), whose political affiliation is never stated, and a beautiful spy (Madeleine Carroll), who workers for "the other side." The Loyalists and the Fascists were never identified by name and viewers had difficulty knowing whether Fonda was a Loyalist or merely a humble advocate for the universal rights of man.

While Hollywood could not quite come out in favor of the left-wing Loyalists in *Blockade*, it could still make fun of Communists in *Ninotchka* (1939) and *Comrade X* (1940). In the former film, for example, Greta Garbo's dogmatic Soviet official is easily seduced away from the party line by the luxuries of capitalism—in particular, by a frivolous hat which she sees in a store window.

Populist films that exposed the predicament of the working class took pains to make it clear that the support of labor was not to be confused with Communist propaganda. Ford's adaptation of John Steinbeck's *The Grapes of Wrath* (1940) explores the ways in which migrant farm workers were exploited, but it carefully distances itself from anything that might be considered un-American. Thus Tom Joad (Henry Fonda), though "radicalized" by his experiences at the hands of farm owners and their company police, remains ignorant of the larger political debates that surround the plight of labor in the film. Someone mentions to him that "reds" are suspected of causing trouble by organizing the workers, and he responds by asking, "Who are these 'reds' anyway?"

By the late 1930s, the government had begun to take greater and greater interest in Hollywood's anti-fascism, which was considered to be Communist-inspired. In 1938, Representative Martin Dies, the first chair of the House Un-American Activities Committee (HUAC), declared that those members of the industry who had joined the Hollywood Anti-Nazi League (whose list of sponsors included moguls Carl Laemmle, Jack Warner, and Dore Schary) were "Communist dupes." In 1940, Dies opened hearings to investigate the presence of Communists in Hollywood, naming actors Fredric March, Humphrey Bogart, and James Cagney, and screenwriter Philip Dunne as suspected "reds." All four successfully cleared themselves in testimony given to the Dies Committee, but a precedent had been set. Witch-hunters such as Dies discovered that they could generate enormous publicity by using Hollywood as the target of their investigations.

World War II and Government Policy

During World War II, the government put a hold on its inquiries into communism in Hollywood. Industry personnel had been suspected of being Communists largely because of their participation in anti-Fascist causes and organizations. With American entry into the war, anti-fascism suddenly became national policy, and, with the exception of a brief period during which the Soviet Union and Germany had signed and observed a nonaggression pact (1939–1941), Russia was an ally in America's fight against Germany, Italy, and Japan. For the time being, HUAC kept a low profile.

However, right-wing elements within the Hollywood community continued the anti-Communist campaign which the Dies Committee had begun. In February 1944, they organized themselves into the Motion Picture Alliance for the Preservation of American Ideals, which dedicated itself to purging the industry of "Communists, radicals, and crackpots." Members of the Alliance included director Sam Wood, producer Walt Disney, actors Robert Taylor, Barbara Stanwyck, Adolphe Menjou, Gary Cooper, Clark Gable, John Wayne, and Ward Bond, writers Ayn Rand and Borden Chase, labor representative Roy Brewer of IATSE (the International Alliance of Theatrical Stage Employees), and Lela Rogers, the mother of actress Ginger Rogers.

During the war, the Alliance issued statements calling upon patriotic elements within the film industry to combat "totalitarian-minded groups working within the industry for the dissemination of un-American ideas and beliefs." In response, Dies and his committee returned to Hollywood to investigate the Alliance's charges. In 1945, HUAC, which had originally been a temporary committee, was made permanent, partially in response to the publicity it and the Alliance generated investigating radicals in Hollywood.

During the war, Hollywood produced a number of films designed to give support to American allies. Thus, in addition to celebrating England in *Mrs. Miniver* (1942) and *The White Cliffs of Dover* (1944), the major studios produced

Courtesy of Corinth Films

Actor Adolphe Menjou of the Motion Picture Alliance for the Preservation of American Ideals testifies before the House Un-American Activities Committee about subversives in Hollywood.

several pro-Soviet films, including *Song of Russia* (1943) and *Mission to Moscow* (1943). These works were commissioned, in part, by the U.S. government, which sought to familiarize Americans with the plight of our allies. But these productions would come back to haunt Hollywood in the postwar years, when any support of the Soviet Union was deemed traitorous.

INQUISITION: HUAC, McCARTHY, AND THE HOLLYWOOD TEN

Friends and Foes

Immediately after the war, the long-time tensions that had existed between the United States and the Soviet Union were renewed. In March 1946, former British Prime Minister Winston Churchill gave voice to the concerns of the West in response to the threat of Soviet postwar expansion. After observing the fate of Eastern Europe after its "liberation" by Russia, Churchill declared that "from Stettin in the Baltic to Trieste in the Adriatic, an Iron Curtain has descended across the continent." Churchill identified the spread of communism with the imprisonment of innocent nations behind an "Iron Curtain."

Churchill's phrase succinctly conveyed the fears of the West that it was also in danger of being swallowed up behind the ever-expanding walls of totalitarian oppression. At the same time, communism began to play a greater and greater role in the postwar political landscape of the Far East, especially in North Korea, China, and Indochina.

In the United States, business feared that labor unions would be "taken over" by Communists in a somewhat similar way. In 1945, the Conference of Studio Unions (CSU) (those unions not represented by IATSE) began a strike against the studios which lasted for over eight months. Warner Bros. relied on scabs, fire hoses, tear gas, and other violent means to disperse union pickets and break the strike. During the fall of 1946, another industrywide strike by the CSU resulted in charges, from opponents of the strike, that the unions represented by the CSU had become infiltrated by Communists.

Meanwhile, a nationwide strike by coal miners, which began in April 1946, was followed by a national strike of railway workers in May. These strikes were resolved only after President Harry Truman threatened to draft striking workers into the Armed Forces.

The elections of 1946 witnessed a number of races in which Republican candidates accused the Democratic opponents and the Democratic New Deal administration of Communist sympathies. Both Richard Nixon and Joseph McCarthy relied upon red-baiting to gain their seats in Congress. In 1947, President Truman, in an attempt to demonstrate his administration's own anti-Communist bias, officially declared a "Cold War" against the Soviet Union which was designed to contain the spread of communism abroad. Funds were allocated to assist anti-Communist forces in Greece and Turkey in their struggle against "armed minorities" within their own countries. At the same time, Truman initiated a series of domestic loyalty probes to root out Communist infiltration of government and labor in the United States. As a result of Truman's loyalty review program, between March 1947 and December 1952, over 6.6 million people were investigated and over 500 were dismissed because their loyalty was deemed to be in question.

"Are You Now or Have You Ever Been . . . ?"

It was in this atmosphere of governmental distrust and suspicion that the House Un-American Activities Committee renewed its investigation of subversives within the film industry. Preliminary, closed-door hearings were held in May 1947 by new Committee Chair J. Parnell Thomas. After hearing testimony from members of the Motion Picture Alliance for the Preservation of American Ideals and others, Thomas announced that Hollywood filmmakers "have employed subtle techniques in pictures in glorifying the Communist system and degrading our own system of Government and Institutions." Later that year, in October, Thomas conducted public hearings in Washington DC, during which his committee interviewed 24 "friendly" and 11 "unfriendly" witnesses (18 had been called but only 11 testified). The friendly witnesses, including actors Robert Taylor, Robert Montgomery, Adolphe

Menjou, Ronald Reagan, and Gary Cooper, director Sam Wood, and producer Walt Disney, complained about the subversive activities of Communists within the film industry and identified as many of them as they could by name.

The "unfriendly" witnesses, many of whom had been named as Communists, attended the hearings but refused to cooperate with the Committee, contending that its investigation was illegal and in violation of their rights under the First Amendment of the Constitution. These witnesses included German playwright Bertolt Brecht, who testified that he had never been a member of the Communist Party and then fled the United States on the following day (thus, this eleventh witness avoided making the "Hollywood Ten" the "Hollywood Eleven").

The remaining ten "unfriendly" witnesses were subsequently known as the "Hollywood Ten." They included writer Alvah Bessie (drama critic for *New Masses* and coscreenwriter of *Objective Burma*, 1945); director Herbert

The Hollywood Ten (and their lawyers), January 1948:

Top row (left to right for all rows): Ring Lardner, Jr., Edward Dmytryk, Adrian Scott

Middle row: Dalton Trumbo, John Howard Lawson, Alvah Bessie, Samuel Ornitz

Front row: Herbert Biberman, attorney Martin Popper, attorney Robert Kenny, Albert Maltz, Lester Cole

Courtesy of Corinth Films

Biberman (*Meet Nero Wolfe*, 1936); writer Lester Cole (*Objective Burma*); director Edward Dmytryk (*Crossfire*, 1947); screenwriter Ring Lardner, Jr. (*Woman of the Year*, 1942); founder and first president of the Screen Writers Guild, John Howard Lawson (*Action in the North Atlantic*, 1943); writer Albert Maltz (*Pride of the Marines*, 1945); writer Sam Ornitz; writer-producer Adrian Scott (*Murder, My Sweet*, 1944; *Crossfire*, 1947); and writer Dalton Trumbo (*Thirty Seconds Over Tokyo*, 1944).

They were accompanied to the hearings by an independent group of famous Hollywood celebrities, such as Edward G. Robinson, Humphrey Bogart, Lauren Bacall, Danny Kaye, John Garfield, Gregory Peck, John Huston, and others (such as writer Philip Dunne) who had become members of the Committee for the First Amendment. During the hearings, these celebrities participated in a radio broadcast from Washington, which denounced HUAC and supported the First Amendment, but which gave no direct support to any individual "unfriendly" witnesses with whose confrontational tactics they disagreed.

The Hollywood Ten initially sought to use the hearings as a platform for exposing the dangers of anti-communism and for protesting the way in which the Committee threatened their rights under the First Amendment of the Constitution (although none of the "Ten" chose to invoke the First Amendment, preferring instead to answer the Committee in their own words). Each came with a prepared statement to read, but only one, Albert Maltz, was permitted to present it. They were all asked by members of HUAC, "Are you now or have you ever been a member of the Communist Party?" Because they all refused to answer, they were cited with contempt of Congress, were tried and convicted, and, sentenced to from six months to one year in jail. After exhausting their appeals (and after the U.S. Supreme Court refused to hear their case), they began serving their sentences in 1950.

Blacklisting

Shortly after the October hearings, more than 50 studio executives, members of the Motion Pictures Producers Association, met secretly at the Waldorf-Astoria Hotel in New York to discuss steps that the industry might take to protect itself from the "fallout" from the hearings. In particular, the producers feared threatened boycotts of their films, organized by the Hearst newspapers, the American Legion, and other "patriotic" national organizations. Much as the industry had earlier adopted self-censorship, through the agency of the Hays Office, in order to prevent the creation of external censorship review boards, here it adopted a policy of "self-regulation" which was coupled with the institution of "blacklisting."

Issuing what would be known as "the Waldorf Statement," the studio heads agreed to suspend the Hollywood Ten without pay, deny employment to anyone who did not cooperate with HUAC's investigations, and refuse to hire Communists. In this way, the industry effectively instituted a blacklist of unemployable talent. The numbers of those blacklisted ultimately extended beyond the Hollywood Ten and those who refused to testify before the

Committee at subsequent hearings to include any employees who were suspected of Communist sympathies and who were unable to clear themselves to the satisfaction of the studios. By the mid-1950s over 200 suspected Communists had been blacklisted by the Hollywood studios. The blacklist remained unchallenged from 1947 until 1960, when screenwriter Dalton Trumbo, one of the original Hollywood Ten, worked openly in the industry and received screen credit for his work on producer-director Otto Preminger's *Exodus* (1960) and actor-producer Kirk Douglas' *Spartacus* (1960). However, the blacklist did not begin to give way until the mid-1960s and it remained in effect for a number of artists well into the 1970s.

Alger Hiss, the Rosenbergs, and Senator McCarthy

A second round of HUAC hearings on Hollywood took place in 1951. In the interim, the Cold War had dramatically escalated. A Communist coup had taken place in Czechoslovakia in 1948. In July 1948, a federal grand jury indicted (and subsequently convicted) eleven leaders of the American Communist Party with conspiracy to overthrow the United States government. In 1949, Mao Tse-tung defeated the forces of Chiang Kai-shek and China became a Communist nation. That same year, the Soviets exploded their first nuclear weapon, launching an arms race that would continue for over four decades. In January 1950, former New Deal official Alger Hiss was convicted of perjury charges, stemming from a 1948 accusation by admitted former Communist Whittaker Chambers, a senior editor at *Time* magazine, that Hiss had sold government documents to the Soviets in the 1930s when he worked in the State Department. Hiss' apparent guilt enabled Republicans to portray the Roosevelt administration as thoroughly infiltrated by Communists, a notion that would subsequently be exploited by Senator Joseph McCarthy in his attack on Communists in government. (The release of secret Soviet records in 1992 ultimately cleared Hiss of any association with Communist espionage.)

In February, the British arrested Dr. Klaus Fuchs, an atomic scientist who had worked with the Americans on the A-bomb at Los Alamos, charging that he had spied for the Soviets. The arrest of Fuchs led to the subsequent arrest and conviction of his supposed accomplices, Americans Harry Gold, Morton Sobell, and Julius and Ethel Rosenberg. The Rosenbergs were ultimately executed for espionage in 1953. Several days after the highly publicized arrest of Fuchs, Senator McCarthy launched a witch-hunt of Communists working in government. Speaking in Wheeling, West Virginia, McCarthy declared that he had in his possession a list of 205 names of Communists who were knowingly employed by the State Department.

Even though McCarthy's charges were investigated and proven false by a special committee of the Senate, the press continued to publish his accusations and headline the threat of the red menace until the Army-McCarthy hearings, which were held from April through June 1954. The televised hearings exposed the senator as a bully and a self-serving demagogue, who would do anything to advance his own career. Later that year, in December, the Senate voted to censure McCarthy, whose credibility as a force in national politics quickly crumbled.

Naming Names

During the 1951 HUAC hearings, dozens of former Communists and suspected Communists chose to cooperate with the Committee in an attempt to clear themselves. Unlike the Hollywood Ten, they chose to identify other supposed Communists by name. In April of 1951, Edward Dmytryk, one of the Hollywood Ten, reappeared before HUAC in a carefully orchestrated attempt to clear himself and regain employment in Hollywood. He answered the Committee's questions and identified 24 former Communists. Within a matter of weeks, he was back at work, directing a low-budget film for the King Brothers. The following year, he returned to work at the major studios.

Dozens of other Hollywood artists cooperated with the Committee and chose to name names, although most of them held out for several months or even years before doing so. Screenwriter Martin Berkeley named 155 supposed Communists, director Robert Rossen 54, director Frank Tuttle 36, actor Lee J. Cobb 20, writer Budd Schulberg 15, actor Larry Parks 12, director Elia Kazan 11, composer David Raksin 11, actor Sterling Hayden 7, and writer Clifford Odets 6. The victims of this round of testimony included writers Dashiell Hammett, Paul Jarrico, Michael Wilson, and Carl Foreman; actors Mady Christians, Canada Lee, John Garfield, Larry Parks, Howard da Silva, Paul Robeson, and Gale Sondergaard; and directors Abraham Polonsky, Joseph Losey, and Jules Dassin.

Actor Lionel Stander, who is known to audiences today for his role as the chauffeur in the TV series "Hart to Hart," was perhaps blacklisted for the longest period—from the late 1940s until 1965. Stander's 1951 testimony provided one of the few lighter moments in the saga of the blacklist. When questioned by HUAC, he offered to cooperate with them in exposing "subversive action." Stander declared "I know of a group of fanatics who are desperately trying to undermine the Constitution of the United States by depriving artists and others of Life, Liberty, and the Pursuit of Happiness without due process of law. . . . . I can tell names and cite instances and I am one of the first victims of it. And if you are interested in that and also a group of ex-Fascists and America-Firsters and anti-Semites, people who hate everybody including Negroes, minority groups and most likely themselves . . . and these people are engaged in a conspiracy outside all the legal processes to undermine the very fundamental American concepts upon which our entire system of democracy exists." Stander was referring, of course, to HUAC itself.

The hearings produced very little evidence of Communist influence upon the motion picture industry. One witness recalled that Stander had once whistled the Communist anthem, "The Internationale," in a film while waiting for an elevator. Another noted that screenwriter Lester Cole had inserted lines from a famous pro-Loyalist speech by La Pasionaria about it being "better to die on your feet than to live on your knees" into a pep talk delivered by a football coach.

THE COLD WAR ON SCREEN

Pro-Soviet Wartime Films

Chief targets of HUAC investigators were a handful of pro-Soviet films, such as *The North Star* (RKO, 1943), *Song of Russia* (M-G-M, 1943), *Days of Glory* (RKO, 1944), and *Mission to Moscow* (Warner Bros., 1943), which had been made during the war by major studios as part of the war effort. *The North Star*, which celebrates the resistance of a small Russian village to the Nazis when they are invaded, was written by Lillian Hellman and directed by Lewis Milestone, both of whom were subsequently investigated by HUAC. *Mission to Moscow*, which was based on the autobiography of Joseph Davies, the U.S. Ambassador to the Soviet Union, was supposedly made at the request of Franklin Delano Roosevelt in order "to show American mothers and fathers that . . . the Russians are worthy allies." This piece of obvious pro-Soviet propaganda demonstrated the virtues of our new allies and whitewashed, in the process, their faults, including Stalin's infamous purge trials of the late 1930s.

HUAC focused on this film in particular in an attempt to suggest that the Roosevelt administration was pro-Communist and that Hollywood had served as FDR's unwitting tool, producing pro-Soviet propaganda. But it was difficult to fault Hollywood for its support of an acknowledged American ally in its war against Germany. Indeed, in a 1947 statement delivered to HUAC in defense of the film, producer Jack Warner arged that "if making *Mission to Moscow* in 1942 was a subversive activity, then the American Liberty ships which carried food and guns to Russian allies and the American naval vessels

An American in Russia: Symphony conductor Robert Taylor (a friendly witness for HUAC) falls in love with Soviet musician Susan Peters in *Song of Russia* (1943).

Courtesy of M-G-M

which convoyed them were likewise engaged in subversive activities." In his testimony, Warner "protected" FDR, denying that the President played any role in encouraging the studio to make the film.

However, Warner later named the film's screenwriter, Howard Koch, as a Communist, insisting that whatever pro-Soviet sentiments anyone could find in the film had been slipped into it by Koch. Koch, who had coauthored such patriotic scripts as *Sergeant York* (1941) and *Casablanca* (1942), became, as a result of Warner's desperate need for a "fall guy" on whom to pin responsibility for the film's obvious sympathy for the Soviet Union, yet another victim of the blacklist, remaining out of work for over ten years.

The Anti-Commie Cycle

Ironically, Hollywood produced more films with "subversive" messages after HUAC began its investigations than it did before them. For every anti-Communist picture released in the wake of the first HUAC hearings of 1947, there was another film that attacked the scapegoating and witch-hunting tactics of HUAC and the anti-Communist far right. With films such as *The Iron Curtain* (1948), *The Red Menace* (1949), *The Woman on Pier 13* (aka *I Married a Communist*, 1949), *I Was a Communist for the FBI* (1951), *The Whip Hand* (1951), *Walk East on Beacon* (1952), *My Son John* (1952), *Big Jim McLain* (1952), and *Pickup on South Street* (1953), Hollywood openly condemned Communists, associating them with espionage and with plots involving the violent overthrow of the American government.

The Iron Curtain, which is based on the confessions of a real-life Russian defector, exposes the operations of a Soviet spy ring in Canada. In *The Red Menace*, a disillusioned war veteran falls victim to Communist propaganda, which the film's narrator describes as "Marxian hatred . . . intent upon spreading world dissension and treason." In *Big Jim McLain*, John Wayne plays an FBI agent who tracks down Communist spies in Hawaii for HUAC; the film's end credits even thank the members of the Committee, who "undaunted by the vicious campaign against them" continue to fight against Communist subversion. *Pickup on South Street* portrays Communists as more treacherous and corrupt than common criminals, who at least observe the codes of the underworld. The film's hero, a small-time pickpocket, is no patriot, but he learns that you can't "play footsie" with the "commies," who are even less trustworthy than police stool pigeons and prostitutes.

Us vs. Them: Science Fiction and Paranoia

Few of these blatantly anti-Communist works made a profit at the box office, but virtually every studio made them in order to demonstrate their anti-Communist zeal. Films dealing with the Korean war, such as *The Steel Helmet* (1950) and *Fixed Bayonets* (1951), or with the war in Indochina, such as *China Gate* (1957), provided a more traditional formula for the expression of anticommunism by removing the conflict between "us" and "them" from within the borders of America itself to foreign shores. These movies tended to fare somewhat better with audiences. Even more successful than these overtly anti-Communist films were the covert "war" films—science-fiction films. These works captured the decade's greatest fears—fear of the bomb and fear of a Communist takeover—but did so without the crude tactics of the more flagrantly political films that merely restaged the HUAC hearings in a somewhat more dramatic form or simply reworked recent events that had taken place in Korea.

In *Them!* (1954), gigantic ants, who appear to be mutations produced by nuclear testing, attack Los Angeles, while in *The Incredible Shrinking Man* (1957), a radiation shower serves as the source for human mutation. But instead of producing giant insects, fallout from the bomb actually diminishes the size of the film's hero, who then struggles to survive in a world in which the everyday (in the form of household pets and spiders in the basement) threatens his very existence. Cold War tensions also find expression in films in which invaders from outer space threaten to take over the Earth. In *The Thing* (1951), a creature from outer space that feeds on the blood of its victims and plants seeds that will enable it to reproduce, gives monstrous form to contemporary fears about the spread of communism.

Invaders From Mars (1953) and *Invasion of the Body Snatchers* (1956) exploit the association of communism with "brainwashing," which had developed in the aftermath of the Korean war when American prisoners of war were said to have been indoctrinated with Communist ideology. In *Invaders*, Martians implant crystals in the brains of local citizens, transforming them into slaves

Communism as an alien invasion: In *Invasion of the Body Snatchers* (1956), King Donovan (left), Kevin McCarthy, and Dana Wynter look at a "pod" which has duplicated Donovan's features.

Courtesy of Republic

who do their bidding. In *Invasion*, aliens take over the bodies of the local residents by placing "seed pods" in their houses. The pods copy their features while they sleep, taking them over, "cell by cell." Once they have been taken over by the pods, the film's characters lack individuality, feeling, and emotion; they have, in short, become Communist dupes.

God and Country

Even biblical epics took up the issues of the Cold War. In *The Ten Commandments* (1956), the right-wing director Cecil B. DeMille provides a prologue to the movie in which he asks "whether men are to be ruled by God's law—or whether they are to be ruled by the whims of a dictator." He stresses the relevance of these issues by then asking, "Are men the property of the state? Or are they free souls under God?" And he finally links these issues to the current Cold War by observing that "the same battle continues throughout the world today."

Yet, it is in this same genre that the radical left was able to make a case for the Hollywood Ten and the evils of repressive government. The original script of the first CinemaScope blockbluster, *The Robe* (Fox, 1953), for example, was, according to Philip Dunne who rewrote it and received sole screen credit for the film, written by a blacklisted writer. It casts Caligula as a witch-hunting, McCarthyesque figure and the Christians as persecuted victims of his demonic attempts to purge the Roman empire of potential subversives—that is, of Christians. The hero, Marcellus, is converted to Christianity and publicly tried for treason at the end of the film. The film's Christians meet in underground caverns (i. e., cells) and resist the facism of the Roman state. The pagan villain in *Prince Valiant* (Fox, 1954) captures Prince Valiant and refuses to release him unless he betrays his Christian comrades. The villain literally asks the hero to name names, demanding that the Prince "confirm this list—your father named them all." Needless to say, the Prince stoically refuses, remaining silent in spite of being tortured.

Subversions

Subversive messages also surfaced in the Western. Because he was ultimately blacklisted, Carl Foreman's script for the critically acclaimed, box-office success *High Noon* (1952) emerges as an obvious example of resistance within the industry to outside investigators, such as HUAC. The film's hero, ironically played by a real-life friendly witness, Gary Cooper, is threatened by a gang of cutthroats (HUAC) who are on their way to town (Hollywood). The sheriff-hero is unable to find allies to help him within the (Hollywood) community. He nonetheless confronts and defeats them, waging a battle alone which the townspeople ought to have fought together with him.

A few years earlier, hard on the heels of being blacklisted as one of the original Hollywood Ten, Alvah Bessie wrote the screenplay for *Broken Arrow* (1950), which proved to be one of the highest-grossing films of the year. Bessie was able to accomplish this by using a "front," another screenwriter (Michael Blankfort) who pretended to be the author of the script and who received screen credit for it. (In 1976, Woody Allen starred in a film called *The Front* which dealt with this method of outwitting the blacklist.) The story, which later served as the basis for a highly popular television series of the same name in the mid-1950s, involved the unusual friendship between a white man, Tom Jeffords (James Stewart), and an Apache, Cochise (Jeff Chandler). In befriending the Indians, Jeffords is regarded as a traitor to his own people, who attempt to lynch him. Jeffords, however, is rescued by the Army. He subsequently marries an Indian girl and plays the role of peace-maker between the Apaches and the whites, but the leading citizens of a nearby town attack the Indian camp, killing Jefford's wife in the process.

In Bessie's scenario, Jefford's friendship with the Indians and his campaign for peaceful coexistence between reds and whites marks him as a traitor (a Communist or Communist sympathizer) in the eyes of his own community. The townspeople emerge as barely disguised Communist witch-hunters. The film's sympathies clearly lie with Jeffords, who, like the blacklisted writer, is not only rejected by society but becomes the target of its violence and anger.

A similar scenario crops up in *Johnny Guitar* (1954), which was written by Philip Yordan and directed by one of Hollywood's young rebels, Nicholas Ray. The film's plot reworks the HUAC confrontations between suspected subversives and local vigilantes in terms of a typical Western. Again, the community is seen to be intolerant of those within it who are not like

The anti-HUAC Western: Joan Crawford and Sterling Hayden portray innocent victims of witch-hunting vigilantes in *Johnny Guitar* (1954).

Courtesy of Republic

themselves. And the unconventional, nonconformist hero and heroine are forced to defend themselves against the false accusations of society. The casting of the film makes its allegorical status as an anti-HUAC vehicle even clearer. The hero, whom the town suspects of having robbed the bank, is played by confessed former Communist Sterling Hayden. One of the chief leaders of the vigilantes is played by Ward Bond, a member of Hollywood's most vocal anti-Communist group, the Motion Picture Alliance for the Preservation of American Ideals. The final shoot-out dramatizes the central battle between the forces of conformity and those of nonconformity. However, it does not take place between the two former cold warriors, Bond and Hayden, but between two women, who, in the form of the neurotic and sexually repressive Emma (Mercedes McCambridge) and the former prostitute Vienna (Joan Crawford), reconfigure the political extremes of the film in sexual terms. Though carefully disguised, the anti-HUAC and antiauthoritarian sentiments of the film clearly encourage audiences to root for Hayden and Crawford, as the victims of social oppression.

As in the case of Alvah Bessie, blacklisted writers continued to work secretly in Hollywood and were often drawn to projects that provided a platform for the expression of "liberal" ideas. On more than one occasion, blacklisted writers even won Academy Awards for their work. In 1956, the (unclaimed) Academy Award for best story went to *The Brave One*, which was written by "Robert Rich," one of Dalton Trumbo's aliases. The story deals with the efforts of a Mexican peasant boy to rescue his bull from slaughter in the arena. Next year, the Academy Award for best screenplay went to *The Bridge on the River Kwai* (1957), which explores life in a Japanese prisoner-of-war camp, questions blind obedience to authority, and takes a critical stance toward those who collaborate with the enemy. The script for this box-office blockbuster was signed by Pierre Boule, author of the original novel on which the film was based. Boule, however, did not speak a work of English; the script was actually written by two blacklisted writers, Carl Foreman and Michael Wilson.

The secret work of blacklisted writers tended to fare better at the box office than did the one or two projects which directly attacked the system. In 1954, a group of blacklisted filmmakers, including Herbert Biberman, Michael Wilson, and Paul Jarrico, worked on an independently made feature, *Salt of the Earth*, which was a prolabor film dealing with the 1951–1952 strike by Mexican-American zinc miners. The film exposes a double standard whereby minority workers were paid less than their white coworkers and were forced to work under hazardous conditions. In addition, it celebrates the efforts of the miners' wives in winning the strike. Its feminist narrative perspective, unique for the 1950s, provided a model for Barbara Kopple's *Harlan County, U.S.A.* (1977), a documentary about a strike by Kentucky coal miners.

American immigration officials attempted to halt production of *Salt of the Earth* by deporting its Mexican star as an illegal alien before the film was completed. Laboratory technicians and projectionists, members of the anti-Communist IATSE union, refused to process prints of the film or to project them in theaters. And right-wing organizations, such as the American Legion, threatened to organize boycotts if exhibitors attempted to show the film. As a result, the film played in only a limited number of situations in the United States.

Chaplin in Exile

The most overt attack on HUAC came from Charles Chaplin, whose prior association with "known Communists" such as composer Hanns Eisler and writer Bertolt Brecht put him under suspicion as a Communist sympathizer. In 1952, Chaplin's apolitical, semiautobiographical drama about a music hall comic, *Limelight*, became the target of a nationwide boycott, organized by the American Legion. Chaplin, who had never become an American citizen, had embarked on a worldwide tour to promote the film, after first securing a permit from the State Department to reenter the United States on his return. In September, 1952, shortly after Chaplin had left the country, the U.S. Attorney General suddenly revoked Chaplin's reentry permit on the grounds that Chaplin was an "unsavory" character. The Attorney General insisted that Chaplin answer questions about his political beliefs before he would be granted permission to reenter the United States.

A few weeks later, the American Legion denounced Chaplin as a Communist "fellow traveler" and launched a boycott of *Limelight*, vowing to sustain their protest until Chaplin returned to the United States to answer questions about his political sympathies. Refusing to submit himself to the ordeal undergone by other members of the Hollywood community who had been forced to testify before HUAC, Chaplin gave up his residence in the United States and moved to Switzerland, where he lived until his death in 1977. Chaplin did not return to the United States until 1972—20 years later—when he journeyed to New York City, where he was honored by the Film Society of Lincoln Center in a special tribute, and then to Los Angeles to receive an honorary Oscar from the Academy of Motion Picture Arts and Sciences.

During the period of his European exile in the mid-1950s, Chaplin wrote, starred in, and directed *A King in New York* (1957), which was a bitter denunciation of American McCarthyism, in general, and HUAC, in particular. Chaplin, however, did not release the film in the United States until 1973. In the film, Chaplin plays the dethroned king of a fictional European country who flees to the United States. There he meets and befriends a young boy, whose parents are Communists who have been called to testify before HUAC. The boy, played by Chaplin's son, Michael, denounces the government for its totalitarian behavior, including acts similar to Chaplin's own experiences, such as depriving citizens of passports to travel. Chaplin's king shields the boy from HUAC, which has subpoenaed him to testify about his parents' political beliefs and loyalties. The FBI eventually tracks the boy down, takes him into custody, and forces him to "name names" in order to secure the release of his parents.

Because he has helped the boy, the king is called to appear before HUAC to explain his actions and to give testimony about his political sympathies. On his way to the hearings, the king's finger becomes accidentally caught in the nozzle of a fire hose, which he is forced to bring into the hearing room with him. The water is turned on and the king "inadvertently" ends up dousing the members of HUAC with a stream of water. In spite of this mishap, the Committee clears the king of the charges that he is a subversive. He is, after all, a monarch and thus, by profession, an anti-Communist. However, at the end of the film, Chaplin's king decides to return to Europe rather than live in a society dominated by the forces of fear and political repression.

In Defense of the Informers: *On the Waterfront*

Perhaps the most curious film to be "inspired" by the HUAC hearings, however, was *On the Waterfront* (1954), which was written by Budd Schulberg and directed by Elia Kazan. Both Schulberg and Kazan were friendly witnesses who had named names when they testified before HUAC. Voted Best Picture of the Year by the Academy, *Waterfront* functions as a cleverly disguised defense of those members of the Hollywood community who informed on their colleagues. In the film, ex-prizefighter Terry Malloy (Marlon Brando) is a union (read "Communist") "dupe" who slowly discovers just how corrupt and vicious the local longshoremen's union actually is. The union leadership, which is dominated by mobsters, is seen to be responsible for the death of a potential "stool pigeon," who threatens to inform on them. It also exploits the very workers it claims to protect. Near the end of the film, union boss Johnny Friendly orders the murder of Terry's protective brother Charley (Rod Steiger) and Terry then testifies against the union in hearings held by the Waterfront Crime Commission. The film concludes with Terry's return to the docks, where he openly confronts the union's hired thugs, who beat him up. Terry's defiance of the union, however, wins him the support of the other workers, who join him in his repudiation of the union leadership. The message of the film was clear: it's not only okay to inform, but those who do are the real heroes.

AFTERMATH

The Fight Continues

By the late 1950s, the political power of HUAC and Senator McCarthy had declined. In 1953, the Soviet Union's hard-line premier, Joseph Stalin, died and the Korean war came to a conclusion. At the end of 1954, the Senate voted to "condemn" McCarthy for his verbal abuse of fellow senators and for his contempt for the Senate itself. McCarthy's influence quickly faded, and he died three years later. During the early 1960s, Hollywood slowly began to abandon the blacklist, openly acknowledging the work of Trumbo (*Exodus*, *Spartacus*) and other blacklisted individuals.

However, Hollywood continued to fight the Cold War, though the hysterical anti-communism of the 1950s quickly gave way to a cooler, more calculated manipulation of Cold War fears for dramatic effect rather than for political propaganda. In other words, Communists began to function more as traditional villains than as real-life threats to our national security. The paranoid vision of *The Manchurian Candidate* (1962) suggests that brainwashed Korean prisoners of war have been programmed to assassinate American political candidates. Yet, the film also condemns a McCarthyite politician who is, ironically, revealed to be an unwitting pawn in the larger game plan the Communists have devised to take over the United States.

Rabid anticommunism and nuclear anxiety are still strong enough in the mid-1960s—the Barry Goldwater era—to provide the stuff of black humor in Stanley Kubrick's *Dr. Strangelove* (1964), which explores the political "fallout" after a fanatical anti-Communist in the American military deliberately launches a nuclear attack on the Soviets. In the 1970s, Dalton Trumbo's adaptation of Henri Charriere's novel about unjust imprisonment in a French Guiana penal colony, *Papillon* (1973), includes a sequence in which the hero (played by Steve McQueen) refuses to betray the name of a friend and concludes with a comparison of McQueen's defiance of authority with costar Dustin Hoffman's complicit resignation to it.

John Wayne's *The Green Berets* (1968) takes a hard line against those who oppose the war in Vietnam, suggesting that they are the unfortunate victims of Communist propaganda. Even more recently, *Rambo: First Blood Part II* (1985) attempts to keep the Cold War alive by mixing old-fashioned, us-vs.-them anti-communism with a new ingredient—the relevation of treachery from within. As a result, Rambo takes on not only the Vietcong and its Russian military advisers, but also the American CIA and the political establishment, who attempt to undermine Rambo's mission to rescue POWs. Sylvester Stallone successfully manipulates anti-Communist sentiment again that same year in *Rocky IV* (1985), which pits Rocky against a Soviet boxer who is responsible for the ring death of Rocky's old friend, Apollo Creed.

Red Dawn (1984), a right-wing fantasy written and directed by John Milius, imagines what it would be like if the Cubans and the Soviets invaded the United States, transforming rural Colorado into a battleground in which American teenagers wage a guerrilla war with the Communist invaders. Cold War tensions also fuel *Top Gun* (1986), in which Navy pilots test their mettle against Soviet migs, and *No Way Out* (1987), in which Russian agents are found working in the Pentagon. The fact that the latter film was a remake of an apolitical film noir, *The Big Clock* (1948), further illustrates the way in which the Cold War had been reduced to the status of a timely convention, which could be plugged into virtually any traditional narrative formula.

The rise to power of Mikhail Gorbachev in the Soviet Union in 1985 and the advent of the era of *glasnost* further served to undermine the viability of Cold War rhetoric in American films. *Rambo III* (1988) attempts to prolong the anti-Soviet sentiments which had helped to make *Rambo II* a box-office hit by sending Rambo to Soviet-occupied Afghanistan to fight Russians, but the film did not do well commercially, putting an end to the highly successful *Rambo* series. By 1990, the relaxation of U.S./Soviet tensions could be dramatically seen in the adaptation of Tom Clancy's 1984 Cold War novel, *The Hunt for Red October*, into a suspense melodrama in which Sean Connery's Soviet submarine commander emerges as the film's hero, successfully outwitting both his Soviet superiors and his American counterparts.

Win, Lose, or Draw?

From the vantage point of the 1990s, the Cold War, the HUAC hearings in Hollywood, and the blacklist emerge as nightmarish aberrations which properly belong to another time, another place, and another generation. Recent attempts to recreate this world, such as *Guilty by Suspicion* (1991) in which Robert De Niro plays a director forced to give testimony to HUAC, have failed to connect with contemporary filmgoers who find little in these dramatic situations with which they can identify. Even before the Cold War officially concluded, Hollywood discovered that audiences could not care less about the supposed "red menace" threatening us from without and from within. If then-President Ronald Reagan, an old Cold Warrior from the 1950s, could come to terms with the "evil empire" of the Soviet Union, then so could the rest of us.

During the presidential campaign of 1992, George Bush insisted that the United States had "won" the Cold War, forcing the collapse of communism. What is more likely is that both the United States and the USSR "lost" it by spending themselves into a state of economic disaster, characterized by rampant inflation, recessions, and escalating deficits. Day by day, the Cold War is emerging as a common enemy of the peoples of both the United States and

The end of the Cold War: Soviet submarine commander Marko Ramius (Sean Connery) plots to defect to the Americans in *The Hunt for Red October* (1990).

Courtesy of Paramount

the Soviet Union. At any rate, this appears to be the message that Hollywood is sending in films like *The Hunt for Red October* in which lower-echelon officers in the Soviet navy, such as nuclear submarine commander Marko Ramius (Sean Connery), and in the American CIA, such as analyst Jack Ryan (Alec Baldwin), join forces to outwit the doomsday scenario being written by their political superiors and to establish the grounds for a post–Cold War alliance of Soviet and American peoples.

Set "shortly before Gorbachev came to power," the film documents the attempts of Ramius and his fellow officers to defect from the Soviet Union and the political and military responses of both the United States and the Soviet Union. In the final scenes, American and Soviet officers collaborate, jointly serving as the crew of the Soviet typhoon-class submarine, *Red October*, as it evades destruction by Cold War forces which emanate both from within (a KGB saboteur) and from without (an overzealous Soviet submarine commander). Unconventional naval tactics, including the cooperation of an American submarine, result in the self-destruction of the Soviet Union's representative of Cold War philosophy, the promise of a "healthy" revolution in the Soviet Union itself, and the suggestion of peaceful coexistence between the two countries in the future.

HUAC remained in existence until 1975 and the Cold War finally came to an end in the 1990s, but it owes its conclusion not to politicians or governments but to those who have most often been subjected to its tensions—its victims.

SELECT FILMOGRAPHY

Bolshevism on Trial (1919)
Orphans of the Storm (1922)
Trouble in Paradise (1932)
Heroes for Sale (1933)
Blockade (1938)
Ninotchka (1939)
The Grapes of Wrath (1940)
Mission to Moscow (1943)
The North Star (1943)
The Iron Curtain (1948)
The Red Menace (1949)
The Woman on Pier 13 (aka *I Married a Communist*, 1949)
Broken Arrow (1950)
The Steel Helmet (1950)
Fixed Bayonets (1951)
I Was a Communist for the FBI (1951)
Big Jim McLain (1952)

High Noon (1952)
My Son John (1952)
Walk East on Beacon (1952)
Invaders From Mars (1953)
Pickup on South Street (1953)
Johnny Guitar (1954)
On the Waterfront (1954)
Them! (1954)
Invasion of the Body Snatchers (1956)
China Gate (1957)
The Incredible Shrinking Man (1957)
A King in New York (1957)
The Manchurian Candidate (1962)
The Green Berets (1968)
Red Dawn (1984)
Rambo: First Blood Part II (1985)
The Hunt for Red October (1990)

SELECT BIBLIOGRAPHY

Allen, Frederick Lewis. *Only Yesterday: An Informal History of the 1920s.* New York: Harper & Row, 1931.

Bentley, Eric, ed. *Thirty Years of Treason: Excerpts from the Hearings before the House Committee on Un-American Activities, 1938–1968.* New York: Viking, 1971.

Campbell, Russell. "Warners, the Depression, and FDR: Wellman's *Heroes for Sale*," *The Velvet Light Trap*, no. 1 (June 1971).

Ceplair, Larry, and Steven Englund. *The Inquisition in Hollywood: Politics in the Film Community, 1930–1960.* Berkeley: University of California Press, 1983.

Cogley, John. "HUAC: The Mass Hearings," in Tino Balio, ed., *The American Film Industry*, rev. ed. Madison: University of Wisconsin Press, 1985.

Dick, Bernard. *Radical Innocence: A Critical Study of the Hollywood Ten.* Lexington: University Press of Kentucky, 1989.

Dowdy, Andrew. *Movies Are Better Than Ever: The Films of the Fifties.* New York: Morrow, 1973.

Dunne, Philip. *Take Two: A Life in Movies and Politics.* New York: McGraw-Hill, 1980.

Maland, Charles. *Chaplin and American Culture: The Evolution of a Star Image.* Princeton: Princeton University Press, 1989.

Navasky, Victor. *Naming Names.* New York: Viking, 1980.

Norman, Barry. *Talking Pictures: The Story of Hollywood.* London: BBC Books, 1987.

Sayre, Nora. *Running Time: Films of the Cold War.* New York: Dial Press, 1982.

CHAPTER 12

HOLLYWOOD IN
THE AGE OF TELEVISION

THE BIG DECLINE: HOLLYWOOD LOSES ITS AUDIENCE

Something strange happens to American audiences in the postwar era: their 20-year romance with the movies begins to fade. Weekly motion picture attendance, which hits a high of 95 million in 1929, averages 85 million during the war years, and climbs to 90 million in the immediate postwar period of 1945–1948. But attendance falls off dramatically thereafter, sinking to 60 million per week in 1950 and then to 46 million in 1953. During the late 1960s and early 1970s, weekly attendance fell below the 20 million mark, reaching a low of 15.8 million in 1971. By the end of the 1970s, attendance had slowly climbed back to the 20 million mark, where it remains today. But, over a span of a mere 20 years, between 1948 and 1968, Hollywood had lost three-quarters of its audience and the nature of moviegoing in America had evolved from the status of ingrained habit to infrequent diversion.

The reasons for the decline in the popularity of motion pictures are complex. And Hollywood's response to this decrease in attendance is itself quite fascinating. Its attempts to recoup this "lost" audience inaugurated a new era in the cinema—an era of big-budget, widescreen blockbusters which began in the early 1950s and which continues, although in a somewhat less spectacular form, into the present. Contemporary attitudes toward motion pictures in the 1980s and 1990s look back, in part, to this period of readjustment in the 1950s when the industry began to respond, for the first time, to changing conditions in postwar lifestyle and to shifting patterns within leisure-time amusements. American cinema, which had enjoyed the status of *the* mass entertainment medium par excellence for almost 40 years, gradually redefined itself, during the 1950s, as a specialized form of participatorial activity within a larger field of recreational endeavors. The George Lucas and Steven Spielberg productions that dominated the motion picture marketplace in the late 1970s and 1980s have their origin in the special-event, widescreen spectacles that brought audiences (albeit in limited numbers) back to the movie theaters in the 1950s.

AT LEISURE: RECREATION IN POSTWAR AMERICA

The Role of Television

Historians have traditionally assumed that the postwar decline in motion picture attendance is directly related to the advent of television, which provided audiences with entertainment that was both free and readily available in the home. Statistics, however, do not quite bear this out. In 1949–1950, average weekly motion picture attendance decreased by one-third, from 90 to 60 million. This was the largest drop-off to date in the history of moviegoing, which did not plunge as precipitously again until 1965–1967, when it fell by over 50 percent (from 44 to 17.8 million). During 1949–1950, there were only a handful of television stations and relatively few families owned television sets. In 1948, the Federal Communications Commission had placed a freeze on the issuance of licenses for new television stations that lasted until 1952. As a result, there were only 50 stations in operation, and most of these were situated in urban areas (this number increased to 108 by 1952 as stations that were under construction in 1948 and thus not subject to the freeze when it was imposed were completed and went on the air).

The number of television sets did increase significantly during this period from 940,000 (1949) to 3.875 million, but this growth remained modest in comparison to subsequent increases that saw the number of sets jump to 10.3 million in 1951, to 20.4 million in 1953, and to 34.9 million in 1956. By the end of the decade, 90 percent of American homes had television sets. The expansion of television in the 1950s is due, in part, to the termination of the freeze on new stations and to the completion, in 1951, of a network of coaxial cable and microwave links that permitted coast-to-coast hookups and expanded the broadcast range of television transmission to include suburban and rural areas, thus enabling TV networks to reach 40 percent of all American homes. Television undoubtedly played a crucial role, during the 1950–1956 period, in the motion picture industry's redefinition of itself, but it cannot be blamed for the demise of the movies, which had begun several years earlier. Television was merely a highly visible, superficial symptom of a much more profound change in postwar entertainment patterns rather than the direct cause of the movies' downfall; the source of the problem lay elsewhere—in the economic annd sociocultural transformation of blue- and white-collar Americans during the postwar period into the "leisured masses."

Do Something ! : Passive Entertainment vs. Action

During the war years, approximately 25 percent of all the money spent on consumer recreation went for tickets to the movies. By the 1980s, this percentage had fallen to roughly 2.5. Though expenditures for recreation increased (as did ticket prices), less and less of each dollar spent on recreation was paid for admission to the movies. Americans had not just stopped going to the movies, but they had begun doing something else instead. After the war, Americans grew disenchanted with passive entertainment and took a greater and greater interest in participatory recreation—in gardening, golfing, bowling, hunting, fishing, and boating. The workweek dropped from a wartime high of 48 hours to 40 hours in the postwar era and, for the first time in our nation's history, employers began to offer workers one- and two-week paid vacations. Indeed, the length of the average vacation doubled between 1941 and 1953. At the same time, wages increased: disposable personal income rose from $76.1 billion in 1940 to $207.1 billion in 1950, and then to $350 billion in 1960.

With more money to spend and more leisure time in which to spend it, middle- and working-class Americans could devote larger blocks of time to recreation than had ever been possible before. The traditional six-day work-week encouraged the careful budgeting of leisure time, making an evening at the movies an ideal solution to consumers' short-term needs for inexpensive entertainment. However, the new five-day workweek and multiweek paid-vacation plans permitted people to spend weeks on vacation camping in the nation's public parks; to spend weekends hunting, fishing, and boating; to pass the day golfing, gardening, or puttering around the house, working on do-it-yourself, home repair projects. According to one magazine survey, more than 30 million Americans took up gardening in the postwar era. The sale of power tools for use in home workshops increased by almost 700 per-cent; over $175 million was being spent by golfers each year for green fees, $21 million for hunting and fishing licenses, $800 million for sporting goods, and $200 million for musical instruments.

Although television was clearly a passive rather than an active entertain-ment medium, it proved to be remarkably well-suited to the new, active lifestyle of most Americans. TV made continuous live and prerecorded pro-grams available to busy homemakers during the day and to breadwinners in the evening on demand; that is, it could satisfy the needs of an increasingly diverse at-home viewership for a form of spectatorial activity that fit more readily into their daily schedules than did an evening at the movies. In other words, a continuing demand for some passive entertainment persisted within this new era of active involvement, and television ultimately proved to be better tailored to the filling in of short-term leisure-time needs than the movies.

The House, the Car . . .

The decline of the movies is tied, in many ways, to the increasing affluence of the average American, whose newfound "wealth" enabled him and/or her to buy into a radically new lifestyle. The combination of wartime shortages, accumulated savings, and increased earnings led to a postwar spending boom, during which many Americans both literally and figuratively bought their way into a new world. Indeed, the very things that Americans bought took them further and further away from the movies. Through their most important purchases—cars and houses—consumers left urban areas, and the downtown/neighborhood motion picture theater, for the "wide-open" spaces of the suburbs, where inexpensive housing developments, good schools, shopping centers, and freeways back to the city sprang up to service an increasingly young and mobile middle-class population.

New car sales skyrocketed from 69,500 in 1945 to 5.1 million in 1949, 6.7 million in 1950, and 7.9 million in 1955. VA/FHA mortgages and GI loans enabled an unprecedented number of young married couples to purchase houses in the suburbs. These houses were being mass-produced for as little as $8000 a unit by construction entrepreneurs like William J. Levitt on sites near the large metropolitan areas of New York City and Philadelphia. During the 1950s, more than 1.5 million New Yorkers moved out of the city into the surrounding suburbs. Of the 13 million new homes built between 1948 and 1958, 11 million were located in the suburbs.

. . . The Drive-In

The motion picture industry was caught by surprise by this rapid population shift. Motion picture theaters had been concentrated in large urban areas, which traditionally generated the lion's share of box-office revenues. First-run theaters in large urban areas typically accounted for 70 to 80 percent of a film's box-office receipts. Only a handful of theaters were located in the suburbs and it would take time and money to build new theaters in these areas.

An antitrust suit against the majors, known as the Paramount Case, had recently forced the studios to sign a consent decree whereby they agreed to divorce their production and distribution operations from their exhibition chains. At the same time, these chains, which tended to have the most capital for investment in and expansion to new suburban sites, were prevented by the terms of the consent decree from acquiring new theaters. Although several, formerly independent theater chains were free to buy or build new theaters, only a handful of chains could afford to expand, especially given

The Drive-In: The movies follow their vanishing audience to the suburbs.

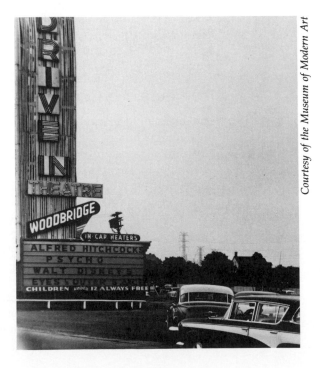

Courtesy of the Museum of Modern Art

declining attendance figures, reduced cash flow, minimal cash reserves, and rampant theater closings.

The quickest and cheapest solution to the problem of theater construction in the suburbs was the drive-in, which involved, in comparison with the construction of indoor theaters, only a modest outlay of capital for land acquisition and development and for the construction of a screen, projection booth, and sound system. As a result, drive-ins popped up all over the map, increasing in number from 554 in 1947 to 4700 in 1958.

Drive-ins adapted themselves as much as possible to the needs of the postwar generation. Instead of hiring a babysitter, dressing up, driving into town, and hunting for a parking space (or paying to put the car in a parking lot), couples with young children took the kids along with them to the drive-in (usually at no extra cost). Many drive-ins provided playgrounds for children to amuse themselves in until the picture started. Parking was, of course, readily available and, since films were viewed from the semiprivacy of one's own car, there was no need to dress up. A number of drive-ins furnished laundry facilities so that families could spend an evening out while completing unfinished household chores at the same time. While drive-ins flourished, urban theaters closed at the rate of roughly two a day, with over 5000 theaters going out of business between 1946 and April 1953.

FEWER, BIGGER, WIDER, DEEPER

This Is Cinerama

The response of the motion picture industry to its sudden loss of a regular, mass audience was characteristically cautious. The studios made fewer, but more expensive films, hoping to lure audiences back to the theater with "quality" product—with lavish biblical spectacles such as *Samson and Delilah* (1949) and *David and Bathsheba* (1951), as well as remakes of tried-and-true historical spectacles such as *Quo Vadis* (1951). It was not so much the Hollywood establishment, however, as the independent producers who engineered a technological revolution that would draw audiences back to first-run, downtown theaters. On September 30, 1952, *This Is Cinerama* opened at the Broadway Theater in New York, launching a widescreen revolution that would permanently alter the shape of the motion picture screen, which had resolutely remained more or less "square" for over 60 years from 1889 to 1952–1953. Less than two months later, another independent effort, the 3-D exploitation picture *Bwana Devil*, premiered in Los Angeles, and audiences stood in lines stretching around the block to catch a glimpse of this new sensation which made lions appear to leap from the screen into the laps of spectators sitting in the theater.

Both Cinerama and 3-D produced enhanced illusions of depth which filmmakers manipulated in order to provide thrills and chills previously unavailable to filmgoers in the past. Cinerama used three cameras mounted alongside of and set at 48-degree angles to one another to film wide, pan-

Courtesy of the Museum of Modern Art

A sketch of the Cinerama system: The Cinerama camera (bottom) records a panoramic image on three strips of film (center), which are then projected, from three separate booths in the theater, onto a deeply curved screen (top).

oramic vistas. Together, these three cameras covered an angle of view of 146 by 55 degrees, which closely approximates that of human vision, which is 160 by 60 degrees. When these three images were projected in the theater by three synchronized projectors onto a deeply curved screen that extended across the full width of most movie palaces, they engulfed audiences, producing a powerful illusion of depth by filling the spectator's field of view, including peripheral vision. Multitrack stereophonic sound, which originated from five speakers situated behind the screen and from a battery of surround speakers placed to the sides of and behind the audience reinforced the spectators' illusion of engulfment, which was described in the press as audience "participation."

The Cinerama experience began with a roller coaster ride, which put spectators in the first car of the Atom Smasher Roller Coaster at the Rockaways Playland amusement park; it ended with a hair-raising, air tour of Bryce Canyon, Yosemite, the Grand Canyon, and Zion Canyon in Zion National Park in which the camera, mounted in the nose of a B-25 bomber, transformed the audience into barnstorming daredevils, hedgehopping through and over sheer canyon walls. World War II flying ace General James Doolittle reportedly clutched his chair during the stunt-flying sequences, and local drugstores made a fortune selling dramamine to spectators who became airsick during the film.

The 3-D Assault

While Cinerama engulfed audiences, pulling them into the action depicted on the screen, 3-D assaulted audiences, hurling spears, shooting arrows, firing guns, and throwing knives at spectators sitting peacefully in their theater seats. The technology of 3-D, unlike that of Cinerama which exploited the phenomenon of peripheral vision, was rooted in the basic principles of binocular vision. By bolting two cameras together so that their lenses were spaced as far apart as human eyes, angling them slightly toward one another, and filming in synchronization, one camera could record action as seen by the right eye and the other that seen by the left. Projected simultaneously through separate, polarizing filters, the "right" and "left" eye records could be "directed" toward the right and left eyes of spectators wearing 3-D glasses. The polarized filters in the glasses permitted the spectator's right eye to receive only right-eye information and the left to see only left-eye information. Synthesizing the two different views, the spectator's brain interpreted the information three dimensionally.

This is Cinerama, which played for more than two years at one theater in New York City and enjoyed similarly lengthy runs in Los Angeles, Detroit, Chicago, and two or three other cities grossed over $20 million and spawned a string of highly successful Cinerama travelogue-adventures, such as *Cinerama Holiday* (1955), *Seven Wonders of the World* (1956), *Search for Paradise* (1957), and *Cinerama South Seas Adventure* (1958), before the first two Cinerama fiction films—*The Wonderful World of the Brothers Grimm* and *How the West Was Won*—were finally released in 1962. By March of 1953, *Bwana Devil* (1952), which was filmed in 3-D in Natural Vision, had grossed over $5 million. Within three weeks of its highly publicized release in April of 1953, *House of Wax,* the first big-budget Natural Vision effort, had grossed over $1 million, and, by the end of its run, had pulled in $3.2 million at the box office. Shortly after the successful opening of *Wax,* a string of cheaply made exploitation pictures were issued in 3-D in 1953, including *Sangaree, It Came From Outer Space, Fort Ti, The Maze,* and *Charge at Feather River.*

The technology required for 3-D production and exhibition, unlike that for Cinerama, was fairly inexpensive, facilitating a boom in the 3-D marketplace. Within a matter of months after the initial release of *Bwana Devil* over 4900 theaters were converted to 3-D, and, during the next two years, 46 films were shot in the process. But for every quality 3-D production, such as *Kiss Me Kate* (1953) or *Dial M for Murder* (1954), there were a half-dozen, low-budget B pictures in 3-D, ranging from *Man in the Dark* and *Robot Monster* (1953) to *The Creature From the Black Lagoon* and *Gorilla at Large* (1954).

By late 1953, the 3-D craze had begun to wane, beset by technological problems that produced eye strain and headaches in spectators, a growing

The 3-D craze: Spectators must wear special polarized glasses in order for the system to produce an illusion of depth.

resistance on the part of moviegoers to the wearing of special 3-D glasses, and the negative association of the process in the public's mind with poorly made exploitation films. As a result, major 1954 3-D productions, such as *Kate* and *Dial M*, were exhibited primarily in "flat" (non–3-D) versions. By the end of 1953, 3-D had given way to Cinerama-like widescreen filmmaking, in particular, to CinemaScope, which had been developed by 20th Century-Fox to duplicate the effect of Cinerama without incurring the tremendous costs associated with that technology.

CinemaScope

Shortly after the premiere of *This is Cinerama* in New York, Fox executives put their research and development department to work, charging them with finding a technology that would reproduce the "participation" effects of Cinerama in a way that would be suitable for adoption by the film industry as a whole (which had refrained from adopting Cinerama because it was designed for usage only in a handful of theaters of appropriate size and location). Fox engineers combined anamorphic lens technology, which had been developed in the 1920s by French scientist Henri Chretien, with multitrack stereo magnetic sound, which had been pioneered by the Cinerama system, and with a highly reflective, slightly curved motion picture screen, which Fox itself had perfected for its theater television system. Chretien's anamorphic lens squeezed a Cinerama-like image possessing an extremely wide angle of view onto a standard strip of 35mm film. Four magnetic soundtracks, placed on the same strip of film that held the image, provided stereo magnetic sound. And, although CinemaScope lacked the compelling illusion of depth provided by Cinerama, its huge, 64-by-24-foot curved screen generated a modest sense of engulfment—so much so that certain roller coaster-type effects, such as the shooting-the-rapids sequence in *River of No Return* (1954), produced pronounced discomfort in audiences.

Between the premiere of *This Is Cinerama* in the fall of 1952 and the release of the first CinemaScope feature, *The Robe*, in September of 1953, the film industry flip-flopped back and forth between 3-D and nonanamorphic wide-screen formats, which ranged in their aspect ratios (or ratio of width to height) from 1.66:1 to 1.85:1. These ratios were achieved by cropping the tops and bottoms of 35mm images in projection. Though the 3-D revolution begun by *Bwana Devil* failed, the widescreen revolution launched by Cinerama and completed by CinemaScope succeeded. Since 1953, every film produced and exhibited in the United States has been shot in one widescreen process or another. Within a matter of one or two years, every country in the world (except for Japan) had abandoned the old "Academy" aspect ratio of 1.37:1 for one or more of the new widescreen formats. By the end of the 1950s, the

The Robe (1953) in CinemaScope: A single projector (lower right) uses 35mm film and an anamorphic lens to project a widescreen image onto a slightly curved screen.

Author's collection

dominant aspect ratios for 35mm projection in the United States were standardized at 1.85:1 (for "flat," nonanamorphic films) and 2.35:1 (for Cinema-Scope, Panavision, and other anamorphic features) while European standards were fixed at 1.66:1 and 2.35:1, respectively. Today, only television retains the old, narrow screen aspect ratio of 1.33:1 (which is only just slightly smaller than the official Academy ratio of 1.37:1).

The projection of widescreen films in color and in stereo sound on theater screens as wide as from 55 to 65 feet and as tall as 24 to 27 feet was undoubtedly meant to provide spectators with a viewing experience dramatically superior to that available at home on narrow, 13- to-19-inch, black-and-white television screens possessing low-fidelity, monaural sound. But the marketing of widescreen cinema to the public proved to be less concerned with comparisons of widescreen to television than it was with the similarities of the widescreen experience to other, highly participatory forms of leisure-time entertainment.

Todd-AO and the Theatrical Experience

If the Cinerama experience resembled an amusement park ride, the Cinema-Scope experience was likened to the legitimate theater where spectators and performers shared the same space. The credits for *The Robe* appeared against a dark red theater curtain, which then opened to reveal the panoramic spectacle of ancient Rome. During the credits of the second CinemaScope feature, *How to Marry a Millionaire* (1953), theater curtains part to disclose the 20th Century-Fox studio orchestra playing an overture to introduce the stage-based comedy that follows. Advertisements for CinemaScope (as well as for 3-D, Cinerama, and Todd-AO) regularly depicted audiences together with the onscreen spectacle as if both spectator and spectacle shared the same space, as in the theater. In describing CinemaScope's "participation effect," publicists repeatedly likened the format's broad image to the oblong *skene* (or stage) of the ancient Greek theater and pointed to the heightened sense of presence whereby the spectators feel that they are actually there, in the midst of the onscreen action.

The appeal to theatrical experience can be seen most clearly in the marketing of the Todd-AO process, which was introduced with the premiere of the motion picture adaptation of Rogers and Hammerstein's long-running Broadway musical, *Oklahoma!*, in October 1955. Advertisements proclaimed, "You're in the show with Todd-AO," and boasted of the enhanced illusion of presence provided by the system, declaring "Suddenly you're there . . . in the land that is grand, in the surrey, on the prairie! You live it, you're a part of it . . . you're in *Oklahoma!*" Todd-AO productions were exhibited, like Cinerama, in select urban theaters at premium prices on a roadshow basis; that is, reserved seat tickets were sold in advance for specific matinee or evening performances on specific days. In other words, *Oklahoma!* in Todd-AO was presented to the public in much the same way that the stage version of *Oklahoma!* had been. Films in Todd-AO were not mere movies, they were semi-legitimate "shows" which appealed to the cinema's carriage trade or movie-going elite.

Todd-AO technology ushered in the first commercially successful wide-film format and, though somewhat ahead of its time, it looked forward to the presentation of motion pictures in 70mm and Dolby stereo that has become a commonplace of contemporary film exhibition practice. A specially built Todd-AO camera, outfitted with a series of nonanamorphic, wide-angle lenses (including a "bug-eye" lens that took in an angle of view of 128 degrees), recorded panoramic action on 65mm (instead of 35mm) film. For exhibition, a 70mm format was used; the 65mm image was accompanied by the six stereo magnetic soundtracks that occupied the additional 5mm on the release print. The widescreen image, which featured an aspect ratio of 2.21:1, was projected upon a deeply curved theater screen, which provided audiences with a sense of engulfment in the image similar to that experienced with Cinerama. *Oklahoma!* exploited this so-called participation effect in its opening sequence when Curly (Gordon MacRae) rides through a field of corn "as high as an elephant's eye" and later, when Laurey (Shirley Jones) is trapped on a roller coaster-like, runaway buckboard. However, these thrills and chills gradually gave way, after the second Todd-AO extravaganza *Around the World in 80 Days* (1956), to less sensational and less obvious

Oklahoma! (1955) in Todd-AO: A single projector (A) produces a widescreen image (without the use of an anamorphic lens) by projecting 70mm film onto a deeply curved screen.

Courtesy of the Academy of Motion Picture Arts and Sciences

participation techniques in subsequent Todd-AO, theatrically based "shows," such as *South Pacific* (1958), *Porgy and Bess* (1959), *Can-Can* (1960), and *The Sound of Music* (1965).

The success of Todd-AO spawned a number of other wide-film processes, including M-G-M Camera 65 [*Raintree County* (1957), *Ben-Hur* (1959)], Super Panavision 70 [*The Big Fisherman* (1959), *Lawrence of Arabia* (1962)], Ultra Panavision 70 [*Mutiny on the Bounty* (1962), *It's a Mad Mad Mad Mad World* (1963)], and Super Technirama 70 [*Spartacus* (1960), *El Cid* (1961), *King of Kings* (1961)]. Twentieth Century-Fox eventually secured ownership of the Todd-AO process in 1958 after Mike Todd's death and used it for the studio's big-budget films [*Can-Can* (1960), *Cleopatra* (1963), *The Agony and the Ecstasy* (1965), *The Sound of Music* (1965)], relegating CinemaScope to second-class status as a format. By 1960, Panavision had replaced CinemaScope as the reigning, 35mm, anamorphic process—a status it continues to hold today.

WAR WITH TELEVISION, PEACE WITH ITS REVENUES

From Villain to Partner

Throughout the 1950s, Hollywood fought a phony war against television, identifying it as the enemy in a conflict that was essentially less with television than it was with other forms of leisure-time entertainment. Film comedies, ranging from the prewidescreen, black-and-white, code-breaking *The Moon Is Blue* (1953) to the Deluxe color, CinemaScope send-up of the advertising game, *Will Success Spoil Rock Hunter?* (1957), poked fun at television commercials. In *Happy Anniversary* (1959), David Niven expresses his outrage at TV by kicking in the screens of one television set after another. In film melodramas as disparate as *All That Heaven Allows* (1955) and *Bigger Than Life* (1956), the presence of television sets function as an indicator of the stultifying nature of a bourgeois, middle-class lifestyle.

But by the mid-1950s, Hollywood's battle with television for an audience had given way to an unspoken truce. In 1954, Disney contracted with ABC to produce a weekly TV show called *Disneyland*, used to promote Disney's theatrical films as well as the Disneyland theme park, which opened in 1955. In 1955, General Teleradio, which had recently acquired the assets of RKO, sold that studio's library of feature films and shorts to television. In 1956, Columbia, Warner Bros., Fox, and M-G-M sold or leased their pre-1948 features to television; and, in 1958, Paramount sold its backlog of old feature films to MCA for television broadcast. At around the same time, Hollywood studios began to produce weekly programs, such as "Warner Bros. Presents," "M-G-M Parade," and "Twentieth Century-Fox Theatre" for television, and entered into negotiations with the major craft guilds (the Screen Actors Guild, the Screen Directors Guild, the Writers Guild of America, and so on) to secure royalty agreements that would enable the studios to release more recent (post-1948) feature films to television. Shortly after an agreement was reached between the producers and the guilds, an era of prime-time broadcast of recent feature films was inaugurated, beginning with "NBC's Saturday Night at the Movies" broadcast of *How to Marry a Millionaire* in September, 1961.

Panning and Scanning: Making CinemaScope Fit on TV

Ironically, the first "contemporary" feature film sold to television had originally been filmed in CinemaScope, which was designed, in part, to provide theatrical viewers with something they could not get at home on television—that is, a widescreen image (and stereo sound). In order to prepare this film for television broadcast, it had to be drastically cropped so that it could fit on the narrow, 1.33:1 television screen. Even more ironically, 20th Century-Fox, which had received an Oscar in 1954 for its development of the CinemaScope process, received another Oscar in 1962 for developing an "anti-Cinema-Scope" process; that is, for perfecting a technique of panning and scanning the original widescreen image so that it could be recomposed for television.

Much as money had driven the original invention, innovation, and diffusion of widescreen processes like CinemaScope, so it also drove its dismantling. The growing reliance of the film industry upon television (and later video) as a subsidiary market for its motion picture product made panning

Courtesy of the Museum of Modern Art

Widescreen films on TV: In order to make a widescreen image (above) of Marilyn Monroe in *How to Marry a Millionaire* (1953) fit the narrow TV screen, the techniques of panning and scanning are used to crop the image (right). Marilyn not only loses her legs, but much of her luxurious apartment as well.

and scanning both necessary and profitable. NBC had paid Fox $25 million to air *Millionaire* and a package of 30 other Fox features—a financial windfall for Fox which was in severe financial straits at the time.

As other networks bargained with other studios for films to air in prime time, the average price per film rose from $180,000 in 1961 to $800,000 by the end of the decade. Recent box-office hits commanded hefty sums; in 1966, ABC paid Columbia $2 million for *The Bridge on the River Kwai* (CinemaScope, 1957); shortly thereafter, ABC bought *Cleopatra* (Todd-AO, 1963) from Fox for $5 million. Though a number of the pricey, prime-time features, such as *The Wizard of Oz* (1939) and *Gone With the Wind* (1939), had been made before the widescreen revolution and posed little problem for TV broadcasters (once the networks had converted to color), widescreen films could not be shown on television without either cropping the sides of the image or showing the tops and bottoms of an image that was supposed to have been cropped in projection in the theater.

The cropping of "flat" widescreen films, designed for exhibition in 1.66:1 or 1.85:1, resulted in image losses of 20 and 28 percent, respectively. With the cropping of anamorphic films, from 44 to 48 percent of the original image was lost. Panning and scanning involves the "extraction" of a 1.33:1 image from a 2.55 to 2.35:1 original image. Since studio guidelines for filming in widescreen processes such as CinemaScope encouraged filmmakers to spread the action (and the actors) across the full width of the frame, panning and scanning tended to cut one or more performers out of the original composition.

For example, in the television version of *It's a Mad Mad Mad Mad World*, which was filmed in Ultra Panavision 70, the Three Stooges are reduced to one as a result of recomposition. In adapting *The High and the Mighty* (Cinema-Scope, 1954) for television, panners and scanners were unable to cover all the action, as a result, one crucial sequence features John Wayne's nose talking to Robert Stack's ear across the empty space of the airplane cockpit which lies between them. More recently, David Lynch's *Blue Velvet* (Panavision, 1986) is reframed for television, dismembering body parts in the process; in the diner sequence, for example, Laura Dern's nose listens attentively to Kyle Mac-Lachlan's explanation of the film's essential mystery. Quite often, recomposition involves editing from one side of the original widescreen frame to another.

In these instances, panners and scanners actually impose an alien editing pattern upon an original sequence that was filmed without any edits whatsoever. For other widescreen images, panners and scanners pan across the frame, introducing a pan that did not appear in the original. In both instances, the preparation of a film for television involves a rereading of it by a laboratory technician or television engineer who had nothing to do with the original work, making the final product similar, in many ways, to a colorized version of an original black-and-white film.

The lucrative television market has played an even more insidious role in the direction of contemporary widescreen films. Knowing that three-quarters of their film's audience will view it on a TV screen (that is, on cable, on videotape or disc, or on network broadcast), filmmakers tend to compose as much for television as they do for widescreen exhibition in the theater. A handful of directors, such as David Lynch, James Cameron, John Carpenter, Brian De Palma, Blake Edwards, John McTiernan, Ridley Scott, and others, use the full width of the widescreen frame, often placing characters at opposite sides of it or including crucial details at its extreme edges. Their work is severely compromised when shown on television. Certain directors, such as Martin Scorsese and Joe Dante, have refused, until recently, to film in 'Scope (a generic term for any movie filmed in an anamorphic process) because of the damage that panning and scanning would do to their work.

Letterboxing

More and more directors are forced to "protect" their original compositions for subsequent television and video playback by avoiding the use of extreme compositions and keeping the major dramatic elements within the "safe-action" area. This means staying within what the American Society of Cinematographers refers to as "that portion of the picture area inside the camera aperture borders within which all significant action should take place for 'safe' or full reproduction on the majority of black-and-white and color home receivers." In other words, they compose in such a way that no essential information appears at the edges of the frame, ensuring that their films will "work" on television. Milos Forman, George Lucas, Sydney Pollack, and Steven Spielberg have played a crucial role in the Directors Guild's campaign against panning and scanning and they have recently begun to insist, following the example of Woody Allen with *Manhattan* (Panavision, 1979), that their films be released on video in the letterbox format, which preserves the original aspect ratio of a film by reducing the height of the image so that its edges can fit on the TV screen without significant cropping.

Letterboxing enables films to be shown on television in their proper aspect ratio, but many viewers initially objected to it because it resulted in a reduction in the size of the image and the presence of blue or black masking above and below it. The gradual acceptance of letterboxing as a viable alternative to panning and scanning among producers, directors, and audiences has, however, contributed to a revival of interest in widescreen. Over the past few years, a growing market for letterboxed films has arisen not only among videophiles but also within discriminating sectors of the general audience as well. As a result, directors who work in 'Scope can now do so with the assurance that, because of letterboxing, there will be greater protection for their compositions when they are released on video. At the same time, letterboxing provides them with an incentive to maximize the potential of the widescreen frame when they film for theatrical exhibition. Recently, directors like Scorsese have begun to reconsider their earlier refusal to use the 'Scope format; the result is *Cape Fear* (Panavision, 1991), which recalls, in its extreme compositions, the early years of aesthetic experimentation that characterized the first era of widescreen filmmaking in 1953–1956.

BLOCKBUSTERS

Big Event Pictures

The heyday of the widescreen blockbuster extended from the mid-1950s to the mid-1960s and included films such as *War and Peace* (VistaVision, 1956), *Around the World in 80 Days* (Todd-AO, 1956), *The Ten Commandments* (VistaVision, 1956), *South Pacific* (Todd-AO, 1958), *Ben-Hur* (M-G-M Camera 65, 1959), *Spartacus* (Technirama-70, 1960), *Exodus* (Panavision-70, 1960), *El Cid* (Technirama-70, 1961), *Mutiny on the Bounty* (Panavision-70, 1962), *Lawrence of Arabia* (Panavision-70, 1962), *Cleopatra* (Todd-AO, 1963), and *The Sound of Music* (Todd-AO, 1965).

However, spiraling production costs and a string of box-office disasters, such as *Dr. Dolittle* (1967), *Star!* (1968), *Hello Dolly* (1969), *Paint Your Wagon* (1969), *Darling Lili* (1970), and *Tora! Tora! Tora!* (1970), heralded the end of the big-budget, widescreen spectacle. In 1963, Cinerama abandoned its original, three-strip system for a single-strip 70mm format, losing much of earlier Cinerama's powerful illusion of engulfment and participation in the process. Though the trade name "Cinerama" continued to serve as a draw at the box office and certain Cinerama productions, such as *2001: A Space Odyssey* (1968), proved to be both critical and commercial successes, Cinerama ultimately became virtually indistinguishable from other, super-70mm processes.

At around the same time (ca. 1963), Panavision developed a laboratory process that enabled producers to blow 35mm anamorphic prints up to 70mm without significant loss in quality. This technology, which was introduced with Otto Preminger's *The Cardinal* (1963), permitted producers to film in the less expensive 35mm format and to release films in 70mm, if their estimation of the box-office potential of the finished film warranted it. In permitting any film to become a potential 70mm blockbuster, the 70mm blowup tended to undermine the very notion of the widescreen blockbuster.

The long-standing association of the blockbuster with extravagance, costly sets and costumes, high-priced stars, and lavish production values gave way to a decidedly less exclusive product that included both big and small pictures. At one end stood David Lean spectacles such as *Doctor Zhivago* (1965) and costume pictures, such as *Becket* (1964) and *Camelot* (1967) and at the other were more or less standard genre pictures, ranging from musicals [*Bye Bye Birdie* (1963) and *Sweet Charity* (1969)] to Westerns [*The Professionals* (1966), *The Wild Bunch* (1969), *Two Mules for Sister Sara* (1970), and *Wild Rovers* (1971)].

The redefinition of the nature of the motion picture experience that took place in the 1950s succeeded in the short term but failed over the long haul. Dwindling audiences did return to theaters, but the appeal to participation did little to halt the slow erosion of the traditional, prewidescreen motion picture audience. As those habitual moviegoers disappeared, Hollywood attempted to shore up its losses by instituting a new kind of entertainment and a new pattern of moviegoing, both of which resemble, to a certain extent, the content and form of the legitimate theater. This pattern of infrequent moviegoing could only sustain the industry in an era of blockbusters—an era in which each film became a special event that drew the sometime spectator away from other leisure-time activities back into the movie theater. However, over the years, widescreen has lost its impact; it has become the norm for all production and, thus, no longer enjoys any status as a revolutionary new technology.

Narrowing Expectations

Though certain contemporary films, especially the work of Steven Spielberg and George Lucas, continue to revive the notion of participation, presenting themselves as "events," the notion of participation has become degraded, descending to a fairly primitive experience in which spectators respond in a programmatic way to predictable stimuli. Participation has gradually become more and more passive. The infrequent consumption of motion pictures has become more and more automatic and habitual, especially in today's small-screen theaters and multiplexes which are only a fraction of the size of and provide only a fraction of the experience of yesterday's movie palaces. In the age of television, we have narrowed both our sights and our expectations, reconciling ourselves to a postrevolutionary cinema that holds few, if any, surprises, thrills, or chills as a medium. Of course, the current craze for special effects has restored, in part, the special status of the medium to overwhelm the spectator with the sort of "attractions" that lured spectators to it at the turn of the century. Though we continue to be excited by the content of the movies, their basic format, which has remained unchanged for the past 30 years, has lost much of its power to engage us as participants in a dramatically new audio-visual sensory experience.

SELECT FILMOGRAPHY

Bwana Devil (3-D, 1952)
This Is Cinerama (Cinerama, 1952)
House of Wax (3-D, 1953)
Kiss Me Kate (3-D, 1953)
The Robe (CinemaScope, 1953)
Dial M for Murder (3-D, 1954)
River of No Return (Cinema-Scope, 1954)
White Christmas (VistaVision, 1954)
Oklahoma! (Todd-AO, 1955)
Around the World in 80 Days (Todd-AO, 1956)
The Searchers (VistaVision, 1956)
The Ten Commandments (VistaVision, 1956)
Will Success Spoil Rock Hunter? (CinemaScope, 1957)

South Pacific (Todd-AO, 1958)
Ben-Hur (M-G-M Camera 65, 1959)
Exodus (Panavision-70, 1960)
Spartacus (Technirama-70, 1960)
El Cid (Technirama-70, 1961)
Lawrence of Arabia (Panavision-70, 1962)
Mutiny on the Bounty (Panavision-70, 1962)
Cleopatra (Todd-AO, 1963)
The Sound of Music (Todd-AO, 1965)
2001: A Space Odyssey (Cinerama, 1968)
Manhattan (Panavision, 1979)
Blue Velvet (Panavision, 1986)

SELECT BIBLIOGRAPHY

Balio, Tino, ed. *Hollywood in the Age of Television.* Boston: Unwin Hyman, 1990.

Belton, John. *Widescreen Cinema.* Cambridge: Harvard University Press, 1992.

Carr, Robert E., and R. M. Hayes. *Wide Screen Movies: A History and Filmography of Wide Gauge Filmmaking.* Jefferson, NC: McFarland, 1988.

Hilmes, Michele. *Hollywood and Broadcasting: A History of Economic and Structural Interaction from Radio to Cable.* Champaign: University of Illinois Press, 1990.

CHAPTER 13

THE 1960s: THE COUNTERCULTURE STRIKES BACK

YOUTH AND CHALLENGE

During the 1960s, war was waged on several fronts. From 1964, when North Vietnamese torpedo boats reportedly attacked American destroyers in the Gulf of Tonkin, to 1975, when the United States evacuated its military forces from Saigon, the United States, together with its South Vietnamese allies, fought the Viet Cong and the North Vietnamese in Southeast Asia. On the home front, one generation of Americans battled another. "Youth," a term that tended to be reserved for those who were under age 30, found itself in an ideological battle with "age." They differed with one another over not only the war but also a host of other issues, such as sexual mores, race relations, lifestyle, and just plain "style." They belonged to two different cultures. The older members of the "establishment" and the youth movement liked different kinds of music, dressed differently, and wore their hair at different lengths. Indeed, hair became a symbol of the 1960s counterculture and served as a point of departure for one of the decade's most popular stage musicals, *Hair*, the tribal rock opera that ran on Broadway for four years from 1968 to 1972. Hair became a running gag in the Beatles' first film, *A Hard Day's Night* (1964). And it was hair that triggered the redneck violence against the hippie heroes in *Easy Rider* (1969).

The younger, postwar generation, known as "baby boomers," had been raised according to the new permissiveness advocated by Dr. Benjamin Spock, whose *Baby and Child Care* had originally been published in 1946. Indeed, Spock himself subsequently took responsibility for his "children" and became a spokesperson for the antiwar movement in the 1960s. According to Vice President Spiro Agnew, the "problem children" of the 1960s were the fault of Dr. Spock whose book, according to Agnew, "threw discipline out the window." The products of this revolution in childrearing grew up to challenge the repressive codes established by their more conservative elders, who had been brought up in the hard times of the Great Depression. The children of parents who fought the good and just war against Hitler and fascism in the 1940s questioned the American ideology that had involved the nation on what was apparently the wrong side of a seemingly unjust war in Southeast Asia. And they looked with suspicion upon the appeals to patriotism that had been used to defend that war.

THE KENNEDY ERA

"The New Frontier"

The 1960s began not with violent confrontation but with the orderly transfer of power from one generation to another. In 1961, the 43-year-old John F. Kennedy, a liberal Democrat from Massachusetts, was sworn in as President of the United States, replacing the 70-year-old Republican Dwight David Eisenhower. As the youngest President in American history, Kennedy brought the energy and intensity of youth to his program for a New Frontier in American political life. In his inaugural address, Kennedy noted that "the torch has been passed to a new generation of Americans" and called for a new activism, appealing to Americans to "ask not what your country can do for you" but "what you can do for your country."

With Kennedy, a new emphasis upon sophistication, style, and wit entered national politics. Jack and his wife Jackie became the ideal couple, and Kennedy's admirers likened his administration to King Arthur's mythical court of Camelot, casting him as both Arthur and Lancelot and Jackie as Queen Guenevere. The White House became their castle and Washington was transformed into a utopian kingdom full of dreams about the creation of an ideal, once and future world. Just prior to Kennedy's inauguration, in December 1960, Alan J. Lerner and Frederick Loewe's musical, *Camelot*, had opened on Broadway. And Kennedy's New Frontier naturally evoked Camelot, a world governed by acts of chivalry, trust, passionate idealism, and romance.

With Kennedy, the style of government changed. Kennedy invited noted artists such as cellist Pablo Casals to play in the East Room of the White House. New England poet Robert Frost, who was asked to read one of his poems at the inauguration, became Kennedy's poet laureate. The President's interest in literature ranged from Frost and Shakespeare to Ian Fleming. Fleming's slickly written spy novels about the exploits of secret agent 007, James Bond, doubled in popularity after JFK's fascination with them became public knowledge. At the same time, Kennedy cultivated the image of a movie star, bringing glamour to the White House. The President socialized with members of the movie colony—with his "Rat Pack" buddies, including brother-in-law Peter Lawford, Frank Sinatra, Dean Martin, and Sammy Davis, and with Marilyn Monroe.

However, the novelty of the Kennedy style did not necessarily make him the spokesperson of 1960s youth, who questioned the substance of his political program. With the notable exception of his creation of the Peace Corps, Kennedy's foreign policy won him few supporters in the new left student movement. His attempted invasion of Fidel Castro's Cuba, in April 1961, at the Bay of Pigs resulted in severe criticism of his tactics by student activists and others. His handling of the Cuban Missile Crisis in October 1962 escalated Cold War tensions and the danger of nuclear war, infuriating antinuclear protestors at home. Under Kennedy's leadership, the presence of

American military advisors in Vietnam dramatically increased, expanding an involvement of Americans in Southeast Asia that would ultimately result in the Vietnam war.

The Civil Rights Movement

Kennedy's domestic policy, which focused attention on civil rights, was readily embraced by liberal high school and college students across the nation. The civil rights movement became the cornerstone of 1960s activism, setting an agenda and establishing a strategy of nonviolent intervention that would inform subsequent student protests against the Vietnam war and other political and social problems. But the civil rights movement was well under way even before Kennedy took office. In 1960, four black students staged a peaceful sit-in at an all-white lunch counter at Woolworth's in Greensboro, NC. By the end of the year, these nonviolent protests had successfully integrated lunch counters in over 126 southern cities. In 1962, James Meredith became the first black student to attend the University of Mississippi, though he needed the assistance of federal marshals to attend classes. In support of demands for civil rights set by black organizations such as SNCC and CORE, black and white students marched on Washington in 1962 and 1963. They registered black voters in the South during the summers of 1963 and 1964; the latter became known as "Freedom Summer." In 1964, three civil rights workers named Michael Schwerner, Andrew Goodman, and James Cheney were murdered in Mississippi—a crime that became the subject of investigation in Alan Parker's *Mississippi Burning* (1988).

After a summer of civil rights work in the South, Mario Savio returned to Berkeley in 1964 where he set up a table to recruit additional volunteers. When university officials banned him from organizing on campus and outlawed all other political activity as well, Savio and others protested, launching the Berkeley "Free Speech" movement. When eight student leaders were summarily suspended by the university administration, students, using sit-in tactics developed by the civil rights movement in the South, passively protested the university's violation of their freedom of speech. Over the course of the strike, 814 Free Speech Movement supporters were jailed before Berkeley faculty finally voted to permit political activity on campus.

Civil rights marches by Martin Luther King and others led to the passage of the Civil Rights Act of 1964, the Voting Rights Act of 1965, and the Civil Rights Act of 1968, which prohibited discrimination on the basis of color, race, religion, or national origin in public places, at the polls, and in housing. Nonviolence, however, soon gave way to violence. Kennedy was assassinated in November 1963. Blacks rioted in Harlem in the summer of 1964. Malcolm X was killed in February 1965. Blacks rioted in Watts in August 1965, and in Newark and Detroit in 1967. In 1966, Huey P. Newton and Bobby Seale founded the Black Panthers, a black militant organization that advocated violence as a means to secure black liberation and favored separatist objectives instead of integration. Martin Luther King was gunned down in April 1968, and Robert Kennedy was slain in June 1968.

Against the War

In the mid-1960s, as students shifted attention from purely domestic to foreign issues, they adopted the techniques of symbolic protest that had proven effective in the civil rights movement. In 1965, they organized a "March on Washington to End the War in Vietnam," which drew national attention to the antiwar movement. By 1968, the escalation of the Vietnam war, the complicity of Columbia and various other universities with war research, and continuing racial injustice at home prompted students at Columbia University to escalate the "sit-in" into the "strike." Students occupied administration buildings and other university property in an attempt to focus attention upon the war and racism. When the administration had the students forcibly and violently removed by police, a strike ensued in which students protested the administration's action by shutting down the university. A number of other university campuses followed suit in 1968 and 1969 and, in May of 1970, after President Nixon announced a further escalation of the war—an "incursion" of U.S. forces into Cambodia—there was a nationwide strike on over 200 college campuses. At Kent State University, Ohio National Guardsmen fired into a crowd of student protestors, killing four of them and wounding nine others. Meanwhile, during the summer of 1968, antiwar protestors at the Democratic National Convention in Chicago were savagely beaten by police while network news cameras looked on. Live broadcast of the spectacle in the streets shocked home viewers who were outraged at the excessive violence employed by the Chicago police in arresting the demonstrators. These events subsequently served as the background for Haskell Wexler's *Medium Cool* (1969), which followed the movements of a fictional television news camerman who was caught up in the police riots.

Courtesy of M-G-M

Campus unrest and the student strike at Columbia University serve as the basis for *The Strawberry Statement* (1970), which portrays police response to the student occupation of university buildings.

Liberation: The Women's Movement

Conflict resulting from generational and racial differences provided a broad background against which traditional relationships between the sexes underwent a reevaluation. In 1963 Betty Friedan published *The Feminine Mystique*, in which she examined the ways women had been disempowered and repressed. Women in the new left soon found that the student movement was as sexist and patriarchal (that is, male-dominated) as the larger society and began to set up their own activist organizations, such as the National Organization of Women (NOW), which was formed in 1966 with Friedan as its president.

For feminists, the traditional oppression of women was seen as rooted in the institution of marriage, which confined them to the home, and in the dominance of certain cultural assumptions about women, which excluded middle-class women from the workplace and restricted working-class women to a narrow range of permissible jobs. Certain sectors of this institutional oppression relaxed somewhat in the 1960s. The availability of the first reliable oral contraceptive for women (introduced with the marketing of Enovid in 1960) gave women more control over their bodies than they had ever known before, enabling them to choose whether or not to have children and when to have them. Political activism during the 1960s resulted in the overthrow of antiabortion laws in a number of states, with New York at the forefront in 1969.

At the same time, more and more women enrolled in and graduated from college; their numbers increased by 47 percent in the 1950s and 168 percent in the 1960s. As college graduates, women entered the work force qualified for white-collar jobs traditionally held by men. Working women had been a factor in the American economy throughout the twentieth century, but middle-class women had never entered the work force in great numbers prior to the 1960s. The women's movement served as an advocate for equality in the workplace, demanding equal pay for equal work, and campaigned to make women economically self-sufficient.

Yet women's liberation entailed new forms of subjugation. Radical feminists complained that the sexual revolution proved more of a benefit for men, who had a field day, than it did for women, who became victims of sexual exploitation. The pill may have liberated women but it also changed the attitudes of men toward women, who were now expected to be more accessible than they had been in the past. In other words, it became harder for a women to just say no to a man. Nor was the trade-in of unpaid domestic drudgery as a homemaker for a 40-hour workweek necessarily liberating, especially when men began to expect women to be both breadwinners and lovers, as well as homemakers.

The 1960s saw some success for the civil rights movement, which put an end to (overt) segregation in schools, public places, and housing, and for the antiwar movement, which helped to force American troops out of Vietnam. The limited success of the women's movement, however, was undercut by their larger disempowerment within patriarchy. The women's movement's chief political victory proved to be its legalization of abortion, which came in the 1973 U.S. Supreme Court's *Roe v. Wade* decision. Its chief political failure was its inability to secure the passage of the Equal Rights Amendment, which would have guaranteed women the same "equality of rights" enjoyed by men under the Constitution and the Bill of Rights.

PROJECTIONS: WOMEN ON SCREEN

As far as the films of the 1960s were concerned, the women's movement became the sexual revolution; that is, its political agenda was translated into a series of superficial changes in sexual mores. Women are depicted as sexually liberated or aggressive. But Hollywood's women are modeled less after the revolutionary women who fought for equal rights in NOW than after the centerfolds found in the misogynistic pages of *Playboy*. *Lolita* (1962), and *Cleopatra* and *Irma la Douce* (both 1963) celebrate the sexual power of the new woman as does *Barbarella* (1968), the futuristic film in which Jane Fonda revolutionizes life in the 41st century by making love "the old-fashioned way." James Bond films introduce a host of sexually available women, including Pussy Galore (Honor Blackman) in *Goldfinger* (1964). The sexual revolution culminates (for men, at least) in the wife-swapping craze celebrated in *Bob & Carol & Ted & Alice* (1969).

The backlash against 1960s feminism: Sexual politics becomes translated onto the screen in terms of sexual display. Sue Lyons as the title character in *Lolita* (1962).

Courtesy of M-G-M

Hollywood's response to the women's movement involves more backlash than backing. Parts for women revert to stereotype: actresses play either madonnas or whores. The only working women are motherly governesses or prostitutes. Julie Andrews enjoys a spectacular career as the former, playing nannies in both *Mary Poppins* (1964) and *The Sound of Music* (1965). Jane Fonda excels as the latter, playing an unfaithful wife in *The Chase* (1966) and prostitutes in *Walk on the Wild Side* (1962) and *Klute* (1971). As one of the few white-collar women workers, Doris Day successfully straddles the fence in *Lover Come Back* (1961) in which she plays an account executive for an advertising firm. But she also pays the price, winning the screen persona of a sexual tease, that is, a madonna-whore. An exception that proves the rule is Sandy Dennis in *Up the Down Staircase* (1967), who plays an inner-city school teacher, Sylvia Barrett. Engaged in one of the few professions traditionally open to respectable women, her dedicated English instructor combines the nineteenth-century idealism of the nanny-to-the-aristocrats with the twentieth-century, down-to-earth realism necessary for survival in the New York public school system.

It was not until the late 1970s and early 1980s that white- and blue-collar working women made it back to the screen. Films such as *Network* (1976), in which Faye Dunaway plays a ruthless television executive; *The China Syndrome* (1979), in which Jane Fonda plays a television reporter; and *Norma Rae* (1979), in which Sally Field is a textile worker, reflect the real-life achievements of professional working women and lead the way for the new image of the independent woman that dominates the 1980s in films starring actresses such as Sigourney Weaver, Meryl Streep, Glenn Close, Kathleen Turner, Whoopi Goldberg, Debra Winger, Cher, Sissy Spacek, Diane Keaton, Bette Midler, Shelly Long, and Melanie Griffith.

YOUTH FILMS: ACTIVISM AS LIFESTYLE

Women's liberation was not the only movement to fare poorly in its representation on the movie screen. With one or two exceptions—that is, in certain noncommercial works produced by the alternative media—the student movement tended to find itself reduced to confused college kids whose ideas were half-baked and who were drawn to political activism and protests in search of sex and cheap thrills. Documentary and student filmmakers brought some seriousness to the underlying issues, covering peace marches, protests, and student strikes, while radical filmmaking groups, such as New York Newsreel and San Francisco Newsreel, attempted to represent the perspectives of minority groups and student radicals in films like *Black Panther* (1968) and *Columbia Revolt* (1968). *Medium Cool* (1969), which was made independently but distributed by Paramount, straddles the fence between documentary honesty and Hollywood glitz, combining the raw fervor of the new left with the stylish trappings of old-fashioned narrative cinema. It deals with the adventures of a television news cameraman whose encounters with black militants, affair with a woman whose husband was killed in Vietnam, and experiences during the police riots at the 1968 Democratic Convention radicalize him.

At the very end of the decade, the student protest movement gave rise to a number of fairly conventional Hollywood features designed to exploit the new youth market. In 1970, after the astounding commercial success of youth-cult movies such as *The Graduate* (1967), which looks at postgraduation career angst, and *Easy Rider* (1969), which glamorizes counterculture lifestyles, the major studios released a series of films concerned with student protest, including *Zabriskie Point, Getting Straight*, and *The Strawberry Statement*, as well as *The Magic Garden of Stanley Sweetheart, The Revolutionary*, and *R.P.M.* (all 1970). *Pursuit of Happiness* (1971) rounded out this unusual, short-lived subgenre dealing with the equally short-lived student movement. In *The Strawberry Statement*, which was based on the Columbia protests, a student becomes involved in campus demonstrations because he is interested in a girl who belongs to the movement. In *Getting Straight*, its hero, a former civil rights worker and Vietnam veteran, returns to school, discovers that demonstrations are "sexy," and becomes a committed radical only when victimized by the bureaucracy of the academic establishment and unprovoked police brutality.

Though somewhat more interesting, Michelangelo Antonioni's *Zabriskie Point* similarly obscures the underlying political issues that prompted student unrest. The film reduces student radicalism into an extremely generalized and universal male anxiety, suggesting that the age-old identity crisis is what has

Would-be student radicals in jail: Mark Frechette (left) embodies the hipness of alienated youth in *Zabriskie Point* (1970).

Courtesy of M-G-M

been at the bottom of student unrest in 1960s America. Its hero, an innocent suspect in a cop killing, sets off on a cross-country flight in a stolen airplane from the west coast. Easily distracted from his goal by a girl driving on the highway below, he lands and joins her on her trip to Zabriskie Point in Death Valley. At the end of this absurdist reworking of Alfred Hitchcock's *North by Northwest* (1959), he returns to California to surrender to the police but is killed before he can give himself up. The circular story pattern demonstrates the futility of student activism and its politically incorrect conclusion suggests that the pleasures of mental revolt can be more satisfying than material action in the real world. The film ends with the girl's fantasmatic, imaginary destruction of the symbols of American materialism: as the girl looks at the house of her bourgeois boss, it explodes, and close-up, slow-motion shots of commercial products fill the screen. In other words, the heroine's psychic act of rebellion proves to be as powerful as, and even more powerful than, the hero's physical acts of rebellion.

Finally, *Pursuit of Happiness* documents the identity crisis of a former student activist who campaigned for Gene McCarthy in 1968, who was arrested at the police riots in Chicago that summer, but who gradually became more and more alienated from the movement, his girl friend, and his family, and from the identity each of them tries to impose upon him. Again, politics are papered over and the film becomes a depoliticized, more individualized saga about the hero's flight from society and search for a personal utopia. The hero gives up on his efforts to change the world and flees it instead, after declaring, "There's a nervous breakdown going on out there and I don't want to be part of it!"

"SOLVING" THE RACE PROBLEM

Neither the women's movement nor the student movement found adequate representation within mainstream American cinema. The controversial political issues they both raised were transformed into the melodramatic stuff of conventional film narratives. Equal rights for women became sexual liberation and war resistance became existential adolescent angst. Race relations tended to be dealt with a bit more directly, but even well-meaning liberal films, such as Stanley Kramer's Academy Award winning *The Defiant Ones* (1958), "solved" racial problems without uncovering their root causes in the fundamental political and economic inequality that existed between blacks and whites. In the Kramer film, two convicts—one a white bigot (Tony Curtis) and the other a bitter black (Sidney Poitier)—flee the police while handcuffed together and learn that the survival of each depends upon the assistance and cooperation of the other.

Hollywood films of the 1960s expose bigotry and racism but do so without exposing their sources. The major studios ignore the *politics* of racism. Their films contain no sit-ins, no marches on Washington, no campaigns to register black voters, no attempts to integrate schools and colleges, and no exposés of racial discrimination in housing. There is one notable exception in this silence. *A Raisin in the Sun*, distributed by Columbia Pictures in 1961, treats the attempts of a black family to move into a white neighborhood in Chicago. However, a handful of non-Hollywood films, including documentaries (*King: A Filmed Record . . . Montgomery to Memphis*, 1970) and independently made features (*A Man Called Adam*, 1966), attempt to deal with many of these issues. Unfortunately, they never found wide distribution.

Hollywood concerned itself with racism but did so on its own terms. For Hollywood, racism was not an economic or political but, rather, a human problem. As such, it could be solved through dramatic means. It was isolated, identified, recognized, and rejected; an Aristotelean catharsis then followed during which a tenuous accord was reestablished between the races suggesting that all would be well in the future. Mere acknowledgment of the problem meant that the problem was somehow solved. Sidney Poitier emerges as a perfect problem solver. His skin color provokes racism, but his class status solves whatever problems whites have with his blackness. Playing middle- and upper-middle-class professionals such as a journalist (*The Bedford Incident*, 1965), a doctor (*Guess Who's Coming to Dinner*, 1967), an engineer/school teacher (*To Sir, With Love*, 1967), and a homicide detective (*In the Heat of the Night*, 1967), Poitier is equal, if not superior to any of his white antagonists, who are forced to recognize his abilities and to purge themselves of their own racism.

In other instances, the cure for racism proves to be white paternalism. The liberal lawyer (Gregory Peck) in *To Kill a Mockingbird* (1962) intervenes to save an innocent black man (Brock Peters) from a white lynch mob, as does a young, white priest in *The Cardinal* (1963). Toward the end of the decade, blacks and whites are seen onscreen working together, against a common enemy, as is the case in *Hurry Sundown* (1967), in which two young southern farmers—one white and one black—join forces to defeat a white bigot who wants their land. And in *Change of Habit* (1969), black and white nuns work together at a free clinic in the slums to help disadvantaged blacks and Hispanics. These latter two films dramatize the cooperation that takes place between blacks and whites working within the civil rights movement, but remove this spirit to a different time (*Sundown* is set in the post–World War II South) and place (*Habit* is set in a northern city). In this way, the films are made more marketable to a contemporary southern (white) audience not quite ready for films dealing with events from the recent past or with ongoing civil rights issues.

ON THE OFFENSIVE: MONEY, FILMS, AND CHANGING MORALITY

Controversy and Conservatism

The political conservatism of Hollywood in the 1960s was, in large part, driven by economics. The industry was still making films for a general audience, in spite of a growing awareness that the traditional movie-going audiences of the past had begun to disappear in the 1950s, replaced by a younger, better-educated, and more diverse audience. The economics of the general audience explain Hollywood's reluctance to tackle subject matter that is politically controversial. It might offend some sector of the viewing public —such as the South. The big money-making films of the 1960s reflect this conservative taste. They include war films, such as *The Guns of Navarone* (1961) and *The Longest Day* (1962); widescreen historical spectacles, such as *El Cid* (1961), *How the West Was Won* (1962), *Lawrence of Arabia* (1962), and *Cleopatra* (1963); Disney family films, such as *One Hundred and One Dalmations* (1961), *The Absent-Minded Professor* (1961), *The Sword in the Stone* (1963), and *Mary Poppins* (1964); and musicals, such as *West Side Story* (1961), *The Music Man* (1962), *My Fair Lady* (1964), and *The Sound of Music* (1965).

In the previous decade, the restriction on controversial social subjects such as sex and drugs had been relaxed. But the films that spearheaded this challenge to the Production Code, *The Moon is Blue* (1953), *The Man With the Golden Arm* (1955), and *Baby Doll* (1956), did not rank among the top-ten box-office attractions of their respective years. Sex continues to sell in the 1960s with the release of films such as *Lolita* (1962), *Cleopatra* and *Irma La Douce* (1963), and the James Bond films, especially *Goldfinger* (1964), *Thunderball* (1965), and *You Only Live Twice* (1967). But other forms of social controversy, such as violence, drug use, and the open rebellion of contemporary youth against the conformity of the older generation, remain relegated to the marginal status of cheaply made, exploitation films. As such, they rarely appear on the big screens of major theaters and, thus, rarely make enormous sums of money. But all this begins to change in the late 1960s, when a viable market opened up for "exploitation" films, that is, for films that contain sex, violence, drugs, and willfully disobedient youth (of the sort found in low-budget teen-pics of the 1950s and 1960s made for drive-ins by Roger Corman and American International Pictures). The change is gradual.

A New Vocabulary

In 1966, Warner Bros. tested the waters, as it were, with its film adaptation of noted playwright Edward Albee's prestigious play *Who's Afraid of Virginia Woolf?* Directed by Broadway director Mike Nichols, it features language that violates even the tolerant Production Code of the mid-1950s. Its stars, Richard Burton and Elizabeth Taylor, trade expletives back and forth that had never been heard on the screens of first-run theaters before. There are eleven "goddamns," five "sons of bitches," seven "bastards," as well as "screw you," "hump the hostess," and "up yours." Rated "R" (restricted to those over the age of 18), the film grossed over $14.5 million, was nominated for thirteen Academy Awards, and won five. But Albee was hardly exploitation material.

The next year, Avco/Embassy earned over $44 million with another Mike Nichols picture, *The Graduate* (1967). Though its hero, played by Dustin Hoffman, engages in an adulterous relationship with the sex-starved wife of his father's business partner, the film violates few taboos. Yet, it foregrounds the situation of disaffected youth in ways that appealed to the under-30 market. None of the adults in the film understand Hoffman's alienation; all of them, including his parents and the infamous Mrs. Robinson (Anne Bancroft) who seduces him, try to manipulate him or shape his future. But he simply refuses and, finally, rebels against them.

Live Fast, Die Young: *Bonnie and Clyde*

That same year, Warner Bros. released *Bonnie and Clyde,* an outlaw-couple film that earned almost $30 million. Combining large doses of sex (or, more accurately, sexual frustration) and violence, the film appealed to an emerging audience that was both young and antiestablishment. Posters and other publicity material for the film proclaimed that its central characters were "young," "in love," and "kill[ed] people." Depression-era folk heroes cast in the mold of figures from populist mythology, such as Robin Hood and Jesse James, Bonnie and Clyde rob the banks that foreclosed on rural farmers. At the same time, in living out their lives moment by moment, they look back to the more recent, existentialist, anti-heroes of the films of the French New Wave, such as the Jean-Paul Belmondo character in Jean-Luc Godard's *Breathless* (1959), who is also an outlaw on the run.

Bonnie and Clyde's cross-country spree captures the spirit and energy of the youth movement and epitomizes the revolt against institutional authority that found support among young moviegoers of the mid-1960s. The stars of the film, Warren Beatty and Faye Dunaway, even made the cover of *Time* magazine. The characters they played were immediately appropriated as cult figures by the new generation of college-age audiences who were fascinated by their style—by the way they dressed, by the way they talked, by the way they defied custom and convention, and by the way they died. Young men and women began wearing fashions from the 1930s, and the "Bonnie Parker look," which consisted of a V-neck sweater, midiskirt, shoulder-length hair, and beret, became the rage in women's fashion magazines.

And audiences were profoundly moved by the romantic way in which Bonnie and Clyde died. Caught in a police ambush in a hail of bullets, they first look at one another and then rush for one final embrace. Filmed in slow motion, they jerk spasmodically as the bullets tear into them. It is as if they are in the throes of some great passion or of some ultimate sexual experience. Overnight, they became the counterculture's Romeo and Juliet—star-crossed lovers who lived fast, died young, and left good-looking (but bullet-ridden) corpses.

The increasing violence of mainstream Hollywood films like *Bonnie and Clyde* (1967) tested the limits of what had traditionally been permissible on the American screen. The *New York Times* critic, Bosley Crowther, condemned the film's violence and apparent glorification of criminals—two aspects of the film that clearly violate the old Production Code. But the cultural context within which the film had been made differed dramatically from that in which the original Production Code had been written (ca. 1930). John F. Kennedy had been shot in 1963, and his spasms, as the bullets entered his body, had

Courtesy of Warner Bros.

The outlaw couple in *Bonnie and Clyde* (1967): Bonnie (Faye Dunaway) and Clyde (Warren Beatty) are young, in love, and they kill people.

been recorded on film and seen by millions of Americans, who also saw Jack Ruby shoot Lee Harvey Oswald in front of television cameras. By the mid-1960s, the Vietnam war had begun to escalate, along with its nightly coverage on the network news. Finally, in the spring of 1968, a few months after the film's release, Martin Luther King and Robert F. Kennedy were assassinated; RFK's shooting was also captured, in part, by television cameras and replayed for shocked audiences.

Sex, Violence, and Ratings

The sexual explicitness of both foreign and domestic films, such as *La Dolce Vita* (Italy, 1960), *Two Women* (Italy, 1961), *Kiss Me, Stupid* (1964), and *Who's Afraid of Virginia Woolf?* (1966), increased, responding, in part, to changes in the popular perception of acceptable sexual behavior. However, what proved acceptable in one culture or community was not necessarily acceptable in another. In April 1968, the Supreme Court delivered two decisions that proved crucial to ongoing debates over the definition of obscenity, permitting local communities to establish their own censorship guidelines. These changes immediately prompted the MPPA (the Motion Picture Producers Association) to transform its time-worn Production Code review process (which was preliminary to the granting or withholding of its seal of approval) into a ratings system.

By clearly distinguishing films from one another in terms of the potentially objectionable nature of their content, the film industry hoped to head off any attempts on the part of local governments to establish their own forms of censorship. At the same time, the new ratings system provided categories for films that would never have received seals of approval in the past. By acknowledging the existence of such films, the MPPA officially admitted them into the marketplace, paving the way for more American films that deal with mature subject matter.

Under the rating system, which took effect on November 1, 1968, a "G" means that a film is suitable for general audiences; all ages are admitted to theaters showing such a film. An "M" (which was subsequently changed to "PG") designates the film to be suitable for mature audiences; that is, for adults and, subject to the guidance of their parents or to "parental guidance" (PG), for children. An "R" means that a film is restricted to adults; children under age sixteen (an age that was later changed to seventeen) are admitted only if accompanied by an adult. In the case of an "X" rating, no one under sixteen (later seventeen) is admitted. The PG rating was subsequently modified, broken down into PG and PG-13, after the release of *Indiana Jones and the Temple of Doom* (1984), which contained graphic violence that was subsequently deemed unsuitable for children under age thirteen.

In 1969, sex and violence hit unprecedented heights on the screen. *Sexual Freedom in Denmark,* a foreign import, became the first pornographic film to play in a commercial theater in New York; previously, porno films had been shown only in theaters reserved exclusively for hard-core films. Another import, *I Am Curious (Yellow),* pulled in $6.5 million in rentals that year at the box office, becoming the first porno film to rank among the top twelve grossing attractions of the year. Hollywood also tested the waters. *Midnight Cowboy,* a prestige production directed by John Schlesinger and released by United Artists, contained an explicit sex act, which automatically earned it an X, making it one of the first big-budget Hollywood films to receive that rating. In spite of the X, which not only limited admission to it but also restricted advertising for it (many papers, including the *New York Times,* refused to accept advertising for X-rated films), *Midnight Cowboy* earned over $20 million and won Academy Awards for Best Picture, Best Director, and Best Screenplay. That same year saw the release of Sam Peckinpah's apocalyptic Western, *The Wild Bunch,* which was rated R because of the violence of its opening and closing gun battles and blood baths. Here, as in *Bonnie and Clyde,* slow motion aestheticizes the violence, making it both more graphic and more balletic.

The Great Teen-Pic: *Easy Rider*

Drugs, sex, and violence provided much of the spectacle that turned actor/director Dennis Hopper's low-budget ($555,000), R-rated motorcycle picture, *Easy Rider* (1969), into a big hit, which grossed over $60 million worldwide. Although distributed by Columbia, the film is essentially an exploitation teen-pic, modeled on AIP (American International Pictures) biker movies such as *The Wild Angels* (1966). Yet, at the same time, the film's intentions went beyond those of the conventional B picture. It looks like an underground film, employing stylistic practices found in the nonnarrative, experimental cinema of Stan Brakhage, Bruce Baillie, and Kenneth Anger. Hopper uses flash frames and cuts that flash forward from one sequence to the next; shots filmed with a hand-held camera; squeezed, anamorphic images; and a hallucinatory, psychedelic dream sequence. Advertisements for the film, which described its theme, give some sense of its artistic ambitions: "A man went looking for America and couldn't find it anywhere."

This rambling motorcycle film serves as a picaresque portrait of 1960s America, ranging from utopian hippie communes to bigoted small-town communities in the South. The film's young heroes become countercultural knights in search of a contemporary Holy Grail, journeying from drug deals in the modern wasteland of Los Angeles to a spaced-out Mardi Gras in the old world city of New Orleans, where, under the influence of LSD, the film's heroes wander through a graveyard. The characters' idealistic search for the

Dennis Hopper (left), Peter Fonda, and Jack Nicholson go looking for America in *Easy Rider* (1969).

Courtesy of Columbia

American dream proves to be a failure—or, as Wyatt (Peter Fonda) confesses to Billy (Dennis Hopper) near the end of their trip, "We blew it." They search, but they find nothing.

TRANSFORMATION: THE COUNTERCULTURE GOES MAINSTREAM

The financial success of *Easy Rider* established the existence of a specialized youth market. By the mid-1960s, the traditional movie audience had changed from a middle-aged, high school-educated, middle- to lower-class viewing group to a younger, college-educated, more affluent, middle-class audience. By the mid-1970s, 76 percent of all moviegoers were under the age of 30; the majority of these—64 percent—came from affluent families and had gone to college. *Bonnie and Clyde* and *The Graduate* had suggested that a younger audience with a taste for more adult themes could dramatically increase the box-office revenues for a major studio production. But *Easy Rider* proved that even a cheaply made, exploitation film that was pitched solely to the college-age crowd could make a great deal of money.

Easy Rider revolutionized the industry, demonstrating that spectacular returns could be realized on a rather modest investment, if the film appealed to this new audience. *Easy Rider* led to a series of youth-cult films, including a number of films from those who had been involved in its production. Producer Bert Schneider parlayed the success of *Easy Rider* into a production company, BBS Productions, a distribution deal with Columbia, and a string of films, including *Five Easy Pieces* (1970), *The Last Picture Show* (1971), *A Safe Place* (1971), *Drive, He Said* (1971), *The King of Marvin Gardens* (1972), and, finally, the antiwar, Academy Award-winning documentary about Vietnam, *Hearts and Minds* (1974).

Director Dennis Hopper was given a more or less blank check to make his next film, *The Last Movie* (1971), a self-reflexive, antiestablishment Western about the exploitation of third-world cultures, which was filmed and set in a remote Indian village in Peru. Jack Nicholson, who played a cameo role in *Easy Rider* that brought him instant stardom, was cast as a hippie in *On a Clear Day You Can See Forever* (1970) and played a series of offbeat types in *Five Easy Pieces*, *Carnal Knowledge* (1971), *A Safe Place*, *Drive, He Said*, and *The King of Marvin Gardens* before landing his starring, Academy Award-winning role as the nonconformist mental patient, Randel P. McMurphy, in the film adaptation of the ultimate 1960s antiauthoritarian novel, Ken Kesey's *One Flew Over the Cuckoo's Nest* (1975).

In the case of Hopper, Nicholson, and Schneider, the counterculture moved into the mainstream of Hollywood production, though only Nicholson remained there for any length of time. A handful of directors, such as Michelangelo Antonioni (*Blow-Up*, 1966; *Zabriskie Point*, 1970), and Arthur Penn (*Bonnie and Clyde*, 1967; *Alice's Restaurant*, 1969; *Little Big Man*, 1970), give dramatic form to the lifestyles and beliefs of the dissident generation that fought war abroad and racism at home, but the majority of films that tried to deal with the 1960s youth culture, the civil rights movement, the student protest movement, or the women's movement depoliticized their agenda or disguised it in such as way that it no longer possessed any confrontational power.

As the films became more and more expensive and less and less exploitational, they lost their dissident status as attacks on the mainstream from the fringe and became mainstream themselves. Even *Easy Rider* soft-pedaled the politics of the antiestablishment left and focused upon the style rather than the content of the revolt of youth in the 1960s. Westerns like *Little Big Man, Soldier Blue* (1970), and *Ulzana's Raid* (1972) implicitly criticize American involvement in Vietnam by suggesting that the genocidal warfare by whites against Native Americans in the old West is comparable to that of whites against Asians in Southeast Asia. But their antiwar stance remains hidden beneath the surface of seemingly conventional genre pictures. In other words, in spite of the production of films specifically targeted for younger audiences, it is through the disguised medium of genre pictures that the counterculture got its message into the mainstream of Hollywood production.

BLAXPLOITATION AND BEYOND

An Emerging Black Audience

One or two of the most radical films of this era came disguised as genre vehicles. In fact, it was again in the area of exploitation films that the counterculture found the least compromised and most powerful presentations of its political concerns. The most compelling instance of this was to be found in the short-lived cycle of black action pictures made between 1970 and 1973, which were referred to as "blaxploitation" films by both contemporary trade magazines such as *Variety* and critics. The phenomenal success of three Sidney Poitier films made in 1967—*In the Heat of the Night, To Sir, With Love*, and *Guess Who's Coming to Dinner*—indicated to Hollywood that black was not only beautiful but box office as well. Polls indicated that one-quarter of all regular moviegoers in the late 1960s and early 1970s were black. This statistic was reinforced by the box-office figures for Poitier's films, but it was confirmed by the amazing success of a number of more or less routine, cheaply made genre pictures starring relatively unknown black actors that made money in the wake of Poitier's success.

Between 1970 and 1972, over 50 feature films were made specifically for a black audience. In 1970, United Artists began to cultivate this emerging black audience with its release of Ossie Davis' adaptation of a Chester Himes detective novel, *Cotton Comes to Harlem*, which starred Godfrey Cambridge, Raymond St. Jacques, and Calvin Lockhart and which earned a hefty $15.4 million, largely in urban markets where there were large numbers of black viewers. In 1971, Melvin Van Peebles' independently made, outlaw-on-the-run, X-rated picture *Sweet Sweetback's Baadasssss Song*, which cost only $500,000 to make, earned over $10 million. Also in 1971, *Shaft*, a private-eye picture directed by the son of still photographer Gordon Parks and released by M-G-M, grossed over $7 million.

Poitier's big-budget A pictures were targeted at a general audience, comprised of both blacks and whites who shared the more or less middle-class values embodied in Poitier's screen persona. This is the same audience that came to see former Supreme, Diana Ross, play Billie Holiday in Paramount's lavish production of *Lady Sings the Blues* (1972) and Cicely Tyson as a southern sharecropper in *Sounder* (1972). Both *Lady* and *Sounder* were directed by whites and earned over $9 million each in rentals. The boom in big-budget black films went bust in 1978 with the disappointing returns from the filmed adaptation of the Broadway musical, *The Wiz*, starring Diana Ross, Michael Jackson, Nipsey Russell, and others. The film, which cost Universal more than $24 million to produce, returned only $13.6 million in domestic rentals, emerging as one of the biggest flops of the late 1970s.

Blaxploitation films, on the other hand, were inexpensively made exploitation films pitched primarily to middle- and lower-class urban blacks. White audiences, raised on a steady diet of sex and violence found in gangster films, such as *Bonnie and Clyde* (1967), war films, such as *The Dirty Dozen* (1967), and Westerns, such as *The Wild Bunch* (1969), were drawn in considerable numbers to black crime pictures, which featured similarly strong doses of sex, violence, and gritty realism. Though blaxploitation films were often merely the reworking and recasting of traditionally white stories, plot situations, and character types for black audiences with black actors, many of them nonetheless addressed the concerns of the black community in ways which were unprecedented on the American screen.

A Revolutionary Film: *Sweet Sweetback's Baadasssss Song*

Sweet Sweetback (1971), which was produced, written, edited, scored, and directed by its star, Melvin Van Peebles, emerges as one of the most revolutionary films of this era. The film's hero evolves from a cynical, self-absorbed, morally corrupt superstud into an angry black militant. Sweetback becomes a political outlaw when he intervenes on behalf of a black radical, who is being beaten by the police. He fights back and seriously wounds two cops by hitting them on the head with his handcuffs. The radicalized figure of Sweetback emerges as a cult hero for the black power movement. Black Panther chief, Huey Newton, proclaimed the film "the first truly revolutionary Black film made."

Like the hero of Godard's *Breathless*, Sweetback is an outlaw on the run. But his rebelliousness is more political than existential—he resists white authority on behalf of the larger, oppressed black community whom he realizes he now represents. At the end of the film, he miraculously escapes across the border into Mexico where (the film suggests) he will recover from his wounds and continue his struggle against the white establishment. The film ends with a title that promises things to come: "A BAADASSSSS NIGGER IS COMING BACK TO COLLECT SOME DUES."

Courtesy of Cinemation

Pursued by the Los Angeles police, Sweetback (Melvin Van Peebles) becomes a black folk hero in *Sweet Sweetback's Baadasssss Song* (1971).

Radical hostility underscores many blaxploitation films in which whites tend to be cast as bigots and villains. Even in Poitier's first film as a director, *Buck and the Preacher* (1972), black homesteaders are tracked down and ruthlessly slaughtered by white bounty hunters. Their sole allies prove to be another oppressed group, Indians, who ride to their rescue at the last minute, playing the part usually performed by the U.S. Cavalry, who rescue settlers from attacking Indians in countless white Westerns. White police officers, like Mattelli (Anthony Quinn) in *Across 110th Street* (1972) or McKinney in *Black Caesar* (1973), tend to be both corrupt cops who take bribes from black gangsters and brutal racists, who abuse their authority as police officers to beat up defenseless blacks.

Outlaws or Role Models?

Black Caesar, directed by the white Larry Cohen, serves as an allegory for racial conflict. Its hero, Tommy Gibbs (Fred Williamson), rises from shoeshine boy to small-time hood to hitman for the Mafia. His rise to power is symbolized by his "overthrow" of the white lawyer for whom his mother worked as a maid. Gibbs quite literally takes the lawyer's place, buying him out of his apartment and even buying the clothes off his back; then he "frees" his own mother from servitude. Gibbs' quest for power leads him to take on the Mafia itself. He and his henchmen wipe out the Mafia family for whom he works and take its place.

Near the end of the film, in a showdown with McKinney, the white cop picks up a handy shoeshine box—the film's first symbol of black oppression by whites—and begins to beat Gibbs with it. Though the hero ultimately defeats the representatives of white power and racism—the Mafia and McKinney—he nonetheless falls from power himself in traditional gangster fashion. Abandoned by friends and family and wounded in a series of gun battles with the Mafia, which have wiped out his gang, Gibbs, now suddenly vulnerable for the first time in his life, is knifed to death in the rubble of a slum tenement by a gang of black teenagers.

Critics within the black community, including representatives from the NAACP, complained that the heroes of blaxploitation films did not represent the black community in a postive manner. These heroes tended to be violent criminals (*Black Caesar*), superstuds and pimps (*Sweet Sweetback*), or drug dealers (*Superfly*, 1972). The title characters in *Shaft* (1971) and *Cleopatra Jones* (1973) prove to be more traditional heroes, working as a private detective and a government agent, respectively. In fact, Cleopatra Jones provides an image of black womanhood that is considerably more liberated than that found in other blaxploitation films. And the black policeman in *Across 110th Street*, Pope (Yaphet Kotto), is steadfastly incorruptible. But the criminality of the majority of black heroes makes them unacceptable to middle-class black audiences.

However, blaxploitation heroes epitomize the outlaw status that the more aggressive and revolutionary members of the black power movement enjoy in the eyes of both the black and white middle class. In other words, it is perversely appropriate for the black counterculture to find itself identifying with, and identified as, outlaws. Thus, while the white counterculture identifies with Bonnie and Clyde or with the drug-dealing anti-heroes of *Easy Rider*, black (and white) revolutionaries make folk heroes out of black outlaws who overthrow white authority. Though the majority of Hollywood productions garble the message of the counterculture, it finds a voice—albeit marginal—in a handful of exploitation films that permit it to strike back against the more conservative mainstream.

SPLIT SCREEN: THE TWO 1960s

In *Field of Dreams* (1989), the heroine (Amy Madigan) lashes out during a PTA meeting at a conservative neighbor who wants to ban the books of a (fictional) radical black writer, Terence Mann (James Earl Jones), who was an inspiration to the youth movement in the 1960s. She accuses the would-be book burner of never having experienced the sixties, insisting that, instead, she had had two fifties and then had gone right on to the seventies. The 1960s has come to mean the civil rights, student protest, antiwar, and women's liberation movements. It has also become the stuff of nostalgia for television sitcoms, such as "The Wonder Years," which presented the 1960s as an age of innocence and idealism.

But the 1960s cannot be so easily labeled. For moviegoers, there were at least two 1960s. There was a 1960s for the conservative, middle-aged, middle-class mainstream, who went to big-budget historical spectacles, lavish musicals, Doris Day and Rock Hudson sex comedies, Disney family pictures, and cartoonlike, gadget-filled James Bond spy thrillers. This 1960s was essentially the second of the two 1950s referred to by Amy Madigan in *Field of Dreams*. But there was also a different 1960s for a younger, more liberal, middle- and lower-class audience—the audience that was moved by the books of writers like the fictional Terence Mann. These viewers were gradually drawn away from their parents' movies to films like *The Graduate, Bonnie and Clyde*, and *Easy Rider*, to films that attempted to address an under-30 age group. For them, the 1960s began sometime after JFK's assassination—after the nostalgic days of Buddy Holly and before the fanatic hysteria that greeted the arrival of the Beatles in the United States. In other words, the 1960s began, for them, when the "happy days" depicted in George Lucas' *American Graffiti* (1973) came to a close—at the end of the summer of 1962. For this generation of moviegoers, the 1960s stretched beyond the end of the decade into the early 1970s and lasted until the end of the Vietnam war. But their movies did not catch up with them until the late 1960s. Even when they did, few films—with the possible exception of the animated Beatles' film *Yellow Submarine* (1968)— conveyed the spaced-out, utopian pacifism of the hippies and/or flower children who followed Timothy Leary's advice, took LSD, and "tuned in, turned on, and dropped out." Nor did many major Hollywood productions capture the anger or intensity of the new left, the antiwar movement, or black militants.

By the mid-1970s, the cynicism of Dr. Spock's baby boomers had won the day. A number of their parents' movies—all of them musicals—began to flop one after the other at the box office, beginning with *Dr. Dolittle* (1967), which cost $20 million and earned $6 million; then *Star!* (1968), which cost $15 million and earned $4 million; *Hello Dolly* (1969), which cost $24 million and earned $15 million; and *Darling Lili* (1970), which cost $22 million and earned only $3 million. Meanwhile, films for the college-age crowd became more and more popular, with *The Graduate* (1967), *Bonnie and Clyde* (1967), *2001: A Space Odyssey* (1968), and *Easy Rider* (1969) returning huge profits to their producers. Bitter social satires and genre send-ups, such as Robert Altman's *M*A*S*H* (1970) and *McCabe and Mrs. Miller* (1971); Mike Nichols' adaptation of Joseph Heller's comic novel about military bureaucracy, *Catch-22* (1970); Arthur Penn's anti-Western, *Little Big Man* (1970); and Stanley Kubrick's adaptation of Anthony Burgess' study of amorality, violence, and repression, *A Clockwork Orange* (1971), found a ready audience among a disenchanted, increasingly skeptical youth, who had been raised on the black humor of nightclub comedian Lenny Bruce, cartoonist Jules Feiffer, and novelists Terry Southern, Joseph Heller, John Barth, and Kurt Vonnegut, Jr.

REJUVENATION

Hollywood filmmaking slowly adjusted to its new audience in the 1960s, but, for many, the system moved too slowly. The majority of those who produced, wrote, and directed motion pictures in the 1960s were themselves products of much earlier eras. As Richard Corliss noted, "for most of the Sixties, movies were a business for middle-aged (or old) men: from 1957 to 1966, the Best Film Oscar went to movies directed by men whose average age was 52." Within ten years, that statistic had changed and the average age of Oscar-winning (still male) directors had fallen to 38. During the early 1970s, a new generation of filmmakers appeared—filmmakers who had gone to school in the 1960s and who, therefore, belonged to that generation of filmgoers: Francis Ford Coppola (UCLA, 1958–1968); George Lucas (USC, ca. 1967); Brian De Palma (Columbia, 1962; Sarah Lawrence, 1964); Stephen Spielberg (California State, ca. 1968); and Martin Scorsese (NYU, 1964, 1966).

Although products of the 1960s, these filmmakers came from varied backgrounds and represented a broad political spectrum. De Palma had roots in the 1960s counterculture that cropped up in both *Greetings* (1968), which deals with the draft and the antiwar movement, and in its sequel, *Hi, Mom!* (1970), which contains a powerful sequence dealing with race relations. A filmmaker like Coppola, on the other hand, eluded easy categorization. His script for *Patton* (1970) combines idolatry for the World War II military hero with a sympathetic critique of the general's authoritarian behavior. Coppola describes the Mafia in *The Godfather* (1972) as "a metaphor for America" and suggests that his film is an exposé of the greed and violence that underlie the capitalist system. But, in exposing the criminal underworld's corruption and abuse of power, Coppola also celebrates the "family values," loyalty, and sense of justice that lie at the heart of the charisma that made the Corleones attractive to audiences.

Although Hollywood's filmmakers had become younger, the audiences for Hollywood films had grown even younger still. By the mid-1970s, almost half the movie-going public was between the ages of 12 and 20. In other words, the college-age spectators of the 1960s had given way to a high school-age audience in the 1970s. By the end of the 1970s, the five top-grossing films of all time—*Star Wars, Jaws, The Godfather, Grease,* and *Close Encounters of the Third Kind*—had all been directed by men under the age of 35. But the combination of young directors and even younger audiences had resulted in a cinema that was stylistically youthful and inventive but politically conservative. Exploitation-type genre films continued to dominate the marketplace, but in the 1970s they cost much more to make and much more was at risk if they failed. As a result, their potential for subversive statements had been severely restricted. If, in the late 1960s and early 1970s, the counterculture had struck back, then by the mid-1970s it found itself seriously compromised by changes in the marketplace, which heralded yet another turn in the revolutionary progress of the cinema.

SELECT FILMOGRAPHY

Lolita (1962)
Cleopatra (1963)
Irma la Douce (1963)
Goldfinger (1964)
Who's Afraid of Virginia Woolf? (1966)
Bonnie and Clyde (1967)
The Graduate (1967)
Up the Down Staircase (1967)
Bob & Carol & Ted & Alice (1969)

Easy Rider (1969)
Medium Cool (1969)
Getting Straight (1970)
The Strawberry Statement (1970)
Zabriskie Point (1970)
Klute (1971)
Sweet Sweetback's Baadasssss Song (1971)
Black Caesar (1973)

SELECT BIBLIOGRAPHY

Anon. "The Violent Years," in Ann Lloyd, ed., *70 Years at the Movies: From Silent Films to Today's Screen Hits.* New York: Crescent, 1988.

Bogle, Donald. *Toms, Coons, Mulattoes, Mammies, and Bucks: An Interpretive History of Blacks in American Films* (new expanded edition). New York: Continuum, 1989.

Cagin, Seth, and Philip Dray. *Hollywood Films of the Seventies: Sex, Drugs, Violence, Rock 'n Roll and Politics.* New York: Harper & Row, 1984.

Corliss, Richard. "We Lost It at the Movies: The Generation that Grew Up on *The Graduate* Took Over Hollywood—and Went into Plastics," *Film Comment* **16,** no. 1 (January–February, 1980).

Cripps, Thomas. *Black Film as Genre.* Bloomington: Indiana University Press, 1978.

Gitlin, Todd. *The Sixties: Years of Hope, Days of Rage.* New York: Bantam, 1987.

Haskell, Molly. *From Reverence to Rape: The Treatment of Women in the Movies.* New York: Holt, 1973.

Hillier, Bevis. *The Style of the Century: 1900–1980.* New York: Dutton, 1983.

James, David. *Allegories of Cinema: American Film in the Sixties.* Princeton: Princeton University Press, 1989.

Mordden, Ethan. *Medium Cool: The Movies of the 1960s.* New York: Knopf, 1990.

CHAPTER 14

THE FILM SCHOOL GENERATION

THE NEW WAVE

During the late 1940s and early 1950s, Henri Langlois screened old movies seven times a day in his small, 50-seat theater at the Cinémathèque Française in Paris. He ran every kind of film from every country in the world that produced motion pictures. Here a new generation of moviegoers saw the silent films of D. W. Griffith, Carl Dreyer, Sergei Eisenstein, F. W. Murnau, Eric von Stroheim, Maurice Stiller, and others for the first time since their initial releases in the 1910s and 1920s. It was here that they discovered the American sound films of Howard Hawks, John Ford, Alfred Hitchcock, and Orson Welles. It was here that they also obtained a sense of their own cinematic heritage by watching the work of Louis Lumière, Georges Méliès, Louis Feuillade, Jean Renoir, and others.

The Cinémathèque became the meeting place for a handful of film fanatics who came to see everything that Langlois showed. Five young men in particular attended regularly, eventually met one another there, and became the center of an emerging film culture. They watched films, talked and argued with one another about them, wrote passionately about them in a new film journal, *Cahiers du cinéma,* and brought their knowledge of the cinema to films they themselves made. Their names were François Truffaut, Jean-Luc Godard, Eric Rohmer, Jacques Rivette, and Claude Chabrol. They became central figures in what critics referred to as the New Wave, the explosion of films made by young, first-time French directors that took place at the end of the decade.

The New Wave began in 1958, when Chabrol directed his first feature, *Le Beau serge.* Then, in 1959, Truffaut's *The Four Hundred Blows* and Godard's *Breathless* not only won international acclaim but also earned huge profits at the box office. Their financial success opened the doors for others and, over the next two years, 67 journalists, academics, writers, and students directed their first films in France. New Wave directors did not apprentice for years in the film industry before getting their first film to direct, but many of them had *studied* films for years. They had learned about the cinema in film clubs, at the Cinémathèque , and in movies houses in Paris. Many of the films they made reflected this alternative form of apprenticeship.

A film like *Breathless* was hardly academic, but it is informed by an understanding of film history that was rarely seen on motion picture screens prior to the advent of the New Wave. It was dedicated to Monogram, an American studio that produced B films in the 1930s and 1940s. It contains a tribute to

Humphrey Bogart, at whose photograph the hero stares intently, as if looking at himself in a mirror. A poster for Bogart's last film, *The Harder They Fall* (1956), is prominently displayed outside a neighborhood theater (as well as a poster for a recent film, starring Jack Palance and directed by Robert Aldrich). The narrative resembles that of an American crime film, and the film's characters, an existential hero on the run (Jean-Paul Belmondo) hopelessly in love with a femme fatale (Jean Seberg), belong to the world of American film noir. And the hero's death alludes to the final sequences in old Cagney and Bogart pictures directed by Raoul Walsh (*The Roaring Twenties*, 1939; *High Sierra*, 1941). Although the film is also full of allusions to more traditional art forms and artists, such as Dylan Thomas, William Faulkner, Rainer Maria Rilke, W. A. Mozart, Paul Klee, Pierre Auguste Renoir, Pablo Picasso, and others, it steadfastly refuses to distinguish between high and low forms. As far as Godard is concerned, Bogart stands on equal footing with Mozart.

THE AUTEUR THEORY: DIRECTORS AS STARS

Cahiers du cinéma and Andrew Sarris

Godard, and other French critics who worked for *Cahiers du cinéma*, rewrote the traditional film canon, which had consisted largely of classic, European art films. They included within it commercial American films made by directors (such as Howard Hawks, Alfred Hitchcock, Vincente Minnelli, and Samuel Fuller), who were then generally considered to be mere Hollywood hacks. An American critic, Andrew Sarris, adopted the tactics of the *Cahiers* group, bringing their writings, opinions, and polemics to the United States in the form of what Sarris termed "the auteur theory." Sarris' book on American directors, *The American Cinema* (1968), argued that directors were the principal authors of motion pictures and set forth a new canon of great filmmakers. More important, the book forced a wholesale reevaluation of American cinema by critics, scholars, students, and film buffs. A cagey journalist, Sarris inspired controversy (and, thus, secured attention for his project) by ranking directors, who belonged to the "Pantheon," "Far Side of Paradise," "Expressive Esoterica," "Less Than Meets the Eye," "Strained Seriousness," and other categories. But Sarris' chief contribution, as an educator, was to provide a map of the existing terrain for others to follow, add to, correct, and challenge.

Sarris forced Americans to take their own cinema seriously—and he had the critical clout, prestige, and intellectual appeal of the New Wave (and its *auteur* theory) behind him. Though not everyone agreed with Sarris' taste, many were so persuaded by the New Wave's enthusiasm for American cinema that further research into current and past Hollywood product was considered necessary. If Truffaut idolized Hitchcock, then Hitchcock must be an artist of considerable talents. American intellectuals rushed to Truffaut's self-effacing, book-length interview with Hitchcock (1968) to find out what all the stir was about.

Retrospective: America Discovers Its Cinematic Past

While Sarris was rediscovering new film *auteurs* (authors) in his weekly newspaper column (which began in 1960), American museums and revival theaters began to conduct extensive retrospectives of major directors' work. In New York City, Peter Bogdanovich, influenced by Sarris' criticism, mounted extensive retrospectives of the works of Welles, Hawks, and Hitchcock during the early 1960s at the Museum of Modern Art. Around the same time, Daniel Talbot (along with Bogdanovich, Sarris, and second-string *New York Times* film critic, Eugene Archer) programmed a series of film retrospectives at the New Yorker Theater on New York's Upper West Side. Like the *Cahiers* group, Sarris, Bogdanovich, and Archer wrote extensively about the cinema and argued on behalf of neglected American *auteurs*. Like the critics-turned-directors of the New Wave, Bogdanovich became a director himself. After a brief apprenticeship with Roger Corman, he made *Targets* (1968), a movie about a serial killer who murders his family and then terrorizes the patrons of a drive-in theater that is showing a Boris Karloff horror picture. Karloff's presence in the film inspires Bogdanovich to introduce a cinematic quote—a clip of Karloff from an early Hawks film, *The Criminal Code* (1931), which the actor is watching on television. Bogdanovich's psychopathic killer serves as the focus for a number of allusions to Hitchcock films, such as *Psycho* (1960) and *Strangers on a Train* (1951). After *Targets*, Bogdanovich made a documentary for the American Film Institute about John Ford, *Directed by John Ford* (1971). Tributes to Hawks and Ford filled Bogdanovich's next feature film, an adaptation of a Larry McMurtry novel, *The Last Picture Show* (1971); while the film after that, a screwball comedy starring Barbra Streisand and Ryan O'Neal called *What's Up, Doc?* (1972), was a loose remake of Hawks' *Bringing Up Baby* (1938).

Peter Bogdanovich evokes the world of John Ford in *The Last Picture Show* (1971), casting a familiar Fordian actor, Ben Johnson, as Sam the Lion, who represents the spirit of the past.

Courtesy of Columbia

The Critic as Filmmaker

Bogdanovich proved to be something of an exception—American film critics did not follow their French counterparts to take up positions behind the camera. Two *Esquire* (nonfilm) critics, Robert Benton and David Newman, collaborated on the screenplay of *Bonnie and Clyde,* which they tried to get first Truffaut and then Godard to direct before turning to Arthur Penn. Benton subsequently became a director (*Bad Company,* 1972; *The Late Show,* 1977; *Kramer vs. Kramer,* 1979), but, though movie wise, he never indulged in the sort of cinematic allusionism found in Bogdanovich's early work. After retiring from the *New York Times,* critic Bosley Crowther became an executive at Columbia Pictures. In 1979, *New Yorker* critic Pauline Kael enjoyed a brief stint in Hollywood as a production executive, courtesy of producer-actor Warren Beatty, but her time there did not result in projects that were ever filmed.

The only American *film* critics to make it in Hollywood as creative talents came from much earlier eras and served as unselfconscious screenwriters for Old Wave directors. Frank Woods left the *New York Dramatic Mirror* to write for Griffith in the teens (*The Birth of a Nation,* 1915); *New York Times* reviewer Frank Nugent wrote Westerns for John Ford in the late 1940s, as well as *The Quiet Man* (1952); and the film critic for *Time* and *Nation,* James Agee, scripted John Huston's Humphrey Bogart and Katharine Hepburn adventure picture, *The African Queen* (1951) and later Charles Laughton's gothic chase film, *The Night of the Hunter* (1955).

Training Ground: The Rise of Film Schools

Film critics tended to have little status in the eyes of the American film industry, which found them more annoying than enlightening. Indeed, Nugent was reportedly hired by 20th Century-Fox in order to prevent him from writing negative reviews of that studio's pictures. But Hollywood tended to look upon film students who studied at major film schools and desperately wanted to enter the industry with a more favorable eye. They appeared to be uncritical of the industry, eager to succeed within it, and appreciative of its history. They could also be paid (at first) considerably less than older, more experienced directors. At the same time, with the collapse of the studio system, film schools tended to provide a pool of semiskilled talent upon which the industry could draw whenever there was a need for new blood. And during the 1960s, an unprecedented number of would-be *auteurs* enrolled in film schools to study the craft and (hopefully) follow in the footsteps of their favorite *auteurs,* whether they be Hitchcock, Hawks, Ford, Welles, or another neglected giant of commercial cinema.

Film gradually became a feature of a contemporary liberal arts education, and more and more talented young filmmakers took up the study of film and television on both an undergraduate and graduate level. In 1967, 200 American colleges and universities offered roughly 1500 courses in film and television. Eleven years later, over 1000 schools listed 10,000 such courses.

Graduate programs at the University of California at Los Angeles, the University of Southern California, and New York University produced a new generation of filmmakers, such as Francis Ford Coppola (UCLA), George Lucas (USC), and Martin Scorsese (NYU), while the American Film Institute's Center for Advanced Film Studies trained Paul Schrader, David Lynch, and others.

At the same time, the rise of film study in the university produced a new generation of film-smart moviegoers, who had taken one or more film courses in college or even in high school. This new young audience sought out films that addressed their interest. Like Coppola, Lucas, and Scorsese, they had grown up on the movies, watching them on television, in campus film societies, or in film courses. They not only appreciated the work of the film school generation because it grew out of the same cultural experiences as theirs, but also understood many of the allusions to earlier films and filmmakers that peppered the movies directed by the members of the American New Wave.

THE COLOR OF MONEY: YOUNG DIRECTORS AND THE BOX OFFICE

Youth Films and Economics

However, it was not entirely the growth in cinematic literacy that opened Hollywood's doors in the late 1960s and early 1970s to a new crop of filmmakers. It was economics that enabled young directors to get their start. During the period 1969–1972, the seven major studios had record losses totaling over $500 million. Experienced directors had bombed with big-budget flops like *Star!* (Robert Wise, 1968) and *Darling Lili* (Blake Edwards, 1970). At the same time, the phenomenal success of the low-budget, youth-cult film *Easy Rider* (1969), directed by 33-year-old Dennis Hopper, demonstrated to studio executives that experience was not always as profitable as youthful energy. Meanwhile, a number of youth-oriented films (most made by older directors), such as *Butch Cassidy and the Sundance Kid* (1969), *Woodstock* (1970), *Love Story* (1970), and *Summer of '42* (1971), enjoyed outstanding financial success. And Hopper was not the only young filmmaker involved in the making of a hit. Francis Ford Coppola won an Academy Award for his screenplay for *Patton* (1970), one of the top-grossing films of the year. At the same time, Bogdanovich's *Last Picture Show* and *What's Up, Doc?* were both among the top ten box-office hits of 1971 and 1972. More important, many of the films produced by this younger crop of filmmakers fared extremely well at the box office. USC once boasted that "as of December 1983, 41 of the 42 all-time highest grossing films have USC alumni affiliated with them."

Though Spielberg was not from USC, his films, including some produced by Lucas, topped the charts; *E.T.* earned $228.6 million, *Jaws* $129.5 million, *Raiders of the Lost Ark* $115.6 million, and the two *Indiana Jones* sequels $115.5 and $109 million. Lucas' *Star Wars* films dominated the top-ten all-time film rental champs, earning $193.5 million, $168 million, and $141.6 million. In-

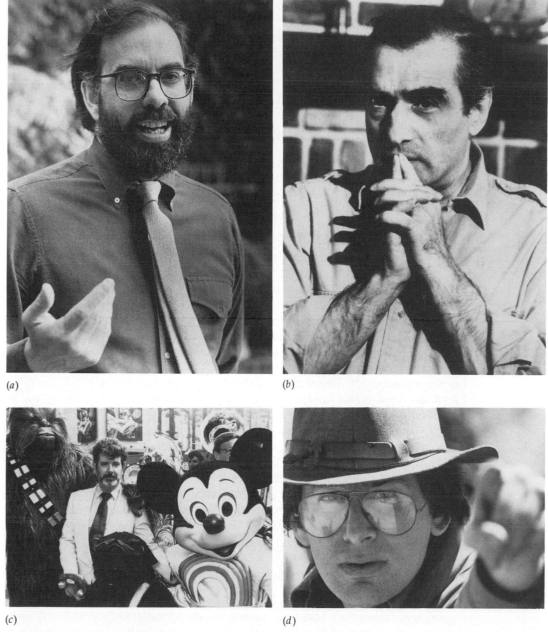

(a)

(b)

(c)

(d)

The Most Likely to Succeed of the Film School Generation: (*a*) Francis Ford Coppola, (*b*) Martin Scorsese, (*c*) George Lucas, and (*d*) Steven Spielberg.

dustry analysts read the box-office statistics of the 1969–1972 period against their own research data, which told them that the age of the average moviegoer had gotten younger. By 1970–1971, over 43 percent of all viewers were between the ages of 12 and 20. (By the end of the 1970s, this figure had climbed to roughly 50 percent.) An additional 30 percent of the total audience

303

were between the ages of 21 and 29, making almost 75 percent of the film audience under age 30. Given the age of the audience, the success of youth films, and the promising track record of young filmmakers like Hopper, Bogdanovich, and Coppola, the studios turned to the source of much of this new talent in search of the next generation of filmmakers.

The Roger Corman School

Hopper, Bogdanovich, and Coppola had all received practical experience in filmmaking by working for the master of the exploitation film, Roger Corman, who produced and directed cheaply made horror films, Westerns, and motor-cycle and gangster pictures for American International Pictures.

Hopper had starred in a number of Corman teen-pics, as had his costars in *Easy Rider*, Peter Fonda and Jack Nicholson. Corman not only gave Bog-danovich a start but also made it possible for a film school type such as Coppola to make his first feature-length film, *Dementia 13* (1963); for Martin Scorsese to direct his second, *Boxcar Bertha* (1972); and for John Milius to direct his first film, *Dillinger* (1973). AIP even gave Woody Allen his start, bankroll-ing his *What's Up, Tiger Lily?* (1966). A few years later, Corman helped Jonathan Demme and Jonathan Kaplan make their first films. Demme's back-ground in exploitation has recently resurfaced in his picaresque sexual odys-sey, *Something Wild* (1986), with Jeff Daniels and Melanie Griffith, and in his horror mystery, *The Silence of the Lambs* (1991), with Jodie Foster and Anthony Hopkins. Kaplan also fared quite well in the exploitation mode with his gang-rape exposé, *The Accused* (1988), starring Jodie Foster; and with his stalker film, *Unlawful Entry* (1992), starring Kurt Russell and Ray Liotta.

In looking to Corman protégés, the major studios tacitly acknowledged a significant shift in the nature of the traditional Hollywood film. During the 1970s, the industry, led by the film school generation, would turn more and more frequently to the kinds of pictures made by Corman—genre pictures. It would draw upon the subject matter that had previously been the sole province of the exploitation market—gangster films, teen hot-rod flicks, sci-ence-fiction adventures, monster pictures, and horror films.

Exploitation on a Grand Scale

However, in undertaking these low-budget subjects, Hollywood gave them a big-budget treatment. Thus, Corman's *Bloody Mama* (1970), which explores the gangster family of bloody Ma Barker and her equally bloodthirsty boys, gives way to Coppola's more operatic and more lavish family melodrama, *The Godfather* (1972). George Lucas' *American Graffiti* (1973) is a souped-up hybrid of an Annette Funicello–Frankie Avalon *Beach Party* movie (1963) and films like *Hot Rod Girl* (1956), which document the 1950s teen world of drag-strip racing and juke joints. Lucas' *Star Wars* (1977) and Steven Spielberg's *Close Encounters of the Third Kind* (1977) look back to Flash Gordon serials and science-fiction films of the 1950s. Spielberg's *Jaws* (1975) draws on familiar monster pictures such as *The Creature From the Black Lagoon* (1954), *Attack of the Crab Monsters* (1957), and *Frogs* (1972). Brian De Palma's *Carrie* (1976), an adaptation of a Stephen King novel about a young girl with telekinetic powers, has roots not only in De Palma's own AIP shocker *Sisters* (1973), but also in earlier teen monster films, such as *I Was a Teenage Frankenstein* (1957) or *I Was a Teenage Werewolf* (1957).

Many of the big hits of the 1970s were low-budget genre pictures in disguise. Some of the biggest, like William Friedkin's lavishly produced gross-out horror picture, *The Exorcist* (1973), which earned $89 million, even dropped the disguise. The industry marketed these films according to methods that had proven effective in the exploitation field. Hollywood abandoned its traditional release pattern whereby a film would first open in one or two theaters in the nation's largest cities; then, several weeks later, as word-of-mouth reports from spectators on the quality of the film spread, it would be placed by the distributor in additional theaters, in other cities and in the suburbs, with the number of theaters in which to play it calculated in accordance with audience response.

Starting with *Jaws*, the major studios adopted the distribution patterns developed in the exploitation market. The film was released nationwide in approximately 600 theaters at the same time. In addition to saturating the market with prints of the film, Universal (its distributor) saturated the television and radio airwaves with national and local advertising for the film as well. They soon discovered that, in a wide-release situation, when advertising (and advertising expenditures) were doubled, the returns at the box office increased by at least three or four times. Thereafter, big-budget exploitation films opened in from 800 to 1000 theaters simultaneously and advertising budgets increased dramatically, averaging about 50 percent of the film's negative cost (that is, what it cost to make the film).

REFERENCES, MEANING, AND POSTMODERNISM

The Art of Allusion

Though exploitation films provided models for the new Hollywood, young filmmakers were equally drawn to the classics—the European art cinema, *Citizen Kane* (1941), popular American genres, film noir, and an emerging canon of filmmakers and films. Like Godard in *Breathless*, they refused to distinguish between high and low art, borrowing from both with equal abandon. Thus *American Graffiti* looks back to AIP teen-pics, but it also borrows crucial elements, including its basic plot, from Federico Fellini's *I Vitelloni* (1953). Fellini's semiautobiographical film tells the story of the mundane activities of adolescents living boring lives in a provincial Italian village and concludes with the hero's departure for a challenging future in the big city. At the end of *Graffiti*, its central character, Curt (Richard Dreyfuss), similarly escapes the deadening routine of small-town life in California and heads East to go to college. *Raiders of the Lost Ark* (1981) brought Saturday afternoon serials back to life, but it also invoked *Citizen Kane,* suggesting in its last shot that the lost ark is as ultimately unattainable as was Rosebud.

Hitchcock, Hawks, and Ford inspired filmmakers, who patterned their own films after the films of these American masters. *Rear Window* (Hitchcock, 1954), for example, serves as the source for Michelangelo Antonioni's *Blow-Up* (1966); Hitchcock's story of voyeurism in Greenwich Village and Antonioni's investigation of perception and photographic truth in London inform Coppola's study of surveillance in San Francisco, *The Conversation* (1974); and all three provide the background for De Palma's thriller about an accidental eavesdropper in *Blow Out* (1981). *The Searchers* (Ford, 1956), *Vertigo* (Hitchcok, 1958), *Rio Bravo* (Hawks, 1959), *Psycho* (Hitchcock, 1960), and *The Birds* (Hitchcock, 1963) serve as central texts to which student filmmakers repeatedly allude, quote from, or copy. John Carpenter's *Assault on Precinct 13* (1976), which depicts a desolate Los Angeles police station besieged by scores of terrorists, reworks the plots of both *Rio Bravo*, in which John Wayne defends his jail against a gang of gunslingers, and *The Birds*, in which birds attack a California community and trap the film's central characters in their house.

For his part, Woody Allen acknowledged the influence of Ingmar Bergman (*Interiors*, 1978), Federico Fellini (*Stardust Memories*, 1980), Humphrey Bogart and *Casablanca* (*Play It Again, Sam*, 1972), and the phenomenon of moviegoing (*The Purple Rose of Cairo*, 1985). Even producers became idols of younger directors. Spielberg, for example, fancied himself as the new Disney. *E.T.* (1982) is filled with repeated allusions to Disney's *Mary Poppins. Close Encounters* looks back to the "Night on Bald Mountain" sequence from *Fantasia* (1940) and concludes with Jiminy Cricket's rendition of "When You Wish Upon a Star" from *Pinocchio* (1940). More recently, *Hook* (1991) lays bare Spielberg's own Peter Pan complex and solidifies his identity as the child of Disney.

De Palma and Hitchcock

In *Sisters* (1973), Brian De Palma borrows extensively from *Rear Window* and *Psycho*. Like the James Stewart character in the former film, De Palma's heroine sees a murder committed by her neighbor across the courtyard and spends the rest of the film trying to prove it. The killer turns out to be a Norman Bates–type psychopath who murders men to whom she is attracted. De Palma's *Obsession* (1976), based on a script by Paul Schrader, combines *Vertigo* with *The Searchers*. Its hero (Cliff Robertson) watches helplessly as his wife and daughter are first kidnapped, then (apparently) killed in an explosion. Like the Stewart character in *Vertigo*, after "Madeleine's" (Kim Novak's) supposed death, Robertson is traumatized by what he sees, and his recovery consists of remaking a woman who resembles his wife into the image of his wife. Like his counterpart in *Vertigo*, he remains unaware that this woman is actually his daughter (or "Madeleine" in the Hitchcock film).

The Searchers comes to the rescue of this semi-incestuous melodrama in the form of a final scene in which the hero, like the John Wayne character in the

Courtesy of Columbia

Obsession (1976) begins with an idyllic (Fordian) family ritual: Cliff Robertson and his wife (Genevieve Bujold) put their daughter to bed.

famous Ford Western, recognizes the woman as his long-lost daughter and lifts her into his arms. De Palma's obsession with Hitchcock, to whose films the younger director repeatedly alludes, extends to imitations of specific shots—such as the 360-degree, circular tracking shot from *Vertigo* which crops up in *Obsession* and *Carrie* (both 1976) and even in *The Untouchables* (1987). For De Palma, the borrowing of this shot enables him to adopt the stylistic mask of another behind which he could hide. In effect, De Palma does not "speak" directly to his audiences but instead communicates *through* Hitchcock. Of all the "movie brats" (that is, the generation of filmmakers who grew up watching old movies on television, in repertory houses, or in film school), De Palma proves to be the most "postmodern," though they are all— in varying degrees—products of the postmodern era.

"The Failure of the New"

As Fredric Jameson suggests, contemporary consumer society possesses a culture that is postmodern. By that, Jameson means that postmodernism not only "comes after" modernism but also emerges in reaction to modernism. Although the modernist work of Abstract Expressionists, James Joyce, T. S. Eliot, Igor Stravinsky, and others had once been perceived as revolutionary, modernism has become, over the years, the establishment of the art world. Canonized, it gradually became that against which subsequent artists were forced to revolt in an attempt to say something new and different. As a form of rebellion against the dominant culture of the modernist era, postmodernism ignores traditional distinctions between high culture and popular culture. In terms of stylistic practices, postmodern artists rely upon *pastiche*—a form of imitation of the unique style or content of earlier works that lacks any trace of the satire or parody that characterizes traditional forms of imitation. Pastiche is an entirely *neutral* practice; it conveys no perceptible attitude toward the original. The artist merely adopts a preexistent stylistic mask and speaks blankly (i.e., without expressing any perspective whatsoever toward the work imitated) in the voices of others. De Palma's 360-degree tracking shots epitomize the concept of pastiche. They are expressionless imitations of shots that had been highly charged with romantic feeling in Hitchcock.

Postmodern works also acknowledge the primary obstacle confronting contemporary artists—the inability to say anything that has not already been said, the inability to create or to express that which is unique or novel. It is no longer possible, as it was for D. W. Griffith, Hitchcock, Welles, Ford, and others, to "invent" ways of "writing with cinema." Hollywood's postclassical filmmakers, like De Palma, could only draw upon a preexistent dictionary of shots, situations, themes, and meanings to express themselves. The authentic expression of ideas that took place in the past is today replaced by quotation and allusion to that authentic expression.

Jameson connects this inability to be original or "the failure of the new" with another postmodern trait—nostalgia for the past. Nostalgia films, like *American Graffiti*, embed spectators in a past that is created, in large part, out of the past's imaginary existence. That is, this existence has been created from the way the past has been represented or constructed in cultural artifacts like the movies. The implication is that the past, for this new generation of filmmakers, consists largely of *images* of the past rather than the past itself. Many of the movie brats possess a past that has been permanently fused with the movies they saw in their youth. Thus, images of the past come from earlier films, and they are simply reproduced and recirculated *as* the past in the works of postmodern cinema.

Period films, such as Scorsese's Liza Minnelli musical, *New York, New York* (1977), look like 1940s music dramas such as *Lady in the Dark* (1944), *The Man I Love* (1946), and *My Dream Is Yours* (1949). A number of 1970s films copy the look of film noir in order to establish their 1940s time frame. The most representative of these is Dick Richard's *Farewell, My Lovely* (1975), a Raymond Chandler, private-eye film that starred Robert Mitchum, a familiar face from 1940s and 1950s films noirs.

Schizophrenia and Incoherence

Finally, Jameson sees postmodernism as the art form of the schizophrenic experience. For the postmodern artist, the self is not unified, as it was for classical artists, but fragmented. The self is essentially alienated, cut off from any profound identification with a community. And the self is no longer understood as a whole; rather it is layered or split. As a result, in expressing themselves, postmodern artists convey only the incoherence of their internal reality. At the same time, in transmitting the reality of their social and cultural context, they reproduce only its incoherence.

Certain aspects of Terrence Malick's *Badlands* (1973), an outlaw-couple film based on the real-life 1950s killing spree of Charles Starkweather and his girlfriend, Carol Ann Fugate, capture this sense of incoherence. The voice-over narration by the film's heroine (Sissy Spacek) fails to cohere or make sense of the events seen onscreen. And Malick's distanced, observational, nonjudgmental perspective, which includes extended descriptive passages featuring inanimate objects, plants, and animals, refuses to submit itself to the traditional logic of discrete causes that produce specific effects. More obviously, the temporal and narrative discontinuity of films like *Taxi Driver* (1976), *Looking for Mr. Goodbar* (1977), and *Cruising* (1980) prompt Robin Wood to label them "incoherent texts." Unlike classical cinema, which gives a definite order to experience, these works capture the chaotic spirit of their times. As works that did not know what they wanted to say, they simply reflect the cultural conditions that produced them.

A Postmodern Case Study: *Taxi Driver*

A certain level of incoherence, for example, lies at the heart of *Taxi Driver*, embodied in its central character, Travis Bickle (Robert De Niro). Much as the "hero's" own goals and desires remain unclear and confused, so does the audience's understanding of/attitude toward the character. What does Travis want? The untouchable blonde "angel," Betsy (Cybill Shepherd), whom he irrationally takes to a porno movie on their first big date? The child prostitute, Iris (Jodie Foster), whom he attempts to reform? If he hates the filth of the city and speaks of washing the scum off the streets, why is the target of his assassination attempt the populist politician who has promised to clean up the city? Why does Travis suddenly switch his intended target, killing Iris' pimp instead of the politician?

The incoherence of the character carries over to the audience. Spectators remain uncertain as to whether Travis' "rescue" of Iris at the end of the film, which is accomplished by his brutal murder of her pimp and two of his associates, is to be understood as heroic, as the verbal accounts of it in the press had suggested, or disturbingly psychopathic, as Scorsese's filming of the sequence implies. Travis emerges as the enigmatic product of the various incoherences in the world around him. The film captures the plight of the alienated individual in contemporary consumer society. Surrounded by the conflicting messages of politicians, pimps, and the media and engulfed by filth, crime, and corruption, he attempts to play the part of the old-fashioned Western hero, whose decisive actions would set things right. But traditional heroism is no longer possible in his world; he can only play the part of a somewhat dubious anti-hero, who lashes out at the most obvious and immediate target he can find.

Films like *Taxi Driver* expose the contradictions that inform 1970s America, describing the conditions that produce phenomena such as Vietnam (Travis is a Vietnam veteran) and Watergate (the film's politician would say or do

Courtesy of Columbia

What does Travis (Robert De Niro) want in *Taxi Driver* (1976)?

anything to get elected), but refusing to understand or make sense of those conditions. The film struck a nerve in middle America. One of its repeat viewers was John Hinckley, the ultimate incoherent spectator, who fell in love with Jodie Foster and shot the politician, President Ronald Reagan, rather than the pimp, in an attempt to rewrite the film and give it a better (that is, more coherent) ending. Or perhaps, like Travis, all he wanted to do was get the attention of a girl (Jodie Foster for Hinckley; Betsy for Travis).

REASSURANCE: COMFORT, COMICS, AND NOSTALGIA

A Return to Innocence

Not all 1970s film-school-generation films exposed incoherence. A number of them responded differently. As Wood argues, they "papered over the cracks" instead. If Scorsese enjoyed a modest success at the box office describing the alienation and blankness of American identity in the post-Vietnam, post-Watergate, postindustrial, postmodern era of the mid-1970s, then others reaped hitherto unimaginable rewards by returning to a less-troubled, pre-Vietnam, pre-Watergate world when America was still living in relative socio-political innocence. *Taxi Driver* earned a paltry $12.6 million; but *American Graffiti,* set in 1962, before the assassination of the Kennedys and King, before the national agony of Vietnam, and before the political cynicism of Watergate, grossed $55.6 million.

Raiders of the Lost Ark ($115.6 million) returned us to the innocent action serials of the 1930s and 1940s and restored moral clarity to the screen; we forgot the confusing morality of Vietnam and went back to the clear-cut villainy of Nazis. *Close Encounters* ($82.5 million) encouraged us to regress to the status of children—to play with our food, indulge our whims and obsessions, and engage in a childlike state of wonder. Indeed, the most characteristic image in a Spielberg film turned out to be that of the rapt face of a child looking up in awe (at a UFO, an extra-terrestrial, or some other marvel)—a look which duplicated that of the audience, spellbound in darkness, as it looked up at the screen on which a spectacle of special effects was displayed. *Star Wars* ($193.5 million) was set in a universe "far, far" away and "long, long" ago and, like *Raiders,* evoked the bygone pleasures of children's Saturday matinees at the movies. It also restored the clear-cut distinctions between heroes and villains that had become obscured in post–World War II American cinema. The storm troopers of the (evil) Empire are dressed in Nazi-style uniforms, while Han Solo (Harrison Ford) wears the vest, holster, and boots of a cowboy hero.

Spielberg's sense of wonder dominates *Close Encounters of the Third Kind* (1977): Melinda Dillon and Carey Guffey stare at offscreen alien activities.

Courtesy of Columbia

Opposing Visions

Scorsese is one of the few directors to foreground the predicament of the modern individual cut adrift from traditional forms of identity construction and/or confirmation through reaffirming institutions such as the family and the community. Instead, his films explore the disintegration and fragmentation of any sense of a coherent self. The extreme close-up of an Alka Seltzer tablet dissolving in a glass of water in *Taxi Driver* is emblematic of the status of identity in his work as a whole. His characters, who mirror the doubts and confusions of their time, have no unified sense of who they are. Travis and prizefighter Jake La Motta (*Raging Bull,* 1980) are problematically split or divided characters, who, quite symbolically, talk to themselves in mirrors. In *Goodfellas* (1990), Henry Hill, who wanted to be a "somebody" rather than a "nobody," models his identity on that of the colorful gangsters who lived and worked in his neighborhood when he was a kid. But this identity proves to be more fantasy than fact, and it slowly disintegrates over the course of the film until Henry returns to the status of a "nobody," living anonymously in the witness protection program in the suburbs.

Unlike Scorsese, Lucas and Spielberg give us psychologically noncomplex, comic-book characters. They all know who they are. At the same time, they emerge as decisive individuals, like the Richard Dreyfuss characters in *Graffiti, Jaws,* and *Close Encounters,* who are obsessed by blondes in white T-Birds, sharks, and UFOs, respectively. Luke Skywalker (Mark Hamill) may not have known that Darth Vader was his father or that Princess Leia (Carrie Fisher) was his sister, but he didn't agonize over who he was either. He knew, after all, that he was destined to become a Jedi knight and help destroy the Empire. And even if some of Lucas' or Spielberg's characters initially appear indecisive (like the Dreyfuss characters in *Graffiti* and *Close Encounters*), by the end of the films they have definitely discovered who they are and what they want. They not only "have it all," but, unlike Henry Hill, they keep it all.

In others words, in the mid- to late 1970s and 1980s, the films that proved to be most successful financially were those that reassured rather than disturbed the public. Vietnam, Watergate, and the sociopolitical agenda of 1970s activist America disappeared beneath the surface of the more positive images of an idealized past—of a 1930s, 1940s, or 1950s.

Back in Time

The 1980s saw a nostalgia craze for the 1950s in the form of revivals of 1950s music, fashion, and lifestyles. Teenagers even rediscovered certain 1960s groups, like the Beatles, though the songs that proved most popular tended to be pre–*Sergeant Pepper* (1967). *Grease,* a teen musical set in the 1950s, emerged as the big movie hit of 1978, grossing over $96 million. A few years later, Michael J. Fox, as Marty McFly, took us *Back to the Future* (1985) in one of the first of a series of time-travel films that exploited the nostalgia craze. In this first of what would prove to be (so far) three *Back to the Future* films, the hero returns to the innocence of Eisenhower America in the 1950s.

Taking note of the success of this film, which earned $105 million, Coppola sent Kathleen Turner back to the 1950s to relive her life as a teenager, rethink her subsequent life, and reemerge with renewed hope for the future in *Peggy Sue Got Married* (1986). In both films, the 1950s becomes the site of utopian communities, of baby-boomer Shangri-Las dominated by wholesome values associated with family and community, which had somehow disappeared in succeeding decades. Frank Capra's *Lost Horizon* (1937) had sought a populist paradise amidst the turmoil of the Depression and prewar years that would provide a retreat for Americans during the chaotic period in which American national identity shifted from an agrarian to a corporate base. Nostalgia films of the late 1970s and 1980s perform a similar function, providing a return to a bygone era that had become identified in contemporary culture with more innocent, happier days.

This is accomplished, in part, by invoking the popular culture of that earlier era, especially its music and its films. Films like *Peggy Sue, Stand by Me* (1986), *La Bamba* (1987), *Sea of Love* (1989), *Great Balls of Fire!* (1989), and *Pretty Woman* (1990) borrow their titles (and title songs) from 1950s and 1960s rock-and-roll songs, though not all of them are set in the 1950s. Starting with *American Graffiti* (1973) and continuing through *The Big Chill* (1983), *Baby, It's You* (1983), *The Flamingo Kid* (1984), *Dirty Dancing* (1987), and *Mermaids* (1990), more and more films immerse audiences in 1950s and early-1960s music. Fifties' style rock-and-roll songs on the soundtrack begin to function more and more like a traditional song and dance sequence in a Hollywood musical, serving as an escape from the mundane realities of the present into a more

Returning to the past: Matthew Broderick sings "Twist and Shout" as the title character in *Ferris Bueller's Day Off* (1986).

Courtesy of Paramount

ideal realm associated with the past. Thus, Matthew Broderick's rendition of "Twist and Shout" serves as a utopian centerpiece in *Ferris Bueller's Day Off* (1986), bringing together a community of like-minded rockers who parade together with the hero. And the use of the Righteous Brothers's 1965 version of "Unchained Melody" as the lovers' song in *Ghost* (1990) links their relationship with romantic excesses that more properly belong to their (and post-Watergate America's) youthful past.

Contradictory Impulses

Ironically, the motion pictures to which nostalgia films refer are often themselves less than utopian in their representation of their own times; more often than not, they reflect the contradictory forces that produced them. *Who Framed Roger Rabbit* (1988) employs the stylistic characteristics of film noir (and of *Chinatown,* 1974) to identify the film's temporal setting as that of the 1940s. Noir lighting also proves appropriate to the murder mystery storyline featuring the investigations of private-eye Eddie Valiant (Bob Hoskins). But the elements of film noir used here no longer convey the profound existential anxiety and social alienation experienced by the individual in postwar, 1940s America. They function merely as an allusion to the 1940s rather than as a reflection or expression of it. By the same token, nostalgia films that invoke the 1950s ignore the social turmoil that creeps into that era's sex comedies (see Chapter 7), Westerns (see Chapter 10), melodramas, and other genre pictures. Instead, they tend to cast those periods as more or less idyllic. They become projections of 1980s nostalgia for the 1950s rather than reflections of the actual 1950s (or 1980s).

In another version of the time-travel motif, the future comes back in time to fix the present, which poses a threat to future civilizations. In this scenario, the 1980s are rewritten according to the needs of a larger, utopian project. But what informs both kinds of film is a form of wish fulfillment that denies the present and rewrites the past. Both *Terminator* films (1984, 1991) attempt to escape from the future consequences of past actions by sending agents of the future back into the past to change history. In *Star Trek IV: The Voyage Home* (1986), Captain Kirk (William Shatner) and his crew go back in time to 1980s San Francisco to retrieve a species of whale that has become extinct in the future and that promises to save the Earth from destruction by potential alien invaders. Finally, in *Bill & Ted's Excellent Adventure* (1989), rock-and-rollers from the future dispatch an agent (George Carlin) back to 1980s San Dimas, California, to prevent Bill and Ted (the Wyld Stallyns) from flunking their high school history examination. Their would-be failure threatens to change the course of future civilization, which is rooted in the vision brought about by Bill and Ted's music. Their time travel through past history in a telephone booth enables them to bring back Socrates, Genghis Khan, Napoleon, Joan of Arc, Beethoven, Abraham Lincoln, Billy the Kid, and Sigmund Freud as "show-and-tell" to their final examination, thus guaranteeing not only that they would pass the course but also that inhabitants of the future would "be excellent" to one another.

THE BRAT PACK

One film of the 1980s, which looks back to the 1950s and 1960s, introduces a new generation of actors—"the brat pack"—semitough teens who band together (at least onscreen) in packs and who would prove to upstage and outgross at the box office the earlier generation of directors known as "the movie brats." The film is *The Outsiders* (1983). It is based on an S. E. Hinton novel and directed by an original movie brat, Francis Ford Coppola. It stars Emilio (*Repo Man*, 1984; *Stakeout*, 1987) Estevez, Rob (*St. Elmo's Fire*, 1985) Lowe, C. Thomas (*Soul Man*, 1986) Howell, Matt (*The Flamingo Kid*, 1984) Dillon, Ralph (*The Karate Kid*, 1984) Macchio, Patrick (*Dirty Dancing*, 1987; *Ghost*, 1990) Swayze, and Tom (*Top Gun*, 1986; *Rain Man*, 1988) Cruise. Actually, the brat-pack phenomenon begins several years earlier with the release of two films about troubled teens—Jonathan Kaplan's *Over the Edge* (1979), starring Matt Dillon and Vincent Spano; and Tim Hunter's *Tex* (1982), with Dillon, Estevez, and Meg Tilly, which is also based on an S. E. Hinton novel.

The "brat pack" expands its circle of members in films such as the sequel to *The Outsiders*, *Rumble Fish* (1983), another Hinton/Coppola effort starring Dillon, Mickey Rourke, Vincent Spano, Nicholas Cage, and Christopher Penn. It grows further with *Sixteen Candles* (1984), starring Molly Ringwald; and *The Breakfast Club* (1985), with Ringwald, Estevez, Judd Nelson, and Ally Sheedy. By the late 1980s, members of the brat pack, who had initially represented the rise of a new movement in the group performance—that is, ensemble, non-star acting—had themselves become individual stars performing in vehicles designed especially for them.

"The Brat Pack": *The Outsiders* (1983) groups together (from left to right) future teen stars Emilio Estevez, Rob Lowe, C. Thomas Howell, Matt Dillon, Ralph Macchio, Patrick Swayze, and Tom Cruise.

Courtesy of Zoetrope

THE REAGAN YEARS

"This Time Do We Get to Win?"

If the low-budget exploitation films of the late 1960s and early 1970s capture the chaotic temper of the times, then the big-budget exploitation films of the 1980s reflect the new conservatism of Reaganite America. A handful of films and filmmakers resist this reactionary tide, but, with the exception of Oliver Stone's war film *Platoon* (1986), which earned $70 million and wound up in the top-50 all-time box-office champs, they failed to match the success of the more conservative, mainstream films at the box office. For every *Platoon*, there were a couple of *Rambos* and three or four *Rockys*. As for Stone, he was the exception that proved the rule. He took film courses taught by Scorsese at NYU. He not only refused to paper over the cracks introduced into the American psyche during the 1960s and early 1970s, but also spent the 1980s with his head firmly planted in the 1960s. A Vietnam veteran, he made not only *Platoon* but also *Born on the Fourth of July* (1989). In the 1990s, he continued to look back to the dark side of the 1960s—to Jim Morrison's rise, decline, and death in *The Doors* (1991) and Kennedy's assassination in *JFK* (1991).

Rambo: First Blood Part II (1985) epitomizes the new conservatism, which is based, in part, on the desire to rewrite the recent past and put a positive face on our nation's more negative experiences. Sent on a mission to rescue American prisoners of war held captive in Southeast Asia, Sylvester Stallone's John Rambo, referring back to the original Vietnam conflict, asks his superior, "This time do we get to win?" The plot of the film is a symbolic reworking of the American right wing's perception of the war—Rambo's mission is undermined by political bureaucrats, military brass, and the CIA, who didn't want him to win. If America lost the Vietnam war back in 1975 on both the military and political fronts, Rambo won it for us in the mid-1980s, single-handedly killing hundreds of the enemy and rescuing a chopperful of American MIAs. President Ronald Reagan led the cheering section for the film. After Lebanese terrorists released 39 American hostages, Reagan declared, "I saw *Rambo* last night. I know what to do the next time this happens."

A similar sort of heroic defiance lies at the heart of the *Rocky* series (1976, 1979, 1982, 1985, 1990), though in these films it is not so much history that is being reversed as it is the fortunes of the underdog. Through hard work, exhaustive physical training, and a tenacious determination to win, Rocky Balboa's lower-class, down-and-out prizefighter battles against all odds to win fight after fight and to prove, contrary to whatever Scorsese might have suggested in *Raging Bull*, that the American dream still works. Unfortunately, as Robin Wood has suggested, this dream is bound up with certain reactionary values, including racism and sexism. White racists cheer as Rocky, the Italian Stallion, defeats Apollo Creed (Carl Weathers) for the championship in the first film; and although Rocky and Apollo become friends in subsequent films in the series, Apollo plays the acknowledgedly inferior sidekick to

Rocky's obviously superior ethnic hero. If boxing history sees Rocky's proto-type, Rocky Marciano, eclipsed by black heavyweights such as Floyd Patterson, Sonny Liston, Joe Frazier, and Muhammed Ali (on whom the character of Apollo was based), the movies reverse that chronology, making Rocky the great white hope of the 1980s.

Physical Culture: Biology as Destiny

Musclemen Stallone and Arnold Schwarzenegger emerge as the ultimate figures of male adolescent fantasy in the 1980s. These He-Men of the Universe provide a form of bodily spectacle and visual pleasure that answers the growing obsession with technology and special effects that dominate the science-fiction film. Rambo returns us to basics; he dresses like a Native American and his chief weapon is an enormous knife. With these simple tools, he takes on the superior technology of the enemy. Rocky merely uses his fists. Schwarzenegger's initial success as *Conan the Barbarian* (1982) and *Conan the Destroyer* (1984) depends, in part, upon his swordplay. And as the Terminator, Schwarzenegger comes into the world unarmed and naked, although he himself is supposedly a high-tech cyborg. Special effects enhance the *Terminator* films, but it should not go unnoticed that when Arnold finally gets to play the good guy in *Terminator 2* (1991), his Terminator is technologically inferior to (and thus more "human" than) his liquid metal antagonist. Rooted in the most rudimentary form of the celebration of the individual—the fetishization of the (male) body—the new conservatism of the 1980s elevates biology to the status of destiny. Both success and survival depend more upon physical might than political, social, or economic right. The rugged individualist rules.

ANOTHER GENERATION

The 1980s witness the advent of a new generation of filmmakers. Lucas, Spielberg, De Palma, and Scorsese continue to make films inspired, directly or indirectly, by Hollywood in its heyday. But they have been joined by a new wave of directors, screenwriters, and actors who are the products of a different cultural experience. A number of the hot new directors, including Martin (*Beverly Hills Cop*, 1984) Brest, John (*Die Hard*, 1988) McTiernan, Spike (*Do the Right Thing*, 1989) Lee, Joel (*Miller's Crossing*, 1990) Coen, Susan (*Desperately Seeking Susan*, 1985) Seidelman, Alex (*Repo Man*, 1984) Cox, Penelope (*Wayne's World*, 1992) Spheeris, and John (*Boyz N the Hood*, 1991) Singleton, went to film school. But they had not grown up, as the earlier generation of movie brats had, on the films of the 1950s, nor did their films contain extensive allusions to earlier American cinema. Indeed, they didn't have the same sort of unlimited access to old Hollywood movies enjoyed by these earlier directors. In the 1970s, commercial television had more or less abandoned old films in favor of made-for-TV movies. When this new crop of directors did pay homage to the past, they tended to cite the seminal works of their own youth, such as television sitcoms, rather than films like *The Searchers*, which their predecessors had seen a generation earlier in movie theaters. At the same time, the new generation of audiences grew up on sitcoms and made-for-TV movies rather than on the classic films of the 1950s. Their expectations of what the cinema could be tended to be radically different from those of their parents.

A spin-off of "Happy Days," which was itself a television adaptation of Lucas' *American Graffiti*, "Laverne and Shirley" becomes the source for a series of gags in films such as Spheeris' *Wayne's World*, while one of the sitcom's stars, Penny Marshall, brought her TV experience to bear on her direction of successful screen comedies such as *Big* (1988) and *A League of Their Own* (1992), and melodramas such as *Awakenings* (1990). Other young directors, such as Tim (*Batman*, 1989) Burton, Ivan (*Ghostbusters*, 1984) Reitman, James (*The Terminator*) Cameron, and Chris (*Home Alone*, 1990) Columbus, not only lack formal training in film school but also betray few, if any, classical influences on their work. By the mid-1980s, the fascination with the cinema of studio-era 1930s to 1950s Hollywood that had inspired the French New Wave and the original film school generation had dissipated. Film schools no longer produced would-be Hitchcocks, Hawkses, and Fords. They found that their students wanted to be Lucases, Spielbergs, Coppolas, and Scorseses. Hitchcock, Hawks, and Ford had all died in the 1970s, becoming "history" in the most negative sense of the term. Young filmmakers found they had little patience for the films of D. W. Griffith, F. W. Murnau, Ernst Lubitsch, Frank Capra, Ford, Hawks, or even Hitchcock, who belonged to earlier eras when films were silent, black and white, or both.

At the same time, the demands of the marketplace become more and more constrictive. Negative costs escalate and exhibition and distribution strategies become more and more geared toward the new techniques of exploitation marketing. Though everyone wanted to make a new *Citizen Kane*, they also wanted it to gross $100 million or more, make a bundle on T-shirts and tie-ins, and become immortalized by having their film transformed into a ride at Disneyland, Disney World, or Universal Studio Tours. Contemporary Hollywood stopped looking back to the past and began to look to its future—to cable television sales, video sales and rentals, network broadcasts, and syndication. In other words, filmmakers who had been raised on television began to look *through* television for their audiences. Since the great majority of the viewers of their films would see them in one form or another on the tube, more and more films began to define themselves in relation to the contemporary world of television rather than to the suddenly old-fashioned world of film. By the 1980s, the continuity of the Hollywood tradition had begun to fall apart. Each new film existed in an aesthetic vacuum, though it continued to compete with the box-office statistics of its predecessors. Audiences who expected little were enthralled by the little they got. And they had even less with which to compare. If you have never seen *Intolerance*, *Sunrise*, *Citizen Kane*, *The Searchers*, or *Vertigo*, you can't expect more than *Batman Returns*.

CREDITS: THE FILM SCHOOL GENERATION AND THEIR FILMS

American Film Institute Center (AFI) for Advanced Film Studies served as a training ground for young filmmakers such as:

Martin Brest (*Beverly Hills Cop, Midnight Run*)
Caleb Deschanel (*The Black Stallion, The Right Stuff, The Natural*)
Amy Heckerling (*Fast Times at Ridgemont High, Look Who's Talking*)
Tim Hunter (*Tex, The River's Edge*)
Jeremy Paul Kagan (*The Chosen, The Adventures of Natty Gann*)
David Lynch (*Eraserhead, The Elephant Man, Blue Velvet*)
Terrence Malick (*Badlands, Days of Heaven*)
John McTiernan (*Die Hard, Hunt for Red October*)
Tom Rickman (*Coal Miner's Daughter*)
Matthew Robbins (*The Sugarland Express, Batteries Not Included*)
Paul Schrader (*Taxi Driver, Hardcore, Mishima*)
Ed Zwick (*"Thirtysomething," Glory*)

New York University (NYU) has produced:

Joel Coen (*Blood Simple, Barton Fink*)
Jonathan Kaplan (*White Line Fever, The Accused, Unlawful Entry*)
Spike Lee (*Do the Right Thing, Jungle Fever, Malcolm X*)
Martin Scorsese (*Taxi Driver, Raging Bull, Goodfellas*)
Susan Seidelman (*Desperately Seeking Susan*)

The University of California at Los Angeles (UCLA) educated the following filmmakers:

Carroll Ballard (*The Black Stallion*)
Paul Bartel (*Eating Raoul, Scenes From the Class Struggle in Beverly Hills*)
Charles Burnett (*Killer of Sheep, To Sleep With Anger*)
Francis Ford Coppola (*The Godfather, The Conversation, Apocalypse Now*)
Alex Cox (*Sid and Nancy, Repo Man*)
Colin Higgins (*The Best Little Whorehouse in Texas, Foul Play, 9 to 5*)
Gloria Katz (*American Graffiti*)
Paul Schrader (see AFI)
Penelope Spheeris (*The Decline of Western Civilization II, Wayne's World*)

Alumni of the University of Southern California (USC) included:

Hal Barwood (*Sugarland Express*)
Ben Burtt (*Star Wars*)
John Carpenter (*Halloween, Escape From New York*)
Walter Hill (*48 Hours, The Warriors*)
Willard Huyck (*American Graffiti, Howard the Duck*)

Irwin Kershner (*The Eyes of Laura Mars, The Empire Strikes Back*)
Randal Kleiser (*Grease, The Blue Lagoon*)
Gary Kurtz (*Star Wars, The Empire Strikes Back*)
Michael Lehmann (*Heathers, Hudson Hawk*)
George Lucas (*American Graffiti, Star Wars*)
Paul Mazursky (*Bob & Carol & Ted & Alice, Down and Out in Beverly Hills*)
John Milius (*Conan the Barbarian, The Wind and the Lion*)
Walter Murch (*The Conversation, Apocalypse Now, Return to Oz*)
Kevin Reynolds (*Robin Hood: Prince of Thieves*)
John Singleton (*Boyz N the Hood*)
Robert Zemeckis (*Romancing the Stone, Back to the Future, Who Framed Roger Rabbit?*)

SELECT FILMOGRAPHY

The Last Picture Show (1971)
The Godfather (1972)
American Graffiti (1973)
The Conversation (1974)
Jaws (1975)
Assault on Precinct 13 (1976)
Carrie (1976)
Taxi Driver (1976)

Close Encounters of the Third Kind (1977)
Star Wars (1977)
Grease (1978)
Apocalypse Now (1979)
The Empire Strikes Back (1980)
Raiders of the Lost Ark (1981)

SELECT BIBLIOGRAPHY

Byron, Stuart. "Industry," *Film Comment* **16**, no. 1 (January–February 1980), 38–39.

Cagin, Seth, and Philip Dray. *Hollywood Films of the Seventies: Sex, Drugs, Violence, Rock 'n Roll and Politics.* New York: Harper & Row, 1984.

Carroll, Noel. "The Future of Allusion: Hollywood in the Seventies (and Beyond)," *October* **20** (Spring 1982): 51–81.

Corliss, Richard. "The Seventies: The New Conservatism," *Film Comment* **16**, no. 1 (January–February 1980), 34–38.

Jacobs, Diane. *Hollywood Renaissance.* Cranbury, NJ: Barnes, 1977.

Jameson, Fredric. "Postmodernism and Consumer Society," in Hal Foster, ed., *The Anti-Aesthetic.* Seattle: Bay Press, 1983.

Monaco, James. *American Film Now.* New York: Oxford University Press, 1979.

Pye, Michael, and Lynda Myles. *The Movie Brats: How the Film Generation Took Over Hollywood.* New York: Holt, 1979.

Rogin, Michael. *Ronald Reagan: The Movie.* Berkeley: University of California Press, 1987.

Von Gunden, Kenneth. *Postmodern Auteurs: Coppola, Lucas, De Palma, Spielberg and Scorsese.* Jefferson, NC: McFarland, 1991.

Wood, Robin. *Hollywood from Vietnam to Reagan.* New York: Columbia University Press, 1986.

CHAPTER 15

INTO THE 1990s: BRINGING IT ALL BACK HOME

CONTRADICTIONS: FROM THE GIPPER TO *BLUE VELVET*

The American cinema of the 1980s and early 1990s is far too recent a phenomenon for us to grasp clearly and completely. Its relationship to contemporary American experience remains obscure—in part, because that relationship is still in the process of taking shape. To some extent, films of this era convey the social, political, and cultural landscape of the Reagan/Bush and Bush/Quayle political administrations, which set a national agenda of sorts for the period 1980–1992. "Reaganite" entertainment, as the films of this period have been dubbed, is, in part, a cinema of reassurance, optimism, and nostalgia—qualities embodied in the political persona of Ronald Reagan.

As Robin Wood has argued, national traumas of the 1970s, in particular the Vietnam war and Watergate, served to undermine public confidence in the nation's leaders. Reagan attempted to restore this lost confidence. He did this, in part, by encouraging Americans to forget Watergate and to view Vietnam less as a national defeat than as a failure in American resolve to win, caused, in part, by a loss of faith in traditional American values. Reagan represented a restoration of those values. As a public figure, he evoked an earlier, more "innocent" era of American social, political, and cultural identity with which he was himself, as a former movie star, identified. As "acting" president, Reagan created for himself a political persona that was built, in part, on his earlier screen persona and, in part, on the more immediate demands of rekindling popular trust in national leadership.

His screen persona was that of the optimist; the upwardly mobile, self-made man; the war hero; the rugged yet God-fearing individualist, the Western hero who dies saving the life of his best friend; and (offscreen) the dedicated anti-Communist. As a politician, Reagan even began to play the patriarch who, like Notre Dame football coach Knute Rockne (whom Pat O'Brien played opposite Reagan's George Gipp in *Knute Rockne, All American*, 1940), could charismatically rejuvenate the spirits of all Americans by imploring them (as Reagan repeatedly did in political speeches) "to win one for the Gipper." This persona is itself a product of the pre-Vietnam, pre-Watergate 1940s and 1950s when it was constructed. Reagan, as president, automatically evoked this earlier period for most Americans who grew up with him as a Hollywood movie star. To many, Reagan symbolized the 1950s—at least, the idyllic, small-town, 1950s Eisenhower America as it existed in the popular imagination. Thus, when Marty McFly (Michael J. Fox) time-travels back to 1955 in *Back to the Future* (1985), a Ronald Reagan Western, *Cattle Queen of Montana* (1954) is playing at the small, downtown movie theater.

"Reaganite" cinema exploits many of the values and qualities that Reagan himself espoused, as well as the conservative concerns of an emerging, new right—the young, upwardly progressive, professionals—the so-called yuppies of the "me" generation. Indeed, one of the goals of Michael J. Fox (who starred as the young Republican Alex Keaton on a television sitcom, "Family Ties") in the 1950s segment of *Back to the Future* is typical of the concerns associated with the "me" generation: he serves as a matchmaker between his future mom and dad and thus ensures his own birth.

Yet, the films of the 1980s and early 1990s cannot be identified entirely in terms of the policies of one or two particular political regimes. They also embrace major liberal countercurrents that undermine the conservative thrust associated with Reagan's agenda for handling foreign policy and domestic affairs. In fact, the Reaganite cinema that dominated the early 1980s seemed to spawn an oppositional cinema that set forth a dramatically different image of America in the late 1980s. During the middle of the decade, around the time of public disclosures concerning the Iran-Contra, "guns-for-hostages" affair (1986), more and more films are being made in Hollywood that are increasingly skeptical of this Reaganite vision of America. They include films that are highly critical of life in 1980s, small-town America. Thus, David Lynch's *Blue Velvet* (1986), as well as his short-lived television series "Twin Peaks," depict a world of brutality, vice, and corruption that lie beneath the surface of everyday life in an apparently innocent and deceptively ordinary

Reaganite cinema: Adapting himself to the 1950s, Marty McFly (Michael J. Fox) does his Chuck Berry imitation at a 1955 high school dance in *Back to the Future* (1985).

Courtesy of Universal

small town in middle America. The world that his characters inhabit is inane and absurd. Tim Hunter's *River's Edge* (1986), a chillingly distanced portrait of teenagers growing up in the deadening atmosphere of contemporary American suburbs, looks at the boredom, the banality, and the selfish insensitivity that characterizes the lives of a flaked-out, younger generation of lower-middle-class Americans who are not so much heroic rebels without a cause as dysfunctional misfits without feelings.

REAGANITE CINEMA: "MORNING IN AMERICA"

Regeneration

During his presidential campaigns, Ronald Reagan attacked the pessimism of his Democratic opponents; once elected, Reagan pronounced that the long night of Democratic misrule was over and that "it's morning in America." This 1984 Republican campaign theme attempted to renew national identity and unity and tell Americans that they were about to witness a new beginning, an economic and spiritual rebirth. Reagan promised to bring America back to life, much as he himself bounced back after John Hinckley's unsuccessful attempt to assassinate him in 1981. Reagan's own recovery served as a symbolic enactment of things to come; his presidency would make the light in the nation's heart go back on, much as it did near the end of *E.T.: The Extra-Terrestrial* (1982), when the sympathetic alien miraculously recovers from apparent death.

The notions of rejuvenation and starting over inform countless films of this period. In *Cocoon* (1985), three senior citizens in their seventies (that is, about Reagan's age) accidentally discover a fountain of youth in a Florida swimming pool where aliens have stored mysterious cocoons. The film, however, ultimately criticizes their desire for an unnatural, physical youth. The secret of rejuvenation, it insists, lies not in any fountain of youth but in spiritual renewal. In 1986, wealthy businessman Rodney Dangerfield goes *Back to School* where he enjoys a second childhood while attempting to provide a role model for his wayward son.

The rejuvenation theme even finds its way into a Cold War science-fiction saga dealing with the threat of a nuclear holocaust. In *Star Trek II: The Wrath of Khan* (1982), "we" (i.e., the United States), including Admiral Kirk (William Shatner) and the crew of the starship Enterprise, battle "them" (i.e., the USSR), led by the vengeful Khan (Ricardo Montalban) who relies on Soviet-like mind-control techniques, for possession of a missile-shaped device developed by the Genesis Project. If used properly (i.e., by us) and exploded on a "dead" planet, the Genesis Effect could transform the planet into a Garden of Eden; if the device falls into the wrong hands (i.e., the Russians) and is set off on an inhabited planet, it would do the same thing, but would destroy all existing life in the process. Although Captain Spock (Leonard Nimoy) sacrifices his own life to save those of his comrades, the film concludes with a Reaganite happy ending—with the successful creation of a new world out of a barren, lifeless planet.

Nostalgia: Coming of Age in the Past

More often than not, new beginnings in Reaganite cinema involve a nostalgic return to the past in which the clock is turned back. The magic of the movies enables audiences to go back in time in an attempt to recover the small-town, affluent American paradise of the Eisenhower era, before poverty, crime, homelessness, and the demise of both the family and the community began to erode the American dream. Indeed, much of Reagan's domestic economic policy looks back to an even earlier era—to that of the Calvin Coolidge administration in the 1920s, when "the business of America was business." At any rate, a number of films, in particular the highly successful *Back to the Future* series (1985, 1989, 1990) and *Peggy Sue Got Married* (1986), feature characters who return to the golden age of the 1950s and come back to the present full of the promise and spirit of this idyllic past, reenergized and ready to confront the future.

A time warp of sorts also lies at the heart of *Field of Dreams* (1989). In this film, the hero, Ray Kinsella (Kevin Costner), responds to a mysterious, unseen voice that tells him "if you build it, he will come" and constructs a baseball field in the middle of a cornfield in 1980s Iowa. His apparently irrational behavior blindly reaffirms the essential innocence of America and Americans—in large part through his celebration of the country's national pastime, baseball. But in *Field of Dreams,* the central character doesn't go back in time. Instead, he builds the field and the past comes to him. Famous (dead) ballplayers from different decades in the past, including Shoeless Joe Jackson (Ray Liotta), gather together to play baseball on his field in the present. Yet, the effect of this particular variation on the time-travel motif remains the same—contact with the past renews the spirits of those in the present.

The pre-Vietnam era serves as the time frame for a number of more realistic 1980s films, ranging from *Diner* (1982) and *The Right Stuff* (1983) to *Stand by Me* (1986). Although the 1950s of *Diner* and *Stand by Me* is experienced primarily from below—that is, from the perspective of lower- and lower-middle-class teenagers, these films nonetheless present a nostalgic and somewhat romanticized vision of coming of age in Eisenhower America before the traumatic events of the 1960s and 1970s. Both films depict an intense male camaraderie within a disparate group of (white) boys from somewhat different ethnic and social backgrounds and, thus, reaffirm the mythic notion of an American melting pot.

Paradise Lost/Paradise Regained

The theme of innocence regained takes a variety of forms. One involves a rejection of life in the big city for that in the suburbs, in rural America, or in the untouched world of nature. During the Reagan-Bush period, the shift in population that had begun in the post–World War II years finally resulted in the creation of a new national demographic profile. For the first time in our history, more Americans lived in the suburbs than in either the city or the country. Shopping malls replaced cities as centers of American "culture." From one perspective, the suburbanization of America marks a return to small-town values. City slickers, like those in the 1991 film of the same name, find a renewed sense of community and a new, more positive sense of themselves as a result of their encounter with a more primitive, more inno- cent, rustic America.

Reworking a basic situation presented in the television series "Northern Exposure," *Doc Hollywood* (1991) exploits the urban anxieties of an ambitious young doctor who is accidentally trapped in an out-of-the-way, rural town. The doctor, played by Michael J. Fox, desperately seeks to escape this impos- sibly provincial place in order to take up a lucrative practice as a plastic surgeon in Los Angeles. The film climaxes with his ultimate discovery that he belongs in this backwoods Garden of Eden. *Return of the Jedi* (1983) concludes with the victory of the rebels over the forces of the Empire on the forest moon of Endor, where the furry Ewoks live in a utopian world of nature. The *Crocodile Dundee* films (1986, 1988) present the legendary hunter/adventurer (played by Paul Hogan) whose values have been shaped by his contact with nature and who serves, along with the globe-trotting archeologist Indiana Jones (Harrison Ford), as a paradigm for the new, masculine hero of the 1980s.

The back-to-nature drive reaches its climax in a series of more or less "liberal" films that reject the values of urban and suburban America. *Witness* (1985) and *The Mosquito Coast* (1986), for example, imagine a more innocent world—Amish Pennsylvania and the jungles of a Caribbean island—in which the hero (Harrison Ford in both films) recovers a simplicity and naivete which

Back to nature: Allie Fox (Harrison Ford), his wife (Helen Mirren), and his children (River Phoenix, Hilary Gordon, and Rebecca Gordon) abandon civilization for a remote island in the Caribbean in *The Mosquito Coast* (1986).

Courtesy of Warner Bros.

are absent in contemporary urban America. Indeed, *Mosquito Coast* emerges as an implicit indictment of the anti-environmental policies of the Reagan and Bush administration. For Ford, this return-to-innocence scenario culminates in an urban drama, *Regarding Henry* (1991), in which he plays an aggressive, cutthroat, yuppie lawyer whose near-death experience forces him to restart his life from scratch and reject his earlier behavior. In a similar vein, in *Medicine Man* (1992) Sean Connery lives in the slowly disappearing rain forests of South America, where he discovers (and loses) a cure for cancer while he also instructs research scientist Lorraine Bracco in the ways of nature, which ultimately prove more attractive than those of civilization.

The most obvious attempts by filmmakers to return to a world of nature that was responsible for bringing characters back to life or for introducing vitality into their otherwise humdrum lives can be found in films such as *Out of Africa* (1985), Danish author Isak Dinesen's semiautobiographical account of her life in Kenya in the 1910s and 1920s; *Crocodile Dundee* (1986), which juxtaposes the relative innocence of the Australian outback to the manifest decadence of New York City; *Gorillas in the Mist* (1988), which looks at anthropologist Dian Fossey's efforts to study and protect African gorillas; *Dances With Wolves* (1990), in which Kevin Costner's Lieutenant John Dunbar rejects his own, supposedly more advanced culture for that of the Sioux Indians; and *City Slickers* (1991), in which three middle-aged New Yorkers become cowhands on a cattle drive.

At the opposite end of the nature/culture spectrum, the less edifying world of the shopping mall provides a background for the narratives of a number of teen dramas, including *Fast Times at Ridgemont High* (1982), *Bill & Ted's Excellent Adventure* (1989), and *Scenes from a Mall* (1991). Though the mall can be fun, as Genghis Khan, Joan of Arc, and Beethoven discover in *Bill & Ted*, it is nonetheless a space of ultimate conformity where everyone's leisure-time activity is the same—shopping. Malls represent the rampant consumerism that drives the 1980s economy, and provide a semiautonomous setting in which the individuality of those who frequent them gives way to a dehumanizing anonymity. The love-hate relationship that mall shoppers routinely have with malls finds unique expression in these films, which both exploit and expose the shallowness of mall culture.

Striking Back

Strands of Reaganite conservatism can be found in the no-nonsense action films starring super-heroes Sylvester Stallone (in the *Rocky* and *Rambo* films) and Arnold Schwarzenegger (in the *Conan* and *Terminator* films). This ideology even crops up in the rugged individualism of less muscular types such as Paul Hogan in the *Crocodile Dundee* films (1986, 1988) and Bruce Willis in the *Die Hard* films (1988, 1990).

Even would-be antiestablishment action movies of the 1980s, such as Eddie Murphy's *Beverly Hills Cop* films (1984, 1987) and Mel Gibson's and Danny Glover's string of *Lethal Weapon* films (1987, 1989, 1992), come down firmly on the side of mainstream values. They promote law and order, interracial harmony, police camaraderie, and a celebration of the family. At the same time, they realize widely held, popular desires to strike back at what the Reagan administration identified as the chief threats to the security and well-being of 1980s America—terrorism and drug trafficking.

Of course, Murphy's comic irony and street-smart wit is worlds apart from the single-minded tenacity and straightforwardness of a Schwarzenegger or Stallone. But the fact is that the character of Axel Foley in *Beverly Hills Cop* was originally written as a part for Stallone. Though rewritten for Murphy, the role retains traces of a moral righteousness, a bitter desire for vengeance, and a brutal violence more closely associated with a Rocky or a Rambo than with a Billy Ray Valentine from *Trading Places.*

CASTLES IN THE AIR: REIMAGINING TRADITIONAL INSTITUTIONS

Having It Both Ways

In the Vietnam and Watergate era, the movies dramatize the essential hostility that underlies the relationship between individuals and the system. This earlier cinema celebrates outlaws and nonconformists, as seen in *Bonnie and Clyde* (1967), *Easy Rider* (1969), *The Wild Bunch* (1969), *Butch Cassidy and the Sundance Kid* (1969), and *One Flew Over the Cuckoo's Nest* (1975). By exposing the decadence and corruption of lifestyles in the 1980s, motion pictures reaffirm traditional populist values and proclaim their own independent status as critics of the system. The female characters in *9 to 5* (1980), for example, encounter a corrupt system in the workplace which they then make better by change from within.

In Reaganite entertainment, the system works. *Wall Street* (1987) lets us indulge our own desires for success while condemning those ruthless junk bond speculators, like Michael Douglas' Ivan Boesky-like, inside-trader Gordon Gekko. Thus, audiences can identify with Gekko's ambitious young informant, Bud Fox (Martin Sheen), who uses insider information to rise to the upper strata of the Wall Street elite. But, unlike Gekko, Fox has second thoughts about the morality of his actions; he renounces his ways, and uses his skill as a trader to help the government get the goods on his former boss. *Wall Street* demonstrates American business both at its worst and at its best, but its chief message is that the business community remains principled; it can, it will, and it does clean up its own act.

In a similar way, *Broadcast News* (1987) lets us criticize the news media, in the person of the handsome but empty-headed news anchorman, Tom Grunick (William Hurt). At the same time, we are also encouraged to appreciate those within television journalism who are either first-rate reporters, like Albert Brooks' Aaron Altman, or hotshot producers, like Holly Hunter's Jane Craig, who also criticize the network's preference for style over substance in its quest for ever-greater ratings. Because it presents the news media as its own worst critic, the film restores our faith in the essential honesty of the institution of television news as a whole. It's okay because it acknowledges its faults.

Trading Places (1983) seems to criticize the inhumanity of the Duke brothers, played by Ralph Bellamy and Don Ameche, who are Philadelphia stock futures manipulators; but the film refuses to indict the economic system that produces characters like the Dukes. The Dukes emerge as eccentric aberrations of an industry that proves to be perfectly capable of regulating itself. Thus, the film depicts as villains the Dukes, who treat both Eddie Muphy's Billy Ray Valentine and Dan Ackroyd's Louis Winthorp III quite callously. Yet, it does not condemn capitalism. Indeed, it endorses the aggressive, market-manipulating strategies of Valentine and Winthorp, who use the system to destroy the Duke brothers and, more important, to enrich themselves. It's okay for some people—for the good guys, in particular—to make a lot of money. Capitalism is not inherently evil; in fact it even has a sense of humor. What's more, the system can be "conned" by the have-nots of this world, such as a formerly homeless and impoverished black street beggar (Murphy) and a destitute blue-blood turned street person (Ackroyd). In other words, the system works; it rewards those with initiative and industry and punishes those who abuse their power and position for purely personal reasons.

Although Reaganomics did not always provide a stimulus for small business, it did promote individual enterprise. Entrepreneurial experimentation provides the background to *Risky Business* (1983), a teen comedy in which Joel Goodsen (Tom Cruise) targets admission to an Ivy League college as his goal in order to pursue a career in business. While his parents are out of town, Joel enters the world of business on the ground floor with a local corner on the world's oldest profession—prostitution. His success wins him the admiration of a college recruiter who secures his admission to Princeton. The lesson: greed and ingenuity pay, provided they are attractively packaged in the form of Tom Cruise. (In Marshall Brickman's original script, Joel doesn't get into college at the end. This downbeat conclusion was filmed and tested on preview audiences who clearly preferred a happy ending, which was then tacked onto the film.)

Being All That You Can Be

The image of another institution—the military, which had been tarnished as a result of Vietnam—undergoes both revision and glamorization in the 1980s. Films about Vietnam, such as Oliver Stone's *Platoon* (1986) and *Born on the Fourth of July* (1989) and Brian De Palma's *Casualties of War* (1989), continue to portray the insanity of the American military establishment, but non-Vietnam service films present a different face. The military is humanized somewhat when it becomes the site for comedy in *Private Benjamin* (1980) and *Stripes* (1981). In the former film, Jewish princess Goldie Hawn joins the "new" Army, which includes more and more women. And in the latter film, Bill Murray and Harold Ramis turn the Army into a fraternal organization of

Animal House types who spearhead an unauthorized invasion of Czechoslovakia.

Hot-shot pilots become something of a movie staple in the 1980s. In *An Officer and a Gentleman* (1982), audiences root for Zack Mayo (Richard Gere) in his attempt to get through the Naval Aviation Officer's Candidate School and for Debra Winger's local factory girl, whose pride prevents her from trapping an officer (Zack) into marriage and, thus, from realizing her ambition to better her lot. For the first time in decades, life in the Navy began to look attractive. *The Right Stuff* (1983) documents the early days of the space program when military and civilian pilots trained to become astronauts. Though the film looks somewhat satirically at the politics and public relations that inspired the Mercury flights and debunks the mystique of NASA's first astronauts, it also celebrates the more traditional heroism of the legendary test pilot, Chuck Yeager (Sam Shepard), who definitely has "the right stuff."

Top Gun (1986), which was filmed with the full cooperation of the Navy, emerges as the cinematic equivalent of a Navy recruitment poster. Directed by Tony Scott, who was a veteran in the field of television commercials, the film stars Tom Cruise as Maverick, a trainee in the Navy's elite Fighter Weapons School. The drama hinges around Maverick's competition with his archrival, Ice (Val Kilmer), for the coveted status of "top gun" in the squadron and around his affair with an astrophysics instructor (Kelly McGillis). Trans-

Recruitment posters: In *Top Gun* (1986), Maverick (Tom Cruise) has it all, finding adventure and romance (with Kelly McGillis) as a hot-shot pilot in the Navy's Fighter Weapons School.

Courtesy of Paramount

formed by the film into the military's equivalent of a rock star, Maverick shoots down a couple of Russian MIGs and also wins the heart of McGillis. After the film's release, the Air Force instructed its ad agency to produce commercials with the *Top Gun* look.

The restoration of public confidence in the military, which begins onscreen in revisionist celebrations of the military like *An Officer and a Gentleman* and *Top Gun,* culminates offscreen in the 1983 invasion of Grenada, which was celebrated in Clint Eastwood's *Heartbreak Ridge* (1986); the "liberation" of Panama in 1989; and the 1990–1991 Persian Gulf war with Iraq. American intervention in third-world countries is perhaps best represented in the cycle of *Indiana Jones* films, which look back to the neocolonialist spirit of turn-of-the-century Europe and the United States (a spirit remarkably captured in Spielberg's television spin-off series, "The Young Indiana Jones Chronicles"). As Peter Biskind points out, the *Indiana Jones* films celebrate "the figure of the dashing colonialist adventurer who plunders and pillages antiquities from Third World countries for First World collectors." Indy raids the jungles of South America, the mountainous wastes of Tibet, and the deserts of Egypt in search of the Ark of the Covenant in *Raiders of the Lost Ark* (1981). He visits the Far East (somewhere beyond the Himalayas) where he matches wits with Asian thuggees in *Indiana Jones and the Temple of Doom* (1984). And in *Indiana Jones and the Last Crusade* (1989), he quests after the Holy Grail in the Holy Lands of the Middle East.

Oedipus with a Happy Ending: The Return of the Father

The hidden agenda behind the Indiana Jones films, as well as that behind the *Star Wars* films; the numerous nostalgic returns to the pre-Vietnam past, from *Back to the Future* (1985) to *Dirty Dancing* (1987); the eager demonstrations that the system works in films like *Trading Places* and *Broadcast News*; and the recruiters' visions of the military that can be found in *An Officer and a Gentleman* and *Top Gun,* become clearer as the decade moves to a close and as Lucas' and Spielberg's trilogies move toward their resolutions. As Robin Wood notes, the dominant tendency of Reaganite cinema is "the restoration of patriarchal authority."

Films of the late 1960s and 1970s, ranging from *Bonnie and Clyde* (1967) and *Easy Rider* (1969) to *The Graduate* (1967) and *One Flew Over the Cuckoo's Nest* (1975), dramatize the generation gap and celebrate the defiance of authority. Nonconformist youth in *Alice's Restaurant* (1969), *Getting Straight* (1970), *Zabriskie Point* (1970), and *Hair* (1979) struggle against the system. Children in *The Graduate, A Clockwork Orange* (1971), *Badlands* (1973), *The Exorcist* (1973), and *Carrie* (1976) rebel against their parents (or against parental figures). But in the 1980s, the younger generation seeks to repair the relationship between themselves and their parents that had been ruptured in the films of the previous decade.

Most significantly, one of the chief leaders of the (1970s) rebellion against the symbolic father (the repressive Empire) in *Star Wars* (1977), Luke Skywalker (Mark Hamill), makes his peace with his father in the 1980s. In *The*

Empire Strikes Back (1980), Luke discovers that his archenemy, Darth Vader, is really his father; and in *Return of the Jedi* (1983), as Vader dies, father and son are reconciled. Thus, as the series comes to an end, Luke redeems his father, winning him back to the good side of the Force. For Spielberg, the evolution is significant. *Close Encounters of the Third Kind* (1977) looks at the inadequacy of the family, which both little children and parents (Richard Dreyfuss' Roy Neary) abandon in quest of the utopian world of the aliens. *E.T.: The Extra-Terrestrial* (1982), which is situated in a "broken" home, is all about the quest for the absent father, whose place is filled, in part, by the alien E.T. In *Indiana Jones and the Last Crusade* (1989), Indy's long-standing hostility toward his father, with whom he has not spoken in over 20 years, is put aside as the two join forces to achieve a common goal. Or, rather, they agree to give up that goal—the Holy Grail—in order to save one another.

The ritualistic nature of the restoration of the father finds its most magical expression in *Field of Dreams* (1989), in which the oedipal conflict of the 1960s and 1970s is quite literally resolved in the 1980s. Ray Kinsella (Kevin Costner), a former student activist, who left home after ridiculing his father's passion for baseball, hears voices and, as a result, compulsively builds a baseball diamond in the middle of an Iowa cornfield. Soon, his dead father's favorite baseball players from the past show up, like Shoeless Joe Jackson (Ray Liotta), and begin to play ball on the field. Meanwhile, Ray hunts down his own alternate father figure, black activist writer Terence Mann (James Earl Jones), and brings him back to Iowa where black and white, radical and conservative, and father and son resolve their differences by playing baseball together. (Of course, none of the legendary ballplayers who play on the field of dreams are black, a fact which undermines Mann's stirring speech at the end about baseball and the American dream). In the final scene of the film, Ray plays a game of catch with his father, who has come back as a young catcher in his twenties. In this way, the film symbolically effects a reconciliation between

Fathers and sons: (*a*) Indiana Jones (Harrison Ford, right) and his father (Sean Connery) embark on a joint quest for the Holy Grail in *Indiana Jones and the Last Crusade* (1989). (*b*) Ray Kinsella (Kevin Costner, right) is reconciled with his dead father (Dwier Brown) on the *Field of Dreams* (1989).

(a)   *(b)*

the older and younger generations that Vietnam and other social, political, and cultural issues had previously cast into opposite camps.

As Wood and Britton note, a surprising number of films from this period have, as their central project, the reaffirmation of the father. In several films, including *Kramer vs. Kramer* (1979), *Ordinary People* (1980), *3 Men and a Baby* (1987), and *Boyz N the Hood* (1991), this restoration of the father takes place at the expense of the mother, who either abandons or otherwise gives up her children and leaves them to the father or to other males. Father figures, including trainers such as Burgess Meredith's Mickey in the *Rocky* films, Yoda and Obi-Won Kenobi in the *Star Wars* films, and Pat Morita's Mr. Miyagi in *The Karate Kid* films (1984, 1986, 1989); or mentors such as Christopher Lloyd's Dr. Emmett Brown in the *Back to the Future* films or Jones' Terence Mann in *Field of Dreams,* serve as crucial agents for change, providing the necessary stimulus for heroes to realize their goals and desires.

Films of the 1980s regularly deal with the melodramatics of family relations, with the (attempted) reconstitution of the nuclear family. *Terms of Endearment* (1983) explores the love-hate relationship between a domineering mother (Shirley MacLaine) and her independent-minded daughter (Debra Winger), who rediscover their affection for one another as they both grow older. In a reworking of *Terms of Endearment, Nothing in Common* (1986) explores a similar relationship between a father (Jackie Gleason) and his somewhat distant son (Tom Hanks), who have even less in common than MacLaine and Winger. In 1988, the reunification of separated brothers serves as the basis for the melodramatic comedy of *Rain Man* and for the more improbable comedy of *Twins,* in which Arnold Schwarzenegger and Danny DeVito play twins separated at birth. The family melodrama also provides a vehicle for the representation of more unconventional female characters. In *A League of Their Own* (1992), which deals with the creation of the short-lived, All-American Girls Professional Baseball League, highly competitive sisters, played by Geena Davis and Lori Petty, battle with one another for recognition as athletes. They eventually go their separate ways, but the film climaxes with their emotional reconciliation years later.

Parents and Babies: A Wide Spectrum

The obsession of recent cinema with questions of family comes as no surprise. During the late 1970s and 1980s, the baby boomers began to have babies themselves. Parenting, whether conventional (i.e., by married, heterosexual couples) or unconventional (i.e., by single parents, unmarried couples, homosexual couples), becomes one of the dominant experiences of the post-Vietnam, post-Watergate era of national recuperation. The cycle begins with *Kramer vs. Kramer* (1979), in which Dustin Hoffman, abandoned by his wife, learns how to become a father to his six-year-old son. This semimelodramatic scenario is comically reworked more than a decade later—in *Hero* (1992), which also features Hoffman's attempts to be a good father to his estranged son. In between these two works lies an astounding spectrum of parenting situations. *Baby Boom* (1987) deals with a workaholic management consultant, J. C. Wiatt (Diane Keaton), who inherits a twelve-month-old baby from her cousin, who dies in a traffic accident. Like Hoffman in *Kramer,* her attempts to be a good mother come at the cost of her career at a high-powered public relations firm, but inadvertently lead her into another career, making and bottling baby food.

One of the subplots of Lawrence Kasdan's nostalgic requiem for the 1960s, *The Big Chill* (1983), involves a thirtysomething, unmarried corporate lawyer, Meg (Mary Kay Place), who is racing against her own biological clock and who wants to have a baby, fathered, if possible, by one of her former college friends. In *3 Men and a Baby* (1987), a six-month-old baby girl is left on the doorstep of three bachelors, played by Tom Selleck, Steve Guttenberg, and Ted Danson. This national obsession with getting kids finds its wackiest expression in Joel and Ethan Coen's parody of the parental urge, *Raising Arizona* (1987). In this tongue-in-cheek comedy, a small-time crook (Nicholas Cage) and his parole officer/wife (Holly Hunter) are unable to have children so they kidnap a baby from a couple who just had quintuplets.

A string of films about parenting were released in 1988, including *She's Having a Baby* and *The Good Mother.* After the notoriety of the Baby M case, Jonathan Kaplan gave us *Immediate Family* (1989), a film about a childless couple in Seattle who contract with a pregnant teenager to adopt her baby. Amy Heckerling's *Look Who's Talking* (1989) and *Look Who's Talking Too* (1990)

Parenting: Peter (Tom Selleck, left) and Michael (Steve Guttenberg) fill in as fathers in *3 Men and a Baby* (1987).

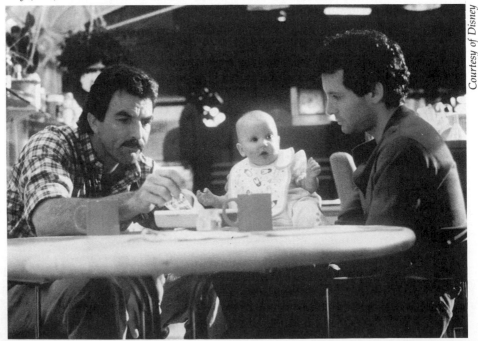

Courtesy of Disney

detail the adventures in parenting of an unwed mother (Kirstie Alley) and the New York cabby (John Travolta) who drives her to the hospital and sticks around to help her out with raising her son (whose voice is provided by Bruce Willis).

Former child star, now director, Ron Howard explores somewhat more conventional family structures in *Parenthood* (1989), which stars Steve Martin as a comically conscientious family man who tries to become the father he never had. His costar, Rick Moranis, follows in Martin's footsteps, playing a comic inventor who accidentally changes the size of his family in a pair of extremely successful family comedies, *Honey, I Shrunk/Blew Up the Kids* (1989, 1992). At the same time, two *Home Alone* films (1990, 1992), which play upon parental nightmares involving lost children and look at the remarkable survival skills of contemporary kids, have proven to be phenomenal hits among preteen, teen, and post-teen viewers at the box office. Meanwhile, the baby boom runs rampant on television, which clogs the airwaves with family sitcoms featuring cute little kids, such as "Full House," the short-lived "Baby Talk," and "Baby Boom"; cute young kids, such as "The Wonder Years," "Doogie Howser," and "Blossom"; and a variety of cute family situations, ranging from single mothers ("Kate and Allie"), single fathers ("Full House"), and heterosexual "arrangements" ("Who's the Boss?") to more traditional nuclear families ("The Cosby Show," "Roseanne," and "The Simpsons").

COUNTERCURRENTS

Martin Scorsese: Against the Grain

The Reagan-Bush years do feature a number of filmmakers and films that undermine the feel-good, happy-ending cinema of America in the 1980s. As noted in the previous chapter, Martin Scorsese's films lack the optimism, reassurance, and box-office grosses of the era's blockbusters, and continue to go against the dominant grain. *Raging Bull* (1980) deconstructs the cult of male machismo which Stallone had fostered through his highly successful celebrations of the Rocky character's come-from-behind victories against superior opponents. Robert De Niro's Jake La Motta emerges as a brutally violent, physically abusive, self-destructive "hero" whose success in the ring is ironically framed by his subsequent attempts to exploit that image in his act as a nightclub entertainer.

The King of Comedy (1983) inverts the return-of-the-father scenario, which runs through so many films of the Reagan-Bush era, by focusing upon oedipal conflict that remains unresolved. As would-be TV comic Rupert Pupkin, Robert De Niro both loves and hates a father figure, the comic, late-night television host Jerry Langford, who is played by real-life, substitute host for the Johnny Carson show, Jerry Lewis. Rupert overthrows the father, kidnapping Jerry and taking his place on TV, but his victory is brief for he is eventually caught and sent to jail. Though he has achieved fame of sorts,

Rupert is reduced at the end of the film to the status of a freak whose celebrity derives primarily from his notoriety in the media rather than from his talents as a stand-up comic.

Scorsese looks at the dark side of the American dream in *After Hours* (1985), *The Color of Money* (1986), and *Goodfellas* (1990). He explores and calls into question the process of mythmaking in *The Last Temptation of Christ* (1988), in which Christ, doubting that he is *the* Christ, undergoes the same sort of identity crisis experienced by Travis Bickle, Jake La Motta, Henry Hill, and other Scorsese heroes. Even *Cape Fear* (1991), Scorsese's most popular film in terms of the box-office, portrays a nightmare vision of middle America, in which a yuppie lawyer (Nick Nolte) and his somewhat dysfunctional family are terrorized by a former convict, Max Cady (Robert De Niro), who is a demonic embodiment of all the violence and sexuality which mainstream Reaganite cinema attempts to hold in check.

At the same time, Scorsese's earlier films—in particular, *Mean Streets* (1973)—and other offbeat films of the 1970s continue to inspire a number of younger filmmakers whose work combines a similar interest in violent exploitation genres and independently made art cinema. For example, Ethan and Joel Coen's *Blood Simple* (1984), like *Mean Streets,* looks back, but in a decidedly more self-conscious way, to the themes and visual style of film noir, while ironically transposing Scorsese's vision of violent urban relationships to the unlikely, wide-open spaces of Texas. It also captures the visual look and eccentric narrative perspective of Terrence Malick's philosophically meditative *Badlands* (1973). *Miller's Crossing* (1990), released the same year as *Goodfellas,* also explores the inner workings of the mob, but the story is again transposed from an urban setting to a midwestern no-man's-land that resembles the Personville of Dashiell Hammett's proto-noir, hardboiled novel *Red Harvest.* And, unlike The Scorsese film (or Coppola's *Godfather* films), it gives the gangster genre an existential twist. For the Coens, traditional genres and audience expectations about genre serve as the background against which they can perform their surfacy, postmodernist reworkings of conventions.

As Jim Hoberman points out, both Nick Gomez's *Laws of Gravity* (1992) and Quentin Tarantino's *Reservoir Dogs* (1992) look back to the disturbing, noncathartic verbal and visual violence that becomes Scorsese's trademark in films such as *Mean Streets. Laws of Gravity* documents life in the world of two small-time Brooklyn crooks, second cousins to Scorsese's Charlie (Harvey Keitel) and Johnny Boy (Robert De Niro). *Reservoir Dogs,* which stars a familiar Scorsese icon, Harvey Keitel (as well as Tim Roth, Steve Buscemi, Chris Penn, Michael Madsen, and Lawrence Tierney), and which reworks an old Stanley Kubrick film, *The Killing* (1956), deals with the violent aftermath of a failed robbery in a way that recalls the intensity of early Scorsese films.

The Gay New Wave

Minorities have consistently been represented either marginally or not at all in Hollywood films. During the 1980s, however, a handful of minority filmmakers began making films that enjoyed both critical acclaim and (limited) success at the box-office. There has always been a gay underground, but during the postwar era, it becomes increasingly prominent, especially in the "Beat" movement and, in particular, in the poetry of Allen Ginsberg. By the 1980s, it has finally broken into the mainstream. Elements of underground movies of the 1960s by gay filmmakers, such as Jack Smith, Andy Warhol, and George Kuchar, crop up in what Hoberman refers to as the "queer" cinema of Gus Van Sant's *Drugstore Cowboy* (1989) and *My Own Private Idaho* (1991), Todd Haynes's *Poison* (1991), Tom Kalin's *Swoon* (1992), and Gregg Araki's *The Living End* (1992). The notion of "queer cinema" refers to a deliberately oppositional stance that certain gay filmmakers take toward conventional Hollywood cinema. In *Idaho*, which is a male hustler's version of Shakespeare's *Henry IV, Part I,* Van Sant combines fantasy sequences, à la Smith's *Flaming Creatures*, with the road exploits of his two *Easy Rider*-like heroes.

Poison interweaves three unrelated stories—or, as Haynes puts it, "three tales of [homoerotic] transgression and punishment." One tale takes the shape of a documentary interview with a woman who tells how her seven-year-old son murdered his father and then magically flew off out a second-story bathroom window. Another, cast in the form of a science-fiction thriller, follows a scientist who experiments upon himself and then turns into a leprous serial killer. The third, set in a prison, involves a sadomasochistic

Dr. Graves (Larry Maxwell) distills the sex drive, a formula which will later accidentally transform him into the Leper Sex Killer, as a female admirer, Dr. Olson (Susan Norman), looks on in *Poison* (1991).

Courtesy of Zeitgeist

relationship between two male prisoners. Set in the 1920s, *Swoon* redrama-tizes the real-life Richard Leob and Nathan Leopold affair, detailing how the homosexual couple kidnap and murder a young boy, and exploring the general public's homophobic reaction to their crime over the course of their subsequent trial and execution.

Spike Lee: Into the Mainstream

Somewhat less marginalized in terms of their status within the film industry than these homosexual filmmakers, a number of black directors moved from the fringes of independent filmmaking to the mainstream of commercial cinema during the 1980s and 1990s. NYU graduate Spike Lee won critical success with his first feature, *She's Gotta Have It* (1986), and soon found financial support for his projects from major studios such as Universal, which distributed *Do the Right Thing* (1989) and *Jungle Fever* (1991), and Warner Bros., which handled *Malcolm X* (1992). Lee can be credited with preparing the stage for the rise of a new generation of black filmmakers in the 1980s and 1990s, including John Singleton (*Boyz N the Hood*, 1991; *Poetic Justice*, 1993), Mario Van Peebles (*New Jack City*, 1991), and Lee's own cameraman, Ernest Dickerson (*Juice*, 1992).

Driven by desire: Spike Lee's *She's Gotta Have It* (1986).

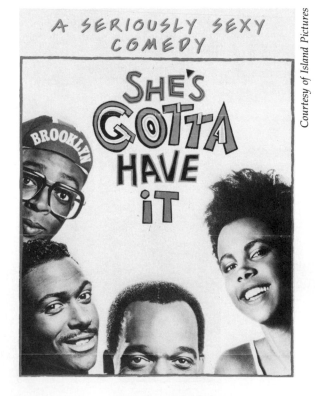

Courtesy of Island Pictures

Lee prefaces *Gotta Have It* with a quote from Zora Neale Hurston that distinguishes between the desires of men and women, concluding that the dreams of men are "mocked to death by time," but that the dreams of women are "the truth." Lee's central character is Nola Darling (Tracy Camilla Johns), whose birthday is the same as that of Malcolm X.

Lee's films are all about desire. In *Gotta Have It*, his central character learns that she can't have it all, that she must make painful choices, grow up, and give up the pleasures of the status quo in favor of a commitment to one of her three male lovers. By the same token, in *Do the Right Thing* (1989) Mookie (Spike Lee) finally discovers that he cannot continue to play the field, juggling his obligations to his Italian boss, Sal (Danny Aiello), to his former girlfriend, Tina (Rosie Perez), and to the racially tense, black community of Bedford-Stuyvesant. At the end of the film, he commits to his community. Reacting to the death of a friend at the hands of the police, he leads a neighborhood riot against the local pizza shop where he works for Aiello, subscribing to the violence preached by Malcolm X rather than to the passive nonviolence prescribed by Martin Luther King.

Like Spike Lee, NYU film student Susan Seidelman successfully combined the techniques of independent and commercial cinema in her second feature, *Desperately Seeking Susan* (1985; her first film, *Smithereens*, 1982, remained largely an underground classic). Seidelman provides a portrait of suburban society and its stifling effects upon a middle-class New Jersey housewife, Roberta (Rosanna Arquette). Intrigued by a personal advertisement "desperately seeking Susan," Roberta is drawn to New York's lower east side, where she develops a case of amnesia and lives the more liberated and adventurous life of Susan (Madonna). Though her memory is ultimately restored, by the end of the film she realizes the she can now never return to her former existence as a yuppie housewife.

Jim Jarmusch and Julie Dash: On the Fringe

Not all independent filmmakers of the 1980s move into the mainstream. Another NYU graduate, Jim Jarmusch, who directed *Stranger Than Paradise* (1984), *Down By Law* (1986), *Mystery Train* (1989), and *Night on Earth* (1991), continues to work on the fringes of the film industry. Though his films rely upon story and character, his narrative exposition remains minimal. Things happen to one set of characters, then they or similar things happen again to a different set of characters. Thus, in *Down By Law*, a New Orleans pimp, Jack (John Lurie), is set up by his enemies and sent to jail; then a local drunk, Zack (Tom Waits), is framed for a murder and winds up in the same cell as Jack. They escape, along with another cell mate, only to find themselves hiding out in a room that looks exactly like their former prison cell.

Often, as in *Down By Law* and *Mystery Train*, a foreigner observes what takes place, providing a somewhat estranged perspective on the proceedings. Roberto (Roberto Benigni), an Italian who speaks only broken English, plays this role in *Law*. This alien perspective resembles that of the director himself, who looks on bemusedly at the absurdity of the narrative conventions that

Julie Dash, director of *Daughters of the Dust* (1991).

govern most Hollywood films. Thus, Roberto comments, after they make good their miraculous jailbreak, that it was "just like they do in American movies."

Daughters of the Dust (1991), one of the more successful independent films of the early 1990s, provides new models for independent filmmaking. It gives a voice to a group that has traditionally been either unrepresented or misrepresented in mainstream cinema—black women. But it also made money, earning more than $1.6 million and remaining on *Variety's* list of top-grossing films for over 30 weeks. As Jacqueline Bobo points out, Julie Dash's film was promoted by a dedicated group of two black women and one black man, who publicized it by direct mailings to black churches and social organizations, black radio and television stations, and black newspapers. In other words, the film did not just find its audience—an audience was found for it.

Set at the turn of the century, *Daughters of the Dust* looks at an African-American family living on an island off the coast of the southern United States on the eve of its departure for the North. The narrative examines the unique world of the Gullah, the people who inhabit the island, and lovingly observes their customs, many of which will be left behind when they leave the island. Like the photographer in the film, *Daughters of the Dust*, which takes the shape of a family album, functions as a means of recording a cultural memory, reconstructing it out of a world that has long since disappeared and transmitting it to a new generation of viewers.

HOME ALONE WITH HOME VIDEO

The Cable Revolution

While a handful of filmmakers worked on the fringe, more and more film viewers moved the mainstream experience of film-"going" to a new center—the home. At the same time, more and more films begin to bear the stamp of these dramatic changes that take place in the field of home entertainment.

In 1975, Home Box Office (which commenced its operations in 1972) began transmitting recent motion pictures and other entertainment programs via satellite to cable subscribers. HBO thus introduced a "premium" service that augmented the "basic" cable service, which for several decades had enjoyed a marginal existence by supplying network programming to customers with poor reception in out-of-the-way places.

In 1977, Ted Turner followed HBO's example, relying upon satellite transmission to expand the audience for his "superstation," TBS, which broadcast older movies, sporting events, and other shows. Shortly thereafter, Showtime (1978) and The Movie Channel (1979) entered the home movie channel marketplace, joining forces in 1983.

VCRs and Couch Potatoes

1975 also witnessed the mass marketing of another home video technology, which transformed the face of the entertainment industry—the VCR, or videocassette recorder. In November 1975, Sony introduced the Betamax, which could record television programs off the air; about a year later, another Japanese company, Matsushita, began selling a home-recording machine that used a noncompatible VHS, or video home system, format. By the mid-1980s, basic and premium cable television were reaching over 40 million households and over 30 million households had VCRs. Between 1983 and 1986, a home-video rental market exploded, as dealers around the country began to rent prerecorded videocassettes, which they had purchased from the Hollywood studios, to customers, who watched them at home on their VCRs.

The sale and rental of prerecorded videocassettes (which consisted mostly of movies and a few self-help, i.e., workout, tapes) climbed from approximately $4 billion in 1986 to roughly $11 billion in 1992. During the same period, theatrical box-office receipts rose from $3.75 billion to roughly $5 billion; thus, home video now brings in more than twice the amount of money generated by theatrical exhibitors.

Home video not only initiated a new form of distribution; it also created a new mass audience—the home viewer. By the end of 1992, 98 percent of all American homes had television sets and 78 percent possessed VCRs. The motion picture industry began, in turn, to court this home audience, making films that appealed to it as well as to the loyal audience of moviegoers who regularly went to see movies in theaters. Roughly 35 to 40 percent of *theater* audiences consisted of teenagers and two-thirds were between the ages of 12 and 29. For these age groups, violent action pictures (like the *Indiana Jones*, Arnold Schwarzenegger, Sylvester Stallone, *Beverly Hills Cop, Star Wars, Die Hard*, and *Lethal Weapon* films) continued to serve as highly attractive vehicles, combining adventurous male heroes with spectacular action and special-effects sequences.

But these films also appealed to a somewhat older audience, aged 29 to 39, who constituted yet another 18 percent of the regular movie-going audience but who also subscribed to cable, owned VCRs, and rented tapes. This older audience had grown up on the "event cinema" of Steven Spielberg and George Lucas in the 1970s; in the mid-1980s, they began to bring that "event cinema" home to watch on TV. More important, the generation of young producers, directors, and screenwriters who led the film school generation in its friendly takeover of the film industry in the 1970s were themselves growing older, having families, and, as we have already seen, making films about families.

Movie-"Going"

The advent of the home audience transformed traditional theatrical exhibition in three significant ways. It virtually eliminated second-run theaters, repertory cinemas, and porno houses (though a handful of repertory houses, such as New York's Film Forum, continue to thrive in the nation's largest cities and one or two porno houses still show X-rated videos). After a film's initial release, it no longer played a subsequent run in cheaper neighborhood theaters but went directly into video distribution, finding its next audience on premium cable channels and in video rental outlets. Revival houses were unable to compete with video stores, which made older films available to home viewers virtually whenever they wanted to see them. Meanwhile, the porno industry converted almost entirely to tape, providing X-rated films that customers could view in the privacy of their own homes—that is, in a more congenial atmosphere than ever before.

Even for theatrical audiences, the experience of going to the movies became less and less distinct from watching them at home on television. The size of movie theaters and of movie screens, especially in multiplexes and mall cinemas, grew smaller and smaller. Audiences, shaped by the conditions of the home viewing experience, began more and more frequently to talk during movies, providing the sort of play-by-play commentary on the on-screen action characteristic of television sports announcers. Ironically, movie-"going" in the 1990s recalls that of the 1890s, when members of the audience watched films individually on the minuscule, peep-show screen of Edison's Kinetoscope, as well as that of the nickelodeon era (ca. 1905), when spectators looked at movies in small storefront theaters which were about the size of some of today's smaller multiplexes. Of course, contemporary multiplexes tend to provide better, cleaner surroundings than did storefront nickelodeons (as well as state-of-the-art sound systems), but they lack the sense of showmanship associated with the neighborhood theaters of the

Courtesy of Universal

The future lies with video: Max Renn (James Woods) get hooked on cable in the 1983 horror classic *Videodrome*.

1930s, 1940s, and 1950s. The days of the movie palace, when going to the movies was as much of a unique experience as the movie itself, are clearly over.

For better or worse, the future of the movies lies with cable and video. The advent of pay-per-view cable, which can provide its customers with four or five films five or six times a day, may eventually eliminate the neighborhood video store. At-home audiences can order the film they want, when they want to see it, and simply be billed for it along with their monthly cable charges. This form of distribution has an obvious appeal to Hollywood studios, who would retain greater control over their own product and would enjoy a steady flow of rental income from films that are now sold outright to video rental stores.

In years to come, more and more films will be shot using high-definition television (HDTV) cameras, which many engineers insist will produce images equivalent to those of 35mm motion picture film. In the home, HDTV television sets will display widescreen images that are several feet high and roughly $1^3/_4$ times wider than they are high.

Much as the advent of the movies did not destroy the theater and that of television did not destroy the movies, the rise of home video is unlikely to kill off the movies. Indeed, industry analysts note that more Americans are watching movies today than they have since the 1950s—largely because home video has extended the potential audience for movies and now reaches those viewers who lost the movie-going habit in the postwar era.

The movies—that is, motion pictures projected on a screen for mass audiences in theaters—will undoubtedly survive as a popular entertainment experience. But they will just as certainly differ from movies of the past in significant ways because of the new life they have found in home video. The movies have survived for over 100 years, in part, because they have satisfied the demands of an ever-changing mass audience, whose initial need for its own form of mass-produced entertainment brought the movies into being and whose continuing need for amusement governs the transformations in the movies and in the movie-going experiences that are described in this book.

SELECT FILMOGRAPHY

Kramer vs. Kramer (1979)
The Empire Strikes Back (1980)
Ordinary People (1980)
Raging Bull (1980)
Raiders of the Lost Ark (1981)
E.T.: The Extra-Terrestrial (1982)
An Officer and a Gentleman (1982)
Star Trek II: The Wrath of Khan (1982)
The Big Chill (1983)
The King of Comedy (1983)
Return of the Jedi (1983)
Trading Places (1983)
Beverly Hills Cop (1984)
Blood Simple (1984)
Back to the Future (1985)
Desperately Seeking Susan (1985)
Blue Velvet (1986)

Down By Law (1986)
Peggy Sue Got Married (1986)
River's Edge (1986)
She's Gotta Have It (1986)
Top Gun (1986)
Baby Boom (1987)
Broadcast News (1987)
Raising Arizona (1987)
3 Men and a Baby (1987)
Wall Street (1987)
Rain Man (1988)
Twins (1988)
Bill & Ted's Excellent Adventure (1989)
Do the Right Thing (1989)
Field of Dreams (1989)
Parenthood (1989)
Daughters of the Dust (1991)
Poison (1991)
Laws of Gravity (1992)
Medicine Man (1992)
Reservoir Dogs (1992)

SELECT BIBLIOGRAPHY

Biskind, Peter. "Blockbuster: The Last Crusade," in Mark Crispin Miller, ed., *Seeing Through Movies*. New York: Pantheon, 1990.

Bobo, Jacqueline. *Credible Witness: Black Women, Film Theory, Spectatorship*. New York: Columbia University Press, 1994.

Britton, Andrew. "Blissing Out: The Politics of Reaganite Entertainment," *Movie* **31/32** (1984).

Brodie, Douglas. *The Films of the Eighties*. New York: Citadel Press, 1990.

Combs, James E. *American Political Movies: An Annotated Filmography of Feature Films*. New York: Garland, 1990.

Gomery, Douglas. *Shared Pleasures: A History of Movie Presentation in the United States*. Madison: University of Wisconsin Press, 1992.

Hoberman, Jim. "Back on the Wild Side," *Premiere* (August 1992).

———. "Out and Inner Mongolia," *Premiere* (October 1992).

O'Brien, Tom. *The Screening of America: Movies and Values from Rocky to Rain Man.* New York: Continuum, 1990.

Prince, Stephen. *Visions of Empire: Political Imagery in Contemporary American Film.* New York: Praeger, 1992.

Rogin, Michael Paul. *Ronald Reagan, the Movie, and Other Episodes in Political Demonology.* Berkeley: University of California Press, 1987.

Ryan, Michael, and Douglas Kellner. *Camera Politica: The Politics and Ideology of Contemporary Hollywood Film.* Bloomington: Indiana University Press, 1988.

Wood, Robin. "80s Hollywood: Dominant Tendencies," *CineAction*, no. 1 (Spring 1985).

———. *Hollywood from Vietnam to Reagan.* New York: Columbia University Press, 1986.

GLOSSARY OF TECHNICAL AND OTHER TERMS

Academy ratio The shape of the image projected on a screen or, more accurately, the aspect ratio or ratio of the width to height of the projected image as it was standardized (at 1.37:1) by the Academy of Motion Picture Arts and Sciences circa 1930. See also *Aspect ratio*.

Anamorphic lens A special lens used for filming and projecting widescreen images. The anamorphic lens in a camera records a wide, panoramic field of view onto standard 35mm film by compressing the image in the horizontal plane. In the theater, an anamorphic projection lens unsqueezes this compressed image, spreading it across a theater screen to produce an image with an aspect ratio of 2.35:1. See also *CinemaScope* and *Panavision*.

Art direction The designing and building of the studio sets and the selection of nonstudio locations on which a film will be shot. Also called "set design."

Aspect ratio The ratio of width to height of the projected image. Before 1930, the standard aspect ratio of silent films was 1.33:1; that is, the width of the projected image was 1.33 times that of its height, resulting in a somewhat rectangular image. The 1930 Academy ratio, which remained a standard until 1953, was, at 1.37:1, more or less identical to the silent film aspect ratio. Starting with Cinerama in 1952, which featured a 2.77:1 aspect ratio, American films were filmed and/or projected in a variety of more or less extremely rectangular, widescreen formats, ranging from 1.66:1 (VistaVision) to 2.35:1 (CinemaScope) and 2.77:1. The current American widescreen standards are 1.85:1, 2.21.1 (70mm), and 2.35:1 (anamorphic Panavision). See also *Academy ratio*.

B films Quickly made motion pictures, usually produced to fill the second half of a double bill that also features an A film. B films generally have a budget (and a running time) that is significantly less than that of A films.

Back light Light used to illuminate the space between characters and their backgrounds to separate the characters from their backgrounds. See also *Three-point lighting*.

Biopic A biographical film based on the life of a famous historical figure. This genre is generally associated with studios such as 20th Century-Fox (*Young Mr. Lincoln*, 1939) and Warner Bros. (*The Life of Emile Zola*, 1937) during the 1930s and 1940s, though other studios also made biopics and the genre survives today (*Malcolm X*, Warner Bros., 1992).

Blaxploitation films A term coined by *Variety* to describe a series of Hollywood genre films made in the early 1970s, featuring black performers, that were produced for a black audience.

Blind bidding A distribution system in which exhibitors are forced to contract for the rental of films prior to seeing them.

Block booking A distribution system in which exhibitors are forced to contract for the rental of groups of (two or more) films in order to secure the permission to exhibit any one film distributed by a particular studio.

Cable television A system for the transmission of television signals that uses cable wires or fiber optics instead of radio waves broadcast through the air.

Camera angle The angle at/from which the camera looks at the action. In a low-angle shot, the camera looks up from below at the action. In a high-angle shot, the camera looks down from above at the action. In an eye-level shot, the camera looks at the action head-on, from a position that is chest or head high.

Camera distance The relative distance of the camera from the action being filmed, e.g., extreme close-up, close-up, medium shot, long shot, and so on. The scale upon which the distance is measured is generally that of the human body. (The content of the shots need not be restricted to human or even animate forms. Each film will establish its own scale of distances, depending, in part, upon the subject matter of the film.) Thus, an extreme close-up presents only a portion of the face. A close-up frames the entire head, hand, foot, or other object. Medium close-ups give a chest-up view of individuals, as seen in most sequences in which two characters converse with one another, while medium shots tend to show the body from the waist up. Shots of characters that frame them from the knees up are referred to as medium long shots, while long shots range from full-figure images of characters, to inclusion of some of the surrounding space immediately above and below them. In extreme long shots, the human body is overwhelmed by the setting within which it is placed, as in Westerns in which distant figures are seen as specks in a larger landscape.

Camera movement The physical movement of the camera, either through its rotation on an axis (that is, a pan or tilt shot) or through its movement on a track, a dolly, a crane, or other movable camera support. See also *Crane shot, Dolly shot, Pan, Tilt*, and *Tracking shot*.

CinemaScope A widescreen process, developed in 1953 by 20th Century-Fox, that relies on an anamorphic camera lens to squeeze a panoramic view onto standard 35mm film and an anamorphic projection lens to display the original view on a theater screen, producing an image with an aspect ratio of 2.35:1. The system was initially accompanied by four-track, magnetic stereo sound. See also *Aspect ratio*.

Cinerama A widescreen process, independently developed and introduced in 1952, that employs three interlocked cameras to record a wide, panoramic view on three separate strips of 35mm motion picture film. In the theater, three interlocked projectors projected the three film strips side by side on a deeply curved screen. This projection produced an aspect ratio of 2.77:1. A separate strip of film carried the stereo magnetic sound, which consisted of six tracks that supplied sound to five speakers behind the screen and additional surround speakers, and a seventh track which was used to control the other six. See also *Aspect ratio*.

Classical Hollywood cinema A mode of production associated with American cinema that involves certain narrative and stylistic practices. Narratives are structured around characters who have specific, clearly defined goals and deal with their triumph over various obstacles that stand in the way of the attainment of those goals. These narratives are presented in a manner that is both as efficient and as (stylistically) invisible as possible.

Close-up An image in which the size of the object shown is relatively large. See also *Camera distance*.

Continuity editing A system of editing that attempts to create the illusion of temporal and spatial coherence, unity, and/or continuity. It relies on the *180-degree rule*, the *Shot/reverse shot*, and various matches.

Costume design The style or design of the clothing to be worn by the actors and actresses who appear in a film.

Crane shot A moving shot in which the camera, mounted on a crane, rises and/or descends as it views the action.

Crosscutting A form of editing that involves cutting back and forth between two or more separate scenes. See also *Parallel editing*.

Cut A simple break in the film where two shots are joined together. In *Rear Window* (1954), there is a cut from James Stewart looking to a shot of what he sees (Miss Torso).

Deep focus A style of filming that relies upon a wide-angle lens, coated lenses (lenses that have been treated with a special substance that enables them to transmit more light), fast film (i.e., film that is more sensitive to light and thus requires less exposure time than "slow" film), and powerful illumination to produce an image that possesses extreme depth of field (that is, in which the extreme foreground and extreme background appear in sharp focus). See also *Depth of field*.

Depth of field The range in front of an individual lens within which objects will appear in sharp focus. Depending upon the focal length of the lens used, this range of sharp focus will be shallow, moderate, or deep.

Diegetic sound   Sound which comes from the world depicted in the film, including dialogue, sound effects, and music (from radios, record players, or other onscreen sources). This sound is produced within the space of the film and can be (or could be) heard by any characters who inhabit that space. *Diegetic sound* is to be distinguished from *nondiegetic sound*.

Dissolve   A fluid form of shot transition that involves fading out on one shot while simultaneously fading in on another; for a brief moment, at the midpoint of the dissolve, both images will be visible on the screen at the same time.

Dolly shot   A shot in which the camera, mounted on a mobile platform or camera support with wheels, moves in any of a variety of different directions parallel to the floor.

Editing   A process that involves the selection of images (in the form of unedited takes or shots) and sounds for subsequent inclusion in the film and the assemblage of this material to produce a finished film. Though some editing occurs during *production*, the bulk of a film's editing takes place during the *postproduction* stage. Editing also refers to the sequence of shots in the finished film.

Establishing shot   A shot that functions to present the spatial parameters within which the subsequent action of a scene takes place or otherwise introduce a scene.

Eye-level shot   See *Camera angle*.

Eye-line matching   This feature of continuity editing involves two shots in which a character in the first shot looks offscreen at another character or object. The next shot then shows what that character is looking at from a position that reflects, in its angle, the character's position and the direction in which he or she has looked, but remains more or less objective (as opposed to subjective) in nature. *Point-of-view editing* is a form of *eye-line matching* in which the second shot shows what is being looked at from the character's exact position.

Fade   The gradual darkening of the image until it becomes black (the fade-out) or the gradual brightening of a darkened image until it becomes visible (the fade-in).

Fill light   A light used to fill in shadows cast by the key lights. See also *Three-point lighting*.

Film noir   Literally meaning "black film," film noir refers to a style or mode of filmmaking, which flourished between 1941 and 1958, that presents narratives involving crime or criminal actions in a manner that disturbs, disorients, or otherwise induces anxiety in the viewer.

Flashback   A shot or sequence that shows events which take place at an earlier moment than the present time in the film.

Focal length   The distance from the center of a lens to the plane of the film. The focal lengths of lenses vary from relatively short lengths in *wide-angle lenses* to relatively long lengths in *telephoto lenses*.

Genre   A category of filmmaking which is recognized as a "type," possessing familiar narrative and stylistic conventions. Standard genres are the melodrama, Western, war film, musical, and comedy.

Graphic match   A technique used in continuity editing in which the major features of the composition in one shot are duplicated or matched in the next shot, providing a graphic continuity that serves to bridge the edit.

High-angle shot   See *Camera angle*.

High-key lighting   A style of lighting, found in comedies, musicals, and other upbeat films, in which the fill light eliminates dark shadows cast by the key light, producing an image that is brightly and evenly lit. See also *Three-point lighting*.

Iris-in/iris-out   A major transition in the silent cinema in which an adjustable aperture on the camera would gradually open, in an iris-in, to reveal more and more image within an expanding, geometrically shaped frame, or would gradually close down, in an iris-out, to narrow the field of view, which is surrounded by more and more blackness.

Key light   The chief or brightest source of light in a scene. See also *Three-point lighting*.

Letterboxing A video format that enables wide-screen films to be seen on television in (more or less) their original *aspect ratio*. It involves a reduction in the height of the image so that the full width of the image can be seen on the somewhat narrow television screen. If a film has been letterboxed, black (or blue) masking appears above and below the original wide-screen image.

Lighting The illumination of the set or filming location by means of natural or artificial lights. See also *Three-point lighting*.

Long take A shot that continues for a relatively long period of time (e.g., 20 or more seconds).

Low-angle shot See *Camera angle*.

Low-key lighting A style of lighting, found in film noir, suspense, or horror films, in which there is little fill light, resulting in a dark or shadow-filled image. See also *Three-point lighting*.

Match on action A technique of continuity editing that uses the carryover of physical movement from one shot to the next in order to conceal cuts. Thus, as a character begins to sit down in medium long shot, an editor will often cut in to a closer shot as the action continues.

Medium shot An image in which the size of the object or scene shown lies somewhere in between that of a close-up or medium close-up and a medium long shot or long shot. In terms of the human body, a shot that frames characters roughly from the knees up. See *Camera distance*.

Mise-en-scene A French term that literally means "putting on the stage." Mise-en-scene encompasses a variety of "theatrical" categories related to the staging of action for the camera. These range from purely theatrical areas of expression, such as set design, costume design, the blocking of actors, performance, and lighting to purely filmic techniques, such as camera movement, camera angle, camera distance, and composition. Strictly speaking, mise-en-scene includes the relation of everything within the shot to everything else within the shot—of actors to the decor, of decor and actors to the lighting, of actors, decor, and lighting to the camera position, and so forth.

Mode of production The particular system within which films are made. These systems range from home movies, in which amateur equipment is used by individuals to record everyday events for family viewing, to Hollywood productions, in which state-of-the-art equipment and experienced professionals (screenwriters, directors, actors, and other craftspersons) are used to produce commercial products for a mass audience.

Montage The French word for "editing." A style of editing associated with Soviet films of the late 1920s.

Montage sequence A sequence in a film that relies upon editing to condense or expand action, space, or time. In a travel montage, for example, a lengthy journey of a character might be condensed to a handful of shots of various places which that character has visited that are connected by a series of dissolves. This kind of montage can be seen in *Mr. Smith Goes to Washington* (1939), when Jefferson Smith (James Stewart) takes a sight-seeing bus around Washington, D.C., and shots of various buildings and monuments are edited together to reflect his tour of the nation's capital. On the other hand, the shower sequence in Alfred Hitchcock's *Psycho* (1960) is also a montage sequence. It breaks the action down into over 75 separate shots, relying upon montage to expand (and thus magnify the horror of) the brutal murder of the film's heroine.

Movie palace An enormous motion picture theater with lavish, often exotic decor. Located in large urban areas, a movie palace typically had enough seats for several thousand spectators at once. The New York Roxy, for example, had 6200 seats. The first movie palaces were built in the 1910s.

Multiplex A cluster of several theaters under a single roof, economically operated by the same size staff required to run a single theater. Typically, three or four small theaters, each seating about 200 spectators, will be grouped around a single large theater, seating about 500–800, to form a movie arcade.

Nickelodeon A small, storefront motion picture theater, approximately 25 feet wide and 75–100 feet long, seating about 200 spectators.

Introduced in about 1905, nickelodeons were so named because they charged customers a nickel (or a dime) for a full program of motion picture entertainment.

Nondiegetic sound Sound (generally music) that does not originate in the world depicted onscreen but comes from the space occupied by a nondramatized narrator. The music provided by the film's composer that underscores dramatic action (and that is not heard by the characters in the film) is nondiegetic. Voice-over narration provided by someone who is not a character in a film, such as the "voice-of-God" narration found in newsreels and certain documentaries, is nondiegetic.

Normal lens A camera lens that possesses an angle of view which is somewhat similar to that of the human eye and which thus provides a view of the action that seems less exaggerated or distorted than that provided by a *wide-angle* or *telephoto lens*. The range for normal lenses is roughly 40mm–50mm.

180-degree rule A convention observed in filmmaking that ensures continuity in screen position and screen direction from one shot to the next. In cutting from shot to shot, the camera remains on one side of an imaginary line (the 180-degree line) that runs through the main actors or action. If the camera were to cross this line during a conversation sequence, for example, the screen position of players in the first shot would be reversed in the second.

Pan A camera movement in which the camera rotates horizontally on its axis, presenting a panoramic view of the scene by rotating from right to left (or from left to right) a certain number of degrees to reveal what lies before the camera on either side.

Panavision An anamorphic, widescreen process similar to *CinemaScope*. Panavision replaced CinemaScope as an industry standard for anamorphic filmmaking during the early 1960s.

Panning and scanning A process employed in the adaptation of widescreen motion pictures for broadcast on television. In the transfer from original motion picture to television master, a special telecine device crops the film to make it fit on the television screen, introducing edits and pans from one part of the original image to another.

Parallel editing A style of editing that involves cutting back and forth between two or more scenes in which the action is taking place simultaneously or in which one action is either compared or contrasted with another. See also *Crosscutting*.

Pay-per-view A *cable television* distribution system that enables cable companies to charge home viewers a fee for watching an individual film rather than a subscription fee for a particular premium cable channel, such as HBO or Showtime.

Persona The "mask" or projected personality of an actor or star.

Point-of-view editing A form of eye-line matching that involves a series of three separate shots—a shot of a character looking offscreen, a point-of-view shot of what the character sees, and a reaction shot of the character as he or she reacts to the thing that has been seen.

Point-of-view shot A shot that is clearly marked as subjective in nature and which duplicates the optical perspective of a specific character in the film.

Populism A dominant myth that celebrates a certain kind of American identity based upon preindustrial, agrarian ideals, such as that of Jefferson's yeoman farmer, the small businessperson, the opponent of big government, the anti-intellectual, and the good neighbor.

Postproduction The phase of motion picture production during which footage filmed during production is edited and assembled, special effects are created, music is composed and recorded, and the sound track is mixed.

Preproduction The phase of motion picture production during which a screenplay is written, parts are cast, a crew is assembled, and sets and costumes are designed and constructed.

Production The phase of motion picture production during which actual filming takes place.

Production code Rules and regulations, established (and subsequently revised) at various periods during the history of the studio system, that indicated particular subjects, ranging from nudity, white slavery, drug addiction, and other criminal acts to miscegenation, that were not permitted to be represented on the screen.

Ratings A system of film classification that rates films on the basis of the amount of sex, violence, or objectionable language contained within them. The Motion Picture Association of America has six ratings: G (suitable for a general audience), PG-13 (parental guidance recommended for children under the age of thirteen), PG (parental guidance suggested), R (restricted to persons over seventeen unless accompanied by an adult), NC-17 (no child under 17 permitted), and X (prohibited to persons under seventeen). The difference between NC-17 and X is that the former rating is used for "serious" films with mature themes, such as *Henry and June* (1990), and the latter is now used solely for pornographic films.

Roadshowing A specialized distribution system, modelled on the legitimate theater, in which a film is shown at first-run theaters and tickets are sold, in advance, on a reserved-seat basis.

Runs, zones, and clearances A pattern of exhibition in which certain theaters secure the rights to exhibit films before other theaters are permitted to show them. *Runs* are broken down into first run, second run, and subsequent runs. New films are initially licensed only to first-run theaters, which are thus protected from competition with second- and subrun theaters. Only one theater in a certain *zone* or geographical area will be permitted to exhibit the film in any particular run. And between each run, a certain period of time or *clearance* will be established to enable the various runs to maximize profits.

Scene The film's smallest dramatic unit; it consists of one or more shots that present an action which is spatially and temporally continuous.

'Scope A shortening of the term "CinemaScope." It has become a generic term for any film made in an anamorphic process. See also *CinemaScope*.

Segmentation The breaking down of a film into its basic parts for purposes of analysis of the relationship of one part or segment to another.

Set design See *Art direction*.

Shot An unbroken strip of film made by an uninterrupted running of the camera and edited at the beginning and end in preparation for its inclusion in a film. See also *Take*.

Shot/reverse shot A multishot system (involving at least two shots) frequently used in filming conversations and other kinds of sequences, which observes the 180-degree rule. The shots alternate back and forth between an angled shot from one end of the 180-degree line and another from the other end. The second shot views the action from the same angle as the first, though that angle is now "reversed," that is, the shot is taken from the opposite direction. In other words, the shot/reverse shot pattern involves an initial shot, from one angle favoring one character, followed by another shot, from another angle favoring the other character. The relative screen positions of both characters will be maintained from shot to shot and the camera will remain on the same side of the 180-degree line that runs through the center of the action.

Sound mixing The combination, during the phase of postproduction, of three different categories of film sound—dialogue, sound effects, and music.

Stereo magnetic sound A sound system that relies on magnetic recording and playback in the theater, using magnetically striped projection prints to produce stereo sound coming from three or more speakers in the theater.

Take An unbroken strip of yet unedited film made by an uninterrupted running of the camera. To be distinguished from a *long take*.

Telephoto lens A camera lens that has a long focal length and takes in a relatively narrow angle of view in comparison to a *normal lens*. Any lens that is longer (e.g., 75mm, 100mm) than the standard 40–50mm normal lens is a telephoto lens.

3-D A system of motion picture production and exhibition, (re-)introduced in the 1950s, that involved the creation of an illusion of depth/

emergence, which was based on the principles of binocular vision.

Three-point lighting The standard lighting set-up employed in Hollywood. The "three points" to which the term refers are the dominant sources of illumination—the key light (or chief directional light source), the fill light (or weaker light source that "fills in" the shadows cast by the key light), and the back light, the minor light that illuminates the space between the back of the set and the characters in order to separate or distinguish the characters from the background.

Tilt A form of *pan* in which a stationary camera tilts upward or downward on its axis.

Tracking shot A shot in which the camera, mounted on any one of a variety of mobile camera supports (e.g., cranes, dollies, Steadicams, or tracks), moves bodily through space in any of a variety of directions parallel to the floor. In some situations, the camera is literally placed on tracks laid down upon the floor or built into the ceiling.

VCR An abbreviation for "video cassette recorder."

Vertical integration A system of motion picture production, distribution, and exhibition in which these three sectors are controlled by a single economic entity, such as a studio, which both makes and distributes a product that is exhibited in its own theaters. This particular structure was outlawed by the courts in 1948.

VHS An abbreviation for "video home system," the initials refer to a special system of *VCR*s and tapes that rely upon a half-inch videotape format.

VistaVision A widescreen process, developed by Paramount in 1954. It relies on a special 35mm camera that exposes two frames of film horizontally (rather than one frame exposed vertically as in standard cameras) in order to record a panoramic view. It produced an extremely sharp image that was projected in an aspect ratio of 1.66:1.

Voice-over narration Speech that accompanies a previously filmed sequence but does not come from the sequence itself. The voice may be that of a character within the film who is describing onscreen events that are seen in a flashback or it may be that of an omniscient, unseen, offscreen commentator whose voice accompanies onscreen images, as in newsreels and certain forms of documentaries.

Wide-angle lens A camera lens that possesses a short focal length and takes in a fairly wide angle of view, relative to that captured by a *normal lens*. A 25mm lens (or any lens shorter than the 40–50mm normal lens) is a typical wide-angle lens.

Widescreen Any film production or projection format that uses an *aspect ratio* greater than the *Academy ratio*, that is, an aspect ratio of 1.66:1 or more.

Wipe A form of shot transition in which the second shot appears to wipe the first shot off the screen.

Zoom A special lens that possesses a variety of different focal lengths which range from wide-angle to telephoto. Manipulation of the lens produces the impression of movement toward or away from objects by shifting from wide-angle to telephoto focal lengths or vice versa. These shifts simply enlarge or decrease the apparent size of the image but involve no actual movement of the camera.